# BIRDS

## of

# NEW YORK
# STATE

*To Wendy, artist and gardener*

*Invite birds to your garden and enjoy. Go farther afield to the parks and preserves to build your experiences and become more appreciative of the wondrous world around us.*

*Bob Budliger*

*Robert E. Budliger*
*Gregory Kennedy*

*with contributions from*
*Chris Fisher & Andy Bezener*

LONE
PINE

Lone Pine Publishing International

**The Distributor: Lone Pine Publishing**
1808 B Street NW, Suite 140
Auburn, WA, USA  98001

**Website:** www.lonepinepublishing.com

**National Library of Canada Cataloguing in Publication**
Budliger, Robert E., 1935-
 Birds of New York State / Robert E. Budliger & Gregory Kennedy.


 Includes bibliographical references and index.

 ISBN-13: 978-1-55105-326-4.  ISBN-10: 1-55105-326-8


 1. Birds—New York (State)–Identification.  I. Kennedy, Gregory, 1956–   II. Title.
QL684.N7B82 2005        598'.09747      C2003-906884-6


*Cover Illustration:* Gary Ross
*Illustrations:* Gary Ross, Ted Nordhagen, Ewa Pluciennik
*Separations & Electronic Film:* Elite Lithographers Co.


PC: 13

# CONTENTS

# ACKNOWLEDGMENTS

Our knowledge and understanding of the birds of New York are greatly increased by the legions of binocular-toting people who go afield to study them, and then take the time and effort to report their observations. We are indebted to the birders who do organized Christmas bird counts, Breeding Bird Survey routes and Breeding Bird Atlases, as well as those who individually report their sightings to regional compilers of birding journals such as the *Kingbird* and *North American Birds*. An important debt is owed the organizers and compilers of these efforts. We are particularly indebted to the species account authors and editor of *Bull's Birds of New York*, which recently pulled all the distributional information together in one place. Thanks also go to John Acorn, Chris Fisher, Andy Bezener and Eloise Pulos for their contributions to previous books in this series. In addition, thank you to Gary Ross, Ted Nordhagen and Ewa Pluciennik, whose skilled illustrations have brought each page to life.

My own growth as a birder has been encouraged and supported by many, but I am especially grateful for the encouragement of Scoutmaster Stan Babcock, the friendship of "birding buddies" Bill Reeves and Bill Lee, the mentoring of Cornell professor Richard Fischer, the opportunities offered by the National Audubon Society and the strong support of a too-often neglected family—Carol, Kurt and Amy.

—Bob Budliger

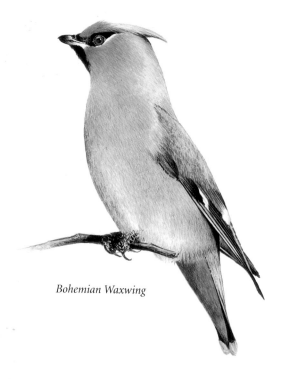

*Bohemian Waxwing*

**Greater White-fronted Goose**
size 30 in • p. 36

**Snow Goose**
size 30 in • p. 37

**Canada Goose**
size 34 in • p. 38

**Brant**
size 25 in • p. 39

**Mute Swan**
size 60 in • p. 40

**Tundra Swan**
size 51 in • p. 41

**Wood Duck**
size 17 in • p. 42

**Gadwall**
size 20 in • p. 43

**Eurasian Wigeon**
size 18 in • p. 44

**American Wigeon**
size 20 in • p. 45

**American Black Duck**
size 23 in • p. 46

**Mallard**
size 23 in • p. 47

**Blue-winged Teal**
size 15 in • p. 48

**Northern Shoveler**
size 19 in • p. 49

**Northern Pintail**
size 23 in • p. 50

**Green-winged Teal**
size 14 in • p. 51

**Canvasback**
size 20 in • p. 52

**Redhead**
size 20 in • p. 53

**Ring-necked Duck**
size 16 in • p. 54

**Tufted Duck**
size 17 in • p. 55

**Greater Scaup**
size 17 in • p. 56

**Lesser Scaup**
size 17 in • p. 57

**King Eider**
size 22 in • p. 58

**Common Eider**
size 24 in • p. 59

**Harlequin Duck**
size 16 in • p. 60

**Surf Scoter**
size 18 in • p. 61

**White-winged Scoter**
size 21 in • p. 62

**Black Scoter**
size 19 in • p. 63

**WATERFOWL**

Long-tailed Duck
size 18 in • p. 64

Bufflehead
size 14 in • p. 65

Common Goldeneye
size 18 in • p. 66

Barrow's Goldeneye
size 18 in • p. 67

Hooded Merganser
size 17 in • p. 68

Common Merganser
size 24 in • p. 69

Red-breasted Merganser
size 23 in • p. 70

Ruddy Duck
size 16 in • p. 71

**GROUSE & ALLIES**

Gray Partridge
size 12 in • p. 72

Ring-necked Pheasant
size 30 in • p. 73

Ruffed Grouse
size 17 in • p. 74

Spruce Grouse
size 15 in • p. 75

Wild Turkey
size 36 in • p. 76

Northern Bobwhite
size 10 in • p. 77

Red-throated Loon
size 25 in • p. 78

Common Loon
size 32 in • p. 79

**DIVING BIRDS**

Pied-billed Grebe
size 13 in • p. 80

Horned Grebe
size 14 in • p. 81

Red-necked Grebe
size 19 in • p. 82

Northern Fulmar
size 18 in • p. 83

Cory's Shearwater
size 19 in • p. 84

Greater Shearwater
size 18 in • p. 85

Sooty Shearwater
size 17 in • p. 86

Wilson's Storm-Petrel
size 7 in • p. 87

Northern Gannet
size 36 in • p. 88

American White Pelican
size 63 in • p. 89

Double-crested Cormorant
size 29 in • p. 90

Great Cormorant
size 36 in • p. 91

American Bittern
size 25 in • p. 92

Least Bittern
size 13 in • p. 93

Great Blue Heron
size 50 in • p. 94

Great Egret
size 39 in • p. 95

Snowy Egret
size 24 in • p. 96

Little Blue Heron
size 24 in • p. 97

Tricolored Heron
size 26 in • p. 98

Cattle Egret
size 20 in • p. 99

Green Heron
size 18 in • p. 100

Black-crowned Night-Heron
size 25 in • p. 101

Yellow-crowned Night-Heron
size 24 in • p. 102

Glossy Ibis
size 23 in • p. 103

Black Vulture
size 25 in • p. 104

Turkey Vulture
size 29 in • p. 105

Osprey
size 24 in • p. 106

Bald Eagle
size 31 in • p. 107

Northern Harrier
size 19 in • p. 108

Sharp-shinned Hawk
size 12 in • p. 109

Cooper's Hawk
size 17 in • p. 110

Northern Goshawk
size 23 in • p. 111

Red-shouldered Hawk
size 19 in • p. 112

Broad-winged Hawk
size 16 in • p. 113

Red-tailed Hawk
size 21 in • p. 114

Rough-legged Hawk
size 21 in • p. 115

Golden Eagle
size 35 in • p. 116

American Kestrel
size 8 in • p. 117

Merlin
size 11 in • p. 118

Peregrine Falcon
size 17 in • p. 119

**RAILS, COOTS & CRANES**

Clapper Rail
size 14 in • p. 120

Virginia Rail
size 10 in • p. 121

Sora
size 9 in • p. 122

Common Moorhen
size 13 in • p. 123

American Coot
size 15 in • p. 124

Sandhill Crane
size 45 in • p. 125

**SHOREBIRDS**

Black-bellied Plover
size 12 in • p. 126

American Golden-Plover
size 10 in • p. 127

Semipalmated Plover
size 7 in • p. 128

Piping Plover
size 7 in • p. 129

Killdeer
size 10 in • p. 130

American Oystercatcher
size 18 in • p. 131

American Avocet
size 17 in • p. 132

Greater Yellowlegs
size 14 in • p. 133

Lesser Yellowlegs
size 10 in • p. 134

Solitary Sandpiper
size 8 in • p. 135

Willet
size 15 in • p. 136

Spotted Sandpiper
size 7 in • p. 137

Upland Sandpiper
size 12 in • p. 138

Whimbrel
size 18 in • p. 139

Hudsonian Godwit
size 15 in • p. 140

Marbled Godwit
size 18 in • p. 141

Ruddy Turnstone
size 9 in • p. 142

Red Knot
size 10 in • p. 143

Sanderling
size 8 in • p. 144

Semipalmated Sandpiper
size 6 in • p. 145

**Western Sandpiper**
size 6 in • p. 146

**Least Sandpiper**
size 5 in • p. 147

**White-rumped Sandpiper**
size 7 in • p. 148

**Baird's Sandpiper**
size 7 in • p. 149

**Pectoral Sandpiper**
size 9 in • p. 150

**Purple Sandpiper**
size 9 in • p. 151

**Dunlin**
size 8 in • p. 152

**Stilt Sandpiper**
size 8 in • p. 153

**Buff-breasted Sandpiper**
size 8 in • p. 154

**Short-billed Dowitcher**
size 11 in • p. 155

**Long-billed Dowitcher**
size 12 in • p. 156

**Wilson's Snipe**
size 11 in • p. 157

**American Woodcock**
size 11 in • p. 158

**Wilson's Phalarope**
size 9 in • p. 159

**Red-necked Phalarope**
size 7 in • p. 160

**Red Phalarope**
size 8 in • p. 161

GULLS & ALLIES

**Pomarine Jaeger**
size 21 in • p. 162

**Parasitic Jaeger**
size 18 in • p. 163

**Laughing Gull**
size 16 in • p. 164

**Little Gull**
size 10 in • p. 165

**Black-headed Gull**
size 16 in • p. 166

**Bonaparte's Gull**
size 13 in • p. 167

**Ring-billed Gull**
size 19 in • p. 168

**Herring Gull**
size 24 in • p. 169

**Iceland Gull**
size 22 in • p. 170

**Lesser Black-backed Gull**
size 21 in • p. 171

**Glaucous Gull**
size 27 in • p. 172

**Great Black-backed Gull**
size 30 in • p. 173

**GULLS & ALLIES**

Sabine's Gull
size 13 in • p. 174

Black-legged Kittiwake
size 17 in • p. 175

Gull-billed Tern
size 14 in • p. 176

Caspian Tern
size 21 in • p. 177

Royal Tern
size 20 in • p. 178

Roseate Tern
size 12 in • p. 179

Common Tern
size 14 in • p. 180

Arctic Tern
size 12 in • p. 181

Forster's Tern
size 15 in • p. 182

Least Tern
size 9 in • p. 183

Black Tern
size 9 in • p. 184

Black Skimmer
size 18 in • p. 185

Razorbill
size 17 in • p. 186

Black Guillemot
size 13 in • p. 187

**DOVES, PARROTS & CUCKOOS**

Rock Pigeon
size 12 in • p. 188

Mourning Dove
size 12 in • p. 189

Monk Parakeet
size 11 in • p. 190

Black-billed Cuckoo
size 12 in • p. 191

Yellow-billed Cuckoo
size 12 in • p. 192

**OWLS**

Barn Owl
size 15 in • p. 193

Eastern Screech-Owl
size 8 in • p. 194

Great Horned Owl
size 21 in • p. 195

Snowy Owl
size 23 in • p. 196

Barred Owl
size 20 in • p. 197

Long-eared Owl
size 15 in • p. 198

Short-eared Owl
size 15 in • p. 199

Northern Saw-whet Owl
size 8 in • p. 200

Common Nighthawk
size 9 in • p. 201

Chuck-will's-widow
size 12 in • p. 202

Whip-poor-will
size 9 in • p. 203

Chimney Swift
size 5 in • p. 204

Ruby-throated Hummingbird
size 4 in • p. 205

Belted Kingfisher
size 12 in • p. 206

Red-headed Woodpecker
size 9 in • p. 207

Red-bellied Woodpecker
size 10 in • p. 208

Yellow-bellied Sapsucker
size 8 in • p. 209

Downy Woodpecker
size 6 in • p. 210

Hairy Woodpecker
size 9 in • p. 211

American Three-toed Woodpecker
size 8 in • p. 212

Black-backed Woodpecker
size 9 in • p. 213

Northern Flicker
size 13 in • p. 214

Pileated Woodpecker
size 18 in • p. 215

Olive-sided Flycatcher
size 7 in • p. 217

Eastern Wood-Pewee
size 6 in • p. 218

Yellow-bellied Flycatcher
size 6 in • p. 219

Acadian Flycatcher
size 6 in • p. 220

Alder Flycatcher
size 6 in • p. 221

Willow Flycatcher
size 6 in • p. 222

Least Flycatcher
size 5 in • p. 223

Eastern Flycatcher
size 7 in • p. 224

Great Crested Flycatcher
size 8 in • p. 225

Eastern Kingbird
size 8 in • p. 226

**SHRIKES & VIREOS**

Northern Shrike
size 10 in • p. 227

White-eyed Vireo
size 5 in • p. 228

Yellow-throated Vireo
size 5 in • p. 229

Blue-headed Vireo
size 5 in • p. 230

Warbling Vireo
size 5 in • p. 231

Philadelphia Vireo
size 5 in • p. 232

Red-eyed Vireo
size 6 in • p. 233

**JAYS & CROWS**

Gray Jay
size 12 in • p. 234

Blue Jay
size 12 in • p. 235

American Crow
size 19 in • p. 236

Fish Crow
size 15 in • p. 237

Common Raven
size 19 in • p. 238

Horned Lark
size 7 in • p. 239

Purple Martin
size 7 in • p. 240

Tree Swallow
size 5 in • p. 241

**LARKS & SWALLOWS**

Northern Rough-winged Swallow
size 5 in • p. 242

Bank Swallow
size 5 in • p. 243

Cliff Swallow
size 5 in • p. 244

Barn Swallow
size 7 in • p. 245

**CHICKADEES, NUTHATCHES & WRENS**

Black-capped Chickadee
size 5 in • p. 246

Boreal Chickadee
size 5 in • p. 247

Tufted Titmouse
size 6 in • p. 248

Red-breasted Nuthatch
size 4 in • p. 249

White-breasted Nuthatch
size 6 in • p. 250

Brown Creeper
size 5 in • p. 251

Carolina Wren
size 5 in • p. 252

House Wren
size 5 in • p. 253

Winter Wren
size 4 in • p. 254

Sedge Wren
size 4 in • p. 255

Marsh Wren
size 5 in • p. 256

Golden-crowned Kinglet
size 4 in • p. 257

Ruby-crowned Kinglet
size 4 in • p. 258

Blue-gray Gnatcatcher
size 4 in • p. 259

Eastern Bluebird
size 7 in • p. 260

Veery
size 7 in • p. 261

Gray-cheeked Thrush
size 7 in • p. 262

Bicknell's Thrush
size 7 in • p. 263

Swainson's Thrush
size 7 in • p. 264

Hermit Thrush
size 7 in • p. 265

Wood Thrush
size 8 in • p. 266

American Robin
size 10 in • p. 267

Gray Catbird
size 9 in • p. 268

Northern Mockingbird
size 10 in • p. 269

Brown Thrasher
size 11 in • p. 270

European Starling
size 8 in • p. 271

American Pipit
size 6 in • p. 272

Bohemian Waxwing
size 8 in • p. 273

Cedar Waxwing
size 7 in • p. 274

Blue-winged Warbler
size 5 in • p. 275

Golden-winged Warbler
size 5 in • p. 276

Tennessee Warbler
size 5 in • p. 277

Orange-crowned Warbler
size 5 in • p. 278

WOOD-WARBLERS & TANAGERS

Nashville Warbler
size 5 in • p. 279

Northern Parula
size 4 in • p. 280

Yellow Warbler
size 5 in • p. 281

Chestnut-sided Warbler
size 5 in • p. 282

Magnolia Warbler
size 5 in • p. 283

Cape May Warbler
size 5 in • p. 284

Black-throated Blue Warbler
size 5 in • p. 285

Yellow-rumped Warbler
size 5 in • p. 286

Black-throated Green Warbler
size 5 in • p. 287

Blackburnian Warbler
size 5 in • p. 288

Yellow-throated Warbler
size 5 in • p. 289

Pine Warbler
size 5 in • p. 290

Prairie Warbler
size 5 in • p. 291

Palm Warbler
size 5 in • p. 292

Bay-breasted Warbler
size 5 in • p. 293

Blackpoll Warbler
size 5 in • p. 294

Cerulean Warbler
size 5 in • p. 295

Black-and-white Warbler
size 5 in • p. 296

American Redstart
size 5 in • p. 297

Prothonotary Warbler
size 5 in • p. 298

Worm-eating Warbler
size 5 in • p. 299

Ovenbird
size 6 in • p. 300

Northern Waterthrush
size 6 in • p. 301

Louisiana Waterthrush
size 6 in • p. 302

Kentucky Warbler
size 5 in • p. 303

**Mourning Warbler**
size 5 in • p. 304

**Common Yellowthroat**
size 5 in • p. 305

**Hooded Warbler**
size 5 in • p. 306

**Wilson's Warbler**
size 5 in • p. 307

**Canada Warbler**
size 5 in • p. 308

**Yellow-breasted Chat**
size 7 in • p. 309

**Summer Tanager**
size 7 in • p. 310

**Scarlet Tanager**
size 7 in • p. 311

**Eastern Towhee**
size 8 in • p. 312

**American Tree Sparrow**
size 6 in • p. 313

**Chipping Sparrow**
size 6 in • p. 314

**Clay-colored Sparrow**
size 6 in • p. 315

**Field Sparrow**
size 6 in • p. 316

**Vesper Sparrow**
size 6 in • p. 317

**Savannah Sparrow**
size 6 in • p. 318

**Grasshopper Sparrow**
size 5 in • p. 319

**Henslow's Sparrow**
size 5 in • p. 320

**Saltmarsh Sharp-tailed Sparrow**
size 5 in • p. 321

**Seaside Sparrow**
size 6 in • p. 322

**Fox Sparrow**
size 7 in • p. 323

**Song Sparrow**
size 6 in • p. 324

**Lincoln's Sparrow**
size 5 in • p. 325

**Swamp Sparrow**
size 5 in • p. 326

**White-throated Sparrow**
size 7 in • p. 327

**White-crowned Sparrow**
size 7 in • p. 328

**Dark-eyed Junco**
size 6 in • p. 329

**Lapland Longspur**
size 6 in • p. 330

**Snow Bunting**
size 7 in • p. 331

**Northern Cardinal**
size 8 in • p. 332

**SPARROWS, GROSBEAKS & BUNTINGS**

Rose-breasted Grosbeak
size 8 in • p. 333

Blue Grosbeak
size 7 in • p. 334

Indigo Bunting
size 5 in • p. 335

Dickcissel
size 6 in • p. 336

**BLACKBIRDS & ALLIES**

Bobolink
size 7 in • p. 337

Red-winged Blackbird
size 8 in • p. 338

Eastern Meadowlark
size 9 in • p. 339

Rusty Blackbird
size 9 in • p. 340

Common Grackle
size 13 in • p. 341

Boat-tailed Grackle
size 16 in • p. 342

Brown-headed Cowbird
size 7 in • p. 343

Orchard Oriole
size 7 in • p. 344

Baltimore Oriole
size 7 in • p. 345

**FINCHLIKE BIRDS**

Pine Grosbeak
size 9 in • p. 346

Purple Finch
size 5 in • p. 347

House Finch
size 5 in • p. 348

Red Crossbill
size 6 in • p. 349

White-winged Crossbill
size 6 in • p. 350

Common Redpoll
size 5 in • p. 351

Hoary Redpoll
size 5 in • p. 352

Pine Siskin
size 5 in • p. 353

American Goldfinch
size 5 in • p. 354

Evening Grosbeak
size 8 in • p. 355

House Sparrow
size 6 in • p. 356

# INTRODUCTION

## BIRDING IN NEW YORK

In recent decades, birding has evolved from an eccentric pursuit prac-
ticed by a few dedicated individuals to a continent-wide activity that
boasts millions of professional and amateur participants. There
are many good reasons why birding has become so popular.
Many people find it relaxing, while others enjoy the out-
door exercise that it affords. Some see it as a rewarding
learning experience, an opportunity to socialize with
like-minded people and a way to monitor the health
of the local environment. Still others watch birds to
reconnect with nature. A visit to any of New York's
premier birding locations, such as the Montezuma
National Wildlife Refuge, Bear Mountain State
Park, Jamaica Bay Wildlife Refuge or Montauk
Point State Park, would doubtless uncover still
more reasons why people watch birds.

*Osprey*

We are truly blessed by the geographical
and biological diversity of New York. In addi-
tion to supporting a wide range of breeding birds and year-round residents, our state
hosts a large number of spring and fall migrants that move through our area on the
way to their breeding and wintering grounds. In all, 460 bird species have been seen
and recorded in New York. Out of these, 325 or so species make regular appearances
in the state.

## BEGINNING TO LEARN THE BIRDS

### The Challenge of Birding

Birding (also known as "birdwatching") can be
extremely challenging and getting started is
often the most difficult part. Learning to recognize
all the birds in New York is a long process. But fear
not! The species pictured in this guide will help
you get started. Although any standard North
American field guide will help you identify
local birds, such guides can be daunting
because they cover the entire continent and
present an overwhelming number of species.
By focusing specifically on the bird life of New
York, we hope to make the introduction to the
world of birding a little less intimidating

*Red-winged
Blackbird*

### Classification: The Order of Things

To an ornithologist (a biologist who studies birds), the
species is the fundamental unit of classification because
the members of a single species look most alike and they
naturally interbreed with one another. Each species has a

scientific name, usually derived from Latin or Greek and always italicized, that designates genus and species, as well as a single accredited common name, so that the different vernacular names of a species do not cause confusion. A bird has been properly identified only when it has been identified "to species," and most ornithologists use the accredited common name. For example, "American Coot" is an accredited common name, even though some people call this bird "Mudhen." *Fulica americana* is the American Coot's scientific name (*Fulica* is the genus, or generic name, and *americana* is the species, or specific name).

Ornithologists have arranged all the species in a standard sequence beginning with the waterfowl (order Anseriformes), which are thought by many to be most like the evolutionary ancestors of modern birds. This sequence ends with those species thought to have been most strongly modified by evolutionary change and most departed from the ancestral form. We have organized this book according to this standard sequence.

## TECHNIQUES OF BIRDING

Being in the right place at the right time to see birds in action involves both skill and luck. The more you know about a bird—its range, preferred habitat, food preferences and hours and seasons of activity—the better your chances will be of seeing it. It is much easier to find a Northern Saw-whet Owl in the northern forest than elsewhere, especially at night in spring, when adults are calling for mates. Snowy Owls, however, are most often seen on fence posts or in fields during the day in winter.

Generally, spring and fall are the busiest birding times. Temperatures are moderate then, and a great number of birds are on the move, often heavily populating small patches of habitat before moving on. Male songbirds are easy to identify on spring mornings as they belt out their courtship songs. Throughout much of the year, diurnal birds are most visible in the early morning hours when they are foraging, but during winter they are often more active in the day when milder temperatures prevail. Timing is crucial because summer foliage often conceals birds and cold weather drives many species south of our region for winter. Birding also involves a great deal of luck. You often happen to cross paths with an unusual bird as you visit a variety of sites.

*Snowy Owl*

### Birding by Ear

Recognizing birds by their songs and calls can greatly enhance your birding experience. When experienced birders conduct breeding bird surveys in the summer, they rely more on their ears than their eyes, because listening is far more efficient. There are numerous tapes and CDs that can help you learn bird songs, and a portable player with headphones can let you quickly compare a live bird with a recording.

18

## BIRDING BY HABITAT

New York can be separated into several ecological region or "ecozones": Coastal Plain, Hudson-Taconic Highlands, Appalachian Plateau, Great Lakes Plain, St. Lawrence–Champlain Plain, Adirondacks–Tug Hill and Hudson-Mohawk Valley. Each ecozone is composed of a number of different habitats. Each habitat is a community of plants and animals supported by the infrastructure of water and soil and regulated by the constraints of topography, climate and elevation.

Simply put, a bird's habitat is the place in which it normally lives. Some birds prefer open water, some are found in cattail marshes, others like mature coniferous forest, and still others prefer abandoned agricultural fields overgrown with tall grass and shrubs. Knowledge of a bird's habitat increases the chances of identifying the bird correctly. If you are birding in wetlands, you will not be identifying tanagers or towhees; if you are wandering along the beaches of the Coastal Plain, do not expect to meet Northern Saw-whet Owls or Tundra Swans. Only in migration, especially during inclement weather, do some birds leave their usual habitat.

## BIRD LISTING

Many birders list the species they have seen during excursions or at home. It is up to you to decide what kind of list—systematic or casual—you will keep, and you may choose not to make lists at all. However, lists may prove rewarding in unexpected ways. For example, after you visit a new area, your list becomes a souvenir of your experiences there. By reviewing the list, you can recall memories and details

*Baltimore Oriole*

that you might otherwise have forgotten. Keeping regular, accurate lists of birds in your neighborhood can also be useful for local researchers. It can be interesting to compare the arrival dates and last sightings of hummingbirds and other seasonal visitors, or to note the first sighting of a new visitor to your area.

## BIRDING ACTIVITIES

### Birding Groups

We recommend that you join in on such activities as Christmas bird counts, birding festivals and the meetings of your local birding or natural history club. Meeting other people with the same interests can make birding even more pleasurable, and there is always something to be learned when birders of all levels gather. If you are interested in bird conservation and environmental issues, natural history groups and conscientious birding stores can keep you informed about the situation in your area and what you can do to help. Bird hotlines provide up-to-date information on the sightings of rarities, which are often easier to relocate than you might think. The following is a brief list of contacts that will help you get involved:

*Tundra Swan*

## Organizations

**Audubon New York**
200 Trillium Lane
Albany, NY 12203
518-869-9731
ny.audubon.org
nasnys@audubon.org

**New York State Ornithological Association**
P.O. Box 95
Durhamville, NY 13054
www.nybirds.org

**Cornell Laboratory of Ornithology**
159 Sapsucker Woods Road
Ithaca, NY 14850
1-800-843-BIRD (1-800-843-2473)
www.birds.cornell.edu
cornellbirds@cornell.edu

**Hotlines**
Niagara Frontier (Buffalo)
716-896-1271
Genesee Region (Rochester)
585-425-4630
Syracuse 315-637-0318
Hudson-Mohawk Region (Albany)
518-439-8080
New York City–Long Island
212-979-3070

## Useful Websites
www.birdingonthe.net
www.vitualbirder.com
www.birdzilla.com

## Bird Conservation

New York abounds with bird life. There are still large areas of wilderness here, including parks, wildlife refuges and public lands. Nevertheless, agriculture, forestry and development for housing have reduced viable bird habitat throughout the region. It is hoped that more people will learn to appreciate nature through birding, and that they will do their best to protect the natural areas that remain. Many bird enthusiasts support groups such as the National Audubon Society and the Nature Conservancy, which help birds by providing sanctuaries or promoting conservation of the natural world.

Landscaping your own property to provide native plant cover and natural foods for birds is an immediate and personal way to ensure the conservation of bird habitat. The cumulative effects of such urban "nature-scaping" can be significant. If your yard is to become a bird sanctuary, you may want to keep the neighborhood cats out—cats kill millions of birds each year. Check with the local Humane Society for methods of protecting both your feline friends and wild birds.

## Bird Feeding

Many people set up backyard bird feeders or plant native berry- or seed-producing plants in their garden to attract birds to their yard. The kinds of food available will determine which birds visit your yard. Staff at birding stores can suggest which foods will attract specific birds. Hummingbird feeders are popular in summer to attract the Ruby-throated Hummingbird and are filled with a simple sugar solution made from one part sugar and three to four parts water.

Contrary to popular opinion, birds do not become dependent on feeders, nor do they subsequently forget to forage naturally. Winter is when birds use feeders the most, but it is also difficult to find food in spring before flowers bloom, seeds develop and insects hatch. Birdbaths will also entice birds to your yard at any time of year, and heated birdbaths are particularly useful in the colder months. Avoid birdbaths that have exposed metal parts because wet birds can accidentally freeze to them in winter. There are many good books written about feeding birds and landscaping your yard to provide natural foods and nest sites.

## Nest Boxes

Another popular way to attract birds is to set out nest boxes, especially for House Wrens, Eastern Bluebirds, Tree Swallows and Purple Martins. Not all birds will use nest boxes: only species that normally use cavities in trees are comfortable in such confined spaces. Larger nest boxes can attract kestrels, owls and cavity-nesting ducks.

## Cleaning Feeders and Nest Boxes

Nest boxes and feeding stations must be kept clean to prevent birds from becoming ill or spreading disease. Old nesting material may harbor a number of parasites, as well as their eggs. Once the birds have left for the season, remove the old nesting material and wash and scrub the nest box with detergent or a 10 percent bleach solution (1 part bleach to 9 parts water). You can also scald the nest box with boiling water. Rinse it well and let it dry thoroughly before you remount it.

Feeding stations should be cleaned monthly. Feeders can become moldy and any seed, fruit or suet that is moldy or spoiled must be removed. Unclean bird feeders can also be contaminated with salmonellosis and possibly other avian diseases. Clean and disinfect feeding stations with a 10 percent bleach solution, scrubbing thoroughly. Rinse the feeder well and allow it to dry completely before refilling it. Discarded seed and feces on the ground under the feeding station should also be removed.

We advise that you wear rubber gloves and a mask when cleaning nest boxes or feeders.

## West Nile Virus

Since the West Nile Virus first surfaced in North America in 1999, it has caused fear and misunderstanding—some people have become afraid of contracting the disease from birds, and health departments in some communities have advised residents to eliminate feeding stations and birdbaths. To date, the disease affects at least 138 species of birds. Corvids (crows, jays and ravens) and raptors have been the most obvious victims because of their size, though the disease also affects some smaller species. The virus is transmitted to birds and to humans (as well as to some other mammals) by mosquitoes that have bitten infected birds. Not all mosquito species can carry the disease and birds do not get the disease from other birds. As well, humans cannot contract the disease from casual contact with infected birds. According to the Centers for Disease Control and Prevention (CDC), only about 20 percent of people who are bitten and become infected will develop any symptoms at all and less than 1 percent will become severely ill.

Because mosquitoes breed in standing water, birdbaths have the potential to become mosquito breeding grounds. Birdbaths should be emptied and the water changed at least weekly. Drippers, circulating pumps, fountains or waterfalls that keep water moving will prevent mosquitoes from laying their eggs in the water. There are also bird-friendly products available to treat water in birdbaths. You can contact your local nature store or garden center, or do some research on-line, for more information on these products.

## TOP BIRDING SITES IN NEW YORK

There are hundreds, if not thousands, of good birding areas throughout New York. The following areas have been selected to represent a broad range of bird communities and habitats, with an emphasis on accessibility. Common birds are included in these accounts, as well as exciting rarities.

### Roger Tory Peterson Nature Center

Named for the hometown boy who is credited with making nature more accessible to the masses by inventing the modern filed guide, the Roger Tory Peterson Nature Center in Jamestown is surrounded by old fields, upland woods, swamp forests and several ponds. The center has an observation tower from which the ponds can be scoped for Great Blue Herons, Green Herons, Mallards, Ring-necked Ducks and Hooded Mergansers. Feeders attract many migrant and wintering sparrows, including the Song, White-throated, White-crowned, Fox, Field and American Tree sparrows. Over 30 species of warblers are seen or heard each May, and flycatchers, vireos and thrushes are common. Great Horned Owls nest, as do Red-tailed Hawks. One of the few Long-eared Owl nests found in the state was discovered here. A visit to the nature center should be coupled with a stop at the Roger Tory Peterson Institute (RTPI), which houses much of the artist's work and is becoming an important national institution for inspiring nature study by conducting teacher education projects.

*Red-tailed Hawk*

### Niagara River Corridor

In New York, the Niagara River flows 36 miles from Lake Erie to Lake Ontario and forms part of our border with Canada. Justifiably called the "Gull Capital of North America," this portion of the river is ice-free in winter and provides a good source of food for the large numbers of gulls that turn up in late fall, many of which linger until spring. As many as 12 species of gulls have been seen in a day. Herring, Ring-billed, Bonaparte's and Great Black-backed gulls make up the bulk of the birds. Glaucous, Iceland, Little and Black-headed gulls, as well as Black-legged Kittiwakes, are often seen. Among the rarities are Franklin's, Lesser Black-backed, California and Thayer's gulls. Some birders get better views from the Canadian side of the river to add species to their state list. Harlequin Ducks, King Eiders, Barrow's Goldeneyes and Purple Sandpipers are among the non-gull quarry to be searched out.

*Black-legged Kittiwake*

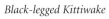

## Iroquois National Wildlife Refuge–Tonawanda Wildlife Management Area–Oak Orchard Wildlife Management Area

These three areas make up the 20,000-acre "Alabama Swamp," one of the largest wetland complexes in the state. Several large streams, swamp forests, open-water impoundments, upland woods and farm fields attract a great diversity of birds. Over 250 species are on the official checklist. Managed principally for migrating waterfowl—Canada Geese, Snow Geese, Tundra Swans and a variety of dabbling and diving ducks—these wetlands are also valuable for Great Blue Herons and Green Herons. This remains the best site in New York for King Rails, which are reported here annually, and a pair of Bald Eagles also nests in the area. Oak Orchard Creek remains one of the easiest sites in the state in which to find the rare southern Prothonotary Warbler. Several small, difficult-to-identify flycatchers—the *Empidonax* or "empies"—nest here, among them the more southern Acadian Flycatcher.

## Letchworth State Park

The Genesee River exposed a million years of rock layers when it carved the "Grand Canyon of the East." Deep, cool ravines surrounded by upland hardwood forests give the 20-mile-long Letchworth State Park its diversity of habitats. Cool northern hardwood forests are juxtaposed with drier oak-hickory forests. The park naturalist claims the largest list of breeding species of wood-warblers in the northeastern U.S.—Blue-winged, Golden-winged, Nashville, Yellow, Chestnut-sided, Black-throated Blue, Black-throated Green, Magnolia, Pine, Prairie, Hooded, Cerulean and Blackburnian warblers show a mix of northern and southern species. The edges of the park abut some of the best farmland in the state and surrounding open areas harbor Eastern Meadowlarks, Bobolinks and a number of grassland sparrows, among them the Savannah, Vesper, Grasshopper and Henslow's sparrows.

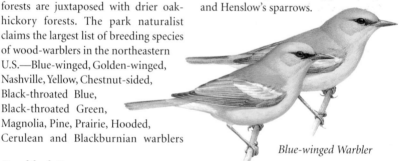

*Blue-winged Warbler*

## Braddock Bay

State and town park land make up this Lake Ontario shore landscape of beach, marsh, pond and woodland. Together with neighboring Hamlin Beach State Park, Braddock Bay is an outstanding place to watch migration—hawks and songbirds in spring, and gulls, jaegers and waterfowl in fall. Braddock Bay is the site of an important spring hawk watch, and large numbers of Red-tailed, Broad-winged, Rough-legged and Red-shouldered hawks, as well as eagles, falcons, Northern Harriers and Ospreys, pass over in March and April. Also in spring, a patch of conifer woods hosts Northern Saw-whet Owls and Long-eared Owls that, reluctant to fly out over open water, settle to roost. The large cattail marshes are home to Red-winged Blackbirds, Swamp Sparrows and Marsh Wrens. Black Terns, rare breeders in New York, also nest in the marshes. Purple Martins use nest boxes erected for them and all the eastern swallow species can be seen in large migratory flocks in August and September.

## Derby Hill

Located on a Lake Ontario bluff, Derby Hill is one of the state's premier spring hawk watch sites. The Onondaga County Audubon Society employs a hawk counter who, with a number of volunteers, tallies the thousands of raptors that pass down the lakeshore. All three *Accipiter* species, Red-tailed, Red-shouldered and Broad-winged hawks, three species of falcons, Osprey, Northern Harriers and Bald Eagles are common. Numbers are sometimes astonishing—totals exceed 40,000 raptors annually, and one April day, 18,000 Broad-winged Hawks were counted. Extreme rarities tantalize—Swainson's Hawks, Mississippi Kites and once even a White-tailed Eagle, a vagrant from Eurasia, which has been dubbed the "bird of the century." In fall, birders focus their attention on the lake to watch the passage of gulls, Pomarine Jaegers, Parasitic Jaegers, Red Phalaropes and Red-necked Phalaropes. By late fall, the wintering assemblage of diving ducks—Common Goldeneyes, Buffleheads, scaups, scoters and mergansers—have shown up. Among them are the occasional Barrow's Goldeneye or Harlequin Duck. Gull flocks often contain Black-headed Gulls or Little Gulls.

## Cape Vincent–Point Peninsula

Cape Vincent is a large area of open agricultural land interspersed with woodlots that borders the east end of Lake Ontario and the St. Lawrence River. The best time of year for birding is winter, when northern raptors visit to feed on the abundant mice. Resident Red-tailed Hawks and Great Horned Owls are then joined by Rough-legged Hawks in sometimes impressive numbers, as well as Short-eared Owls. Gyrfalcons have been seen along the shores of Point Peninsula, site of a state park. Open water on the lakeshore harbors large numbers of Common Goldeneyes, Buffleheads and Long-tailed Ducks, as well as several species of dabbling ducks. Horned Larks, Snow Buntings and Lapland Longspurs are frequently seen feeding in freshly manured farm fields and visit roadsides for grit. Small coveys of New York's only established population of Gray Partridge may be found in these same fields and roadsides, and often visit backyard feeders.

## Montezuma National Wildlife Refuge

The Montezuma National Wildlife Refuge is a 7000-acre remnant of once-vast marshes located at the north end of Cayuga Lake. The refuge was established in the late 1930s to provide a stopover for huge numbers of migrating waterfowl, particularly Canada Geese. People drive the 5-mile tour road in fall to view the 100,000 or so waterfowl resting and feeding on the Main Pool. The refuge also contains swamp forest, upland woods and agricultural areas. Warbler migration in May is often quite good and a number of these "butterflies of the bird world" stay to breed, among them the rare Prothonotary Warbler and the Cerulean Warbler. Fall migration is equally good for birders. May's Point Pool and Benning Marsh are managed for the shorebirds that visit in late summer and fall—Greater Yellowlegs, Lesser Yellowlegs, Short-billed Dowitchers, Black-bellied Plovers and American Golden-Plover, as well as an assortment of small "peep" sandpipers, are easily found. Montezuma also has nesting Bald Eagles, the result of a restoration program that began here in the 1970s. One nest is easily seen from the observation tower at the Tschache Pool. An Osprey nest is located near the entrance and visitor center.

## Sapsucker Woods–Cornell Laboratory of Ornithology

Every birder must visit the "Lab of O" at least once in a lifetime. This is *the* national center of bird research and education, and a large, modern facility has replaced the outgrown lab founded by Arthur A. Allen, America's first professor of ornithology. Visitors can see the artwork of Louis Agassiz Fuertes, watch waterfowl on a small pond, view songbirds coming to feeders through a large gallery window and walk the trails of Sapsucker Woods.

Sapsucker Woods is a wet woodland adjacent to the Cornell Lab, surrounded by old fields. There are 4.2 miles of self-guided trails and the area attracts a variety of birds—the checklist has more than 200 species on it. Ruffed Grouse, Pileated Woodpeckers, Wood Thrushes, Veeries, Red-eyed Vireos, American Redstarts, Northern Waterthrushes and a number of other common species nest here. American Woodcocks can be heard courting in April.

## Ferd's Bog–Moose River Plains

Every New York birder eventually travels to the small fen in the western Adirondacks known as Ferd's Bog, usually in May and June to search out boreal specialties. A quarter-mile-long path through a northern hardwood forest and balsam swamp leads to a short board-walk out onto the bog mat. This is the only easily visited site in which to find both American Three-toed and Black-backed woodpeckers. The dense forests around the bog are home to breeding Hermit Thrushes, Blue-headed Vireos, Red-eyed Vireos, Winter Wrens and a number of wood-warbler species. Hairy Woodpeckers, Downy Woodpeckers, Yellow-bellied Sapsuckers and Broad-winged Hawks are also found here. An Osprey pair nests at the edge of the bog.

The Moose River Plains are a vast wild area nearby, and many of the same species can be found there. It was the last place in New York to have a Golden Eagle nest, in the 1970s, and there is hope for the species' return as populations of this raptor increase in eastern Canada. A visit to the area in May or June requires long sleeves, head nets and bug repellent—the black flies can be fierce.

## Essex-Westport

Centered around the two Lake Champlain shore villages of Essex and Westport are a number of excellent birding sites that can be visited by driving side roads off NY 22. Winter birding along the lakeshore and in open farm areas turns up a surprise on every visit. Open water has Common Loons, Horned Grebes, Canada Geese, Mallards, American Black Ducks, Common Goldeneyes, Buffleheads, Common Mergansers and Long-tailed Ducks. Rarities such as the Eared Grebe and Barrow's Goldeneye may be present. Red-tailed Hawks, Rough-legged Hawks, Horned Larks, Snow Buntings and Lapland Longspurs can be found in open country. Northern Shrikes occur frequently. In irruption years, there is no better region for Bohemian Waxwings. Migrant shorebirds rest along the shoreline in late summer and fall. Gulls and jaegers can be seen in late fall and into winter. Large skeins of Canada Geeses and Snow Geese fly south along the lake and stop on farm fields to feed on waste grain. An occasional Greater White-fronted Goose may occur with them.

## Five Rivers Environmental Education Center

Because of its proximity to Albany, the 350-acre Five Rivers Environmental Education Center has become an important center for education. The variety of habitats—ponds, streams, woodlands, conifer plantations, old fields and a cool ravine—and the ease with which they can be visited by birders means that the center's bird list is quite large. Great Blue Herons and Green Herons feed in the ponds that are also home to nesting Canada Geese, Mallards and Wood Ducks. Ruffed Grouse and Wild Turkeys nest in the deeper woods. Great Horned Owls and Eastern Screech-Owls nest here, and Long-eared Owls and Short-eared Owls visit in winter. Eastern Bluebirds responded to a nest-box program and are now common. Open fields are home to the Bobolink, Savannah Sparrow and Eastern Meadowlark. An annual bird list is started on a public walk on New Year's Day and tallies the first 30 or so of the 150-plus species that can be found in the area. During the height of migration in May, more than 90 species have been counted, including as many as 20 species of wood-warblers.

## Shawangunk Grasslands National Wildlife Refuge

Born in controversy, the new Shawangunk Grasslands National Wildlife Refuge is a square mile of grassland and scrub surrounded by farms. Once an army airfield, with concrete runways still visible, the site was used in the past by parachutists from West Point, the FBI for car chase training and model airplane flyers. The refuge was established in 1999, with 400 acres set aside as grassland. Now visitors are kept to the old runways and plans for access will limit usage to nonintrusive nature recreation. The refuge is now being kept at a very early successional stage to provide habitat for a number of rarities. Eastern Meadowlarks, Bobolinks and several grassland sparrows—Savannah, Vesper, Grasshopper and Henslow's—nest here. Several Northern Harriers, a Northern Shrike or two and up to a dozen Short-eared Owls spend the winter feeding on mice. Neighboring farms may be birded from roadways. Barn Owls nest in nearby buildings and likely use the area for feeding. Red-headed Woodpeckers nest at a nearby horse farm. Turkey Vultures and Black Vultures are often seen soaring over the valley.

## Bashakill Wildlife Management Area

The Bashakill Wildlife Management Area is composed of over 2000 acres of marsh, swamp woods and uplands, and contains the largest freshwater marsh in southern New York. A stream that runs through the middle of the marsh gives canoe access, which is wonderful way to see the more secretive marsh denizens such as Pied-billed Grebes, American Bitterns, Least Bitterns, Virginia Rails, Sora and Common Moorhens. A walking trail traverses the wooded eastern edge of the area and gives access to both upland and marsh birds. A full day in May can easily turn up 100 species. The composite list for the area has over 220 species and includes most of the eastern woodpeckers, swallows, vireos, wood-warblers and thrushes. Typically southern species such as the Acadian Flycatcher, Prothonotary Warbler and Yellow-breasted Chat have also been seen here. All three accipiters—the Cooper's Hawk, Sharp-shinned Hawk and Northern Goshawk—as well as Red-tailed, Broad-winged and Red-shouldered hawks, fly down the valley on fall migration.

## Bear Mountain State Park

Two sites within Bear Mountain State Park provide the best birding—Iona Island marshes and Doodletown. Iona Island in the Hudson River is connected to the park by a large cattail marsh that is home to the Least Bittern, Virginia Rail, Marsh Wren and Common Yellow-throat. It is also a winter roosting site for Black Vultures and the occasional Turkey Vulture. Wintering Bald Eagles are frequently seen on the river. Uphill, along an old overgrown roadway, is the site of a Revolutionary War–era village, Doodletown. As in much of the park, the surrounding forest is dominated by oak species, and a song-filled May morning will reveal many warblers, including Cerulean, Golden-winged, Blue-winged, Worm-eating and Hooded warblers. The Kentucky Warbler and White-eyed Vireo are two southern specialties that birders seek out. Black-billed Cuckoos and Yellow-billed Cuckoos are often heard, and are particularly common when there are outbreaks of defoliating caterpillars. This is one of the few places in New York where birders must be aware of timber rattlesnakes.

## Marshlands Conservancy–Playland County Park

Marshlands Conservancy and the nearby Playland County Park are two gems tucked away in the middle of highly developed suburbia. Playland is a busy recreation park with a nature sanctuary and a freshwater lake within a few yards of Long Island Sound. It is best visited in winter when several offshore rocks provide views of Great Cormorants, Purple Sandpipers and a variety of gulls. Common Loons, Horned Grebes, Common Goldeneyes, Buffleheads, Red-breasted Mergansers and the three scoter species form rafts on the Sound. The freshwater lake often remains partially open and has the usual dabbling ducks as well as Greater Scaup, Lesser Scaup, Ruddy Ducks, Hooded Mergansers, Common Mergansers, Canvasbacks and an occasional Redhead.

Marshlands Conservancy has a nature center and oak woodlands, a mowed meadow, salt marshes and an open bay. Great Horned Owls nest near the nature center. The marshes harbor Clapper Rails and Saltmarsh Sharp-tailed Sparrows. In fall, migrant Nelson's Sharp-tailed Sparrows give skilled birders an opportunity to discriminate this once "lumped" species pair.

## Central Park, New York City

Central Park is an 843-acre green oasis in the middle of Manhattan that is justifiably world famous as a birding site. Over 190 species visit regularly, and the park's all-time bird list exceeds 275 species. It is almost a rite of passage for a New York birder to make a May trip to Central Park, particularly on a migrant "fallout" day when every copse seems full of vireos, warblers and thrushes. Southern species such as the Summer Tanager, Blue Grosbeak and Orchard Oriole sometimes overfly their destinations and land in this "green spot" in the middle of the concrete canyons. The famous Ramble, 37 acres of thicket, is the place to see these species. Amazingly, there is even a productive fall hawk watch conducted by the New York City Audubon Society and the Urban Park Rangers.

*Blue Grosbeak*

### Jamaica Bay Wildlife Refuge

Jamaica Bay Wildlife Refuge is one of the best birding spots in North America. This 9000-acre mosaic of open bay, tidal flats and saltmarsh-ringed islands lies under the busy flight paths of airlines exiting JFK International Airport. The refuge visitor center sits on an island of fill that has been landscaped with trees and shrubs. Two human-made brackish-water ponds, one of 100 acres and another half the size, dominate the birder's attention. A gravel trail takes visitors around the smaller West Pond, giving good views of the bay and salt marshes, as well as providing a couple of detours into the "gardens," actually groves of trees planted 50 years ago. The East Pond requires boots, since any semblance of trails are simple "herd paths" in the shallow and muddy pond margin. Birding here is excellent year-round. The refuge list has an astounding 330 species, with a couple of dozen "one time only" accidentals. Late summer marks the arrival of southbound shorebirds, and this migration goes on into November. Nearly 30 species of plovers and sandpipers stop to rest and fatten up. Among the rarities have been the Ruff, Curlew Sandpiper, Red-necked Stint and Broad-billed Sandpiper. Herons, egrets and ibises of all kinds nest here. Clapper Rails, Seaside Sparrows, Saltmarsh Sharp-tailed Sparrows, Marsh Wrens and Boat-tailed Grackles are found in the marshes. Barn Owls have taken to the nest boxes mounted on poles in the open marshes and Ospreys commonly nest on pole-mounted platforms. Waterfowl of all kinds are common on the deeper West Pond and in Jamaica Bay. A lone Eurasian Wigeon often joins the flock of American Wigeons. Rafts of Greater Scaup, Common Goldeneyes and Buffleheads winter in the bay. Wintering raptors include Peregrines, which feed off the ducks, and Long-eared Owls and Northern Saw-whet Owls winter in the planed pines.

*Cattle Egret*

## Jones Beach State Park

The western third of a 17-mile barrier island makes up the popular Jones Beach State Park. In all but the busy beach season of July and August, this narrow strip of ocean beach, dunes, thickets, pine woods and salt marshes can be birded with excellent results. Southbound fall migrants, reluctant to set out across the sea, fly west along the beach seeking shelter and food. Shorebirds are seen in great numbers and diversity on mudflats at low tide, and September is the peak of the coastal movement of American Kestrels, Merlins, Peregrine Falcons, Cooper's Hawks and Sharp-shinned Hawks. In May, migrating songbirds blown out to sea land exhausted on the beach. Warblers, vireos, orioles and tanagers decorate the small pines in the dunes like Christmas ornaments. Black Skimmers, Least Terns and Piping Plovers compete with the hundreds of thousands of sun-worshippers for a little of the beach to nest on. Clapper Rails, Marsh Wrens and Seaside Sparrows nest in the salt marsh.

Winter is as good a season as any for birding. Common Loons, Red-throated Loons, Horned Grebes, Red-necked Grebes, Northern Gannets and sea ducks such as Black, Surf and White-winged scoters occur offshore. Jones Inlet at the west end of the park is noted for Harlequin Ducks, Purple Sandpipers and the occasional Little Gull and Black-headed Gull among the huge flocks of Bonaparte's Gulls. Long-eared Owls and Northern Saw-whet Owls winter in the pine thickets, Short-eared Owls can be seen over the marshes and Snowy Owls frequent the dunes.

*Black Skimmer*

## Montauk Point State Park

Montauk Point State Park, located at the eastern end of Long Island, some 130 miles from New York City, can be a cold and windy place in midwinter, though this is the best time to stand at the edge of the sea and scan the large aggregation of sea ducks. As many as 20,000 waterfowl have been counted here in winter. Common Eiders and White-winged, Surf and Black scoters form enormous flocks of constantly flying and diving birds just off the Point. Lesser numbers of Red-breasted Mergansers, Common Goldeneyes, Buffleheads, Long-tailed Ducks and Greater Scaup are common.

There are also the occasional Harlequin Ducks or King Eiders. A sea watch should turn up Northern Gannets, Black-legged Kittiwakes and Razorbills. This is the one place in New York to actively seek out Common Murres, Thick-billed Murres or Black Guillemots. Great Cormorants often fly by the Point. Tubenoses such as Cory's, Greater and Sooty shearwaters and Wilson's Storm-Petrels are occasionally-seen from shore in late summer and early fall. The Point also has a good record of western songbirds that have been blown to the end of land in fall.

## NEW YORK'S TOP 100 BIRDING SITES

1. Ripley Hawk Watch
2. Dunkirk Harbor
3. Roger Tory Peterson Nature Center
4. Allegany SP
5. Tifft Nature Preserve
6. Niagara River Corridor
7. Iroquois NWR–Tonawanda WMA–Oak Orchard WMA
8. Beaver Meadow Nature Center
9. Hanging Bog WMA
10. Letchworth SP
11. Nation's Road Grassland
12. Hamlin Beach SP
13. Braddock Bay
14. Durand-Eastman Park (Rochester)
15. Sodus Bay
16. Howland Island WMA
17. Montezuma NWR
18. Sapsucker Woods–Cornell Laboratory of Ornithology
19. Stewart Park–Cayuga Lake
20. Connecticut Hill WMA
21. Michigan Hollow–Spencer Marsh
22. Spencer Crest Nature Center
23. Oswego Harbor
24. Derby Hill
25. Selkirk Shores SP
26. Whiskey Hollow
27. Beaver Lake CP
28. Whetstone Gulf SP
29. Cape Vincent–Point Peninsula
30. Perch River WMA
31. Wellesley Island SP
32. Upper and Lower Lakes WMA
33. Robert Moses SP
34. Verona Beach–Sylvan Beach
35. Utica Marsh
36. Pharsalia WMA
37. Whitney Point Reservoir
38. Chenango Valley SP
39. Franklin Mountain
40. Ferd's Bog–Moose River Plains
41. Paul Smiths Visitor Interpretive Center (Adirondack Park)
42. Bloomingdale Bog
43. Chubb River Swamp
44. Elk Lake
45. Whiteface Mountain
46. Chazy Landing–Point au Roche SP
47. Ausable Point
48. Essex-Westport
49. Crown Point SP
50. Fort Edward Grassland
51. Saratoga National Historic Park
52. Saratoga Lake
53. Vischer Ferry Nature and Historic Preserve
54. Cohoes–Crescent–Peebles Island SP
55. Partridge Run WMA
56. John Boyd Thacher SP
57. Black Creek Marsh WMA
58. Five Rivers Environmental Education Center
59. Schodack Island SP
60. Cherry Plains SP
61. Lake Taghkanic SP
62. Thompson's Pond–Stissing Mountain
63. Cruger Island–Tivoli Bays
64. Slide Mountain
65. Mohonk Preserve–Minnewaska SP
66. Shawangunk Grasslands NWR
67. Mongaup Valley WMA
68. Bashakill WMA
69. Sterling Forest SP
70. Bear Mountain SP
71. Clarence Fahnestock SP
72. Ward Pound Ridge Reservation
73. Croton Point CP
74. Marshlands Conservancy–Playland CP
75. Pelham Bay Park
76. Inwood Hill Park
77. Central Park

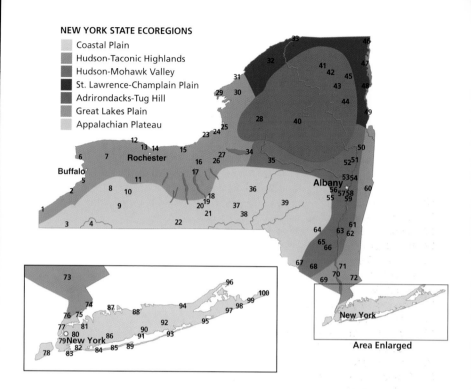

**NEW YORK STATE ECOREGIONS**

- Coastal Plain
- Hudson-Taconic Highlands
- Hudson-Mohawk Valley
- St. Lawrence-Champlain Plain
- Adrirondacks-Tug Hill
- Great Lakes Plain
- Appalachian Plateau

New York

Area Enlarged

**ABBREVIATIONS:**
**CP**–County Park
**NWR** – National Wildlife Refuge
**SP** – State Park
**WMA** – Wildlife Management Area

78. Great Kills Park–Mount Loretto
79. Prospect Park
80. Forest Park
81. Alley Pond Park
82. Jamaica Bay Wildlife Refuge
83. Riis Park–Breezy Point–Fort Tilden
84. Point Lookout–Jones Inlet
85. Jones Beach SP
86. Hempstead Lake SP
87. Caumsett SP
88. Caleb Smith SP–Nissequogue River

89. Fire Island National Seashore
90. Connetquot River SP
91. Heckscher SP
92. Southaven CP–Wertheim NWR
93. Smith Point CP
94. Riverhead Sod Farms
95 Shinnecock Inlet–Dune Road
96. Orient Point SP
97. Mecox Bay
98. Hook Pond
99. Napeague Bay–Hither Hills SP
100. Montauk Point SP

## ABOUT THE SPECIES ACCOUNTS

This book gives detailed accounts of the 320 species of birds that are listed as regular by the Federation of New York State Bird Clubs; these species can be expected on an annual basis. Forty occasional species and species of special note are briefly mentioned in an illustrated appendix. New York birders can expect to see small numbers of these species every few years, brought here either because of anticipated range expansion, migration or well-documented wandering tendencies. The order of the birds and their common and scientific names follow the American Ornithologists' Union's *Check-list of North American Birds* (7th edition, July 1998 and *The Forty-fifth Supplement, 2004*).

One of the challenges of birding is that many species look different in spring and summer than they do in fall and winter. Many birds have breeding and nonbreeding plumages, and immature birds often look different from their parents. This book does not try to describe or illustrate all the different plumages of a species; instead, it focuses on the forms that are most likely to be seen in our area.

**ID:** It is difficult to describe the features of a bird without being able to visualize it, so this section is best used in combination with the illustrations. Where appropriate, the description is subdivided to highlight the differences between male and female birds, breeding and nonbreeding birds and immature and adult birds. The descriptions use as few technical terms as possible, and favor easily understood language. Birds may not have "eyebrows" or "chins," but these and other terms are easily understood by all readers, in spite of their scientific inaccuracy. Some of the most common features of birds are pointed out in the Glossary illustration (p. 369).

*Peregrine
Falcon*

**Size:** The average length of the bird's body from bill to tail, as well as its wingspan, give an approximate measurement of the bird as it is seen in nature. The size of larger birds is often given as a range, because there is variation among individuals. Please note that birds with long tails often have large measurements that do not necessarily reflect "body" size.

**Status:** A general comment, such as "common," "uncommon" or "rare" is usually sufficient to describe the relative abundance of a species. Wherever possible, we have also indicated status at different times of the year. Situations are bound to vary somewhat since migratory pulses, seasonal changes and centers of activity tend to concentrate or disperse birds.

**Habitat:** The habitats we have listed describe where each species is most commonly found. In most cases, it is a generalized description, but if a bird is restricted to a specific habitat, the habitat is described precisely.

**Nesting:** In each species account, nest location and structure, clutch size, incubation period and parental duties are discussed. Remember that birding ethics discourage the disturbance of active bird nests. The nesting behavior of birds that do not nest in our region is not described.

**Feeding:** Birds spend a great deal of time foraging for food. If you know what a bird eats and where the food is found, you will have a good chance of finding that bird. Birds are frequently encountered while they are foraging.

*Red Crossbill*

**Voice:** You will hear many birds, particularly songbirds, which may remain hidden from view. Easily remembered paraphrases of distinctive sounds will aid you in identifying a species by ear. Please note that these paraphrases may only loosely resemble the call, song or sound produced by the bird. Should one of our paraphrases not work for you, feel free to make up your own.

**Similar Species:** Easily confused species are discussed briefly. If you concentrate on the most relevant field marks, the subtle differences between species can be reduced to easily identifiable traits. You might find it useful to consult this section when finalizing your identification; knowing the most relevant field marks will speed up the identification process. Even experienced birders can mistake one species for another.

**Best Sites:** If you are looking for a particular bird, you will have more luck in some locations than in others, even within the range shown on the range map. We have listed places that, besides providing a good chance of seeing a species, are easily accessible. As a result, many nature centers, national wildlife refuges and state parks are mentioned.

**Range Maps:** The range map for each species represents the overall range of the species in an average year. Most birds will confine their annual movements to this range, although each year some birds wander beyond their traditional boundaries. These small maps do not show differences in abundance within the range. They also cannot show small pockets within the range where the species may actually be absent, or how the range may change from year to year.

Unlike most other field guides, we have attempted to show migratory pathways—areas of the region where birds may appear while en route to nesting or winter habitats. The representations of the pathways do not distinguish high-use migration corridors from areas that are seldom used.

## Range Map Symbols

possible breeding area

summer /breeding

year-round

migration

winter

limit of winter dispersal

# NONPASSERINES

Waterfowl

Grouse & Allies

Diving Birds

Heronlike Birds

Birds of Prey

Rails, Coots
& Cranes

Shorebirds

Gulls & Allies

Doves, Parrots &
Cuckoos

Owls

Nightjars, Swifts
& Hummingbirds

Woodpeckers

Nonpasserine birds represent 18 of the 19 orders of birds found in New York, about 71 percent of the species in our region. They are grouped together and called "nonpasserines" because with few exceptions, they are easily distinguished from the "passerines," or "perching birds," which make up the 19th order. Being from 18 different orders, however, means that nonpasserines vary considerably in their appearance and habits—they include everything from the 5-foot-tall Great Blue Heron to the 4-inch-long Ruby-throated Hummingbird.

Generally speaking, nonpasserines do not "sing." Instead, their vocalizations are referred to as "calls." There are also other morphological differences. For example, the muscles and tendons in the legs of passerines are adapted to grip a perch, and the toes of passerines are never webbed. Many nonpasserines are large, so they are among our most notable birds. Waterfowl, raptors, gulls, shorebirds and woodpeckers are easily identified by most people. Some of the smaller nonpasserines, such as doves, swifts and hummingbirds, are frequently thought of as passerines by novice birders, and can cause those beginners some identification problems. With a little practice, however, they will become recognizable as nonpasserines. By learning to separate the nonpasserines from the passerines at a glance, birders effectively reduce by half the number of possible species for an unidentified bird.

# GREATER WHITE-FRONTED GOOSE

*Anser albifrons*

The small numbers of Greater White-fronted Geese that occasionally migrate through New York tend to be overshadowed by their more numerous and more vocal cousins, the Canada Geese, with whom they often travel. The slightly smaller Greater White-fronted Geese can best be distinguished by their bright orange feet, which shine like beacons as the birds stand on frozen spring wetlands and fields. More common farther west, these geese are best seen in our region during spring and fall migration, when they stop to refuel on aquatic plants in shallow ponds and marshes or on freshly sprouted grains in fields and pastures. • Greater White-fronted Geese breed on the arctic tundra and winter in the southern United States and Mexico. • Of the five species of gray geese found in Eurasia, the Greater White-fronted Goose is the only one that is also found in North America. Like most geese, White-fronts are long-lived birds that mate for life, with both parents caring for the young. • This goose is also known as "Speckle Belly."

**ID:** gray brown overall; black speckling on belly; pinkish or yellow orange bill; white around bill and on forehead; white hindquarters; black band on upper tail; orange feet.
**Size:** *L* 27–33 in; *W* 4½–5 ft.
**Status:** rare spring visitor in March and April; rarer in November and through winter; both Canadian pink-billed and Greenland orange-billed races are seen.
**Habitat:** croplands, fields, open areas and shallow marshes.

**Nesting:** does not nest in NY.
**Feeding:** dabbles in water and gleans the ground for grass shoots, sprouting and waste grain and occasionally aquatic invertebrates.
**Voice:** high-pitched "laugh."
**Similar Species:** *Canada Goose* (p. 38): white "chin strap"; black neck; lacks speckling on belly. *Snow Goose* (p. 37): blue morph has white head and upper neck and all-dark breast and belly.
**Best Sites:** Iroquois NWR–Tonawanda WMA–Oak Orchard WMA; Braddock Bay; Montezuma NWR; Hook Pond.

# SNOW GOOSE

*Chen caerulescens*

New York does not receive the staggering numbers of migrating Snow Geese found in other areas, but they are still sure to come in spring and fall. Landing in farmers' fields, these cackling geese fuel up on waste grain from the previous year's crops. In recent years, Snow Goose populations have increased dramatically in North America, as they take advantage of human-induced changes in the landscape and in the food supply. • Snow Geese grub for their food, often targeting the belowground parts of plants. Their strong, serrated bills are well designed for pulling up the root stalks of marsh plants and gripping slippery grasses. Because of their large numbers, there is concern that they may be degrading the sensitive tundra environment that they use for nesting. • Unlike Canada Geese, which fly in V-formations, migrating Snow Geese usually form oscillating, wavy lines. • Snow Goose plumage is sometimes stained rusty red from iron in the water. • Until 1983, this species' two color morphs, a white and a blue, were considered different species.

**ID**: white overall; black wing tips; pink feet and bill; dark "grinning patch" on bill; plumage is sometimes stained rusty red. *Blue morph:* white head and upper neck; dark blue gray body.

**Size:** *L* 28–33 in; *W* 4½ ft.

**Status:** common migrant, often seen in large numbers, from March to April and from October to November; sometimes overwinters along the coast in small numbers; blue morph is more common in western NY.

**Habitat:** shallow wetlands, lakes and fields.

**Nesting:** does not nest in NY.

**Feeding:** grazes on waste grain and new sprouts; also eats aquatic vegetation, grasses, sedges and roots.

**Voice:** loud, constant, nasal *houk-houk* in flight.

**Similar Species:** *Ross's Goose* (p. 357): smaller; shorter neck; lacks black "grinning patch." *Tundra* (p. 41), *Mute* (p. 40) and *Trumpeter swans:* larger; white wing tips. *American White Pelican* (p. 89): much larger bill and body.

**Best Sites:** Iroquois NWR–Tonawanda WMA–Oak Orchard WMA; Montezuma NWR; Perch River WMA; Hook Pond.

# CANADA GOOSE

*Branta canadensis*

Canada Geese are among the most recognizable birds in North America, but they are also among the least valued. Few people realize that at one time these birds were hunted almost to extinction. Populations have since been reestablished and, in recent decades, these large, bold geese have inundated urban waterfronts, picnic sites, golf courses and city parks. Today many people even consider them pests. • Many geese overwinter in more sheltered locations where food is available year-round. Canada Goose pairs mate for life and, unlike most birds, the parents do not sever bonds with their young until the beginning of the next year's nesting. • There are numerous subspecies of Canada Geese that vary considerably in size, though their habits are similar. The smaller races are now known as the Cackling Goose, having been elevated to full species status in 2004, and birders should watch for the very few that straggle here from their normal path between Canada and Texas.

**ID:** long, black neck; white "chin strap"; white undertail coverts; light brown underparts; dark brown upperparts; short, black tail.

**Size:** *L* 21–48 in; *W* 3½–5 ft.

**Status:** common year-round resident; breeds from March to May throughout the state; very common migrant from March to April and from October to November; abundant in winter on Long I. and in Finger Lakes region.

**Habitat:** lakeshores, riverbanks, ponds, farmlands and city parks.

**Nesting:** on an island or shoreline; usually on the ground or on a muskrat lodge; female builds a nest of plant materials and lines it with down; female incubates 3–8 white eggs for 25–28 days while the male stands guard.

**Feeding:** grazes on new sprouts, aquatic vegetation, grass and roots; tips up for aquatic roots and tubers.

**Voice:** loud, familiar *ah-honk,* often answered by other Canada Geese.

**Similar Species:** *Greater White-fronted Goose* (p. 36): brown neck and head; orange legs; white around base of bill; dark speckling on belly; lacks white "chin strap." *Brant* (p. 39): white "necklace"; black upper breast; lacks white "chin strap." *Snow Goose* (p. 37): blue morph has white head and upper neck. *Double-crested Cormorant* (p. 90): lacks white "chin strap" and undertail coverts; crooked neck in flight.

**Best Sites:** Iroquois NWR–Tonawanda WMA–Oak Orchard WMA; Montezuma NWR; Perch River WMA; Hook Pond; Jamaica Bay Wildlife Refuge.

# BRANT
*Branta bernicla*

This cousin of the Canada Goose typically spends most of its time in saltwater environments, but in migration it passes over great expanses of inland habitat, satisfying its hunger with freshwater plants and waste grain. • Most Brant on the Atlantic Flyway are of the white-bellied *hrota* race and are seen in spring and fall, flying low in ragged formation. They make brief stopovers only when the weather is bad. • Brant populations in eastern North America declined by almost 90 percent in the 1930s, when a virulent blight killed much of their winter source of saltwater eelgrass along the Atlantic Coast. Fortunately, many birds switched to eating sea lettuce, a strategy that kept the population from disappearing altogether. Eelgrass has returned in its former abundance to some sites, and this recovery has stabilized Brant numbers. • "Brant" is derived from an Anglo-Saxon word for "burned" or "charred," a reference to this bird's dark plumage.

**ID:** black neck, head and upper breast; dark upperparts; white "necklace," belly and hindquarters; black feet; pale brown sides and flanks. *In flight:* dark wings; dark head; long, white tail coverts conceal black tail; flies in irregular formation or in lines low over water.
**Size:** *L* 25 in; *W* 3½ ft.
**Status:** abundant migrant and winter visitor from October to May on western Long I.; common in migration in May and from October to November along Great Lakes shores and the Hudson Valley.

**Habitat:** lakeshores, agricultural fields and coastal bays and marshes.
**Nesting:** does not nest in NY.
**Feeding:** grazes on aquatic vegetation, primarily eelgrass and sea lettuce; also eats waste grain.
**Voice:** deep, prolonged *c-r-r-r-uk*, with hissing.
**Similar Species:** *Canada Goose* (p. 38): white "chin strap"; brown upperparts and upper breast. *Greater White-fronted Goose* (p. 36): brown neck and head; orange legs; white around base of bill; dark speckling on belly.
**Best Sites:** Hamlin Beach SP; Braddock Bay; L. Champlain; Jamaica Bay Wildlife Refuge; Jones Beach SP.

# MUTE SWAN
*Cygnus olor*

The Mute Swan, a Eurasian bird much admired for its grace and beauty, was introduced to eastern North America in the late 1800s to adorn estates, city parks and zoos. In the 1920s, escaped birds established populations on Long Island and the lower Hudson River. Over the years, these swans have adapted well to their new environment. They have continued to expand their feral populations, and although they are not usually migratory, more northerly nesters have established short migratory routes to milder wintering areas. • Like many nonnative species, Mute Swans are often fierce competitors for nesting areas and food sources. They can be very aggressive toward geese and ducks, often displacing native species. • A reliable long-distance characteristic for distinguishing a Mute Swan from a native swan is the way a Mute Swan holds its neck in a graceful curve with its orange bill hanging down. • In North America, the Mute Swan is one of the heaviest flying birds and is second in size only to the Trumpeter Swan.

**ID:** all-white plumage; orange bill with down-turned tip; black, bulbous knob at base of bill; neck usually held in an S-shape; wings often held in an arch over back while swimming.
**Size:** *L* 5 ft; *W* 6 ft.
**Status:** common year-round resident on Long I., in the New York City area and in the lower Hudson Valley; increasing in scattered upstate localities.
**Habitat:** marshes, lakes, ponds and estuaries.

**Nesting:** on the ground along a shoreline; male helps gather nest material; female builds a mound of vegetation and incubates 5–10 pale green eggs for 34–38 days; both adults raise the young.
**Feeding:** tips up or dips its head below the water's surface for aquatic plants; grazes on land.
**Voice:** generally silent; may hiss or issue hoarse barking notes; loud wingbeats can be heard from up to half a mile away.
**Similar Species:** *Tundra Swan* (p. 41) and *Trumpeter Swan:* lack orange bill with black knob at base; neck usually held straight.
**Best Sites:** Braddock Bay; Marshlands Conservancy–Playland CP; Jamaica Bay Wildlife Refuge; Hook Pond.

# TUNDRA SWAN

*Cygnus columbianus*

Before the last of winter's snows have melted into the fields, Tundra Swans return to New York, bringing us the first whispers of spring. Almost any small pond or lake in the western half of the state will briefly harbor a few Tundra Swans. There are historical accounts of resting swans, exhausted by long migratory flights, being swept over Niagara Falls, but this is apparently a rare occurrence. • Of the three species of North American swans, the Tundra Swan is the one most likely to be seen in the wild. Distinguishing among swan species comes down to the bill: the bright orange bill of the Mute Swan is hard to mistake, while the subtle difference in slope between the bills of the Tundra Swan and the Trumpeter Swan *(C. buccinator)*, and the yellow at the base of the Tundra's bill, can be more difficult to discern. • In the early 19th century, members of the Lewis and Clark expedition collected the first specimen of this bird near the Columbia River, thus its scientific name *columbianus*. • This swan was formerly known as "Whistling Swan."

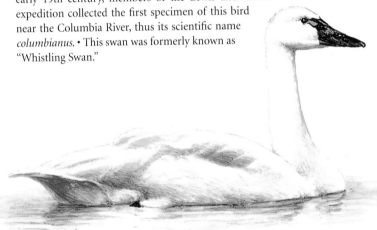

**ID:** all-white plumage; large, black bill; black feet; often shows yellow lores; neck is held straight; neck and head show rounded, slightly curving profile.

**Size:** *L* 4–4½ ft; *W* 6½ ft.

**Status:** common migrant in April in western NY, with large numbers on Chautauqua L., L. Ontario and the Finger Lakes; less common migrant from October to December; rare in winter on Long I.

**Habitat:** shallow areas of lakes and wetlands; also agricultural fields and flooded pastures.

**Nesting:** does not nest in NY.

**Feeding:** tips up, dabbles and surface gleans for aquatic vegetation and invertebrates; grazes for tubers, roots and waste grain.

**Voice:** high-pitched, quivering *oo-oo-whoo* is constantly repeated by migrating flocks.

**Similar Species:** *Trumpeter Swan:* extremely rare; larger; loud, bugling voice; lacks yellow lores; neck and head show more angular profile. *Mute Swan* (p. 40): orange bill with black knob on upper base; neck usually held in an S-shape; down-pointed bill; wings often held in an arch over back while swimming. *Snow Goose* (p. 37): smaller; black wing tips; shorter neck; pinkish bill.

**Best Sites:** Iroquois NWR–Tonawanda WMA–Oak Orchard WMA; Montezuma NWR; Niagara River Corridor; Sodus Bay.

# WOOD DUCK

*Aix sponsa*

The male Wood Duck is one of the most colorful waterbirds in North America, and books, magazines, postcards and calendars routinely celebrate its beauty. • Truly birds of the forest, Wood Ducks will nest in trees that are a mile or more from the nearest body of water. Forced into the adventures of life at an early age, newly hatched ducklings often jump from a height of 20 feet or more out of their nest cavity in a tree to follow their mother to the nearest body of water. The little bundles of down are not exactly feather light, but they bounce fairly well and seldom sustain injury. • Landowners with a tree-lined beaver pond or other suitable wetland may attract a family of Wood Ducks by building a nest box with a predator guard and

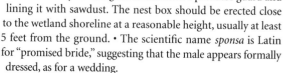

lining it with sawdust. The nest box should be erected close to the wetland shoreline at a reasonable height, usually at least 5 feet from the ground. • The scientific name *sponsa* is Latin for "promised bride," suggesting that the male appears formally dressed, as for a wedding.

**ID:** *Male:* glossy, green head with some white streaks; crest is slicked back from crown; white "chin" and throat; white-spotted, purplish chestnut breast; black-and-white shoulder slash; golden sides; dark back and hindquarters. *Female:* white, teardrop-shaped eye patch; mottled brown breast streaked with white; gray brown upperparts; white belly.

**Size:** *L* 15–20 in; *W* 30 in.

**Status:** common, widespread breeder from March to July; common fall migrant, less common in spring, with migrants arriving in March and departing in October; rare in winter.

**Habitat:** swamps, ponds, marshes and lakeshores with wooded edges.

**Nesting:** in a hollow or tree cavity; may be 30 ft or more above the ground; also in an artificial nest box; usually near water; cavity is lined with down; female incubates 9–14 white to buff eggs for 25–35 days.

**Feeding:** gleans the water's surface and tips up for aquatic vegetation, especially duckweed, aquatic sedges and grasses; eats more fruits and nuts than other ducks.

**Voice:** *Male:* ascending *ter-wee-wee.* *Female:* squeaky *woo-e-e-k.*

**Similar Species:** *Hooded Merganser* (p. 68): slim, black bill; black-and-white breast; male has black head with white crest patch.

**Best Sites:** Iroquois NWR–Tonawanda WMA–Oak Orchard WMA; Montezuma NWR; Upper and Lower Lakes WMA; Southaven CP–Wertheim NWR.

# GADWALL

*Anas strepera*

Male Gadwalls lack the striking plumage of most other male ducks, but they nevertheless have a dignified appearance and a subtle beauty. Once you learn their field marks—a black rump and white wing patches—male Gadwalls are surprisingly easy to identify. • Ducks in the genus *Anas*, the dabbling ducks, are most often observed tipping up their hindquarters and submerging their heads to feed, but Gadwalls dive more often than other ducks in this group. They feed equally during the day and night, a strategy that reduces the risk of predation because the birds avoid spending long periods of time sleeping or feeding. • Gadwall numbers have greatly increased in North America since the 1950s, and this duck has expanded its range throughout the continent. • The majority of Gadwalls winter on the Gulf Coast of the United States and Mexico.

**ID:** white speculum; white belly. *Male:* mostly gray; black hindquarters; dark bill. *Female:* mottled brown; brown bill with orange sides.

**Size:** *L* 18–22 in; *W* 33 in.

**Status:** common breeder on Long I. and rare but increasing breeder inland from May to July; common migrant from March to April and from October to November; uncommon in winter.

**Habitat:** shallow wetlands, lake borders and beaver ponds.

**Nesting:** in tall vegetation, sometimes far from water; well concealed in a scraped-out hollow, often with grass arching overhead; nest is made of grass and other dry vegetation and lined with down; female incubates 8–11 white eggs for 24–27 days.

**Feeding:** dabbles and tips up for aquatic plants; also eats aquatic invertebrates, tadpoles and small fish; grazes on grass and waste grain during migration; one of the few dabblers to dive routinely for food.

**Voice:** *Male:* simple, singular quack; often whistles harshly. *Female:* high *kaak kaaak kak-kak-kak,* in series and oscillating in volume.

**Similar Species:** *American Wigeon* (p. 45): green speculum; male has white forehead and green swipe trailing from each eye; female lacks black hindquarters. *Mallard* (p. 47), *Northern Pintail* (p. 50) and *other dabbling ducks* (pp. 43–51): generally lack white speculum and black hindquarters of male Gadwall and orange-sided beak of female.

**Best Sites:** Montezuma NWR; Jamaica Bay Wildlife Refuge; Iroquois NWR–Tonawanda WMA–Oak Orchard WMA; Braddock Bay.

# EURASIAN WIGEON

*Anas penelope*

Each year in New York, a few fortunate birders discover a conspicuous, chestnut-headed wigeon while scanning a flock of American Wigeons along the shore of a lake or estuary—Eurasian Wigeons are among the most noticeable of the regularly occurring rarities to visit the region. The Eurasian Wigeons that are seen in our region probably represent a small fraction of a large breeding population in Iceland, most of which winter in Europe. Although this species is not recorded as breeding in North America, an increased number of spring sightings suggests that there could be a small breeding population somewhere in Canada, possibly in Labrador. • American Wigeons are also wanderers, and some of these birds have been seen among flocks of Eurasian Wigeons in Europe and eastern Russia. • The scientific name refers to Penelope, the wife of Odysseus, who in Greek legend was thrown into the sea and rescued by seabirds.

**ID:** *Male:* chestnut head; cream forehead; rosy breast; gray sides; black hindquarters; dark feet; black-tipped, blue gray bill. *Female:* rufous hints on mostly brown head and breast; buffy flanks. *In flight:* large, white forewing patch; dusky gray "wing pits."
**Size:** *L* 16–20 in; *W* 31–32 in.
**Status:** rare but regular migrant from March to April and from October to November on Long I.; some overwinter; upstate records are mostly for March and April.
**Habitat:** shallow wetlands, lake edges and ponds; estuaries and larger rivers; occasionally in agricultural fields.

**Nesting:** does not nest in NY.
**Feeding:** primarily vegetarian; dabbles and grazes for freshwater pondweeds and eelgrass; occasionally pirates food from American Coots, which frequently share habitat with this and other dabbling ducks.
**Voice:** *Male:* high-pitched, 2-note whistle: *weeeeeeer. Female:* rough quack.
**Similar Species:** *American Wigeon* (p. 45): white "wing pits"; male has white crown and lacks reddish brown head; female typically has grayer head. *Gadwall* (p. 43), *Mallard* (p. 47) and *Northern Pintail* (p. 49): females lack blue gray bill and appear less buoyant on water.
**Best Sites:** Jamaica Bay Wildlife Refuge; Connetquot River SP; Southaven CP–Wertheim NWR; Hook Pond.

# AMERICAN WIGEON

*Anas americana*

The male American Wigeon's characteristic, piping, three-syllable whistle sets it apart from the wetland orchestra of buzzes, quacks and ticks. Listen carefully, however, and you'll realize where toy makers got the sound for rubber duckies. • Although this bird frequently dabbles for food, nothing seems to please a wigeon more than the succulent stems and leaves of pond-bottom plants. These plants grow far too deep for a dabbling duck, so wigeons often pirate from accomplished divers, such as American Coots, Canvasbacks, Redheads and scaups. In contrast to other ducks, the American Wigeon is a good walker and is commonly observed grazing on shore. • The American Wigeon nests farther north than any other dabbling duck with the exception of the Northern Pintail. Pair bonds are strong and last well into incubation. • The name "wigeon" comes from a French word meaning "whistling duck." Because of the male's bright white crown and forehead, some people call this bird "Baldpate."

**ID:** large, white upperwing patch; cinnamon breast and sides; white belly; black-tipped, blue gray bill; green speculum; white "wing pits." *Male:* white forehead; green swipe extends back from eye. *Female:* grayish head; brown underparts.

**Size:** *L* 18–22½ in; *W* 32 in.

**Status:** uncommon breeder in May and June; common migrant in April and from September to October; very common in winter on Long I.

**Habitat:** shallow wetlands, lake edges and ponds.

**Nesting:** always on dry ground, often far from water; well concealed in tall vegetation; nest is made of grass, leaves and down; female incubates 8–11 white eggs for 23–25 days.

**Feeding:** dabbles and tips up for the leaves and stems of pondweeds and other aquatic plants; also grazes and uproots young shoots in fields; may eat some invertebrates; occasionally pirates food from other birds.

**Voice:** *Male:* nasal, frequently repeated whistle: *whee WHEE wheew. Female:* soft, seldom heard quack.

**Similar Species:** *Gadwall* (p. 43): white speculum; lacks large, white upperwing patch; male lacks green eye swipe; female has orange swipes on bill. *Eurasian Wigeon* (p. 44): gray "wing pits"; male has rufous head, cream forehead, rosy breast and lacks green eye swipe; female usually has browner head.

**Best Sites:** Iroquois NWR–Tonawanda WMA–Oak Orchard WMA; Montezuma NWR; Jamaica Bay Wildlife Refuge; Southaven CP–Wertheim NWR.

# AMERICAN BLACK DUCK

*Anas rubripes*

At one time, the American Black Duck was the most common and widely distributed duck in the region. In recent years, the eastern expansion of the Mallard has come at the expense of this dark dabbler. A male Mallard will aggressively pursue a female American Black Duck, and if she is unable to find a male of her own kind, she will often accept the offer. Hybrid offspring are less fertile and are usually unable to reproduce. To the abundant Mallard it is not a loss, but to the American Black Duck it is a further setback. • This duck usually feeds in shallows where it is able to probe the mud by dabbling, searching below the water's surface with only its rump exposed. In summer, the American Black Duck eats aquatic insects, salamanders, small frogs and anything else that it is able to snatch up. • Male and female American Black Ducks are remarkably similar in appearance, which is unusual for waterfowl. The scientific name *rubripes* means "red foot" in Latin.

**ID:** dark brownish black body; light brown head and neck; bright orange feet; violet speculum. *Male:* yellow olive bill. *Female:* dull green bill mottled with gray or black. *In flight:* whitish underwings; dark body.
**Size:** *L* 20–24 in; *W* 35 in.
**Status:** present year-round; common, widespread breeder from April to June; abundant migrant and winter visitor from October to March.
**Habitat:** lakes, wetlands, rivers, agricultural areas and coastal salt marshes.
**Nesting:** usually on the ground among clumps of dense vegetation near water; female fills a shallow depression with plant material and lines it with down; female incubates 7–11 white to greenish buff eggs for 26–28 days; second clutches are common, usually to replace lost broods.
**Feeding:** tips up and dabbles in shallows for the seeds and roots of pondweeds; also eats aquatic invertebrates, larval amphibians and fish eggs.
**Voice:** *Male:* a croak. *Female:* a loud quack.
**Similar Species:** *Mallard* (p. 49): white belly; blue speculum bordered with white; female is lighter overall and has white outer tail feathers. *Gadwall* (p. 43): male has black hindquarters, white speculum and dark bill.
**Best Sites:** Montezuma NWR; Iroquois NWR–Tonawanda WMA–Oak Orchard WMA; Perch River WMA; Jamaica Bay Wildlife Refuge; Jones Beach SP.

# MALLARD
*Anas platyrhynchos*

The male Mallard, with his iridescent, green head and chestnut brown breast, is the classic wild duck. Mallards can be seen almost any day of the year, often in flocks and always near open water. These confident ducks have even been known to take up residence in local swimming pools. • Wild Mallards will freely hybridize with domestic ducks, which were originally derived from Mallards in Europe. The resulting offspring, often seen in city parks, are a confusing blend of both parents. • The body heat generated by a brooding female is enough to increase the growth rate of nearby grasses, which she will then manipulate to further conceal her precious nest. • Male ducks molt after breeding, losing much of their extravagant plumage. This "eclipse" plumage camouflages them during their flightless period and they usually molt again into their breeding colors by early fall. • Most people think of the Mallard's quack as the classic duck call, and in fact, the Mallard is the only duck that really "quacks."

**ID:** dark blue speculum bordered with white; orange feet. *Male:* glossy, green head; yellow bill; chestnut brown breast; white "necklace"; gray body plumage; black tail feathers curl upward. *Female:* mottled brown overall; orange bill is spattered with black.

**Size:** *L* 20–27½ in; *W* 35 in.
**Status:** common year-round resident; breeds from March to July; abundant migrant in March and from October to November; common in winter.
**Habitat:** lakes, wetlands, rivers, city parks, agricultural areas, sewage lagoons and coastal salt marshes.
**Nesting:** in tall vegetation or under a bush, often near water; nest of grass and other plant material is lined with down; female incubates 7–10 light green to white eggs for 26–30 days.
**Feeding:** tips up and dabbles in shallows for the seeds of sedges, willows and pondweeds; also eats insects, aquatic invertebrates, larval amphibians and fish eggs.
**Voice:** *Male:* deep, quiet quacks. *Female:* loud quacks; very vocal.
**Similar Species:** *Northern Shoveler* (p. 49): much larger bill; male has white breast. *American Black Duck* (p. 46): darker than female Mallard; purple speculum lacks white border. *Common Merganser* (p. 69): blood red bill; white underparts; male lacks chestnut breast.
**Best Sites:** Iroquois NWR–Tonawanda WMA–Oak Orchard WMA; Montezuma NWR; Jamaica Bay Wildlife Refuge; Southaven CP–Wertheim NWR.

# BLUE-WINGED TEAL
*Anas discors*

The small, speedy Blue-winged Teal is renowned for its aviation skills. These teals can be identified in flight by their small size and by the sharp twists and turns that they execute with precision. • Blue-winged Teals migrate farther than most ducks, summering as far north as the Canadian tundra and wintering mainly in Central and South America. They are among the last ducks to return in spring, and the last to establish pair bonds, often waiting until they arrive on their breeding grounds. • Despite the similarity of their names, the Green-winged Teal is not the Blue-winged Teal's closest relative. The Blue-winged Teal is more closely related to the Northern Shoveler and the Cinnamon Teal *(A. cyanoptera)*. These birds all have broad, flat bills, pale blue forewings and green speculums. Female Cinnamon Teals and Blue-winged Teals are so similar in appearance that even ornithologists and expert birders have difficulty distinguishing them in the field.

**ID:** *Male:* blue gray head; white crescent on face; black-spotted breast and sides. *Female:* mottled brown overall. *In flight:* blue forewing patch; green speculum.
**Size:** *L* 14–16 in; *W* 23 in.
**Status:** breeds from May to July in small numbers; common migrant from late April to May and from September to October.
**Habitat:** shallow lake edges and wetlands; prefers areas of short but dense emergent vegetation.
**Nesting:** in grass along a shoreline or in a meadow; nest is built with grass and considerable amounts of down; female incubates 8–13 white or pale olive eggs for 23–27 days.

**Feeding:** gleans the water's surface for sedge and grass seeds, pondweeds, duckweeds and aquatic invertebrates.
**Voice:** *Male:* soft *keck-keck-keck. Female:* soft quacks.
**Similar Species:** *Cinnamon Teal:* female is virtually identical to female Blue-winged Teal, but is richer brown overall and has less distinct eye line. *Green-winged Teal* (p. 51): female has smaller bill, black-and-green speculum and lacks blue forewing patch. *Northern Shoveler* (p. 49): much larger bill with paler base; male has green head and lacks spotting on body.
**Best Sites:** Montezuma NWR; Iroquois NWR–Tonawanda WMA–Oak Orchard WMA; Perch River WMA; Jamaica Bay Wildlife Refuge.

# NORTHERN SHOVELER

*Anas clypeata*

At first glance, the male Northern Shoveler resembles a male Mallard with an extremely large bill. A closer look, however, will reveal other differences—the Northern Shoveler has a white breast and chestnut flanks, while the Mallard has a chestnut breast and white flanks. An extra large, spoonlike bill allows this handsome duck to strain small invertebrates from the water and from the mud on the bottom of ponds. The Northern Shoveler eats much smaller organisms than most other waterfowl, and its intestines are elongated to prolong the digestion of these hard-bodied invertebrates. The shoveler's specialized feeding strategy means that it is rarely seen tipping up, but is more often found in the shallows of ponds and marshes where the mucky bottom is easiest to access. • The scientific name *clypeata* is Latin for "furnished with a shield," possibly for the chestnut patches on the flanks of the male. This species was once placed in its own genus, *Spatula*, the meaning of which needs no explanation.

**ID:** large, spatulate bill; blue forewing patch; green speculum. *Male:* green head; white breast; chestnut brown flanks. *Female:* mottled brown overall; orange-tinged bill.

**Size:** *L* 18–20 in; *W* 30 in.

**Status:** rare and very local breeder; common to abundant migrant from March to May and from September to November; common in winter on Long I.

**Habitat:** shallow marshes, bogs and lakes with muddy bottoms and emergent vegetation, usually in open and semi-open areas.

**Nesting:** in a shallow hollow on dry ground, usually within 150 ft of water; female builds a nest of dry grass and down; female incubates 10–12 pale greenish buff eggs for 21–28 days.

**Feeding:** dabbles in shallow and often muddy water; strains out plant and animal matter, especially crustaceans, aquatic insect larvae and seeds; rarely tips up.

**Voice:** generally quiet; occasionally a raspy chuckle or quack; most often heard during spring courtship.

**Similar Species:** *Mallard* (p. 47): blue speculum bordered by white; lacks pale blue forewing patch; male has chestnut brown breast and white flanks. *Blue-winged Teal* (p. 48): smaller overall; much smaller bill; male has spotted breast and sides.

**Best Sites:** Montezuma NWR; Jamaica Bay Wildlife Refuge; Iroquois NWR–Tonawanda WMA–Oak Orchard WMA.

# NORTHERN PINTAIL
*Anas acuta*

The trademark of the elegant and graceful male Northern Pintail is its long, tapering tail feathers, which are easily seen in flight and point skyward when the bird dabbles. In our region, only the male Long-tailed Duck shares this pintail feature. • Migrating pintails are often seen in flocks of 20 to 40 birds, but some early spring flocks have been known to consist of nearly 10,000 individuals. In spring, flooded agricultural fields tend to attract the largest pintail flocks. Most pintails migrating through New York are heading to or from breeding sites in Alaska, western and northern Canada or the northern Great Plains, although there is a small but growing nesting population in Atlantic Canada. Pintails breed earlier than most waterfowl, though breeding is scattered in New York. • This widespread duck appears to be in an overall decline across its range in central and western North America.

**ID:** long, slender neck; dark, glossy bill. *Male:* chocolate brown head; long, tapering tail feathers; white on breast extends up sides of neck; dusty gray body plumage; black-and-white hindquarters. *Female:* mottled light brown overall. *In flight:* slender body; brownish speculum with white trailing edge.
**Size:** *L* 21–25 in; *W* 34 in.
**Status:** very local breeder upstate; common to abundant migrant from March to April and in October; common in winter on the coast, but rare inland.
**Habitat:** shallow wetlands, fields and lake edges.
**Nesting:** in a small depression in low vegetation; nest of grass, leaves and moss

is lined with down; female incubates 6–12 greenish buff eggs for 22–25 days.
**Feeding:** tips up and dabbles in shallows for the seeds of sedges, willows and pondweeds; also eats aquatic invertebrates and larval amphibians; eats waste grain in agricultural areas during migration; more varied diet than other dabbling ducks.
**Voice:** *Male:* soft, whistling call. *Female:* rough quack.
**Similar Species:** male is distinctive. *Mallard* (p. 47) and *Gadwall* (p. 43): females are chunkier, usually have dark or 2-tone bills and lack tapering tail and long, slender neck. *Blue-winged Teal* (p. 48): green speculum; blue forewing patch; female is smaller. *Long-tailed Duck* (p. 64): head is not uniformly dark; all-dark wings.
**Best Sites:** Iroquois NWR–Tonawanda WMA–Oak Orchard WMA; Montezuma NWR; Perch River WMA; Jamaica Bay Wildlife Refuge.

# GREEN-WINGED TEAL

*Anas crecca*

Green-winged Teals are among the speediest and most maneuverable of waterfowl. When intruders cause these small ducks to rocket up from wetlands, the birds circle quickly overhead in small, tight-flying flocks, returning to the water only when the threat has departed. A predator's only chance of catching a healthy teal is to snatch it from the water or from a nest. • Green-winged Teals often undertake a partial migration before molting into their postbreeding, "eclipse" plumage. In this plumage they are unable to fly because they do not possess a full set of flight feathers. Green-wings are a common migrant, and these lovely little teals often loiter on ponds and marshy wetlands until cold winter weather freezes the water's surface. • Weighing less than a pound, the Green-winged Teal is the smallest dabbling duck in North America.

**ID:** small bill; green-and-black speculum. *Male:* chestnut brown head; green swipe extends back from eye; white shoulder slash; black-spotted, buff brown breast; pale gray sides. *Female:* mottled brown overall; pale belly.
**Size:** *L* 12–16 in; *W* 23 in.
**Status:** uncommon and local breeder in April and May; abundant migrant from March to April and from September to October; common winter visitor from October to March.
**Habitat:** shallow lakes, wetlands, beaver ponds and meandering rivers.

**Nesting:** well concealed in tall vegetation; nest is built of grass and leaves and lined with down; female incubates 6–14 creamy white to pale buff eggs for 20–24 days.
**Feeding:** dabbles in shallows, particularly on mudflats, for aquatic invertebrates, larval amphibians, marsh plant seeds and pondweeds.
**Voice:** *Male:* crisp whistle. *Female:* soft quack.
**Similar Species:** *American Wigeon* (p. 45): male lacks white shoulder slash and chestnut brown head. *Blue-winged Teal* (p. 48) and *Cinnamon Teal:* female has blue forewing patch.
**Best Sites:** Montezuma NWR; Perch River WMA; Jamaica Bay Wildlife Refuge; Southaven CP–Wertheim NWR.

# CANVASBACK

*Aythya valisineria*

While most male ducks sport richly decorated backs, the male Canvasback has a bright, clean back that, appropriately, appears to be wrapped in white canvas. In profile, the Canvasback casts a noble image—the long bill meets the forecrown with no apparent break in angle, allowing birds of either sex to be distinguished at long range. This bird's back and unique profile are unmistakable field marks. • Canvasbacks are diving ducks that are typically found on large areas of open water. Because these birds prefer large lakes and bays and the deepest areas of wetlands, birders often need binoculars to admire the male's wild red eyes and mahogany head. Canvasbacks are most likely to be seen during spring and fall migration, when flocks composed of more than 10,000 individuals occasionally converge on a suitable wetland. • The scientific name *valisineria* refers to one of the Canvasback's favorite foods, wild celery (*Vallisneria americana*).

**ID:** head slopes upward from bill to forehead. *Male:* canvas white back and sides; chestnut brown head and neck; black breast and hindquarters; red eyes. *Female:* duller brown head and neck; gray back and sides.
**Size:** *L* 19–22 in; *W* 29 in.
**Status:** breeds at only 1 Finger Lakes area site, which may originate from introduced birds; common migrant from March to April and in November; common winter visitor.
**Habitat:** marshes, ponds, shallow lakes and other wetlands; large lakes in migration.
**Nesting:** basket nest of reeds and grass is lined with down and suspended above shallow water in dense stands of cattails and bulrushes; may also nest on dry ground; female incubates 7–9 olive green eggs for 24–27 days.
**Feeding:** dives to depths of up to 30 ft (average is 10–15 ft); feeds on roots, tubers, the basal stems of plants, including pondweeds and wild celery, and bulrush seeds; occasionally eats aquatic inverte-brates.
**Voice:** generally quiet. *Male:* occasional coos and "growls" during courtship. *Female:* low, soft, "purring" quack or *kuck;* also "growls."
**Similar Species:** *Redhead* (p. 53): rounded rather than sloped forehead; male has gray back and bluish bill.
**Best Sites:** Montezuma NWR; Iroquois NWR–Tonawanda WMA–Oak Orchard WMA; Niagara River Corridor; Hook Pond.

# REDHEAD
*Aythya americana*

Like the Canvasback, the Redhead is most abundant as a migrant and winter resident. To distinguish a Canvasback from a Redhead, most birders will tell you to contrast the birds' profiles, but the most obvious difference between them is the color of their backs—the Canvasback has a white back, while the Redhead's is gray. • Redheads prefer large marshes for nesting, where they easily blend into the busy goings-on of woodland summer life. Female Redheads usually incubate their own eggs and brood their young as other ducks do, but they occasionally lay their eggs in the nests of other ducks. In our region, the Blue-winged Teal and the Ring-necked Duck may be victims of Redhead egg dumping, also known as "brood parasitism." • The Redhead is a diving duck, but it will occasionally feed on the surface of a wetland like a dabbler.

**ID:** black-tipped, blue gray bill. *Male:* rounded, red head; black breast and hindquarters; gray back and sides. *Female:* dark brown overall; lighter "chin" and "cheek" patches.

**Size:** *L* 18–22 in; *W* 29 in.

**Status:** local breeder as a result of 1950s introductions; common migrant from March to April and from October to November; common in winter, abundant on larger Finger Lakes.

**Habitat:** large wetlands, ponds, lakes, bays and rivers.

**Nesting:** usually in shallow water, sometimes on dry ground; deep basket nest of reeds and grass is suspended over water at the base of emergent vegetation and lined with fine, white down; female incubates

9–14 greenish eggs for 23–29 days; female may lay eggs in other ducks' nests.

**Feeding:** dives to depths of 10 ft; primarily eats aquatic vegetation, especially pondweeds, duckweeds and the leaves and stems of plants; occasionally eats aquatic invertebrates.

**Voice:** generally quiet. *Male:* catlike meow in courtship. *Female:* rolling *kurr-kurr-kurr;* *squak* when alarmed.

**Similar Species:** *Canvasback* (p. 52): clean white back; bill slopes onto forehead. *Ring-necked Duck* (p. 54): female has more prominent white eye ring, white ring on bill and peaked head. *Lesser Scaup* (p. 57) and *Greater Scaup* (p. 56): male has dark head and whiter sides; female has more white at base of bill.

**Best Sites:** Iroquois NWR–Tonawanda WMA–Oak Orchard WMA; Montezuma NWR; Stewart Park–Cayuga L.; Perch River WMA.

# RING-NECKED DUCK

*Aythya collaris*

The Ring-necked Duck's distinctive white bill markings and angular head are field marks that immediately strike an observer. After seeing this duck in the wild, you may wonder why it was not named the "Ring-billed Duck," and you would not be the first birder to ponder this perplexing puzzle. The official appellation is derived from the scientific name *collaris* (collar), which originated with a 19th-century ornithologist looking at an indistinct cinnamon "collar" on a museum specimen, not a birder looking at a live duck through binoculars. • Ring-necked Ducks are diving ducks like scaups, Redheads and Canvasbacks, but they prefer to feed in shallower shoreline waters, frequently tipping up for food like dabbling ducks. Ring-necks are generalized feeders, allowing them to capitalize on the low resources found in the subarctic and boreal settings where they commonly nest. They are even able to nest in boggy areas where a more picky eater would find it hard to eke out a living.

**ID:** *Male:* angular, dark purple head; black breast, back and hindquarters; white shoulder slash; gray sides; blue gray bill with black and white bands at tip; thin, white border around base of bill. *Female:* dark brown overall; white eye ring; dark bill with black and white bands at tip; pale crescent on front of face.

**Size:** *L* 14–18 in; *W* 25 in.

**Status:** local breeder in May and June in the Adirondacks; common to abundant migrant and winter visitor from October to April.

**Habitat:** small lakes, wooded ponds, swamps, marshes and sloughs with emergent vegetation.

**Nesting:** on a floating island or hummock; rarely on a shoreline; frequently over water; bulky nest of grass and moss is lined with down; female incubates 8–10 olive tan eggs for 25–29 days.

**Feeding:** dives underwater for aquatic vegetation, including seeds, tubers and pondweed leaves; also eats aquatic invertebrates and mollusks.

**Voice:** seldom heard. *Male:* low-pitched, hissing whistle. *Female:* growling *churr.*

**Similar Species:** *Lesser Scaup* (p. 57) and *Greater Scaup* (p. 56): lack white ring near tip of bill; male lacks black back; female has broad, clearly defined white border around base of bill and lacks eye ring. *Redhead* (p. 53): rounded rather than peaked head; less white on front of face; female has less prominent eye ring.

**Best Sites:** Montezuma NWR; Perch River WMA; Saratoga L.; Southaven CP–Wertheim NWR.

# TUFTED DUCK
*Aythya fuligula*

The male Tufted Duck looks like a Ring-necked Duck, but lacks the white stripe across the bill and has a long tuft trailing down the back of his head. This European relative of the scaups occasionally ventures into North American waters, and the first sighting in North America was in 1911 in Alaska. This species occurs annually in New York, though it is difficult to be sure that these sighting are not of escaped birds from collections. Increasing numbers of reports lend credence to the belief that these ducks are true vagrants. The Tufted Duck breeds across Eurasia, but there are no North American breeding records. Look for this bird in winter and spring when open fresh water is in short supply. The Tufted Duck can also be seen in coastal bays and estuaries, especially on Long Island and in freshwater habitats.

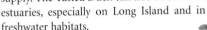

**ID:** *Male:* long, loose tuft at back of head; iridescent, dark purple head and neck; black back, wings, rump and breast; white flanks and belly; black-tipped bill. *Female:* short, brown head tuft; dark brown head, back and wings; reddish brown breast; pale gray brown flanks; white belly; black-tipped bill.
**Size:** *L* 17 in; *W* 25 in.
**Status:** rare but regular migrant and winter visitor from November to April.
**Habitat:** freshwater lakes and ponds until freeze-up; saltwater bays and estuaries in midwinter; also city harbors.

**Nesting:** does not nest in NY.
**Feeding:** dives for plants, crustaceans, mollusks and aquatic insects.
**Voice:** usually silent in winter; male's courtship call is a peeping whistle; female utters a low, growling *err-err-err*.
**Similar Species:** *Ring-necked Duck* (p. 54): white band on bill; lacks head tuft and white wing bar; male has gray flanks; female has white streak behind eye. *Greater Scaup* (p. 56) and *Lesser Scaup* (p. 57): lack head tuft; males have grayer backs and wings; females have more extensive white patch at base of bill.
**Best Sites:** Oswego Harbor; Central Park (NYC); Long I. ponds.

55

# GREATER SCAUP

*Aythya marila*

Since the introduction of zebra mussels into the Great Lakes, large flocks of Greater Scaup have begun wintering here, far away from their traditional wintering grounds on the Atlantic Ocean. • The Greater Scaup is abundant throughout much of the region during spring and fall migration, and some locations boast concentrations of more than 27,000 individuals. • Look for the rounder, not peaked, more greenish head of the Greater Scaup to distinguish it from its Lesser relative. The Lesser Scaup also has a lavender iridescence on its head, making it easy to remember which scaup is which by correlating the color of each duck's head with the corresponding first letter of its name. However, scaups usually raft so far out in the water that specific identification is often not possible. • Scaups are diving ducks and have a heavy bone structure, so they require a running start across the surface of the water to take off. • Both Greater Scaup and Lesser Scaup are known by the nickname "Bluebill."

**ID:** rounded head; golden eyes. *Male:* iridescent, dark green head (may appear black); black breast; white belly, sides and flanks; light gray back; dark hindquarters; black-tipped, blue bill. *Female:* brown overall; well-defined white patch at base of bill. *In flight:* white wing stripe.
**Size:** *L* 16–19 in; *W* 28 in.
**Status:** abundant migrant and winter visitor from October to April on Long I.; smaller numbers winter on the Great Lakes and Niagara R.
**Habitat:** lakes, large marshes and reservoirs; also bays and ocean, usually far from shore.
**Nesting:** does not nest in NY.

**Feeding:** dives underwater to greater depths than other *Aythya* ducks for aquatic invertebrates and vegetation; favors fresh-water mollusks in winter.
**Voice:** generally quiet in migration; alarm call is a deep *scaup*. *Male:* may issue a 3-note whistle and a soft *wah-hooo*. *Female:* may give a subtle "growl."
**Similar Species:** *Lesser Scaup* (p. 57): slightly smaller; shorter white wing stripe in flight; slightly smaller bill; male has peaked, purplish black head; female has peaked head. *Ring-necked Duck* (p. 54): black back; white shoulder slash; white ring around base of bill. *Redhead* (p. 53): male has red head and darker sides; female has less white at base of bill.
**Best Sites:** Niagara River Corridor; Oswego Harbor; Jones Beach SP; Smith Point CP; Montauk Point SP.

# LESSER SCAUP

*Aythya affinis*

The male Lesser Scaup and its close relative, the Greater Scaup, mirror the color pattern of an Oreo cookie: they are black at both ends and light in the middle. Although the two scaup species may occur together on larger lakes during migration, they tend not to mingle. • The Lesser Scaup is one of the most abundant and widespread North American ducks and is most at home among the lakes of forested areas, though this scaup can also be found nesting in marshes. • A member of the *Aythya* genus of diving ducks, the Lesser Scaup leaps up neatly before diving underwater, where it propels itself with powerful strokes of its feet. • The scientific name *affinis* is Latin for "adjacent" or "allied"—a reference to this scaup's close association to other diving ducks. "Scaup" might refer to a preferred winter food of this duck—shellfish beds are called "scalps" in Scotland—or it might be a phonetic imitation of one of its calls.

**ID:** peaked head; yellow eyes. *Male:* purplish black head; black breast and hindquarters; dusty white sides; grayish back; black-tipped, blue gray bill. *Female:* dark brown overall; well-defined white patch at base of bill. *In flight:* white wing stripe.

**Size:** *L* 15–18 in; *W* 25 in.

**Status:** 1 breeding record; abundant migrant from March to April and from October to November; common in winter.

**Habitat:** *Breeding:* woodland ponds, wetlands and lake edges with grassy margins. *In migration:* lakes, large marshes and rivers.

**Nesting:** in tall, concealing vegetation, generally close to water and occasionally on an island; nest hollow is built of grass and lined with down; female incubates 8–14 olive buff eggs for 21–27 days.

**Feeding:** dives underwater for aquatic invertebrates, mostly mollusks, crustaceans and insect larvae; occasionally eats aquatic vegetation.

**Voice:** alarm call is a deep *scaup. Male:* soft *whee-oooh* in courtship. *Female:* purring *kwah.*

**Similar Species:** *Greater Scaup* (p. 56): rounded head; slightly larger bill; longer, white wing stripe; male has greenish black head. *Ring-necked Duck* (p. 54): black and white bands on bill; male has white shoulder slash and black back. *Redhead* (p. 53): male has red head and darker sides; female has less white at base of bill.

**Best Sites:** Montezuma NWR; Marshlands Conservancy–Playland CP; Hempstead Lake SP; Hook Pond.

# KING EIDER
*Somateria spectabilis*

If you want to travel to see a spectacular bird, the dazzling King Eider is worth the effort: the male boasts no less than six bold colors on his magnificent head and bill. When a King Eider is reported at one of its favored winter haunts, birders eagerly bundle up to go look for this impressive duck. Seldom are more than one or two found, and the rather plain female is often overlooked. King Eiders do not breed in New York—they breed primarily in the remote Arctic and their breeding range extends only as far south as northern Ontario, Canada. In fall, the birds are pushed southward by advancing sea ice. • King Eiders are equipped with some of the finest insulation in the bird world (eider down), so they are well adapted for loafing on ice floes and taking deep extended dives into frigid arctic water. • Adverse weather conditions and late break-up of sea ice can cause King Eider numbers to fluctuate dramatically. Because of their remote habitats, much remains unknown about this species.

**ID:** *Male:* blue crown; green "cheek"; orange nasal disc; red bill; black wings; white neck, breast, back, upperwing patches and flank patches. *Female:* mottled, rich rufous brown overall; black bill extends into nasal shield; V-shaped markings on sides.
**Size:** *L* 19–25 in; *W* 3 ft.
**Status:** rare winter visitor from November to April on the Great Lakes and in Atlantic coastal waters.
**Habitat:** at the surf line and beyond off coastal headlands, often farther from shore than Common Eiders and scoters.
**Nesting:** does not nest in NY.

**Feeding:** dives for aquatic mollusks; may dive to depths of more than 150 ft; also takes small insects, crustaceans, echinoderms and some vegetation.
**Voice:** *Male:* soft cooing sounds in courtship. *Female:* low, twanging clucks.
**Similar Species:** male is distinctive. *Common Eider* (p. 59): 1st-winter male has larger, grayer bill; female has evenly barred sides; feathering on sides of long, droopy bill extends to nostrils; immature has white streaking on back. *Scoters* (pp. 61–63): females have solid brown plumage, more bulbous bills, patchier head colors and lack nasal shield.
**Best Sites:** Niagara River Corridor; Sodus Bay; Oswego Harbor; Pt. Lookout–Jones Inlet; Montauk Point SP.

# COMMON EIDER

*Somateria mollissima*

Floating leisurely in rafts of thousands, Common Eiders regularly brave the frigid winter waters of the Atlantic Coast. The largest ducks in North America, these hefty birds are well adapted for living in cold, northern seas. Their high metabolic rate and dense down feathers facilitate their almost entirely marine lifestyle. Long periods of inactivity are punctuated by intense bouts of feeding or short flights to a nearby area, usually situated close to a coastal headland. • During the breeding season, female eiders pluck downy feathers from their own bodies to provide insulation and camou-flage for their eggs. For centuries, people have prized eider down for its superior insulative properties, and down-gathering still goes on in parts of Canada and Scandinavia.

**ID:** *Male:* smoothly sloping forehead; black crown, belly and tail; mostly white upperparts; white flank patch; green tinge on nape and nasal shield. *Female:* gray to rusty brown overall; barred breast, flanks and back; gray bill and nasal shield. *In flight:* flies close to the water's surface with head held low.

**Size:** *L* 24 in; *W* 3–3½ ft.

**Status:** common winter visitor from November to April to eastern Long I., rare elsewhere on Long I.; very rare on Great Lakes.

**Habitat:** shallow coastal waters in all seasons; occasionally seen on large freshwater lakes.

**Nesting:** does not nest in NY.

**Feeding:** pries mollusks, especially blue mussels, from the ocean depths and swallows them whole; may dive deeper than 150 ft; may eat crustaceans, echinoderms, insects and plant material when available.

**Voice:** *Male:* raucous, moaning *he-ho-ha-ho* or *a-o-waa-a-o-waa*. *Female:* Mallard-like *wak-wak-wak-wak-wak;* angry *wh-r-r-r-r*.

**Similar Species:** male is distinctive. *American Black Duck* (p. 46): may appear similar to female Common Eider; much smaller bill; light brown face; purple speculum; white underwing coverts. *Scoters* (pp. 61–63): all lack white back and breast of male and barring of female. *King Eider* (p. 58): male has colorful, blocky head; female has long nasal shield. *Long-tailed Duck* (p. 64), *Bufflehead* (p. 65), *Barrow's Goldeneye* (p. 67) and *Common Goldeneye* (p. 66): lack smoothly sloping facial profile.

**Best Sites:** Montauk Point SP; Orient Point SP; Hither Hills SP.

# HARLEQUIN DUCK
*Histrionicus histrionicus*

The small, surf-loving Harlequin Duck is a scarce but regular migrant and winter visitor to New York, though its numbers have declined over the years. Eastern Harlequin populations have dwindled to only about 1000 birds, initially because of overhunting, but undoubtedly for other reasons as well. • In eastern North America, Harlequins breed along the northeastern Atlantic Coast of Canada, favoring fast-flowing, coastal mountain streams as breeding habitat. After a short breeding season, flocks of Harlequins move southward, wintering along the coast as far south as New York State, with some flocks wandering to the Great Lakes. Though Harlequins stay in New York only briefly, their dynamic appearance never fails to excite and impress fortunate onlookers. • This duck is named after a character from traditional Italian comedy and pantomime, the Harlequin, who wore a diamond-patterned costume and performed "histrionics," or tricks. Some people refer to Harlequins as "Lords and Ladies."

**ID:** small, dark, rounded duck; blocky head; short bill; raises and lowers its tail while swimming. *Male:* blue gray body; chestnut brown sides; white spots and stripes outlined in black on head, neck and flanks. *Female:* dusky brown overall; light underparts; 2–3 light-colored patches on head.
**Size:** *L* 14–19 in; *W* 26 in.
**Status:** rare migrant and winter visitor from November to April on Long I., the Great Lakes and Niagara R.

**Habitat:** Great Lakes shores; rocky jetties.
**Nesting:** does not nest in NY.
**Feeding:** dabbles and dives for aquatic invertebrates, mostly crustaceans and mollusks.
**Voice:** generally silent outside the breeding season.
**Similar Species:** male is distinctive. *Bufflehead* (p. 65): smaller; female lacks white between eye and bill. *Surf Scoter* (p. 61): larger; female has bulbous bill. *White-winged Scoter* (p. 62): female has white wing patch and bulbous bill.
**Best Sites:** Niagara River Corridor; Robert Moses SP; Pt. Lookout–Jones Inlet; Montauk Point SP.

# SURF SCOTER
*Melanitta perspicillata*

W hen spring storms whip up whitecaps on our big lakes, migrating Surf Scoters ride comfortably among the crashing waves. These scoters are most often seen during spring and fall migration, when tired flocks settle on open water in large, dark rafts. Most scoters spend their winters just beyond the breaking surf on both the Atlantic and Pacific coasts, and they are well adapted to life on rough water. The Surf Scoter is the only scoter that breeds and winters exclusively in North America. • Like other species that breed in the Far North, Surf Scoters pair up before arriving on their summer breeding grounds to take advantage of the precious little summer available to them. • The Surf Scoter has the unfortunate distinction of being one of the least-studied waterbirds in North America. Much of the information that is known of its behavior and distribution was documented for the first time only in the latter part of the 20th century.

**ID:** large, stocky duck; large bill; sloping forehead; all-black wings. *Male:* black overall; white forehead and nape; orange bill and legs; black spot, outlined in white, at base of bill. *Female:* brown overall; dark gray bill; 2 whitish patches on sides of head. *In flight:* flies in shallow V-formation or in long lines, usually close to the water's surface.
**Size:** *L* 16–20 in; *W* 30 in.
**Status:** common to abundant migrant and winter visitor from November to April on the coast; less common on inland waters.

**Habitat:** large, deep lakes and large rivers; Great Lakes; coastal waters.
**Nesting:** does not nest in NY.
**Feeding:** dives to depths of 30 ft; eats mostly mollusks; also takes aquatic insect larvae, crustaceans and some aquatic vegetation.
**Voice:** generally quiet; infrequently utters low, harsh croaks. *Male:* occasionally gives a low, clear whistle. *Female:* guttural *krraak krraak.*
**Similar Species:** *White-winged Scoter* (p. 62): white wing patches; male lacks white on forehead and nape. *Black Scoter* (p. 63): male is all black; female has well-defined, pale "cheek" and dark "cap."
**Best Sites:** Montauk Point SP; Jones Beach SP; Hamlin Beach SP; Sodus Bay.

# WHITE-WINGED SCOTER
*Melanitta fusca*

As White-winged Scoters race across lakes, their flapping wings reveal a key identifying feature—the white innerwing patches strike a sharp contrast to the birds' otherwise dark plumage. Because scoters have small wings relative to the weight of their bodies, they require long stretches of water for takeoff. However, once in the air their flight is fast and strong. • The White-winged Scoter is the largest and most abundant of the three scoter species seen in New York, and it is the only scoter seen consistently in moderate numbers throughout winter, usually along Great Lakes shores and on the Atlantic Ocean. • The White-winged Scoter often eats hard-shelled clams and shellfishes whole. It relies upon its remarkably powerful gizzard to crush shells that would require a hammer for us to open. • The name "scoter" may be derived from the way this bird scoots across the water's surface. Scooting can be a means of traveling quickly from one foraging site to another. The name "coot" has also been incorrectly applied to all three scoter species because of their superficial resemblance to this totally unrelated species.

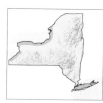

**ID:** stocky body; large, bulbous bill; sloping forehead; base of bill is fully feathered. *Male:* black overall; white patch below eye. *Female:* brown overall; gray brown bill; 2 whitish patches on sides of head. *In flight:* white wing patches.
**Size:** *L* 18–24 in; *W* 34 in.
**Status:** abundant migrant and winter visitor from October to May on the Atlantic Coast; common migrant and winter visitor on the Great Lakes.
**Habitat:** large, deep lakes and large rivers; Great Lakes; Atlantic coastal waters.

**Nesting:** does not nest in NY.
**Feeding:** deep, underwater dives last up to 1 minute; eats mostly mollusks; may also take crustaceans, aquatic insects and some small fish.
**Voice:** courting pair produces harsh, guttural noises, between a *crook* and a quack.
**Similar Species:** *Surf Scoter* (p. 61): lacks white wing patches; male has white forehead and nape. *Black Scoter* (p. 63): lacks white patches on wings and around eyes. *American Coot* (p. 124): whitish bill and nasal shield; red eyes; lacks white patches on wings and around eyes.
**Best Sites:** Montauk Point SP; Orient Point SP; James Beach SP; Hamlin Beach SP.

# BLACK SCOTER
*Melanitta nigra*

Migration is a lengthy and tiring journey, especially after a rigorous breeding season, so many Black Scoters make rest stops on the Great Lakes and the Atlantic Coast as they travel south through our region. These handsome scoters begin arriving as early as September, but the majority arrive through late fall and early winter, just when the frigid cold beckons at our doors. • While floating on the water's surface, Black Scoters tend to hold their heads high, unlike other scoters, which generally look downward. The male is the only North American duck that is uniformly black. • Black Scoters are the most vocal of the scoters, and often reveal their presence with their plaintive, mellow, whistling calls from far out on open water. • Of the three species of scoters in the region, the Black Scoter is the least common. This rarity belies its earlier designation of "Common Scoter," the name still given to the Eurasian *nigra* subspecies.

**ID:** *Male:* black overall; large orange knob on bill. *Female:* light "cheek"; dark "cap"; brown overall; dark gray bill. *In flight:* rather rounded body and wings; silvery wing linings; wings whistle in flight.
**Size:** *L* 17–20 in; *W* 28 in.
**Status:** common migrant and winter visitor from October to April.
**Habitat:** large, deep lakes; Atlantic coastal waters.

**Nesting:** does not nest in NY.
**Feeding:** dives underwater; eats mostly mollusks and aquatic insect larvae; occasionally eats aquatic vegetation and small fish.
**Voice:** generally quiet; infrequently an unusual *cour-loo.*
**Similar Species:** *White-winged Scoter* (p. 62): white wing patches; male has white patch below eye. *Surf Scoter* (p. 61): male has white forehead and nape; female has 2 whitish patches on sides of head.
**Best Sites:** Montauk Point SP; Orient Point SP; Jones Beach SP; Hamlin Beach SP; Dunkirk Harbor.

# LONG-TAILED DUCK
*Clangula hyemalis*

This ancient mariner of the Great Lakes is able to survive violent winter gales on the scale of the great storm that scuttled the unfortunate *Edmund Fitzgerald*. Long-tailed Ducks tend to remain in deeper waters, well away from shore, limiting observers to brief glimpses of their winter finery and the long, slender tail feathers for which the species is named. • Long-tailed Ducks are among the noisiest breeders on the arctic tundra, but during migration and over winter they remain relatively silent. • The breeding and nonbreeding plumages of these arctic-nesting sea ducks are like photo-negatives of each other: their spring breeding plumage is mostly dark with white highlights, while their winter plumage is mostly white with dark patches. • Long-tailed Ducks are among the world's deepest diving waterfowl—they regularly dive to depths of more than 200 feet. • Until recently, this duck was officially called "Oldsquaw," a name that many people still use.

*nonbreeding*

*nonbreeding*

**ID:** *Breeding male:* dark head with white eye patch; dark neck and upperparts; white belly; dark bill; long, dark central tail feathers. *Breeding female:* short tail feathers; gray bill; dark crown, throat patch, wings and back; white underparts. *Nonbreeding male:* pale head with dark patch; pale neck and belly; dark breast; long, white patches on back; pink bill with dark base; long, dark central tail feathers. *Nonbreeding female:* similar to breeding female, but generally paler, especially on head.
**Size:** *L* 17–20 in; *W* 28 in.

**Status:** common migrant and winter visitor from November to April on large lakes, bays and Atlantic waters.
**Habitat:** large, deep lakes, bays and ocean.
**Nesting:** does not nest in NY.
**Feeding:** dives for mollusks, crustaceans and aquatic insects; occasionally eats roots and young shoots; may also take some small fish.
**Voice:** generally silent in migration and winter.
**Similar Species:** *Northern Pintail* (p. 50): thin, white line extends up sides of neck; gray sides.
**Best Sites:** Niagara River Corridor; Hamlin Beach SP; Oswego Harbor; Montauk Point SP; Pt. Lookout–Jones Inlet.

# BUFFLEHEAD

*Bucephala albeola*

Every winter, dozens of species of waterfowl patrol the open waters of the Great Lakes in huge flotillas that are often composed of thousands of birds. Winter imposes many limiting factors on birds, so food and suitable habitat may be scarce at times. Fortunately for the tiny Bufflehead, it is right at home on the water amid its larger relatives. • Buffleheads are active little ducks, often spending as much time chasing each other as they do feeding. Rarely do you see a raft of Buffleheads at rest—it's just not their nature. Activity intensifies as spring approaches because, as with all diving ducks, courtship takes place on the wintering grounds and there is always competition for mates. Buffleheads typically nest on ponds and small lakes, primarily in western and central Canada and north into Alaska. • In migration and in winter, Buffleheads dive for mollusks, mostly snails. If you are lucky, you may even see a whole flock dive at the same time for these tasty morsels.

**ID:** very small, rounded duck; short gray bill; short neck. *Male:* white wedge on back of head; head is otherwise iridescent, dark green or purple, usually appearing black; dark back; white neck and underparts. *Female:* dark brown head; white, oval ear patch; light brown sides. *In flight:* white speculum; very rapid wingbeats.
**Size:** *L* 13–15 in; *W* 21 in.
**Status:** common migrant and winter visitor from November to April.
**Habitat:** open water of lakes, large ponds and rivers; also bays and Atlantic waters.

**Nesting:** does not nest in NY.
**Feeding:** dives for aquatic invertebrates; favors mollusks, particularly snails, and crustaceans in winter; also eats aquatic insect larvae, some small fish and pondweeds.
**Voice:** *Male:* growling call. *Female:* harsh quack.
**Similar Species:** *Hooded Merganser* (p. 68): white crest is outlined in black. *Harlequin Duck* (p. 60): female has several light-colored spots on head. *Common Goldeneye* (p. 66) and *Barrow's Goldeneye* (p. 67): males are larger and have white patch between eye and bill. *Other diving ducks* (pp. 52–71): larger.
**Best Sites:** Hamlin Beach SP; L. Champlain; Pt. Lookout–Jones Inlet; Montauk Point SP.

# COMMON GOLDENEYE

*Bucephala clangula*

The courtship display of the male Common Goldeneye looks much like an avian slapstick routine, although to the bird itself it is surely a serious matter. Courtship begins in winter, when the male performs a number of odd postures and vocalizations, often in front of apparently disinterested females. In one common routine, he arches his puffy, iridescent head backward until his forehead seems to touch his back. Next, he catapults his neck forward like a coiled spring while producing a seemingly painful *peent* sound. • Common Goldeneye females often lay their eggs in the nests of other goldeneyes and cavity-nesting ducks. After hatching, ducklings remain in the nest for one to three days before jumping out of the tree cavity, often falling a long distance to the ground below.

**ID:** steep forehead with peaked crown; black wings with large, white patches; golden eyes. *Male:* iridescent, dark green head; round, white "cheek" patch; dark bill; dark back; white sides and belly. *Female:* chocolate brown head; gray brown body plumage; lighter breast and belly; dark bill is tipped with yellow in spring and summer.
**Size:** *L* 16–20 in; *W* 26 in.
**Status:** rare breeder from April to June in the Adirondacks and Champlain Valley; common migrant and winter visitor from October to April to coastal waters and large lakes.
**Habitat:** *Breeding:* marshes, ponds, lakes and rivers. *In migration* and *winter:* open water of lakes, large ponds and rivers; bays and Atlantic waters.

**Nesting:** in a tree cavity, but will use a nest box; often close to water; cavity is lined with wood chips and down; female incubates 6–10 blue green eggs for 28–32 days; 2 females may each lay a clutch in the same nest if cavities are in short supply.
**Feeding:** dives for crustaceans, mollusks and aquatic insect larvae; may also eat tubers, leeches, frogs and small fish.
**Voice:** *Male:* courtship calls are a nasal *peent* and a hoarse *kraaagh*. *Female:* harsh croak.
**Similar Species:** *Barrow's Goldeneye* (p. 67): male has large, white, crescent-shaped "cheek" patch and purplish head; female has yellow bill and more steeply sloped forehead.
**Best Sites:** Pt. Lookout–Jones Inlet; Montauk Point SP; Marshlands Conservancy–Playland CP; Essex-Westport; Oswego Harbor.

# BARROW'S GOLDENEYE

*Bucephala islandica*

Increasing breeding ranges in Canada probably account for the annual occurrence of this beautiful duck in New York. Look for the Barrow's Goldeneye in shallow water with strong tidal rips or on deep lakes such as Cayuga or Seneca. Most of these goldeneyes breed in western North America, but smaller, highly isolated populations occur in eastern Canada, Greenland and Iceland. These ducks spend the winter in saltwater habitats and coastal estuaries. Wintering sites tend to be restricted, and favored locations are used by about the same number of individuals year after year. • Like the Common Goldeneye, the Barrow's has an amusing foraging style: after taking a deep dive for food, it pops back up to the surface like a colorful cork. The Barrow's Goldeneye also indulges in the same series of acrobatic courtship displays as its less showy cousin. • This diving duck bears the name of Sir John Barrow, secretary to the British Admiralty, who was committed to finding the Northwest Passage.

**ID:** medium-sized, rounded duck; short bill; steep forehead. *Male:* dark purple head; white crescent on "cheek"; white underparts; dark back and wings with white spotting. *Female:* chocolate brown head; yellow bill is tipped with black in spring and summer; gray brown body plumage.
**Size:** *L* 18 in; *W* 28 in.
**Status:** rare migrant and winter visitor from late November to March.
**Habitat:** open lakes, rivers, ponds and lagoons until freeze-up, then moves to salt-water bays and estuaries.

**Nesting:** does not nest in NY.
**Feeding:** dives for mollusks and crustaceans in salt water, insects and aquatic vegetation in fresh water.
**Voice:** generally silent. *Male:* "mewing" call in spring. *Female:* hoarse croaks in spring.
**Similar Species:** *Common Goldeneye* (p. 66): slightly smaller; less steeply sloped head; male has small, round, white "cheek" patch and greenish head; female has darker bill without black tip.
**Best Sites:** Niagara River Corridor; Robert Moses SP; Saratoga L.; occasional from parks along Cayuga L. and Seneca L. shores.

# HOODED MERGANSER

*Lophodytes cucullatus*

Extremely attractive and exceptionally shy, the Hooded Merganser is one of the most sought-after ducks from a birder's perspective. • Most of the time the male Hooded Merganser's crest is held flat, but in moments of arousal or agitation he quickly unfolds his brilliant crest to attract a mate or to signal approaching danger. The drake displays his full range of colors and athletic abilities in elaborate, late-winter courtship displays and chases. • Nationally, Hoodies attain their greatest density in summer in the Great Lakes region, wherever woodlands occur near waterways. • All mergansers have thin bills with small, toothlike serrations to help the birds keep a firm grasp on slippery prey. The smallest of the mergansers, Hoodies have a more diverse diet than their larger relatives. They add crustaceans, insects and even acorns to the usual diet of fish.

**ID:** slim body; crested head; thin, dark, pointed bill. *Male:* black head and back; bold, white crest outlined in black; white breast with 2 black slashes. *Female:* dusky brown body; shaggy, reddish brown crest. *In flight:* small, white wing patches.

**Size:** *L* 16–18 in; *W* 24 in.

**Status:** common breeder from April to June in the Adirondacks; widespread but less common breeder in the rest of the state; common migrant in April and from October to November; winters in New York City area and on Long I.

**Habitat:** forest-edged ponds, wetlands, lakes and rivers.

**Nesting:** in a tree cavity 15–40 ft above the ground; may also use a nest box; cavity is lined with leaves, grass and down; female incubates 10–12 spherical, white eggs for 29–33 days; some females lay their eggs in other birds' nests, including the nests of other species.

**Feeding:** very diverse diet; dives for small fish, caddisfly and dragonfly larvae, snails, amphibians and crayfish.

**Voice:** low grunts and croaks. *Male:* froglike *crrrrooo* in courtship display. *Female:* generally quiet; occasionally a harsh *gak* or a croaking *croo-croo-crook*.

**Similar Species:** *Bufflehead* (p. 65): male lacks black outline to crest and black breast and shoulder slashes. *Red-breasted Merganser* (p. 70) and *Common Merganser* (p. 69): females have much longer, orange bills and gray backs. *Other diving ducks* (pp. 52–71): females lack head crest.

**Best Sites:** Iroquois NWR–Tonawanda WMA–Oak Orchard WMA; Montezuma NWR; Bashakill WMA; Marshlands Conservancy–Playland CP; Southaven CP–Wertheim NWR.

# COMMON MERGANSER

*Mergus merganser*

After a labored takeoff, the Common Merganser flies arrow-straight, low over the water, making broad sweeping turns to follow the meanderings of rivers and lake shorelines. Common Mergansers breed among forest-edged waterways wherever there are cool, clear and unpolluted lakes and rivers. These ducks are cavity nesters, but will also nest on the ground in areas with good fishing and an absence of suitable cavities, such as the shores of the Great Lakes. • Common Mergansers are highly social, and often gather in large groups over winter and during migration. In winter, any source of open water with a fish-filled shoal may support good numbers of these skilled divers. • The Common Merganser is the most widespread and abundant merganser in North America. It also occurs in Europe and Asia, where it is called "Goosander."

**ID:** large, elongated body. *Male:* glossy, green head without crest; blood red bill and feet; white body plumage; black stripe on back; dark eyes. *Female:* rusty neck; crested head; clean white "chin" and breast; orange bill; gray body; orangy eyes. *In flight:* shallow wingbeats; compressed, arrowlike body.

**Size:** *L* 22–27 in; *W* 34 in.

**Status:** common breeder from May to July in the Adirondacks; fairly common breeder on larger river systems; common in winter from October to April wherever there is open water.

**Habitat:** large rivers and deep lakes.

**Nesting:** often in a tree cavity 15–20 ft above the ground; occasionally on the ground or in a large nest box; usually not far from water; female incubates 8–11 pale buff eggs for 30–35 days.

**Feeding:** dives to depths of 30 ft for small fish, usually whitefish, trout, suckers, perch and minnows; young eat aquatic invertebrates and insects, then switch to small fish.

**Voice:** *Male:* harsh *uig-a*, like a guitar twang. *Female:* harsh *karr karr*.

**Similar Species:** *Red-breasted Merganser* (p. 70): male has shaggy green crest and spotted, red breast; female lacks cleanly defined white "chin" and breast. *Mallard* (p. 47): male has chestnut brown breast and yellow bill. *Common Goldeneye* (p. 66): male has white "cheek" patch and stubby, dark bill. *Common Loon* (p. 79): dark bill; white-spotted back.

**Best Sites:** Niagara River Corridor; Hamlin Beach SP; Saratoga L.; Marshlands Conservancy–Playland CP.

# RED-BREASTED MERGANSER

*Mergus serrator*

The Red-breasted Merganser's glossy, slicked-back crest and wild red eyes give it the disheveled, wave-bashed look of an adrenalized windsurfer. Each spring and fall, the shores of the lower Great Lakes host huge congregations of these diving ducks. During peak migration, thousands of Red-breasts may congregate along inshore waters to rest and refuel. • Unlike the other two merganser species, the Red-breasted Merganser prefers to nest on the ground. This bird's lack of dependence on trees enables it to nest where related cavity-nesting species cannot. • Shortly after their mates have begun incubating, males fly off to join large offshore rafts for the duration of summer. During this time, a brief molt makes the males largely indistinguishable from their female counterparts. • Red-breasts will sometimes fish cooperatively, funneling fish for easier capture.

**ID:** large, elongated body; red eyes; thin, orange, serrated, bill; shaggy, slicked-back head crest. *Male:* green head; light rusty breast spotted with black; white "collar"; gray sides; black-and-white shoulders. *Female:* gray brown overall; reddish head; white "chin," foreneck and breast. *In flight:* male has large, white wing patch crossed by 2 narrow, black bars; female has 1 dark bar separating white speculum from white upperwing patch.
**Size:** *L* 19–26 in; *W* 30 in.
**Status:** very rare breeder in widely separated parts of the state; some historical breeding records may be of the Common Merganser; common to abundant migrant from April to May and in November on the Great Lakes and Atlantic Coast; common

winter visitor from November to April on coastal bays and Atlantic waters; less common in winter on the Great Lakes.
**Habitat:** lakes and large rivers, especially those with rocky shorelines and islands; bays and open ocean in winter.
**Nesting:** usually on a rocky island or shoreline; on the ground, well concealed under bushes, driftwood or in dense vegetation; female lines a hollow with plant material and down and incubates 7–10 olive buff eggs for 29–35 days.
**Feeding:** dives underwater for small fish; also eats aquatic invertebrates, fish eggs and crustaceans.
**Voice:** generally quiet. *Male:* catlike *yeow* during courtship and feeding. *Female:* harsh *kho-kha.*
**Similar Species:** *Common Merganser* (p. 69): lacks head crest; male has clean white breast and blood red bill; female's rusty foreneck contrasts with white "chin" and breast.
**Best Sites:** Niagara River Corridor; Hamlin Beach SP; Jones Beach SP; Montauk Point SP.

# RUDDY DUCK

*Oxyura jamaicensis*

Clowns of the wetlands, male Ruddy Ducks display energetic courtship behavior with comedic enthusiasm. The small males vigorously pump their bright blue bills, almost touching their breasts. The *plap, plap, plap-plap-plap* of the display increases in speed to its comical climax: a spasmodic jerk and sputter. In late summer, male Ruddies blend into the crowd, their white "cheeks" the only sign that they were once stars of the show. Their behavior in winter is subdued—they spend hours with their heads tucked into their back feathers and their tails flattened against the water. • Female Ruddies lay an average of eight eggs at a time— a remarkable feat considering that their eggs are bigger than those of a Mallard and that a Mallard is significantly larger than a Ruddy Duck. Females take part in an unusual practice: they often dump their eggs in a communal "dummy" nest that may finally accumulate as many as 60 eggs that will receive no motherly care.

breeding

breeding

**ID:** large bill and head; short neck; long, stiff tail feathers, often held upward. *Breeding male:* white "cheek"; chestnut red body; blue bill; black tail and crown. *Female:* brown overall; dark "cheek" stripe; darker crown and back. *Nonbreeding male:* similar to female but with white "cheek."
**Size:** *L* 15–16 in; *W* 18½ in.
**Status:** rare and local breeder in June and July with greatly fluctuating numbers; common migrant in April and from October to November; winters on Long I.
**Habitat:** *Breeding:* shallow marshes with muddy bottoms and dense emergent vegetation such as cattails or bulrushes. *In migration* and *winter:* sewage lagoons and lakes with open, shallow water.

**Nesting:** in cattails, bulrushes or other emergent vegetation; female suspends a woven platform nest over water; may use an abandoned duck or coot nest, muskrat lodge or exposed log; female incubates 5–10 rough, whitish eggs for 23–26 days; occasional brood parasite.
**Feeding:** dives to the bottom of wetlands for seeds of pondweeds, sedges and bulrushes and for the leafy parts of aquatic plants; also eats a few aquatic invertebrates.
**Voice:** *Male: chuck-chuck-chuck-chur-r-r-r* during courtship display. *Female:* generally silent.
**Similar Species:** *Cinnamon Teal:* lacks white "cheek" and blue bill. *Other diving ducks* (pp. 52–70): females lack long, stiff tail and dark "cheek" stripe.
**Best Sites:** Iroquois NWR–Tonawanda WMA–Oak Orchard WMA; Montezuma NWR; Jamaica Bay Wildlife Refuge; Mecox Bay.

# GRAY PARTRIDGE

*Perdix perdix*

Gray Partridges can be seen "graveling" and picking seeds along quiet country roads, particularly during the early morning and late afternoon. Like other seed-eating birds, they regularly swallow small bits of gravel. These small stones accumulate in the gizzard, a muscular pouch in the digestive system, and help to crush the hard grain and other seeds that these birds feed on. • Gray Partridges travel in groups called "coveys." When flushed, the entire covey bursts suddenly from cover, flapping furiously and then gliding to a safe haven nearby. • During cold weather, Gray Partridges huddle together in a circle to conserve heat, with each bird facing outward, always ready to burst into flight. When incubating their eggs, however, females will sit tightly on their nests and risk being stepped on, rather than attracting attention. • This Eurasian game bird, also known as "Hungarian Partridge" or "Hun," was introduced into our region in the early part of the 20th century.

**ID:** small, rounded body; short tail with chestnut brown outer feathers; chestnut brown barring on flanks; orange brown face and throat; gray breast; mottled brown back; bare, yellowish legs. *Male:* chestnut brown patch on white belly. *Female:* no belly patch; paler face and throat.
**Size:** *L* 11–14 in; *W* 19 in.
**Status:** uncommon year-round resident in a limited range in northern NY; breeds from March to June.
**Habitat:** grassy and weedy fields and agricultural croplands.
**Nesting:** in a hayfield or pasture, or along a grassy fenceline or field margin; on the ground in a scratched-out depression lined with grass; female incubates 15–17 olive-colored eggs for 23–25 days; male helps care for the brood until the following spring.
**Feeding:** at dawn and dusk during summer; throughout the day during winter; gleans the ground for waste grain and seeds; may also eat leaves and large insects; often feeds on manure piles in winter.
**Voice:** at dawn and dusk; sounds like a rusty gate hinge: *kee-uck* or *scirl;* call is *kuta-kut-kut-kut* when excited.
**Similar Species:** *Ruffed Grouse* (p. 74): lacks rusty face and outer tail feathers. *Northern Bobwhite* (p. 77): white crescents and spots edged in black on chestnut brown sides and upper breast; male has white throat and long eye line; female has buff throat and eye line.
**Best Sites:** Cape Vincent–Pt. Peninsula.

# RING-NECKED PHEASANT

*Phasianus colchicus*

A native of Asia, the spectacular Ring-necked Pheasant was introduced to New York in the 1890s as a game bird for hunters. Unfortunately, cold, snowy winters are a problem for this bird because, unlike native grouse, the Ring-necked Pheasant does not have feathered legs and feet to insulate it through the winter months, and it cannot survive on native plants alone. The availability of grain and corn crops, as well as hedgerows and sheltering woodlots, has allowed this pheasant to survive in our region. Populations fluctuate widely in local areas depending on weather conditions, predation and farming practices. • This bird is heard more often than seen, and the male's loud *ka-squawk* call is recognizable near farms, woodlots and brushy suburban parks. • Ring-necked Pheasants are not very strong long-distance fliers, but are swift runners and are able to fly in explosive bursts over small open areas to escape predators.

**ID:** large game bird; long, barred tail; unfeathered legs. *Male:* green head; naked, red face patch; white "collar"; bronze underparts. *Female:* mottled brown overall; light underparts.

**Size:** *Male: L* 30–36 in; *W* 31 in. *Female: L* 20–26 in; *W* 28 in.

**Status:** fairly common year-round resident in the Lake Plains area, Hudson Valley and on Long I.; breeds from April to August.

**Habitat:** *Breeding:* grasslands, grassy ditches, hayfields and grassy or weedy fields; also fencelines and cropland and woodlot margins. *Nonbreeding:* grain and corn fields in fall; woodlots, cattail marshes and shrubby areas close to soybean or corn fields in winter.

**Nesting:** on the ground among grass or sparse vegetation, or next to a log or other natural debris; in a slight depression lined with grass and leaves; female incubates 10–12 olive buff eggs for 23–28 days; male takes no part in parental duties.

**Feeding:** *Summer:* gleans the ground and vegetation for weed seeds, grains and insects. *Winter:* eats mostly seeds, corn kernels and buds.

**Voice:** *Male:* loud, raspy, roosterlike, crowing *ka-squawk. Female:* low, henlike clucking notes.

**Similar Species:** male is distinctive. *Ruffed Grouse* (p. 74): generally smaller; shorter tail than female pheasant.

**Best Sites:** Braddock Bay; Cape Vincent–Pt. Peninsula; Pelham Bay Park (NYC); Shinnecock Inlet–Dune Rd.

# RUFFED GROUSE

*Bonasa umbellus*

Puzzled by the sound of a two-stroke motorcycle or lawnmower engine starting up and stalling in the woods? Actually, what you are hearing is the sound of a "drumming" Ruffed Grouse. Every spring, and occasionally in fall, the male Ruffed Grouse proclaims his territory. He struts along a fallen log with his tail fanned and his neck feathers ruffed, periodically beating the air with accelerating wingstrokes. • The Ruffed Grouse is the most common and widespread grouse in the region, inhabiting a wide variety of woodland habitats ranging from small deciduous woodlots and suburban riparian woodlands to vast expanses of mixedwood and boreal forest. • Populations of Ruffed Grouse seem to fluctuate over a 10-year cycle. Many predators such as the Northern Goshawk that rely on this bird as a food source show population fluctuations that closely follow Ruffed Grouse trends. • During winter, scales grow out along the sides of this bird's toes, giving the Ruffed Grouse temporary "snowshoes."

*red morph*

**ID:** small head crest; mottled rusty brown overall; black feathers on sides of lower neck (visible when fluffed out in courtship displays); darkly barred, reddish tail has broad, dark subterminal band and white tip. *Female:* incomplete subterminal tail band.
**Size:** *L* 15–19 in; *W* 22 in.
**Status:** fairly common year-round resident; breeds from April to June.
**Habitat:** deciduous and mixed forests and riparian woodlands; in many areas favors young second-growth stands with birch and poplar.

**Nesting:** in a shallow depression among leaf litter; often beside boulders, under a log or at the base of a tree; female incubates 9–12 buff-colored eggs for 23–25 days.
**Feeding:** gleans the ground and vegetation; omnivorous diet includes seeds, buds, flowers, berries, catkins, leaves, insects, spiders and snails; may take small frogs.
**Voice:** *Male:* uses wings to produce a hollow, drumming courtship sound of accelerating, deep booms. *Female:* clucks and "hisses" around her chicks.
**Similar Species:** *Spruce Grouse* (p. 75): dark tail lacks barring and white tip; lacks head crest; male has red eye combs.
**Best Sites:** Letchworth SP; Connecticut Hill WMA; Saratoga National Historical Park; John Boyd Thacher SP.

# SPRUCE GROUSE

*Falcipennis canadensis*

The secretive, forest-dwelling Spruce Grouse trusts its cryptic plumage to conceal it from view in its dark, damp, year-round home. Despite its many predators, this grouse often allows people to approach within a few feet, which is the reason it is often called "Fool Hen." Most of the time, however, its camouflage seems to work and more Spruce Grouse probably escape our detection than we notice. • Spruce Grouse spend most of their time in middle-aged spruce-fir stands searching for seasonally available food such as blueberries, flowers, black spruce buds, moss spore capsules and insects. • They are most conspicuous in late April and early May, when females issue their vehement calls and strutting males magically appear in open areas along trails and roadsides. The Spruce Grouse's deep call is nearly undetectable to the human ear, but displaying males attract attention as they transform from their usual dull camouflage to become red-eyebrowed, puff-necked, fan-tailed splendors.

*gray morph*

**ID:** black, unbarred tail with chestnut brown tip; mottled gray, brown and black overall; feathered legs. *Male:* red eye combs; black throat, neck and breast; white-tipped undertail, lower neck and belly feathers. *Female:* barred, mottled underparts.
**Size:** *L* 13–16 in; *W* 22 in.
**Status:** endangered; very rare and seriously declining year-round resident in the Adirondacks; breeds in May and June.
**Habitat:** conifer-dominated forests; sometimes disperses into deciduous forests.

**Nesting:** on the forest floor; in a well-hidden, shallow scrape lined with a few grasses and conifer needles; female incubates 4–7 brown-blotched, buff eggs for 21–24 days.
**Feeding:** live buds and needles of spruce, pine and fir trees; also eats berries, seeds and a few insects in summer.
**Voice:** very low, guttural *krrrk krrrk krrrk*.
**Similar Species:** *Ruffed Grouse* (p. 74): crested head; tail has broad, dark, subterminal band and white tip; lacks black throat and breast.
**Best Sites:** Ferd's Bog–Moose River Plains; Bloomingdale Bog.

# WILD TURKEY
*Meleagris gallopavo*

This charismatic bird is the only native North American animal that has been widely domesticated. The wild ancestors of most other domestic animals came from Europe. • Though it was once abundant in New York, overhunting and habitat loss resulted in the extirpation of the Wild Turkey by the mid-1800s. In the mid-1900s, turkeys from Pennsylvania dispersed into southwestern New York—the first to appear in the region in over 100 years. Relocation programs have since reestablished this bird throughout the state. • Although turkeys prefer to feed on the ground and travel by foot, they are able to fly at speeds of up to 55 miles per hour. • If Congress had taken Benjamin Franklin's advice in 1782, our national emblem would be the Wild Turkey instead of the majestic Bald Eagle.

**ID:** naked, blue red head; dark, glossy, iridescent body plumage; barred, copper-colored tail; mostly unfeathered legs. *Male:* long central breast tassel; colorful head and body; red wattles. *Female:* smaller; blue gray head; less iridescent body.
**Size:** *Male: L 3–3½ ft; W 5½ ft. Female: L 3 ft; W 4 ft.*
**Status:** common year-round resident across the Appalachian Plateau; expanding its range into the Adirondacks; breeds from April to August.
**Habitat:** deciduous, mixed and riparian woodlands; farm fields in late fall and winter.

**Nesting:** in a woodland or on a field edge; in a depression on the ground under thick cover; nest is lined with grass and leaves; female incubates 10–12 brown-speckled, pale buff eggs for up to 28 days.
**Feeding:** in fields near protective woods; forages on the ground for seeds, fruits, bulbs and sedges; also eats insects, especially beetles and grasshoppers; may take small amphibians; occasionally eats waste grain and corn in late fall and winter.
**Voice:** wide array of sounds; courting male gobbles loudly; alarm call is a loud *pert;* gathering call is a *cluck;* contact call is a loud *keouk-keouk-keouk.*
**Similar Species:** all other grouse and grouselike birds are much smaller. *Ring-necked Pheasant* (p. 73): feathered head and neck; long, narrow tail.
**Best Sites:** Allegany SP; Connecticut Hill WMA; Partridge Run WMA.

# NORTHERN BOBWHITE

*Colinus virginianus*

Throughout fall and winter, Northern Bobwhites typically travel in large family groups called "coveys," collectively seeking out sources of food and huddling together during cold nights. When they huddle, members of the covey all face outward, enabling the group to detect danger from any direction. With the arrival of summer, breeding pairs break away from their coveys to perform elaborate courtship rituals in preparation for another nesting season. • The male's characteristic, whistled *bob-white* call, usually issued in spring, is often the only evidence of this bird's presence among the dense, tangled vegetation of its rural woodland home. • Bobwhites benefit from habitat disturbance, using the early successional habitats created by fire, agriculture and forestry. However, as land use has intensified and pesticide use has increased, populations have declined. • The Northern Bobwhite is the only native quail in eastern North America.

**ID:** mottled brown, buff and black upperparts; white crescents and spots edged in black on chestnut brown sides and upper breast; short tail. *Male:* white throat; broad, white "eyebrow." *Female:* buff throat and "eyebrow." *Immature:* smaller and duller overall; lacks black on underparts.
**Size:** *L* 10 in; *W* 13 in.
**Status:** uncommon year-round resident on Long I.; rare in Hudson Valley; breeds from May to September; declining.
**Habitat:** farmlands, open woodlands, woodland edges, grassy fencelines, roadside ditches and brushy, open country; also pine barrens on Long I.

**Nesting:** in a shallow depression on the ground, often concealed by surrounding vegetation or a woven, partial dome; nest is lined with grass and leaves; pair incubates 12–16 white to pale buff eggs for 22–24 days.
**Feeding:** eats seasonally available seeds, berries, leaves, roots and nuts; also takes insects and other invertebrates.
**Voice:** whistled *hoy* is given year-round. *Male:* whistled, rising *bob-white* in spring and summer.
**Similar Species:** *Ruffed Grouse* (p. 74): lacks white throat patch and broad "eyebrow"; long, fan-shaped tail has broad, dark subterminal band; black patches on sides of neck.
**Best Sites:** Connetquot River SP; Shinnecock Inlet–Dune Rd.

# RED-THROATED LOON

*Gavia stellata*

The Red-throated Loon is an easy bird to identify because it typically swims low in the water with its bill held tipped up. • Our smallest loon, the Red-throat is able to leap up from the water directly into flight, stand upright on land and even take off from land. No other loon has these abilities—other loons require 300 feet or more of runway on open water to gain flight. As a result, Red-throated Loons can nest on smaller bodies of water than their larger, less agile relatives. • The Red-throated Loon is an unparalleled diver and obtains most of its food underwater. It can dive to depths of 70 feet, though most dives are shallower, and can vary its buoyancy, making it easier to stay below the surface. • Your best chance of seeing a Red-throated Loon is in spring and fall at any coastal site. These loons breed in the Arctic and winter along the Atlantic and Pacific coasts and occasionally on the Great Lakes. • Native peoples have long considered Red-throated Loons as reliable meteorologists—these birds often become very noisy before the onset of foul weather, possibly sensing changes in barometric pressure.

*nonbreeding*

**ID:** slim bill is held upward. *Breeding:* red throat; gray face and neck; black and white stripes from nape to back of head; plain, brownish back. *Nonbreeding:* white-speckled back; white face; dark gray crown and back of head. *In flight:* hunched back; legs trail behind tail; rapid wingbeats.
**Size:** *L* 23–27 in; *W* 3 ft.
**Status:** very common migrant along the Atlantic Coast and on L. Ontario, and fairly common migrant on large lakes from April to May and from October to November;

common winter visitor from November to March on the Atlantic Coast.
**Habitat:** large freshwater lakes; ocean in winter.
**Nesting:** does not nest in NY.
**Feeding:** dives deeply and captures small fish; occasionally eats aquatic insects and amphibians; may eat aquatic vegetation in early spring.
**Voice:** Mallard-like *kwuk-kwuk-kwuk-kwuk* in flight; distraction call is a loud *gayor-work.*
**Similar Species:** *Common Loon* (p. 79): larger; heavier bill; lacks white speckling on back in nonbreeding plumage.
**Best Sites:** Montauk Point SP; Jones Beach SP; Hamlin Beach SP.

# COMMON LOON

*Gavia immer*

The quavering wail of the Common Loon pierces the stillness of quiet nights, the haunting call alerting cottagers that summer has begun. Loons float very low on the water, disappearing behind swells, then reappearing like ethereal guardians of the lakes. • Common Loons are well adapted to their aquatic lifestyle. These divers have nearly solid bones that make them less buoyant (most birds have hollow bones), and their feet are placed well back on their bodies for underwater propulsion. Small bass, perch, sunfish, pike and whitefish are all fair game for these excellent underwater hunters. On land, however, their rear-placed legs make walking difficult, and their heavy bodies and small wing size mean that these birds require a lengthy sprint over water before taking off. • It is thought that the name "loon" is derived from the Scandinavian word *lom*, meaning "clumsy person," in reference to this bird's awkwardness on land.

*breeding*

**ID:** *Breeding:* greenish black head; stout, thick, black bill; white "necklace"; white breast and underparts; black-and-white upperparts; red eyes. *Nonbreeding:* much duller plumage; sandy brown back; light underparts. *In flight:* long wings beat constantly; hunchbacked appearance; legs trail behind tail.

**Size:** *L* 28–35 in; *W* 3½–4 ft.

**Status:** special concern; fairly common breeder from May to July on Adirondack lakes; common migrant from April to May and from September to November on large lakes; winters in large numbers from November to March on the Atlantic Ocean.

**Habitat:** *Breeding:* large lakes, often with islands that provide undisturbed shorelines for nesting. *Winter:* lakes with open water; Atlantic Ocean.

**Nesting:** on a muskrat lodge, small island or projecting shoreline; always very near water; nest mound is built from aquatic vegetation; pair incubates 1–3 darkly spotted, olive eggs for 24–31 days; pair shares all parental duties.

**Feeding:** pursues small fish underwater to depths of 180 ft; occasionally eats large, aquatic invertebrates and larval and adult amphibians.

**Voice:** alarm call is a quavering tremolo, often called "loon laughter"; contact call is a long but simple wailing note: *where aaare you?*; breeding notes are soft, short hoots; male territorial call is an undulating, complex yodel.

**Similar Species:** *Red-throated Loon* (p. 78): smaller; slender bill; red throat in breeding plumage; sharply defined white face and white-spotted back in nonbreeding plumage.

**Best Sites:** Montauk Point SP; Jones Beach SP; Hamlin Beach SP; any Adirondack lake in summer.

# PIED-BILLED GREBE
*Podilymbus podiceps*

Infrequently heard except when breeding, the Pied-billed Grebe is the smallest, shyest and least colorful of our grebes. It tends to swim inconspicuously in the shallow waters of quiet bays and rivers, only occasionally voicing its strange whinnying call. • An extremely wary bird, this grebe is far more common than encounters would lead you to believe. It is seldom seen in flight because it migrates nocturnally, landing before or at dawn on the nearest body of water. • These grebes build their floating nests among sparse vegetation, so that they can see predators approaching from far away. When frightened by an intruder, they cover their eggs and slide underwater, leaving a nest that looks like nothing more than a mat of debris. Pied-billed Grebes can slowly submerge, leaving only their nostrils and eyes above the water. • The scientific name *podiceps*, which means "rump foot," refers to the way the bird's feet are located toward the back of its body.

*breeding*

**ID:** *Breeding:* all-brown body; black ring on pale bill; laterally compressed "chicken bill"; black throat; very short tail; white undertail coverts; pale belly; pale eye ring. *Nonbreeding:* yellow eye ring; yellow bill lacks black ring; white "chin" and throat; brownish crown.
**Size:** *L* 12–15 in; *W* 16 in.
**Status:** threatened; breeds sparingly from April to July across the state in suitable marshes; common migrant from April to May and from September to October on freshwater bodies; a few winter on Long I. if there is open water; declining owing to habitat disturbance.
**Habitat:** ponds, marshes and backwaters with sparse emergent vegetation.
**Nesting:** among sparse vegetation in a sheltered bay, pond or marsh; floating platform nest of wet and decaying plants is anchored to or placed among emergent vegetation; pair incubates 4–5 white to buff eggs for about 23 days and raises the striped young together.
**Feeding:** makes shallow dives and gleans the water's surface for aquatic invertebrates, small fish and adult and larval amphibians; occasionally eats aquatic plants.
**Voice:** loud, whooping call begins quickly, then slows down: *kuk-kuk-kuk cow cow cow cowp cowp cowp.*
**Similar Species:** *Horned Grebe* (p. 81): seldom seen in summer; red eyes; black-and-white head; golden "ear" tufts and red neck in breeding plumage. *American Coot* (p. 124): all-black body; pale bill extends onto forehead.
**Best Sites:** Iroquois NWR–Tonawanda WMA–Oak Orchard WMA; Montezuma NWR; Jamaica Bay Wildlife Refuge.

# HORNED GREBE

*Podiceps auritus*

A trip to the Great Lakes will provide the best opportunity for observing Horned Grebes in migration and in winter, although these birds can also be seen on other large inland lakes. This compact little bird rides high in the water with its neck somewhat curved or thrust forward when swimming. • The Horned Grebe flies more readily than most grebes, with a strong, direct flight that reveals a large, white patch at the rear of the inner wing. • Like other grebes, the Horned Grebe eats feathers. The feathers pack the digestive tract, and it is thought that they protect the stomach lining and intestines from sharp fish bones or parasites, or perhaps slow the passage of food, allowing more time for complete digestion. • Unlike the fully webbed front toes of most swimming birds, grebe toes are individually webbed, or "lobed"—the three forward-facing toes have individual flanges that are not connected to the other toes. • Both this bird's common name and its scientific name, *auritus* (eared), refer to the golden feather tufts, or "horns," that these grebes acquire in breeding plumage.

*nonbreeding*

**ID:** *Breeding:* rufous neck and flanks; black head; golden "ear" tufts ("horns"); black back; white underparts; red eyes; flat crown.
*Nonbreeding:* black upperparts; white "cheek," foreneck and underparts; lacks "ear" tufts. *In flight:* wings beat constantly; appears hunchbacked ; legs trail behind tail.
**Size:** *L* 12–15 in; *W* 18 in.
**Status:** very common in migration on the Great Lakes and other large inland lakes; migrants arrive in October and depart in April; common in winter on the Atlantic Coast; smaller numbers winter on the Great Lakes and L. Champlain.

**Habitat:** Great Lakes; wetlands and large lakes; Atlantic Ocean.
**Nesting:** does not nest in NY.
**Feeding:** makes shallow dives and gleans the water's surface for aquatic insects, crustaceans, mollusks, small fish and adult and larval amphibians.
**Voice:** silent in migration.
**Similar Species:** *Eared Grebe* (p. 357): black neck in breeding plumage; black "cheek" and darker neck in nonbreeding plumage. *Pied-billed Grebe* (p. 80): thicker, stubbier bill; mostly brown body. *Red-necked Grebe* (p. 82): larger; dark eyes; lacks "ear" tufts; white "cheek" in breeding plumage.
**Best Sites:** Montauk Point SP; Jones Beach SP; Hamlin Beach SP.

# RED-NECKED GREBE

*Podiceps grisegena*

Red-necked Grebes can be seen reliably on Lake Erie and Lake Ontario during fall migration, usually in November. These birds are usually quiet and retiring away from their breeding grounds, so they can be easily overlooked here. • This short-bodied bird has a long, slim neck and a triangular head, which is carried erect. When on the wing it resembles a miniature loon—in flight it stretches its neck and legs to their full extent—but has conspicuous white areas on the leading and rear edges of the inner wing. • The Red-necked Grebe is generally shy. Ordinarily it rides high in the water with its head nodding back and forth as it swims. To escape attention, it can compress its feathers, reducing its buoyancy, and sink out of sight before it is noticed. • The Red-necked Grebe is one of the largest North American grebes. The scientific name *grisegena* means "gray cheek"—a distinctive field mark of this bird in winter plumage.

*nonbreeding*

**ID:** *Breeding:* rusty neck; whitish "cheek"; black crown; straight, heavy bill is dark above and yellow underneath; black upperparts; pale underparts; dark eyes. *Nonbreeding:* grayish white foreneck, "chin" and "cheek."
**Size:** *L* 17–22 in; *W* 24 in.
**Status:** uncommon migrant in April and November on the Great Lakes and larger lakes and rivers; uncommon winter visitor from November to April on the Atlantic Coast.
**Habitat:** open, deep lakes; also ocean in winter.
**Nesting:** does not nest in NY.

**Feeding:** dives and gleans the water's surface for small fish, aquatic invertebrates and amphibians.
**Voice:** silent in migration.
**Similar Species:** *Horned Grebe* (p. 81): smaller; dark "cheek" and golden "horns" in breeding plumage; red eyes, all-dark bill and bright white "cheek" in nonbreeding plumage. *Eared Grebe* (p. 357): smaller; black neck in breeding plumage; black "cheek" in nonbreeding plumage. *Pied-billed Grebe* (p. 80): smaller; thicker, stubbier bill; mostly brown body. *Ducks* (pp. 42–71): all lack the combination of white "cheek" and rusty red neck.
**Best Sites:** Dunkirk Harbor; Hamlin Beach SP; Saratoga L.; Montauk Point SP; Pt. Lookout–Jones Inlet.

# NORTHERN FULMAR

*Fulmarus glacialis*

If it looks like a gull but flies like a shearwater, then it just may be a fulmar. Look twice because, other than a stubby, greenish yellow bill and paler plumage, the Northern Fulmar shares many physical attributes with the closely related shearwater family. It can occur in a spectrum of "color morphs," and the generally all-pale morph is most well represented here. • Specialized for cutting through the wild winds of open ocean expanses, fulmars are fast, skilled flyers. Slim-winged, but thick-necked and bull-headed, these birds roam cooler North Atlantic waters for much of the year, returning to nesting cliffs and offshore sea stacks in summer. In fall and early winter they can be commonly seen on pelagic trips offshore from Long Island. • "Fulmar" is derived from Old Norse and means "foul gull"—when it is disturbed, this bird has a nasty habit of spewing foul-smelling fish oil. • Northern Fulmars have a life expectancy of over 30 years and some are estimated to have lived longer than 50 years.

*light morph*

**ID:** short, pale yellow, "tubed" bill; thick neck; stubby tail; long, tapered wings; pale patch at base of primaries; many birds are intermediate between light and dark morphs. *Light morph:* whitish head and underparts; bluish gray upperparts. *Dark morph:* deep bluish gray overall except for paler flight feathers. *In flight:* alternates rapid, stiff-winged flapping with graceful glides; flies low over waves.
**Size:** *L* 18 in; *W* 3½ ft.
**Status:** fairly common winter visitor from October to April in offshore Atlantic waters.

**Habitat:** favors open ocean waters over upwellings and along the outer continental shelf; rarely approaches the coastline except in fog or during storms.
**Feeding:** will take almost any edible item while swimming; makes shallow plunges beneath the water's surface; eats fish, squid, crustaceans, invertebrates, carrion and marine fishery bycatch.
**Voice:** generally silent; low, quacking call may be given when competing for food.
**Similar Species:** *Shearwaters* (pp. 84–86): more slender; darker plumage and bills; slimmer heads and necks. *Gulls* (pp. 164–75): slimmer necks and bodies; steadier, less stiff wingbeats; many species have black backs or wing tips.
**Best Sites:** pelagic boat trips from Long I. coastal sites, usually Montauk Pt.; some NJ-based boats travel to NY waters.

# CORY'S SHEARWATER

*Calonectris diomedea*

This shearwater was first spotted off the coast of New England in 1880 by Charles Barney Cory, an American ornithologist who believed it to be a new species. Further investigation revealed this seabird to be the North Atlantic race of the Mediterranean Shearwater. Postbreeding individuals disperse from the rocky shores of Mediterranean islands to various areas such as the Indian Ocean or the New England coast. The Cory's Shearwater is the only large shearwater to both breed and winter in the Northern Hemisphere. • Those wishing to see Cory's Shearwater have a challenge ahead of them because these gregarious birds rarely come to investigate nearby vessels. • Though *Calonectris* is Greek for "beautiful swimmer," the Cory's Shearwater exhibits its finest grace in the air, where with languid wingbeats, it is the only shearwater off the Atlantic Coast to occasionally soar upon the ocean breezes. *Diomedea* is a form of the name Diomedes, a Trojan War hero who returned home safely, but whose companions were turned into birds when their ship was lost at sea.

**ID:** gray brown upperparts; white underparts; dark wing tips and tail tip; pale brown head and nape; white throat and lower "cheek"; small, white rump patch; large, yellow bill with small "tube" above upper mandible. *In flight:* white underwings; wings slightly bent downward when gliding.
**Size:** *L* 18–21 in; *W* 3½–4 ft.
**Status:** common visitor from July to November in offshore Atlantic waters.

**Habitat:** open ocean.
**Nesting:** does not nest in NY.
**Feeding:** feeds mostly on the wing; skims low over salt water and dips or makes shallow dives; follows large predatory fish and feeds on small prey forced to the water's surface; takes squid and crustaceans at night; infrequently joins other shearwaters alongside fishing vessels.
**Voice:** mostly silent at sea.
**Similar Species:** *Greater Shearwater* (p. 85): incomplete brown "collar"; dark upperparts; white underparts with smudging on belly; darker bill; narrower wings.
**Best Sites:** Montauk Point SP; Smith Point SP; Fire Island National Seashore.

# GREATER SHEARWATER

*Puffinus gravis*

Commercial fishermen are familiar with these gregarious pirates and refer to them as "Hags" or "Bauks." Working fishing boats are often mobbed by Greater Shearwaters fighting over the opportunity to grab a free meal. Sometimes these shearwaters forage in association with whales and dolphins. • Greater Shearwaters migrate to the North Atlantic for the summer months, but they do not breed here. Their breeding grounds are restricted to islands in the Tristan da Cunha Group, Gough Island and the Falkland Islands in the South Atlantic. • Greater Shearwaters are most common over the outer part of the continental shelf—they tend to avoid nearshore and midocean areas. The most common shearwater in New York waters, Greater Shearwaters follow schools of fish, so their presence is unpredictable. They often come close to shore, and in calm or foggy weather, large flocks can be seen. In dead calm conditions, these birds can only achieve takeoff with great difficulty and are effectively grounded.

**ID:** brown upperparts; white underparts, except for brown belly and undertail coverts; incomplete brown "collar"; usually 1 narrow, white band at base of tail. *In flight:* straight, narrow, pointed wings; dark "wing pits" and markings on wing linings; dark trailing edge on wings.

**Size:** *L* 18 in; *W* 3½ ft.

**Status:** common to abundant visitor from May to December in offshore Atlantic waters.

**Habitat:** open ocean; favors cold waters; most common over the outer portion of the continental shelf; drawn inshore by weather conditions and prey abundance.

**Nesting:** does not nest in NY.

**Feeding:** seizes prey from the water's surface or dives to depths of 30 ft; eats mainly small fish, squid and crustaceans.

**Voice:** generally silent; harsh, gull-like call when feeding.

**Similar Species:** *Cory's Shearwater* (p. 84): lacks brown "collar," belly and undertail coverts; yellow bill. *Manx Shearwater* (p. 357): darker upperparts; white belly and undertail coverts. *Pomarine Jaeger* (p. 162) and *Parasitic Jaeger* (p. 163): more prominent wing patches; longer tails; central tail feathers project in flight.

**Best Sites:** Montauk Point SP; Smith Point CP; Shinnecock Inlet–Dune Rd.

# SOOTY SHEARWATER
*Puffinus griseus*

Each summer, Sooty Shearwaters travel in huge numbers from breeding islands in the Southern Hemisphere to the North Atlantic. During spring and fall, scattered individuals are almost constantly in sight on the open ocean, and concentrations may include tens of thousands of birds. • Various seabird families, including albatrosses, shearwaters and storm-petrels, are widely categorized as "tubenoses"—they all have external tubular nostrils and hooked bills. Sooty Shearwaters, like all tubenoses, have a keen sense of smell that helps them to locate concentrations of food. • The Sooty Shearwater is most abundant along Atlantic coastlines from May through October, although a telescope may be necessary to see them because most birds forage well beyond the surf line. Large concentrations of fish can draw these birds closer to land—the popularity of schooling fish often results in multispecies feeding frenzies that include Sooties and other seabirds. Sooty Shearwaters and Greater Shearwaters dominate most mixed seabird foraging flocks over the continental shelf. • Resident fishermen refer to Sooty Shearwaters as "Black Hags."

**ID:** all-dark body; slender, black bill; silvery patch on underwing linings. *In flight:* long, slender wings; darkly streaked, white wing linings.

**Size:** *L* 17 in; *W* 3–3½ ft.

**Status:** common to abundant visitor in offshore Atlantic waters; most abundant from May to July, but present throughout summer.

**Habitat:** open ocean; concentrates at upwellings and current edges along the continental shelf.

**Nesting:** does not nest in NY.

**Feeding:** gleans the water's surface; makes shallow dives; eats mostly capelin, squid and crustaceans, especially krill; inspects passing boats, quickly forming flocks if food is available.

**Voice:** generally silent; occasionally utters quarrelsome calls when competing for food.

**Similar Species:** *Dark-morph Northern Fulmar* (p. 83): thick, greenish yellow bill; dark wing linings. *Cory's Shearwater* (p. 84) and *Greater Shearwater* (p. 85): variably pale underparts. *Gulls* (pp. 164–75): immatures are paler brown with heavier bills and more flapping flight.

**Best Sites:** Montauk Point SP; Hither Hills SP; Smith Point CP.

# WILSON'S STORM-PETREL

*Oceanites oceanicus*

This long-legged storm-petrel dances over the surface of the water, feet daintily pattering as it hovers, stirring up small crustaceans and fish. The outer portion of the continental shelf is where you are most likely to see the Wilson's Storm-Petrel, but it occasionally wanders close to land—it is often seen from Long Island beaches and has even appeared in New York City's lower bay. Like many marine birds, the Wilson's Shearwater regularly follows fishing boats, grabbing whatever scraps of food are available. • This long-distance migrant travels from the Antarctic to the Grand Banks off Newfoundland, Canada, and back again each year. It nests in the antarctic region and around southern South America on islands and cliffs. • Wilson's Storm-Petrel can be distinguished from Leach's Storm-Petrel by its squared-off tail—the Leach's Storm-Petrel has a forked tail. • Despite their small size, storm-petrels can live to be more than 20 years old. • The name "petrel" is derived from "St. Peter," and the bird is so named because of its seeming ability to walk on water.

**ID:** dark brown overall; white on rump and under-tail coverts; square tail; small, dark, "tubed" bill. *In flight:* shallow, stiff wingbeats; flickering, somewhat erratic flight; toes extend beyond end of tail.
**Size:** *L* 7 in; *W* 16 in.
**Status:** common to abundant visitor from May to September in offshore Atlantic waters.
**Habitat:** open ocean, especially over the continental shelf, but occasionally wanders close to land along coastlines.

**Nesting:** does not nest in NY.
**Feeding:** hovers and skims over the water with its feet "pattering" the surface; snatches food items from the water's surface; takes shrimp and other crustaceans, small fish, squid and marine worms.
**Voice:** usually silent; groups of feeding birds utter soft peeping or chittering calls.
**Similar Species:** *Leach's Storm-Petrel* (p. 357): longer wings; forked tail; may have V-shaped white rump patch; lacks white undertail coverts; erratic flight. *Shearwaters* (p. 84–86): much larger; glide much more often and rarely flap.
**Best Sites:** Montauk Point SP; Hither Hills SP; Jones Beach SP; Jacob Riis Park–Breezy Pt.–Ft. Tilden (NYC).

# NORTHERN GANNET

*Morus bassanus*

Northern Gannets are renowned for their spectacular feeding behavior, often only demonstrated far from the sight of land. Squadrons of gannets soaring at heights of more than 100 feet above the ocean's surface suddenly arrest their flight by folding their wings back, and simultaneously plunge headfirst into the ocean depths in pursuit of schooling fish. These birds have reinforced skulls that have evolved to cushion their brains from diving impacts. • Northern Gannets spend most of the year feeding and roosting at sea. Only during the brief summer breeding season do they seek the stability of land to lay eggs and raise young in large sea-cliff colonies. Gannets do not breed until they are five or six years of age and mate for life. • "Gannet" is derived from the Anglo-Saxon word *ganot*, meaning "little goose." This bird was once classified with the geese and is still known as "Solan Goose" in Europe.

*1st-year juvenile*

**ID:** thick, tapered, pale gray bill; long, narrow wings; pointed tail; white overall with black wing tips and feet; buffy wash on nape. *Immature:* various stages of mottled gray, black and white. *In flight:* white with black primaries; appears pointed at both ends; immature has V-shaped white patch on upper tail.
**Size:** *L* 3 ft; *W* 6 ft.
**Status:** common to abundant migrant from March to April and from October to November in Atlantic coastal waters; occasional migrants occur on the Great Lakes; fairly common in winter from November to April.

**Habitat:** roosts and feeds in coastal and open ocean waters most of year; often seen well offshore.
**Nesting:** does not nest in NY.
**Feeding:** dives for small fish including herring and mackerel; sometimes eats squid; may dive from heights of 100 ft or more above water; occasionally forages by submerging its head while floating on the surface, then diving and swimming once prey is located; regularly scavenges from fishing boats.
**Voice:** usually silent when at sea; feeding flocks may exchange grating growls.
**Similar Species:** *Snow Goose* (p. 37): shorter, pinkish bill; broader wings; long, extended neck in flight.
**Best Sites:** Montauk Point SP; Hither Hills SP; Shinnecock Inlet–Dune Rd.; Jones Beach SP.

# AMERICAN WHITE PELICAN

*Pelecanus erythrorhynchos*

American White Pelicans are a majestic wetland presence with a wingspan only a foot shy of the height of a basketball hoop. Their porous, bucketlike bills are dramatically adapted for feeding. Groups of foraging pelicans deliberately herd fish into schools, then dip their bills and scoop up the prey. As the pelican lifts its bill from the water, the fish are held within its flexible pouch while the water drains out. In a single scoop, a pelican can hold over 3 gallons of water and fish, which is about two to three times as much as its stomach can hold. American White Pelicans eat about 4 pounds of fish per day, but because they prefer nongame fish they do not pose a threat to the potential catches of fishermen. • All other large, white birds with black wing tips fly with their necks extended; the American White Pelican is the only one to fly with its neck pulled back toward its wings.

*nonbreeding*

**ID:** very large, stocky, white bird; long, orange bill and throat pouch; naked, orange skin patch around eye; black primary and secondary wing feathers; short tail. *Breeding:* small, keeled plate develops on upper mandible; pale yellow crest on back of head. *Nonbreeding* and *immature:* white plumage is tinged with brown.
**Size:** *L* 4½–6 ft; *W* 9 ft.

**Status:** rare visitor, usually in April and May, but also from June to November; appears somewhere in NY every year, but is unpredictable.
**Habitat:** large lakes and rivers.
**Nesting:** does not nest in NY.
**Feeding:** surface dips for small fish and amphibians; small groups of pelicans often feed cooperatively by herding fish into large concentrations.
**Voice:** generally quiet; adults rarely issue piglike grunts.
**Similar Species:** no other large, white bird has a long beak with a pouch.
**Best Sites:** Montezuma NWR.

89

# DOUBLE-CRESTED CORMORANT

*Phalacrocorax auritus*

The slick-feathered Double-crested Cormorant is the only North American cormorant that occurs inland in large numbers. Though these birds are seldom seen out of sight of land, their mastery of the aquatic environment is virtually unsurpassed. The Double-crested Cormorant lacks oil glands for water-proofing its feathers, which helps it during underwater dives by decreasing the bird's buoyancy. Instead of floating on the water after a bout of diving, this cormorant is often seen perched on a rock or in a tree with its wings partially spread, a posture thought to aid in drying wet feathers. The cormorant's long, rudderlike tail, excellent underwater vision and sealed nostrils also contribute to the success of its aquatic lifestyle. Once believed to compete with fishermen for the same fish, it is now known that cormorants take undesirables such as alewives, smelt and sculpins. • Double-crested Cormorants migrate in large flocks, flying in a line or in a V-formation like geese.

*breeding*

**ID:** all-black body; long, crooked neck; thin bill, hooked at tip; blue eyes. *Breeding:* throat pouch becomes intense yellow orange; fine, black plumes trail from "eyebrows." *In flight:* rapid wingbeats; kinked neck.
**Size:** *L* 26–32 in; *W* 4½ ft.
**Status:** locally common breeder in June and July on Long I., the Great Lakes and L. Champlain; common migrant from April to May and from September to October; winters in small numbers on Long I.
**Habitat:** large lakes, including the Great Lakes, and large, meandering rivers; also bays and sounds.

**Nesting:** colonial; on the ground on a low-lying island, often with terns and gulls, or precariously high in a tree; nest platform is made of sticks, aquatic vegetation and guano; pair incubates 3–6 bluish white eggs for 25–33 days; young are fed by regurgitation.
**Feeding:** long underwater dives to depths of 30 ft or more when after small schooling fish or, rarely, amphibians and invertebrates; uses bill to grasp prey and bring it to the surface to swallow.
**Voice:** generally quiet; may issue piglike grunts or croaks, especially near nesting colonies.
**Similar Species:** *Great Cormorant* (p. 91): yellow throat bordered by white patch; white flank patches.
**Best Sites:** Dunkirk Harbor; Hamlin Beach SP; Cape Vincent–Pt. Peninsula; Jones Beach SP.

# GREAT CORMORANT

*Phalacrocorax carbo*

The Great Cormorant is the largest of the six cormorant species found in North America. It relies on its superb underwater vision to detect schooling fish beneath the water's surface. Once it locates its prey, the cormorant folds its long wings tight against its body and dives down into the murky depths, propelled only by its large, webbed feet. Like owls, the Great Cormorant coughs up any indigestible parts of its prey in the form of pellets. • Unlike most waterbirds, cormorants lack oil-laden preen glands which aid in the drying-out process. As it swims, a cormorant's feathers become waterlogged and heavy, allowing it to dive more efficiently. However, it must then spend a great deal of its time perched with its wings spread to dry in the sun. This posture makes it instantly recognizable, with the species identifiable by its large size and the yellowish color of its bare throat patch. • The species name *carbo* is Latin for "charcoal" and refers to the generally black plumage of the adult.

*nonbreeding*

**ID:** dark overall; white "chin strap" borders yellow throat pouch; thick neck; heavy bill with hooked tip. *Breeding:* white head plumes and flank patches. *In flight:* flies silently in V-formation.
**Size:** *L* 3 ft; *W* 5–5½ ft.
**Status:** uncommon to common winter visitor from October to April at Long I. coastal sites and on lower Hudson R.; rare winter visitor upstate.

**Habitat:** shallow coastal waters; sheltered bays, estuaries and jetties in winter.
**Nesting:** does not nest in NY.
**Feeding:** dives to depths of 100 ft, but most dives are within 30 ft of the surface; takes a wide variety of fish.
**Voice:** generally silent in winter; occasionally utters low, grunting notes.
**Similar Species:** *Double-crested Cormorant* (p. 90): smaller head and body; orange throat pouch; thinner neck; lacks white "chin strap" and flank patches of breeding Great Cormorant.
**Best Sites:** Montauk Point SP; Pt. Lookout–Jones Inlet; Marshlands Conservancy–Playland CP; Oswego Harbor.

# AMERICAN BITTERN

*Botaurus lentiginosus*

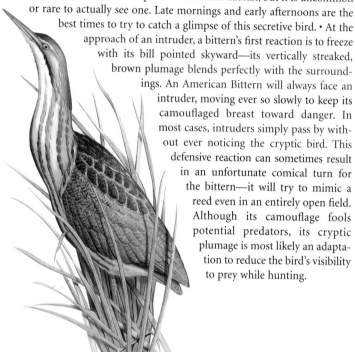

The American Bittern's mysterious booming call is as characteristic of a spring marsh as the sound of croaking frogs, winnowing snipes and nighttime showers. This bittern is common in productive marsh habitat, but it is uncommon or rare to actually see one. Late mornings and early afternoons are the best times to try to catch a glimpse of this secretive bird. • At the approach of an intruder, a bittern's first reaction is to freeze with its bill pointed skyward—its vertically streaked, brown plumage blends perfectly with the surroundings. An American Bittern will always face an intruder, moving ever so slowly to keep its camouflaged breast toward danger. In most cases, intruders simply pass by without ever noticing the cryptic bird. This defensive reaction can sometimes result in an unfortunate comical turn for the bittern—it will try to mimic a reed even in an entirely open field. Although its camouflage fools potential predators, its cryptic plumage is most likely an adaptation to reduce the bird's visibility to prey while hunting.

**ID:** brown upperparts; bold, brown streaking on underparts; straight, stout bill; yellow legs and feet; black outer wings; black streak from bill down neck to shoulder; short tail.

**Size:** *L* 23–27 in; *W* 3½ ft.

**Status:** special concern; very uncommon breeder from May to June in wetlands throughout the state; migrants arrive in April and May and depart by September; very rarely found in Long I. salt marshes in winter.

**Habitat:** marshes, wetlands and lake edges with tall, dense grasses, sedges, bulrushes and cattails.

**Nesting:** above the waterline in dense vegetation; nest platform is made of grass, sedges and dead reeds; often has separate entrance and exit paths; female incubates 3–5 pale olive or buff eggs for 24–28 days.

**Feeding:** patient stand-and-wait predator; strikes at small fish, crayfish, amphibians, reptiles, small mammals and insects.

**Voice:** deep, slow, resonant, repetitive *pomp-er-lunk* or *onk-a-BLONK*; most often heard in the evening or at night.

**Similar Species:** *Black-crowned Night-Heron* (p. 101), *Yellow-crowned Night-Heron* (p. 102), *Least Bittern* (p. 103) and *Green Heron* (p. 100): immatures lack dark streak from bill to shoulder; immature night-herons have white-flecked upperparts.

**Best Sites:** Iroquois NWR–Tonawanda WMA–Oak Orchard WMA; Braddock Bay; Montezuma NWR; Bashakill WMA.

# LEAST BITTERN

*Ixobrychus exilis*

The Least Bittern is the smallest of the herons and one of the most reclusive marsh birds in North America. It inhabits freshwater marshes where tall, impenetrable stands of cattails conceal most of its movements. This bird moves about with ease, its slender body passing freely and unnoticed through dense marshland vegetation. An expert climber, it can often be seen 3 feet or more above water, clinging to vertical stems and hopping about without getting its feet wet. • In our region, where this species approaches the northern limit of its North American range, the Least Bittern pushes the boundaries of its adaptability, particularly its tolerance to chilly summer nights. Least Bitterns are uncommon here and sightings are rare, owing in part to this bird's secretive behavior and solitary lifestyle.

**ID:** rich buff flanks and sides; streaked foreneck; white underparts; mostly pale bill; yellowish legs; short tail; dark primary and secondary feathers. *Male:* black crown and back. *Female and immature:* chestnut brown head and back; immature has darker streaking on breast and back. *In flight:* large, buffy shoulder patches.

**Size:** *L* 11–14½ in; *W* 17 in.

**Status:** threatened; uncommon breeder from May to July, patchily distributed across the state; migrants arrive in April and May and depart by September; very rarely found on Long I. in winter.

**Habitat:** freshwater marshes with cattails and other dense emergent vegetation.

**Nesting:** mostly the male constructs a platform of dry plant stalks on top of bent marsh vegetation; nest site is usually well concealed within dense vegetation; pair incubates 4–5 pale green or blue eggs for 17–20 days; pair feeds the young by regurgitation.

**Feeding:** stabs prey with its bill; eats mostly small fish; also takes large insects, tadpoles, frogs, small snakes, leeches and crayfish; may build a hunting platform.

**Voice:** *Male:* guttural *uh-uh-uh-oo-oo-oo-ooah. Female:* a ticking sound. Both issue a *tut-tut* call or a *koh* alarm call.

**Similar Species:** *American Bittern* (p. 92): larger; bold, brown streaking on underparts; black streak from bill to shoulder. *Black-crowned Night-Heron* (p. 101) and *Yellow-crowned Night-Heron* (p. 102): immatures have dark brown upperparts with white flecking. *Green Heron* (p. 100): immature has dark brown upperparts.

**Best Sites:** Iroquois NWR–Tonawanda WMA–Oak Orchard WMA; Braddock Bay; Montezuma NWR; Cruger I.–Tivoli Bays.

93

# GREAT BLUE HERON
*Ardea herodias*

The sight of a Great Blue Heron is always memorable. Whether you are observing its stealthy, often motionless hunting strategy, or tracking its graceful wingbeats as it returns to a feeding site or its nest, it is difficult not to notice this bird's majesty. • The Great Blue Heron nests in large colonies. Its communal treetop nests, known as rookeries, are sensitive to human disturbance, so if you are fortunate enough to discover a colony, it is best to observe the birds' behavior from a distance. • This heron is often mistaken for a crane, but unlike a crane, which holds its neck outstretched in flight, the Great Blue Heron folds its neck back over its shoulders in an S-shape. • Though mostly a fish eater, this bird may also be found stalking fields and meadows in search of rodents.

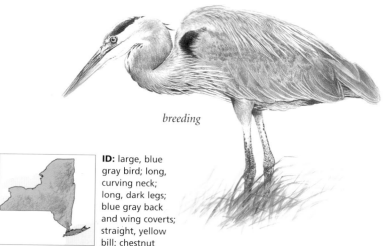

*breeding*

**ID:** large, blue gray bird; long, curving neck; long, dark legs; blue gray back and wing coverts; straight, yellow bill; chestnut brown thighs. *Breeding:* richer colors; plumes streak from crown and throat. *In flight:* neck folds back over shoulders; legs trail behind body; slow, steady wingbeats.
**Size:** *L* 4–4½ ft; *W* 6 ft.
**Status:** breeds from April to June in scattered locales across the state; common migrant from March to April and in September; fairly common in winter where there is open water.
**Habitat:** forages along the edges of rivers, lakes and marshes; also seen in fields and wet meadows.
**Nesting:** colonial; usually in a tree, but occasionally on the ground; flimsy to elaborate stick-and-twig platform is added onto, often over years, and can be up to 4 ft in diameter; pair incubates 4–7 pale blue eggs for about 28 days.
**Feeding:** patient stand-and-wait predator; strikes at small fish, amphibians, small mammals, aquatic invertebrates and reptiles; rarely scavenges.
**Voice:** usually quiet away from the nest; occasionally a deep, harsh *frahnk frahnk frahnk*, usually during takeoff.
**Similar Species:** *Green Heron* (p. 100), *Black-crowned Night-Heron* (p. 101) and *Yellow-crowned Night-Heron* (p. 102): much smaller; shorter legs. *Great* (p. 95), *Snowy* (p. 96) and *Cattle* (p. 99) *egrets:* all are predominately white. *Sandhill Crane* (p. 125): red "cap"; flies with neck outstretched. *Little Blue Heron* (p. 97): smaller; dark overall; purplish head; lacks yellow on bill. *Tricolored Heron* (p. 98): smaller; darker upperparts; white underparts.
**Best Sites:** Iroquois NWR–Tonawanda WMA–Oak Orchard WMA; Montezuma NWR; Bashakill WMA; Jamaica Bay Wildlife Refuge.

# GREAT EGRET

*Ardea alba*

The plumes of the Great Egret and Snowy Egret were widely used to decorate hats in the early 20th century. An ounce of egret feathers cost as much as $32—more than an ounce of gold at that time—and, as a result, egret populations began to disappear. Some of the first conservation legislation in North America was enacted to outlaw the hunting of Great Egrets. These egrets are now recovering and expanding their range, probably to where they formerly nested, though the loss of wetland habitat is on ongoing problem. • Egrets are actually herons, but were given their name for their impressive breeding plumes, referred to as "aigrettes." • Great Egrets are gregarious, feeding and nesting with other Great Egrets, Snowy Egrets and Great Blue Herons. They spend much of their time foraging in shallow water, either wading or standing motionless, waiting for prey. • The Great Egret is the symbol of the National Audubon Society, one of the oldest conservation organizations in the United States.

*breeding*

**ID:** all-white plumage; black legs; yellow bill. *Breeding:* white plumes trail from throat and rump; green skin patch between eyes and base of bill. *In flight:* neck folds back over shoulders; legs extend backward.
**Size:** *L* 3–3½ ft; *W* 4 ft.
**Status:** local breeder from May to June on Long I.; isolated but increasing breeder at a few upstate sites; common summer wanderer.

**Habitat:** marshes, open riverbanks, irrigation canals and lakeshores.
**Nesting:** colonial, but may nest in isolated pairs; in a tree or tall shrub; pair builds a platform of sticks and incubates 3–5 pale blue green eggs for 23–26 days.
**Feeding:** patient stand-and-wait predator; occasionally stalks slowly, stabbing at frogs, snakes and small mammals.
**Voice:** rapid, low-pitched *cuk-cuk-cuk*.
**Similar Species:** *Snowy Egret* (p. 96): smaller; black bill; yellow feet. *Cattle Egret* (p. 99): smaller; orange bill and legs.
**Best Sites:** Jamaica Bay Wildlife Refuge; Jones Beach SP; Shinnecock Inlet–Dune Rd.

# SNOWY EGRET

*Egretta thula*

The Snowy Egret is distinguished by its small size and spotless white plumage. When it reaches adulthood, its black legs with yellow feet make it stand out even more. • In the late 19th century, the Snowy Egret was even more affected by plume hunters than the Great Egret because it was more abundant and widespread, and because its plumes were softer and more delicate. After staging a comeback in the 1960s and 1970s, there were widespread population declines in the late 20th century, likely attributable to the Snowy Egret's sensitivity to a variety of conservation threats. • Herons and egrets, particularly Snowy Egrets, use a variety of feeding techniques. By poking their bright yellow feet in the muck of shallow wetlands, these birds spook potential prey out of hiding places. In an even more devious hunting strategy, Snowy Egrets are known to create shade by extending their wings over open water. When a fish succumbs to the attraction of the cooler shaded spot, it is promptly seized and eaten.

*breeding*

**ID:** white plumage; black bill and legs; bright yellow feet. *Breeding:* long plumes on throat and rump; erect crown; red orange lores. *Immature:* similar to adult, but with more yellow on legs. *In flight:* yellow feet are obvious.
**Size:** *L* 22–26 in; *W* 3½ ft.
**Status:** locally common breeder on Long I. from April to July; migrants arrive in late April and depart by late September; common visitor from southern rookeries in late summer; number of Long I. colonies fluctuates from year to year; 4–20 colonies with 600–1200 pairs in the 1980s and 1990s.

**Habitat:** open edges of rivers, lakes and marshes.
**Nesting:** colonial, often among other herons; in a tree or tall shrub near water; pair builds a solid platform of sticks and incubates 3–5 pale blue green eggs for 20–24 days.
**Feeding:** stirs wetland muck with its feet; stands and waits with wings held open; occasionally hovers and stabs; eats small fish, amphibians and invertebrates.
**Voice:** low croaks; bouncy *wulla-wulla-wulla* on breeding grounds.
**Similar Species:** *Great Egret* (p. 95): larger; yellow bill; black feet. *Cattle Egret* (p. 99): yellow orange legs and bill.
**Best Sites:** Jamaica Bay Wildlife Refuge; Jones Beach SP; Shinnecock Inlet–Dune Rd.

# LITTLE BLUE HERON

*Egretta caerulea*

Because of its dark plumage and lack of aigrette plumes, the Little Blue Heron was only occasionally taken by plume hunters in the 19th century and did not suffer the same population decimation as many of its close relatives. • Although adults of the species look quite different from Snowy Egrets, the white-plumaged young of the two species can be easily confused. It takes two years for Little Blue Herons to reach the completely dark plumage of adult birds. • These herons often occupy saltwater wetlands and will also perch in trees and bushes overhanging slowly moving water-courses. • Though the Little Blue Heron may forage alone, a common practice among egrets and herons is to forage in the company of other wading birds. This improves foraging success because the birds stir up prey for each other in the process of foraging for themselves.

*breeding*

**ID:** medium-sized heron; slate blue overall. *Breeding:* shaggy, maroon-colored head and neck; yellow green legs and feet. *Nonbreeding:* smooth, purple head and neck; dull green legs and feet. *Immature:* white, dusky-tipped primaries; yellowish olive legs; blue gray bill; spotted blue and white when molting to adult plumage.
**Size:** *L* 24 in; *W* 3½ ft.
**Status:** uncommon breeder from May to July on Long I.; uncommon summer visitor; migrants arrive in late April and depart by late September; rarely appears upstate.
**Habitat:** marshes, ponds, lakes, streams and meadows.

**Nesting:** in mixed species colonies; pair builds a large stick nest in a small tree or shrub above water and incubates 3–5 pale blue green eggs for 20–23 days.
**Feeding:** patient stand-and-wait predator; may also wade slowly to stalk prey; eats mostly fish, crabs and crayfish; also takes grasshoppers and other insects, frogs, lizards, snakes and turtles.
**Voice:** generally silent.
**Similar Species:** *Snowy Egret* (p. 96): black bill; black legs; bright yellow feet; immature has yellow lores, entirely dark bill, black legs, greenish yellow feet and lacks dusky primary tips. *Cattle Egret* (p. 99): short, yellow bill; yellow legs and feet; immature is similar to adult, but has black feet.
**Best Sites:** Jamaica Bay Wildlife Refuge; Jones Beach SP.

# TRICOLORED HERON

*Egretta tricolor*

The Tricolored Heron is found only in the New World and is more usually associated with coastal habitats than most other herons or egrets. This large, slender heron is rather spectacular in its tricolored breeding plumage, but a closer inspection will reveal the bird's close affinity to the pure white egrets, with which it often shares a breeding site. • Captains Meriwether Lewis and William Clark were responsible for collecting numerous specimens and bringing them to early ornithologists to be described and named scientifically for the first time. Ornithologist Alexander Wilson favored calling this species "Louisiana Heron," after the place from which it was first collected. Years later, the name Tricolored Heron emerged as this bird's formally recognized common name—derived from the plumage of immature birds, which is a combination of grayish blue, chestnut and white.

*breeding*

**ID:** *Breeding:* long, slender bill, neck and legs; purplish to grayish blue upperparts; yellowish fore-neck; white under-parts; pale rump; long plumes appear on head and back during breeding season. *Immature:* chestnut head, neck and wing coverts. *In flight:* long wings; long legs extend well beyond tail; rather leisurely flight.

**Size:** *L* 26 in; *W* 3 ft.

**Status:** uncommon breeder and summer visitor from May to July on Long I.; very rare elsewhere; migrants arrive in late April and depart by late September.

**Habitat:** coastal saltwater estuaries and protected bays.

**Nesting:** often in multispecies colonies; female uses sticks and vegetation collected by male to build a bulky platform nest in a tree or shrub; pair incubates 3–4 pale greenish blue eggs for 21–23 days.

**Feeding:** uses a variety of waiting, stalking and running techniques to catch prey; eats mostly small fish, plus insects, crustaceans and frogs; occasionally forages by dashing after schools of fish or stirring up bottom sediments with one foot.

**Voice:** generally silent.

**Similar Species:** *Little Blue Heron* (p. 97): dark slate blue overall in nonbreeding plumage; shaggy, maroon neck and dark underparts in breeding plumage.

**Best Sites:** Jamaica Bay Wildlife Refuge; Jones Beach SP.

# CATTLE EGRET

*Bubulcus ibis*

Over the last century—and without help from humans—the Cattle Egret has dispersed from Africa to inhabit every continent except Antarctica. Like most herons, the Cattle Egret is a natural wanderer, but it was probably not until forests had been sufficiently cleared—about 100 years ago—that Cattle Egrets were truly able to colonize the New World. They arrived in Florida in the late 1940s, and first bred in New York in 1970. • The Cattle Egret gets its name from its habit of following grazing animals. Unlike other egrets, its diet consists of terrestrial invertebrates—it feeds on the insects and other small creatures found around ungulates. When foraging, Cattle Egrets sometimes use a "leapfrog" feeding strategy in which birds jump over one another, stirring up insects for the birds that follow. • This bird's scientific name *Bubulcus*, means "belonging to or concerning cattle."

*breeding*

**ID:** mostly white; yellow orange bill and legs. *Breeding:* long plumes on throat and rump; buff orange throat, rump and crown; orange red legs and bill; purple lores. *Immature:* similar to adult, but with black feet and dark bill.
**Size:** *L* 19–21 in; *W* 35–37 in.
**Status:** uncommon breeder in June and July on Long I.; 1 breeding site on L. Champlain; migrants arrive in late April and depart by late September; occasionally seen upstate, most often in spring and summer.
**Habitat:** marshes and agricultural fields.

**Nesting:** colonial, often among other herons; in a tree or tall shrub; male supplies sticks for the female who builds a platform or shallow bowl; pair incubates 3–4 pale blue eggs for 21–26 days.
**Feeding:** picks grasshoppers, other insects, worms, small vertebrates and spiders from fields; often associated with livestock.
**Voice:** generally silent.
**Similar Species:** *Great Egret* (p. 95): larger; black legs and feet. *Snowy Egret* (p. 96): black legs; yellow feet; black bill. *Little Blue Heron* (p. 97): immature has blue gray bill and yellowish olive legs. *Gulls* (pp. 164–75): do not stand as erect; generally have gray mantles.
**Best Sites:** Jamaica Bay Wildlife Refuge; Jones Beach SP; Shinnecock Inlet–Dune Rd.

# GREEN HERON

*Butorides virescens*

This crow-sized heron is far less conspicuous than its Great Blue cousin. The Green Heron eats primarily frogs and small fish, and prefers to hunt in shallow, weedy wetlands, where it often perches just above the water's surface. While hunting, Green Herons sometimes drop small debris, including twigs, vegetation and feathers, onto the water's surface as a form of bait to attract fish within striking range. • If the light is just right, you may be fortunate enough to see a glimmer of green on the back and outer wings of this bird. Most of the time, however, this magical shine is not apparent, especially when the Green Heron stands frozen under the shade of dense marshland vegetation. • Unlike most herons, Green Herons nest singly rather than communally, although they can sometimes be found in loose colonies. • The scientific name *virescens* is Latin for "growing or becoming green," and refers to the greenish highlights in the adult's plumage.

**ID:** green black crown; chestnut face and neck; white foreneck and belly; blue gray back and wings mixed with iridescent green; relatively short, yellow green legs; bill is dark above and greenish below; short tail. *Breeding male:* bright orange legs. *Immature:* heavy streaking along neck and underparts; dark brown upperparts.
**Size:** *L* 15–22 in; *W* 26 in.
**Status:** common and widespread breeder at lower elevations from April to August; migrants arrive in late April and depart by late September; very rare in winter on Long I.
**Habitat:** marshes, lakes and streams with dense shoreline or emergent vegetation.
**Nesting:** nests singly or in small groups; male begins and female completes a stick nest platform in a tree or shrub, usually very close to water; pair incubates 3–5 pale blue green eggs for 19–21 days; young are fed by regurgitation.
**Feeding:** stabs prey with its bill after slowly stalking or standing and waiting; eats mostly small fish; also takes frogs, tadpoles, crayfish, insects, small rodents, snakes, snails and worms.
**Voice:** generally silent; alarm and flight calls are a loud *kowp, kyow* or *skow*.
**Similar Species:** *Black-crowned Night-Heron* (p. 101): larger; white "cheek," foreneck and underparts; 2 long, white plumes trail down from crown; immature has streaked face and white flecking on upperparts. *Least Bittern* (p. 93): buff yellow shoulder patches, sides and flanks. *American Bittern* (p. 92): larger; more tan overall; black streak from bill to shoulder.
**Best Sites:** Montezuma NWR; Bashakill WMA; Jamaica Bay Wildlife Refuge; Jones Beach SP.

# BLACK-CROWNED NIGHT-HERON

*Nycticorax nycticorax*

When the setting sun has sent most wetland waders to their nightly roosts, Black-crowned Night-Herons arrive to hunt the marshy waters and to voice their hoarse squawks. These herons patrol the shallows for prey, which they can see in the dim light with their large, red eyes. They seem unwilling to leave good feeding areas and may remain alongside water until morning, when they reluctantly flap off to treetop roosts. • During the breeding season, the Black-crowned Night-Heron sometimes forages during the day. A popular hunting strategy for day-active night-herons is to sit motionless atop a few bent-over cattails. Anything passing below the perch becomes fair game—even ducklings, small shorebirds or young muskrats. • Young night-herons are commonly seen around large cattail marshes in fall. Because of their heavily streaked underparts, they are easily confused with other immature herons and American Bitterns. • The Black-crowned Night-Heron is the most abundant heron in the world, occurring virtually worldwide.

*breeding*

**ID:** black "cap" and back; white "cheek," foreneck and underparts; gray neck and wings; dull yellow legs; stout black bill; large, red eyes. *Breeding:* 2 white plumes trail down from crown. *Immature:* lightly streaked underparts; brown upperparts with white flecking.

**Size:** *L* 23–26 in; *W* 3½ ft.

**Status:** common breeder on Long I. from April to July; rare and local breeder inland; uncommon in winter on Long I.

**Habitat:** shallow cattail and bulrush marshes, lakeshores and along slowly moving rivers.

**Nesting:** colonial; in a tree or shrub; male gathers nest material and female builds a loose nest platform of twigs and sticks;

pair incubates 3–4 pale green eggs for 21–26 days.

**Feeding:** often at dusk; patient stand-and-wait predator; stabs for small fish, amphibians, aquatic invertebrates, reptiles, young birds and small mammals.

**Voice:** deep, guttural *quark* or *wok,* often heard as the bird takes flight.

**Similar Species:** *Great Blue Heron* (p. 94): much larger; longer legs; blue gray back. *Yellow-crowned Night-Heron* (p. 102): white crown and "cheek" patch on otherwise black head; gray back. *Green Heron* (p. 100): chestnut brown face and neck; blue gray back with green iridescence; immature has heavily streaked underparts. *American Bittern* (p. 92): similar to immature Black-crowned Night-Heron, but bittern has black streak from bill to shoulder and is lighter tan overall.

**Best Sites:** Jamaica Bay Wildlife Refuge; Jones Beach SP; Marshlands Conservancy–Playland CP.

# YELLOW-CROWNED NIGHT-HERON
*Nyctanassa violacea*

The Yellow-crowned Night-Heron's partiality for crustaceans has earned it the name "Crab Eater" in some parts of its range. While in our region, its diet is more varied and also includes frogs, insects and fish. In fall, a return to subtropical and tropical locales will find this heron hunting primarily crabs once again. • Despite its name, the Yellow-crowned Night-Heron commonly feeds by day as well as by night, although poor lighting is a standard criterion for suitable breeding and hunting habitat. During the day, Yellow-crowned Night-Herons usually roost in dense thickets. Its secretive habits, choice of concealing habitats and slow, nearly motionless hunting strategy combine to make this bird a challenge to locate and observe. • During the breeding season, Yellow-crowned Night-Heron pairs greet each other with their crests raised and delicately preen each other's feathers. • Both Yellow-crowned Night-Herons and Black-crowned Night-Herons have bright red eyes in all plumages—possibly an adaptation to their nocturnal foraging.

*breeding*

**ID:** black head; buffy white crown; white "cheek"; dull gray underparts; dark gray upperparts with light feather edges; yellowish legs. *Breeding:* long, white head plumes. *In flight:* feet extend well beyond tail.
**Size:** *L* 24 in; *W* 3½ ft.
**Status:** uncommon breeder from April to July in coastal areas of Long I. and New York City.
**Habitat:** wetlands; along lowland rivers.
**Nesting:** singly or in colonies; in a tree or shrub near water; pair builds a nest of heavy twigs and incubates 2–4 pale greenish blue eggs for 21–25 days.
**Feeding:** stands and waits or wades slowly in shallow water to catch crabs, crayfish, other freshwater invertebrates, fish, frogs and insects; forages alone or in small groups.
**Voice:** a loud *quok!*, less harsh and slightly higher-pitched than the Black-crowned Night-Heron's call.
**Similar Species:** *Black-crowned Night-Heron* (p. 101): black crown and back; shorter legs; thinner bill.
**Best Sites:** Jamaica Bay Wildlife Refuge; Jones Beach SP; Marshlands Conservancy–Playland CP.

# GLOSSY IBIS

*Plegadis falcinellus*

The exotic look of the Glossy Ibis hints at its distant origins. The same power-ful trade winds that drew Christopher Columbus to North America most likely also guided these birds from West Africa to the warm Caribbean only a few centuries ago. The Glossy Ibis probably arrived in North America in the early 1800s. Since the 1930s, this widely distributed Old World bird has estab-lished stable breeding populations as far north as southern Maine from its previously small, concentrated population in the rich marshes of Florida. • The Glossy Ibis is most often seen sweeping its head back and forth through the water, skillfully using its long, sickle-shaped bill like a precision instrument to probe the marshland mud for unseen prey. • This species first nested in New York in 1961 on Long Island. Its population has since increased, but has not expanded beyond the New York City area.

*breeding*

**ID:** long, down-curved bill; long legs; dark skin in front of brown eye is bordered by 2 pale stripes. *Breeding:* glossy, chestnut head, neck and sides; green and purple sheen on wings, tail, crown and face. *Nonbreeding:* dark grayish brown head and neck are streaked with white. *In flight:* appears hunchbacked; neck is fully extended; legs trail behind tail; flocks fly in lines or V-for-mation.

**Size:** *L* 23 in; *W* 3 ft.

**Status:** common but local breeder from May to July on Long I. and in the New York City area; rare spring and summer wan-derer to upstate areas; migrants arrive from late March to April and depart in October and November.

**Habitat:** freshwater and saltwater marshes, swamps, flooded fields and estuaries shallow enough for wading and with adequate shoreline vegetation for nesting.

**Nesting:** colonial, often with egrets and herons; bulky nest platform of marsh vege-tation and sticks is built over water, on the ground or on top of a tall shrub or small tree; pair incubates 3–4 pale blue or green eggs for about 21 days.

**Feeding:** wades through shallow water; probes and gleans for aquatic and terres-trial invertebrates; may also eat adult and larval amphibians, snakes, leeches, crabs and small fish.

**Voice:** cooing accompanies billing and preening during nest relief.

**Similar Species:** *Herons* (pp. 94–102): all lack downcurved bill.

**Best Sites:** Jamaica Bay Wildlife Refuge; Jones Beach SP.

# BLACK VULTURE

*Coragyps atratus*

Much maligned for its morbid feeding habits and somewhat grotesque appearance, this large scavenger is a vital part of a healthy ecosystem. Feeding primarily on carrion, the Black Vulture helps to convert the nutrients of the dead back into nutrients that support the living. • Look for these large birds soaring high among the clouds, scouring the earth below for signs of their next meal. Black Vultures have a less developed sense of smell than Turkey Vultures, so they find their food visually. They are more aggressive than Turkey Vultures and will often take over a carcass, forcing the Turkey Vultures to wait for leftovers. • Unlike vultures in movies, real vultures will not circle above you, waiting for you to take your final breath as you stagger across the desert. However, although they cannot anticipate your time of death, you can be assured that with their keen eyes and superior vantage point, they will be at your side to redistribute your belongings shortly after your departure!

**ID:** all-black plumage; bare, grayish head, legs and feet; base of primaries are whitish; short, square tail; wings are held flat in flight.

**Size:** *L* 25 in; *W* 4½–5 ft.

**Status:** rare but increasing year-round resident in southern NY; first nested in the late 1990s; very rare elsewhere in the state.

**Habitat:** forages over open country throughout its range, but tends to roost and nest in forested areas.

**Nesting:** in a large tree cavity or on the ground in a sheltered site; no nest material is added; pair incubates 2 brown-blotched, buff or pale gray green eggs and raises the young together.

**Feeding:** carrion forms bulk of diet, supplemented with eggs, small reptiles, amphibians and mammals, food waste from garbage dumps and occasionally some plant material.

**Voice:** generally silent; may hiss or grunt at the nest site or around communal food sources.

**Similar Species:** *Turkey Vulture* (p. 105): bare, red head; longer, narrower wings and tail; black wing linings with silver gray flight feathers; wings are usually held in a shallow "V."

**Best Sites:** Shawangunk Grasslands NWR; Sterling Forest SP; Bear Mountain SP.

# TURKEY VULTURE

*Cathartes aura*

Turkey Vultures are unmatched in this region at using updrafts and thermals—they can gain lift from the slightest pocket of rising air and patrol the skies when other soaring birds are grounded. • The Turkey Vulture eats carrion almost exclusively, so its bill and feet are not nearly as powerful as those of eagles, hawks and falcons, which kill live prey. Its red, featherless head may appear grotesque, but this adaptation allows it to remain relatively clean while feeding on messy carcasses. • Vultures seem to have mastered the art of regurgitation. This ability allows parents to transport food over long distances to their young and also enables engorged birds to repulse an attacker or "lighten up" for an emergency takeoff. • Recent studies have shown that American vultures are most closely related to storks, not to hawks and falcons as was previously thought. Molecular similarities with storks, and the shared tendency to defecate on their own legs to cool down, strongly support this taxonomic reclassification.

**ID:** all black; bare, red head. *Immature:* gray head. *In flight:* head appears small; silver gray flight feathers; black wing linings; wings are held in a shallow "V"; rocks from side to side when soaring.

**Size:** *L* 26–32 in; *W* 5½–6 ft.

**Status:** widespread breeder in May and June; common migrant from late March to early April and in October; very rare on the coastal plain.

**Habitat:** usually seen flying over open country; rarely seen over forested areas.

**Nesting:** in a cave crevice or among boulders; rarely in a hollow stump or log; no nest material is used; female lays 2 brown-blotched, dull white eggs on bare ground; pair incubates the eggs for up to 41 days; young are fed by regurgitation.

**Feeding:** entirely on carrion (mostly mammalian); not commonly seen at roadkills.

**Voice:** generally silent; occasionally produces a hiss or grunt if threatened.

**Similar Species:** *Golden Eagle* (p. 116) and *Bald Eagle* (p. 107): lack silvery gray wing linings; do not rock when soaring; head is more visible in flight. *Black Vulture* (p. 104): rare; gray head; silvery tips on otherwise black wings; wings are held flat in flight.

**Best Sites:** Letchworth SP; Braddock Bay; Derby Hill; Bear Mountain SP; Sterling Forest SP.

# OSPREY
*Pandion haliaetus*

The Osprey is superbly adapted for catching fish and is always found near water. It is the only species in its family and is found on every continent except Antarctica. • The Osprey's white undersides disappear against the sky as it flies high above lakes, rivers and bays in search of fish, while its dark "mask" reduces the blinding glare of sunshine skipping off the water. When the bird spies a flash of silver or a slowly moving shadow, it folds its wings and hurls itself in a perilous headfirst dive. An instant before striking the water, the Osprey rights itself and thrusts its feet forward to grasp its prey, often striking the water with a tremendous splash and sometimes disappearing under the water. • The Osprey's feet have two toes facing forward and two facing backward, and the soles are heavily scaled to help the bird clamp tightly onto slippery fish.

**ID:** dark brown upperparts; white underparts; dark eye line; light crown; yellow eyes. *Male:* all-white throat. *Female:* fine, dark "necklace." *In flight:* dark "wrist" patches; brown and white tail bands; long wings are held in a shallow "M."

**Size:** *L* 22–25 in; *W* 5–5½ ft.

**Status:** special concern; common breeder from April to June on Long I.; less common breeder in the Adirondacks; common migrant in late April and in September on the coast and along rivers and lakeshores.

**Habitat:** lakes, slowly flowing rivers and streams, bays and estuaries.

**Nesting:** on a treetop, usually near water; may also use a specially made platform, utility pole or tower up to 100 ft high; massive stick nest is reused over many years; pair incubates 2–4 brown-blotched, yellowish eggs for about 38 days; both adults feed the young.

**Feeding:** dramatic, feet-first dives into water; small fish make up almost all of diet.

**Voice:** series of melodious, ascending whistles: *chewk-chewk-chewk;* also an often-heard *kip-kip-kip.*

**Similar Species:** *Bald Eagle* (p. 107): larger; larger bill with yellow base; yellow legs; clean white head and tail on dark body; lacks white underparts and dark "wrist" patches; holds wings straighter while soaring. *Gulls* (pp. 164–75): white heads; lack dark "wrist" patch.

**Best Sites:** Braddock Bay; Derby Hill; Jamaica Bay Wildlife Refuge; Napeague Bay–Hither Hills SP.

# BALD EAGLE
*Haliaeetus leucocephalus*

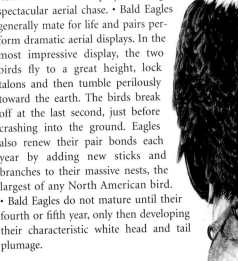

The Bald Eagle is a source of inspiration and wonder for anyone longing for a wilderness experience. Though it cannot compete with the Golden Eagle in strength of talon and character, legends persist that endow it with a mystical quality that is difficult to dispute. • Bald Eagles feed mostly on fish and scavenged carrion. Sometimes an eagle will steal food from an Osprey, resulting in a spectacular aerial chase. • Bald Eagles generally mate for life and pairs perform dramatic aerial displays. In the most impressive display, the two birds fly to a great height, lock talons and then tumble perilously toward the earth. The birds break off at the last second, just before crashing into the ground. Eagles also renew their pair bonds each year by adding new sticks and branches to their massive nests, the largest of any North American bird. • Bald Eagles do not mature until their fourth or fifth year, only then developing their characteristic white head and tail plumage.

**ID:** white head and tail; dark brown body; yellow bill and feet. *1st-year:* dark overall; dark bill; some white in underwings. *2nd-year:* dark "bib"; white in underwings. *3rd-year:* mostly white plumage; yellow at base of bill; yellow eyes. *4th-year:* light head; dark facial streak; variable pale and dark plumage; yellow bill; paler eyes. *In flight:* broad wings are held flat.
**Size:** *L* 31 in; *W* 6½ ft.
**Status:** threatened; breeds from March to May in scattered locations statewide as a result of reintroduction programs; locally common migrant in March and from August to September; locally common visitor from October to March.
**Habitat:** large lakes and rivers.

**Nesting:** usually in a tree near a lake or large river; huge stick nest, up to 15 ft across and 8 ft deep, is often reused for many years; pair incubates 1–3 white eggs for 34–36 days; both adults feed the young.
**Feeding:** eats waterbirds, small mammals and fish captured at the water's surface; frequently feeds on carrion; sometimes pirates fish from Ospreys.
**Voice:** thin, weak squeal or gull-like cackle: *kleek-kik-kik-kik* or *kah-kah-kah.*
**Similar Species:** adult is distinctive. *Golden Eagle* (p. 116): dark overall, except for golden nape; tail may appear faintly banded with white; immature has white patch on wings and at base of tail. *Osprey* (p. 106): similar to 4th-year Bald Eagle; dark "wrist" patches; dark bill; holds wings in "M" in flight.
**Best Sites:** Braddock Bay; Derby Hill; Bear Mountain SP; Croton Point CP.

# NORTHERN HARRIER

*Circus cyaneus*

The Northern Harrier may be the easiest raptor to identify on the wing because no other midsized hawk routinely flies so close to the ground. As it cruises low over fields, meadows and marshes, it grazes the tops of long grasses and cattails, relying on sudden surprise attacks to capture its prey. Although the harrier has excellent vision, its owl-like, parabolic facial disc allows it to hunt easily by sound as well. • The Northern Harrier was once known as "Marsh Hawk" in North America, and it is still called "Hen Harrier" in Europe. Britain's Royal Air Force was so impressed by this bird's maneuverability that it named its Harrier aircraft after this hawk. • Determining the sex of a Northern Harrier is nearly as easy as identifying its species—males are gray, females are brown. • In recent years, this bird's population has declined greatly owing to the loss of its wetland habitat.

**ID:** long wings and tail; white rump; black wing tips. *Male:* blue gray to silver gray upperparts; white underparts; indistinct tail bands, except for 1 dark subterminal band. *Female:* dark brown upperparts; streaky, brown-and-buff underparts. *Immature:* rich reddish brown plumage; dark tail bands; streaked breast, sides and flanks.
**Size:** *L* 16–24 in; *W* 3½–4 ft.
**Status:** threatened; rare breeder from April to June; common migrant in April and from September to October; uncommon in winter.

**Habitat:** open country, including fields, wet meadows, cattail marshes, bogs, croplands and salt marshes.
**Nesting:** on the ground, often on a slightly raised mound; usually in grass, cattails or tall vegetation; shallow depression or platform nest is lined with grass, sticks and cattails; female incubates 4–6 bluish white eggs for 30–32 days.
**Feeding:** hunts in low, rising and falling flights; eats small mammals, birds, amphibians, reptiles and some invertebrates.
**Voice:** most vocal near the nest and during courtship, but generally quiet; high-pitched *ke-ke-ke-ke-ke-ke* near the nest.
**Similar Species:** *Rough-legged Hawk* (p. 115): broader wings; dark "wrist" patches; black tail with wide, white base; dark belly. *Red-tailed Hawk* (p. 114): lacks white rump and long, narrow tail.
**Best Sites:** Braddock Bay; Derby Hill; Cape Vincent–Pt. Peninsula; Jones Beach SP; Shinnecock Inlet–Dune Rd.

# SHARP-SHINNED HAWK

*Accipiter striatus*

After a successful hunt, the diminutive Sharp-shinned Hawk usually perches on a favorite "plucking post," grasping its meal in its razor-sharp talons. This hawk preys almost exclusively on small birds, such as chickadees, finches and sparrows, pursuing them in high-speed chases. • Most people never see a Sharpie nest, because the birds are very tight sitters. Disturb one, however, and you will feel the occupants' wrath. These birds are feisty defenders of their nest and young. • When delivering food to his nestlings, a male Sharp-shinned Hawk is cautious around his mate—she is typically one-third larger than he is and notoriously short-tempered. • Accipiters, named after their genus, are woodland hawks. Their short, rounded wings, long, rudderlike tails and flap-and-glide flight pattern give them the maneuverability necessary to negotiate a maze of forest foliage at high speed.

*immature*

**ID:** short, rounded wings; long, heavily barred, square-tipped tail; dark barring on pale underparts; blue gray back; red horizontal bars on underparts; red eyes. *Immature:* brown overall; yellow eyes; vertical, brown streaking on breast and belly. *In flight:* flap-and-glide flight pattern.

**Size:** *Male: L* 10–12 in; *W* 20–24 in. *Female: L* 12–14 in; *W* 24–28 in.

**Status:** special concern; breeds from April to June throughout the state, but is scattered and secretive, therefore easily overlooked; common migrant in April and from September to October; uncommon in winter.

**Habitat:** dense to semi-open forests and large woodlots; occasionally along rivers and in urban areas; favors bogs and dense, moist, coniferous forests for nesting.

**Nesting:** in a conifer; usually builds a new stick nest each year, but might remodel an abandoned crow nest; female incubates 4–5 brown-blotched, bluish white eggs for 30–35 days.

**Feeding:** pursues small birds through forests; rarely takes small mammals, amphibians and insects.

**Voice:** silent except during the breeding season, when an intense and often-repeated *kik-kik-kik-kik* can be heard.

**Similar Species:** *Cooper's Hawk* (p. 110): larger; more rounded tail tip has broader terminal band; crown is darker than nape and back. *American Kestrel* (p. 117): long, pointed wings; dark "tear streak"; dark "sideburn"; typically seen in open country. *Merlin* (p. 118): pointed wings; rapid wingbeats; dark "tear streak"; brown streaking on buff underparts; dark eyes.

**Best Sites:** Ripley Hawk Watch; Braddock Bay; Derby Hill; Franklin Mt.; Fire Island National Seashore.

# COOPER'S HAWK

*Accipiter cooperii*

Larger and heavier than the Sharp-shinned Hawk, the Cooper's Hawk glides silently through forest clearings, using surprise and speed to snatch its prey from midair. Females have the size and build of male Goshawks and can seize and decapitate birds as large as Ruffed Grouse, which they sometimes pursue on the ground like overweight roadrunners. • These birds are now protected by law and the use of DDT has been banned throughout North America, with the result that the Cooper's Hawk is increasing in numbers and slowly recolonizing former habitats in the region. • Distinguishing the Cooper's Hawk from the Sharp-shinned Hawk is challenging. The Cooper's has a shallower, stiffer-winged flight, while the Sharpie has deeper wingbeats with more bending in the wings. Sharpshins have a square tail, while the Cooper's tail is more rounded.

**ID:** short, rounded wings; long, heavily barred, rounded tail; dark barring on pale undertail and underwings; squarish head; blue gray back; red horizontal barring on underparts; red eyes; white terminal tail band. *Immature:* brown overall; yellow eyes; vertical brown streaks on breast and belly. *In flight:* flap-and-glide flight.
**Size:** *Male:* L 15–17 in; W 27–32 in. *Female:* L 17–19 in; W 32–37 in.
**Status:** special concern; widespread but uncommon breeder from April to June; common migrant in April and from September to October; fairly common in winter.
**Habitat:** mixed woodlands, riparian woodlands and urban woodlots.
**Nesting:** stick-and-twig nest is built 20–65 ft above the ground in a tree, often near a stream or pond; female incubates 3–5 bluish white eggs for 34–36 days.

**Feeding:** pursues prey in flights through forests; eats mostly songbirds; occasionally takes squirrels and chipmunks; uses a "plucking post" or nest for eating.
**Voice:** rapid, woodpecker-like *cac-cac-cac-cac.*
**Similar Species:** *Sharp-shinned Hawk* (p. 109): smaller; squared tail; narrower terminal tail band. *American Kestrel* (p. 117): smaller; long, pointed wings; dark "tear streak"; dark "sideburn"; typically seen in open country. *Merlin* (p. 118): smaller; pointed wings; rapid wingbeats; dark "tear streak"; brown streaking on buff underparts; dark eyes.
**Best Sites:** Braddock Bay; Derby Hill; Franklin Mt.; Jones Beach SP; Fire Island National Seashore.

# NORTHERN GOSHAWK

*Accipiter gentilis*

The Northern Goshawk is an agile, powerful predator that is capable of negotiating lightning-fast turns through dense forest cover. This raptor will prey on any animal it can overtake, dispatching its capture with powerful talons. It has even been known to chase quarry on foot should elusive prey disappear under the cover of dense thickets. • Goshawks are devoted parents that are equally ferocious when defending their nest sites. Unfortunate souls who wander too close to a goshawk nest may be assaulted by an almost deafening, squawking dive-bomb attack. Many biologists who work with these birds wear hard hats while inspecting nests. • The clearing of forests for agricultural and residential development has caused Northern Goshawk populations to decline significantly throughout their range in northern Europe, Asia and parts of North America.

**ID:** rounded wings; long, banded tail with white terminal band; white "eyebrow"; dark crown; blue gray back; fine, gray, vertical streaking on pale breast and belly; gray barring on pale undertail and underwings; red eyes. *Immature:* brown overall; brown vertical streaking on whitish breast and belly; brown barring on pale undertail and underwings; yellow eyes.

**Size:** *Male:* L 21–23 in; W 3–3½ ft. *Female:* L 23–25 in; W 3½–4 ft.

**Status:** special concern; widely distributed but uncommon breeder from April to June; rare to common migrant in March and November; uncommon in winter.

**Habitat:** *Breeding:* mature coniferous, deciduous and mixed woodlands. *Nonbreeding:* forest edges, semi-open parklands and farmlands.

**Nesting:** in deep woods; male builds a large, bulky stick platform in a tree, usually 25–80 ft above the ground; nest is often reused for several years; female incubates 2–4 bluish white eggs for 36–41 days.

**Feeding:** low foraging flights through the forest; feeds primarily on large songbirds, grouse, rabbits and squirrels.

**Voice:** silent except during breeding season, when adults utter a loud, fast, shrill *kak-kak-kak-kak.*

**Similar Species:** *Cooper's Hawk* (p. 110) and *Sharp-shinned Hawk* (p. 109): smaller; reddish breast bars; lack white "eyebrow" stripe; immatures are smaller and have yellow eyes, which become more reddish with age. Buteo *hawks* (pp. 112–15): shorter tails; broader wings; gray or brown eyes.

**Best Sites:** Braddock Bay; Derby Hill; Franklin Mt.; John Boyd Thacher SP.

# RED-SHOULDERED HAWK

*Buteo lineatus*

The Red-shouldered Hawk is a bird of wetter habitats than the closely related Broad-winged Hawk and Red-tailed Hawk. It nests in mature trees, usually along river bottomlands and in lowland tracts of woods alongside creeks. As spring approaches and pair bonds are formed, this normally quiet hawk utters loud, shrieking *key-ah* calls. Be forewarned that Blue Jays have mastered an impressive impersonation of the Red-shouldered Hawk's vocalizations. • During the summer months, the dense cover of the Red-shouldered Hawk's forested breeding habitat allows few opportunities for birders to view this hawk. However, during spring and fall migration, the Red-shouldered Hawk can be found hunting from exposed perches. • If left undisturbed, Red-shouldered Hawks will remain faithful to productive nesting sites, returning yearly. After the parents die, one of the young will carry on the family nesting tradition.

**ID:** chestnut red shoulders on otherwise dark brown upperparts; reddish underwing linings; narrow, white bars on dark tail; barred, reddish breast and belly; reddish undertail coverts. *Immature:* large, brown "teardrop" streaks on white underparts; whitish undertail coverts. *In flight:* dark barring on underside of pale flight feathers and on tail; white crescents or "windows" at base of primaries. **Size:** *L* 19 in; *W* 3½ ft.
**Status:** special concern; uncommon breeder from March to May throughout the state; fairly common migrant from March to April and from October to November; a few birds overwinter.
**Habitat:** mature deciduous and mixed forests, wooded riparian areas, swampy woodlands and large, mature woodlots.
**Nesting:** pair builds a bulky nest of sticks and twigs, usually 15–80 ft above the ground in a deciduous tree (prefers mature maple, ash and beech); nest is often reused; female incubates 2–4 darkly blotched, bluish white eggs for 23–25 days.
**Feeding:** finds prey visually from a fence post, tree or telephone pole and captures it in a swooping attack; may catch prey flushed by low flight; eats small mammals, birds, reptiles and amphibians.
**Voice:** repeated series of high *key-ah* notes.
**Similar Species:** *Broad-winged Hawk* (p. 113): lacks reddish shoulders; wings are broader, more whitish and dark-edged underneath; wide, white tail bands. *Red-tailed Hawk* (p. 114): lacks barring on tail and white "windows" at base of primaries.
**Best Sites:** Ripley Hawk Watch; Braddock Bay; Derby Hill; Franklin Mt.; John Boyd Thacher SP.

# BROAD-WINGED HAWK

*Buteo platypterus*

The generally shy and secretive Broad-winged Hawk prefers different habitat than most other buteos. Shunning the open fields and forest clearings favored by the Red-tailed Hawk, it secludes itself in dense, often wet forests. In this habitat, its short, broad wings and highly flexible tail help it to maneuver in the heavy growth. Most hunting is done from a high perch with a good view. • At the end of the nesting season, "kettles" of buteos and other hawks spiral up from their forest retreats, testing thermals for the opportunity to head south. Broad-winged Hawks are often the most numerous species in these flocks. • By the end of October, most of our region's Broad-winged Hawks will have migrated to the warm climes of Central and South America. In good flight years, thousands of Broad-wings may be observed in an unforgettable single day at inland hawk-watch sites.

*light morph*

**ID:** broad, black and white tail bands; broad wings with pointed tips; heavy barring on rufous brown breast; dark brown upperparts. *Immature:* dark brown "teardrop" streaks on white breast, belly and sides; buff and dark brown tail bands. *In flight:* pale underwings outlined with dark brown.
**Size:** *L* 14–19 in; *W* 32–39 in.
**Status:** common breeder from April to June; abundant migrant in April and in September.
**Habitat:** *Breeding:* dense mixed and deciduous forests and woodlots. *In migration:* escarpments and shorelines; also riparian and deciduous forests and woodland edges.
**Nesting:** usually in a deciduous tree, often near water; bulky stick nest is built 20–40 ft above the ground; usually builds a new nest each year; female incubates 2–4 brown-spotted, whitish eggs for 28–31 days.
**Feeding:** swoops down from a perch for small mammals, amphibians, insects and young birds; often seen hunting from roadside telephone poles in northern areas.
**Voice:** high-pitched, whistled *peeeo-wee-ee;* generally silent during migration.
**Similar Species:** Other Buteo *hawks* (pp. 112–15): broad, dark-edged wings with pointed tips; lack broad banding on tail. Accipiter *hawks* (pp. 109–11): long, narrow tails with less distinct banding.
**Best Sites:** Braddock Bay; Derby Hill; Franklin Mt.; Pelham Bay Park (NYC); Sterling Forest SP.

# RED-TAILED HAWK

*Buteo jamaicensis*

The Red-tailed Hawk is one of the most commonly seen hawks in New York. It is conspicuous year-round, particularly near agricultural lands. An afternoon drive through the country will reveal resident Red-tails perching on exposed tree limbs, fence posts or utility poles overlooking open fields and roadsides. • During their spring courtship, excited Red-tailed Hawks dive at each other, sometimes locking talons and tumbling through the air together before breaking off to avoid crashing to the ground. • This hawk's tail does not turn brick red until the bird matures into a breeding adult. • The Red-tailed Hawk's piercing call is as impressive as the sight of an eagle, and producers of television commercials and movies often cheat by pairing the image of an eagle with the Red-tail's voice.

**ID:** red tail; dark upperparts with some white highlights; dark brown band of streaks across belly. *Immature:* lacks red tail; generally darker; band of streaks on belly. *In flight:* fan-shaped tail; white or occasionally tawny brown underparts and wing linings; dark leading edge on underside of wing; pale underwing flight feathers with faint barring.

**Size:** *Male: L* 18–23 in; *W* 4–5 ft. *Female: L* 20–25 in; *W* 4–5 ft.

**Status:** very common year-round resident; abundant migrant in March and in late October.

**Habitat:** open country with some trees; also roadsides, fields, woodlots, hedgerows, mixed forests and moist woodlands.

**Nesting:** in woodlands adjacent to open habitat; usually in a deciduous tree; bulky stick nest is added to each year; pair incubates 2–4 brown-blotched, whitish eggs for 28–32 days.

**Feeding:** scans for food while perched or soaring; drops to capture prey; rarely stalks prey on foot; eats voles, mice, rabbits, chipmunks, birds, amphibians and reptiles; rarely takes large insects.

**Voice:** powerful, descending scream: *keeearrrr.*

**Similar Species:** *Rough-legged Hawk* (p. 115): white tail base; dark "wrist" patches on underwings; broad, dark, terminal tail band. *Broad-winged Hawk* (p. 113): broadly banded tail; broader wings with pointed tips; lacks dark "belt." *Red-shouldered Hawk* (p. 112): reddish wing linings and underparts; reddish shoulders.

**Best Sites:** Ripley Hawk Watch; Braddock Bay; Derby Hill; Franklin Mt.; Bear Mountain SP.

# ROUGH-LEGGED HAWK

*Buteo lagopus*

The Rough-legged Hawk is truly a bird of the Far North, breeding in arctic and subarctic habitats in North America and across Eurasia. Each fall, Rough-legged Hawks drift south from their breeding grounds into our region. The irregular annual abundance of these hawks in New York results from the interplay of reproductive success, small mammal abundance and the vagaries of early winter weather. When small mammals are common in the north, Rough-legged Hawks may fledge up to seven young, but in lean years one chick is the norm. • Foraging Rough-legs can be easily identified at great distances, even in poor light, because they are one of the few large hawks that routinely hover over prey. • Rough-legged Hawks show great variety in coloration, ranging from a whitish light morph with dark patterning to dark-morph birds that are almost entirely dark with distinctive whitish areas. • The name *lagopus*, meaning "hare's foot," refers to this bird's feathered legs, an adaptation for survival in cold climates.

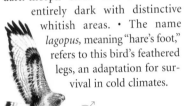

*light morph*

**ID:** white tail base with 1 wide, dark subterminal band; dark brown upperparts; pale flight feathers; legs are feathered to toes. *Dark morph:* dark wing linings, head and underparts. *Light morph:* wide, dark abdominal "belt"; dark streaks on breast and head; dark "wrist" patches; pale underwing linings. *Immature:* lighter breast streaking; bold belly band; buff leg feathers. *In flight:* most show dark "wrist" patches; frequently hovers.
**Size:** *L* 19–24 in; *W* 4–4½ ft.
**Status:** common migrant in November; less common migrant from late February to late March; common winter visitor from

November to March; abundant in some winters during irruption years.
**Habitat:** fields, meadows, open bogs and agricultural croplands.
**Nesting:** does not nest in NY.
**Feeding:** soars and hovers while searching for prey; primarily eats small rodents; occasionally eats birds.
**Voice:** alarm call is a catlike *kee-eer*, usually dropping at the end.
**Similar Species:** *Other* Buteo *hawks* (pp. 112–14): rarely hover; lack dark "wrist" patches and white tail base. *Northern Harrier* (p. 108): facial disc; lacks dark "wrist" patches and dark belly band; longer, thinner tail lacks broad, dark subterminal band.
**Best Sites:** Braddock Bay; Derby Hill; Cape Vincent–Pt. Peninsula; Essex–Westport; Franklin Mt.

# GOLDEN EAGLE

*Aquila chrysaetos*

For centuries, the Golden Eagle has embodied the wonder and wildness of the North American landscape. In the past, with the advent of widespread human development and intensive agricultural practices, this noble bird became the victim of a lengthy persecution. Perceived as a threat to livestock, bounties were offered, encouraging the shooting and poisoning of this regal bird. Today, the Golden Eagle is protected under the Migratory Bird Treaty Act. • The Golden Eagle is actually more closely related to the buteo hawks than it is to the Bald Eagle. Unlike the Bald Eagle, the Golden Eagle is an active, impressive predator, taking prey as large as foxes and geese. • The Golden Eagle is more of a western bird, strongly associated with mountainous areas, and is a rare treat for New York birders. It was previously thought to be nonmigratory, but we now know that birds from northeastern Canada pass through New York on their way to the Appalachians. • Few people ever forget the sight of a Golden Eagle soaring overhead— the average wingspan of an adult exceeds 6 feet!

*immature*

**ID:** very large; brown overall with golden tint to neck and head; brown eyes; dark bill; brown tail has grayish white bands; yellow feet; fully feathered legs. *Immature:* white tail base; white patch at base of underwing primary feathers. *In flight:* short neck; long tail; long, large, rectangular wings; holds wings in a slight "V."
**Size:** *L* 30–40 in; *W* 6½–7½ ft.
**Status:** endangered; former breeder in the Adirondacks; uncommon migrant in March and from October to November; rare winter visitor from November to April.

**Habitat:** *In migration:* along escarpments and lake shorelines. *Winter:* semi-open woodlands and fields.
**Nesting:** does not nest in NY.
**Feeding:** swoops down on prey from soaring flight; eats rabbits, grouse, rodents and foxes; often eats carrion.
**Voice:** generally quiet; rarely a short bark.
**Similar Species:** *Bald Eagle* (p. 107): longer neck; shorter tail; immature lacks white underwing patches and tail base. *Turkey Vulture* (p. 105): naked, reddish head; pale flight feathers; dark wing linings. *Rough-legged Hawk* (p. 115): dark morph has pale flight feathers and white tail base.
**Best Sites:** Derby Hill; Franklin Mt.; Thompson's Pond–Stissing Mt.

# AMERICAN KESTREL

*Falco sparverius*

The American Kestrel is the smallest and most common of our falcons. It hunts small rodents in open areas, and a kestrel perched on a telephone wire or fence post along an open field is a familiar sight throughout the state in summer, and even year-round. • Studies have shown that the Eurasian Kestrel can detect ultraviolet reflections from rodent urine on the ground. It is not known if the American Kestrel has this same ability, but it is frequently seen hovering above the ground while looking for small, ground-dwelling prey. • A helpful identification tip when viewing this bird from afar: the American Kestrel repeatedly lifts its tail while perched to scout below for prey. • This falcon's diminutive size allows it to nest in tree cavities, which helps protect defenseless young kestrels from hungry predators. • Old field guides and old-time birders refer to the American Kestrel as "Sparrow Hawk."

**ID:** 2 distinctive facial stripes. *Male:* rusty back; blue gray wings; blue gray crown with rusty "cap"; lightly spotted underparts. *Female:* rusty back, wings and breast streaking. *In flight:* frequently hovers; long, rusty tail; buoyant, indirect flight style.
**Size:** L 7½–8 in; W 20–24 in.
**Status:** widespread, common breeder from April to June; abundant migrant in April and in September, particularly in fall along coastal beaches; fairly common in winter.
**Habitat:** open fields, riparian woodlands, woodlots, forest edges, bogs, roadside ditches, grassy highway medians, grasslands and croplands.

**Nesting:** in a tree cavity, usually an abandoned woodpecker or flicker cavity; may use a nest box; mostly the female incubates 4–6 finely speckled, white to buff eggs for 29–30 days.
**Feeding:** swoops down from a perch or from hovering flight; eats mostly insects and some small rodents, birds, reptiles and amphibians.
**Voice:** loud, often repeated, shrill *killy-killy-killy* when excited; female's voice is lower pitched.
**Similar Species:** *Merlin* (p. 118): single facial stripe; less colorful; does not hover; flight is more powerful and direct. *Sharp-shinned Hawk* (p. 109): short, rounded wings; reddish barring on underparts; lacks facial stripes; flap-and-glide flight.
**Best Sites:** Braddock Bay; Derby Hill; Jones Beach SP; Fire Island National Seashore.

117

# MERLIN

*Falco columbarius*

Like all its falcon relatives, the main weapons of the Merlin are speed, surprise and sharp, daggerlike talons. This small falcon's sleek body, long, narrow tail and pointed wings increase its aerodynamic efficiency for high-speed songbird pursuits. The elements of speed and surprise work best in open country close to forest edges, and this is where the Merlin is most at home. • Along the coast, where many birds are seen in spring and fall, Merlins make life exciting and sometimes short for such flocking birds as small sandpipers, starlings and blackbirds. Most Merlins migrate to Central and South America each fall, but a few overwinter. • Medieval falconers termed the Merlin "the lady's hawk." Formerly known as "Pigeon Hawk," the Merlin's scientific name *columbarius* comes from the Latin for "pigeon," which it somewhat resembles in flight.

*taiga form*

**ID:** banded tail; heavily streaked underparts; 1 indistinct facial stripe; long, narrow wings and tail. *Male:* blue gray back and crown; rufous leg feathers. *Female:* brown back and crown. *In flight:* rapid, shallow wingbeats.

**Size:** *L* 10–12 in; *W* 23–26 in.

**Status:** rare breeder in the Adirondacks from May to July; common migrant in April and in September, particularly in fall on coastal beaches; rare winter visitor.

**Habitat:** *Breeding:* open and second-growth, mixed and coniferous forests and plantations adjacent to open hunting grounds. *In migration:* open fields, lakeshores and coastal beaches.

**Nesting:** in a tree, crevice or on a cliff; often reuses an abandoned raptor, crow,

jay or squirrel nest; mostly the female incubates 4–5 brown-marked, whitish eggs for 28–32 days.

**Feeding:** overtakes smaller birds in flight; also eats rodents and large insects such as grasshoppers and dragonflies; may also take bats.

**Voice:** loud, noisy, cackling cry: *kek-kek-kek-kek-kek* or *ki-ki-ki-ki;* calls in flight or while perched, often near the nest.

**Similar Species:** *American Kestrel* (p. 117): 2 facial stripes; more colorful; less direct flight style; often hovers. *Peregrine Falcon* (p. 119): larger; well-marked, dark "helmet"; pale, unmarked upper breast; black flecking on light underparts. *Sharp-shinned Hawk* (p. 109) and *Cooper's Hawk* (p. 110): short, rounded wings; reddish barring on breasts and bellies. *Rock Pigeon* (p. 188): broader wings in flight; shorter tail; often glides with wings held in a "V."

**Best Sites:** Braddock Bay; Derby Hill; Franklin Mt.; Jones Beach SP; Fire Island National Seashore.

# PEREGRINE FALCON

*Falco peregrinus*

No bird elicits more admiration than a hunting Peregrine Falcon in full flight, and nothing causes more panic in a tightly packed flock of ducks or shore-birds. Every twist and turn the flock makes is matched by the falcon until it finds a weaker or less-experienced bird. Diving at speeds of up to 220 miles per hour, the Peregrine clenches its feet and then strikes its prey with a lethal blow that often sends both fal-con and prey tumbling. • The Peregrine Falcon's awesome speed and hunting skills were little defense against the pesticide DDT. The chem-ical caused contaminated birds to lay eggs with thin shells, which broke when the adults incubated the eggs. This bird was completely extirpated east of the Mississippi River by 1964. DDT was banned in North America in 1972 and, in the mid-1970s, captive breeding programs were started. These programs have been successful in reestablishing the Peregrine Falcon in the eastern U.S.

**ID:** blue gray back; prominent, dark "helmet"; pale underparts with dark, fine spotting and flecking. *Immature:* brown where adult is blue gray; heavier breast streaks; gray (rather than yellow) feet and cere. *In flight:* pointed wings; long, narrow tail with dark bands.
**Size:** *Male: L* 15–17 in; *W* 3–3½ ft. *Female: L* 17–19 in; *W* 3½–4 ft.
**Status:** reintroduced; endangered; local breeder from March to May, particularly in and near cities as a result of restoration programs; spring migration peaks in April; common migrant in October; occasional winter visitor.

**Habitat:** lakeshores, river valleys, river mouths, urban areas and open fields.
**Nesting:** usually on a rocky cliff or cut-bank; may use a skyscraper ledge or bridge structure; no material is added; nest site is often reused; mostly the female incubates 3–4 heavily speckled, creamy white to buff eggs for 32–34 days.
**Feeding:** high-speed, diving stoops; strikes prey with clenched feet in midair; takes primarily pigeons, waterfowl, shorebirds, flickers and larger songbirds; rarely eats small mammals or carrion; prey is con-sumed on a nearby perch.
**Voice:** loud, harsh, continuous *cack-cack-cack-cack-cack* near the nest site.
**Similar Species:** *Merlin* (p. 118): smaller; lacks dark "helmet"; heavily streaked breast and belly.
**Best Sites:** Braddock Bay; Derby Hill; Franklin Mt.; Jones Beach SP; Fire Island National Seashore.

119

# CLAPPER RAIL

*Rallus longirostris*

The Clapper Rail characteristically flicks its tail as it walks and wades through expanses of cordgrass and glasswort in search of fiddler crabs, small snails and other prey. This bird's slim profile and long, spreading toes allow it to move quickly and efficiently through dense saltwater marshland. • For years, Clapper Rail habitat throughout North America has been under siege by humans hoping to convert "inhospitable" marshland into airports, malls and landfills. Considerably more than half of New York's coastal marshes have been drained and filled, and the rest have been contaminated by a variety of pollutants, which has led to the decline of these marsh denizens. • Because young rails leave the nest within hours of hatching, adults must often split up—one stays on the nest to incubate any remaining eggs, while the other adult moves to a nearby auxiliary nest where the vulnerable, newly hatched young are brooded in safety.

**ID:** long, slightly downcurved bill; four recognized subspecies differ in brightness of coloration; generally darker back feathers have pale edges; grayish brown to cinnamon breast; gray to brown and white vertical bars on flanks; grayish face.

**Size:** L 14½ in; W 19 in.

**Status:** fairly common breeder from April to August in Long I. salt marshes; a few breed along Westchester Co. shores; occasionally found in winter.

**Habitat:** tidal saltwater marshes with glasswort and cordgrass; often feeds along marshy tidal channels during low tide.

**Nesting:** pair builds a cup nest of vegetation in dense cover above or near water; nest usually includes a domed canopy and an entrance ramp; pair incubates 8–10 pale buff eggs for 20–21 days.

**Feeding:** wades in shallow water or among dense marsh vegetation; probes, snatches or gleans aquatic insects, crustaceans and small fish; may also eat seeds, worms and other small items.

**Voice:** *Male:* advertising call is a repeated, clattering *kek-kek-kek;* also repeated *chock* notes, sometimes in a duet with female. *Female: kek-bur* call. Both sexes "purr" during the nesting season; alarm call is series of loud *grip* notes.

**Similar Species:** *Virginia Rail* (p. 121): considerably smaller; more rufous plumage. *King Rail* (p. 359): only very rarely observed in NY; similar size; reddish brown rather than gray.

**Best Sites:** Marshlands Conservancy–Playland CP; Jamaica Bay Wildlife Refuge; Jones Beach SP; Shinnecook Inlet–Dune Rd.; Napeague Bay–Hither Hills SP.

# VIRGINIA RAIL

*Rallus limicola*

The best way to meet a Virginia Rail is to sit alongside a wetland marsh in spring, clap your hands three or four times to imitate this bird's *kidick* calls and wait patiently. If you are lucky, this slim bird will reveal itself for a brief instant, but on most occasions you will only hear this elusive bird. • When pursued by an intruder or predator, a rail will almost always attempt to scurry away through dense, concealing vegetation, rather than risk exposure in a getaway flight. Rails are very narrow birds that have modified feather tips and flexible vertebrae, which allow them to squeeze through the narrow confines of their marshy homes. • The Virginia Rail and its relative the Sora are often found living in the same marshes. The secret of their successful coexistence is in their microhabitat preferences and distinct diets. The Virginia Rail typically favors the dry shoresides of marshes and feeds on invertebrates, while the Sora prefers waterfront property and eats plants and seeds.

*breeding*

**ID:** long, down-curved, reddish bill; gray face; rusty breast; barred flanks; chestnut brown wing patch; very short tail.

**Size:** *L* 9–11 in; *W* 13 in.

**Status:** fairly common breeder from May to July; migrates from April to May and in September; occasionally winters in coastal marshes.

**Habitat:** freshwater wetlands, especially cattail and bulrush marshes.

**Nesting:** concealed in emergent vegetation, usually suspended just over water; loose basket nest is made of coarse grass, cattail stems or sedges; pair incubates 5–13 spotted, pale buff eggs for about 20 days.

**Feeding:** probes into soft substrates and gleans vegetation for invertebrates, including beetles, snails, spiders, earthworms, insect larvae and nymphs; also eats some pondweeds and seeds.

**Voice:** call is an often-repeated, telegraph-like *kidick, kidick;* also "oinks" and croaks.

**Similar Species:** *King Rail* (p. 359): much larger; dark legs; lacks reddish bill and gray face. *Sora* (p. 122): short, yellow bill; black face and throat. *Clapper Rail* (p. 120): much larger; very gray.

**Best Sites:** Iroquois NWR–Tonawanda WMA–Oak Orchard WMA; Braddock Bay; Montezuma NWR; Black Creek Marsh WMA; Bashakill WMA.

# SORA

*Porzana carolina*

The Sora is the most common and widespread rail in North America, and like most rails is seldom seen by birders. Its elusive habits and preference for dense marshlands force most would-be observers to settle for a quick glimpse of this small bird. However, on occasion it has been known to parade around, unconcerned of onlookers, while it searches the shallows for food. • The Sora has two main calls: a clear, whistled *coo-wee* that is easy to imitate and a strange, descending whinny. • The Sora swims quite well over short distances even though its feet are not webbed or lobed. Though it appears to be a weak and reluctant flyer, the Sora migrates hundreds of miles each year between its breeding and wintering wetlands. • The species name *carolina* means "of Carolina" and this bird is also known as "Carolina Rail."

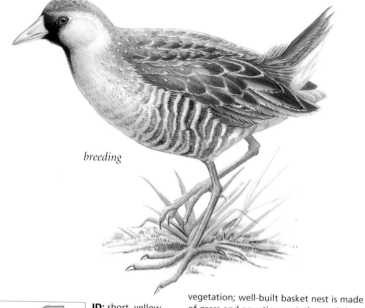

*breeding*

**ID:** short, yellow bill; black face, throat and fore-neck; gray neck and breast; long, greenish legs.
**Size:** *L* 8–10 in; *W* 14 in.

**Status:** formerly very common; drainage of cattail marshes has made this rail an uncommon, but scattered, breeder from May to July; migrates from April to May and from September to October.
**Habitat:** wetlands with abundant emergent cattails, bulrushes, sedges and grasses.
**Nesting:** usually over water, but occasionally in a wet meadow under concealing

vegetation; well-built basket nest is made of grass and aquatic vegetation; pair incubates 10–12 darkly speckled, buff or olive buff eggs for 18–20 days.
**Feeding:** gleans and probes for seeds, plants, aquatic insects and mollusks.
**Voice:** usual call is a clear, 2-note *coo-wee;* alarm call is a sharp *keek;* courtship song begins *or-Ah or-Ah*, descending quickly in a series of maniacal *weee-weee-weee* notes.
**Similar Species:** *Virginia Rail* (p. 121) and *King Rail* (p. 359): larger; long, downcurved bills; chestnut brown wing patches; rufous breasts.
**Best Sites:** Iroquois NWR–Tonawanda WMA–Oak Orchard WMA; Braddock Bay; Montezuma NWR; Black Creek Marsh WMA.

# COMMON MOORHEN

*Gallinula chloropus*

The Common Moorhen is a curious-looking creature that appears to have been assembled from bits and pieces left over from other birds: it has the bill of a chicken, the body of a duck and the long legs and large feet of a small heron. As it strolls around a wetland, its head bobs back and forth in synchrony with its legs, producing a comical, chugging stride. • Unlike most other members of the rail family, the Common Moorhen is quite comfortable feeding in open areas. • For moorhens, the responsibilities of parenthood do not end when their eggs have hatched—parents feed and shelter their young until they are capable of feeding themselves and flying on their own. • Formerly known as "Florida Gallinules," these birds are fiercely argumentative when nesting, but moderate their bombastic tendencies somewhat in migration, when they will feed with American Coots, grebes and ducks. • The scientific name *chloropus* is Greek for "green foot."

*breeding*

**ID:** reddish forehead shield; yellow-tipped bill; gray black body; white streak on sides and flanks; long, greenish yellow legs.
*Breeding:* brighter bill and forehead shield.
**Size:** *L* 12–15 in; *W* 21 in.
**Status:** uncommon and local breeder from May to July; uncommon and local migrant from mid-April to May and from October to mid-November; very rare in winter.
**Habitat:** freshwater marshes, ponds, lakes and sewage lagoons.
**Nesting:** in shallow water or along a shoreline; pair builds a platform or a wide, shallow cup nest of bulrushes, cattails and reeds, often with a ramp leading to the water; pair incubates 8–11 darkly spotted, buff-colored eggs for 19–22 days.
**Feeding:** eats aquatic vegetation, berries, fruits, tadpoles, insects, snails, worms and spiders; may take carrion and eggs.
**Voice:** various sounds include chickenlike clucks, screams, squeaks and a loud *cup;* courting males give a harsh *ticket-ticket-ticket.*
**Similar Species:** *American Coot* (p. 124): white bill and forehead shield; lacks white streak on flanks.
**Best Sites:** Iroquois NWR–Tonawanda WMA–Oak Orchard WMA; Montezuma NWR; Perch River WMA; Jamaica Bay Wildlife Refuge.

# AMERICAN COOT
*Fulica americana*

The American Coot has the bill of a chicken, the lobed feet of a grebe and the body of a duck. With these features, it is not surprising that coots are all-terrain birds that are adept at diving, dabbling, swimming and walking on solid ground. • American Coots squabble constantly during the breeding season, not just among themselves, but also with any waterbird that has the audacity to intrude upon their waterfront property. These odd birds can often be seen scooting across the surface of the water, charging rivals with flailing, splashing wings in an attempt to intimidate. Outside the breeding season, coots gather amicably together in large groups. During spring and fall, thousands congregate at a few select staging sites in our region. These numerous waterfowl are easy to spot because of their pendulous head movements while swimming. • The American Coot is colloquially known as "Mud Hen," and many people mistakenly believe that it is a species of duck.

**ID:** gray black overall; white, chickenlike bill with dark ring around tip; reddish spot on white forehead shield; long, greenish yellow legs; lobed toes; red eyes.

**Size:** *L* 13–16 in; *W* 24 in.

**Status:** local breeder from April to July; common migrant throughout the state; winters on Long I. in fair numbers.

**Habitat:** shallow marshes, ponds and wetlands with open water and emergent vegetation; also sewage lagoons.

**Nesting:** in emergent vegetation; pair builds a floating nest of cattails and grass; pair incubates 6–11 brown-spotted, buffy white eggs for 21–25 days; regularly produces 2 broods in a season.

**Feeding:** gleans the water's surface; sometimes dives, tips up or even grazes on land; eats aquatic vegetation, insects, snails, crayfish, worms, tadpoles and fish; may steal food from ducks.

**Voice:** calls frequently in summer, day and night: *kuk-kuk-kuk-kuk-kuk;* also grunts.

**Similar Species:** *Ducks* (pp. 42–71): lack white, chickenlike bill and uniformly black body. *Grebes* (pp. 80–82): lack white forehead shield and all-dark plumage. *Common Moorhen* (p. 123): reddish forehead shield; yellow-tipped bill; white streak on flanks.

**Best Sites:** Iroquois NWR–Tonawanda WMA–Oak Orchard WMA; Montezuma NWR; Perch River WMA; Jamaica Bay Wildlife Refuge; Southaven CP–Wertheimer NWR.

# SANDHILL CRANE

*Grus canadensis*

Deep, resonant, rattling calls announce the approach of a flock of migrating Sandhill Cranes long before they pass overhead. A coiled trachea adds harmonies to the notes in Sandhill Crane calls, allowing the birds to call louder and farther. At first glance, the large, V-shaped flocks look very similar to flocks of Canada Geese, but cranes circle upward on thermal rises, then slowly soar downward until they find another rise, continuing this pattern all the way to their nesting sites. Migrating flocks of Sandhills consist mainly of mated pairs and close family members. • Cranes mate for life, reinforcing pair bonds each spring with an elaborate courtship dance. • Sandhill Cranes are sensitive nesters, so they prefer to raise their young in areas that are isolated from human disturbance.

**ID:** very large, gray bird with long neck and legs; naked, red crown; long, straight bill; plumage is often stained rusty red from iron oxides in the water. *Immature:* lacks red crown; reddish brown plumage may appear patchy. *In flight:* extends neck and legs; often glides, soars and circles.
**Size:** *L* 3½–4 ft; *W* 6–6½ ft.
**Status:** rare migrant almost anywhere in the state; reported every year, mostly from April to May and from October to November; 1st breeding occurred in May 2003 in the North Montezuma Wetlands; recent reports of breeding in western NY may signal eastward dispersal; regularly seen at spring hawk watches.

**Habitat:** *Breeding:* isolated, open marshes, fens and bogs surrounded by forest or shrubs. *In migration:* agricultural fields and shorelines.
**Nesting:** on a large mound of aquatic vegetation in water or along a shoreline; pair incubates 2 brown-blotched, olive buff eggs for 29–32 days; egg hatching is staggered.
**Feeding:** probes and gleans the ground for insects, soft-bodied invertebrates, waste grain, shoots and tubers; frequently eats small vertebrates.
**Voice:** a loud, resonant, rattling *gu-rrroo gu-rrroo gurrroo.*
**Similar Species:** *Great Blue Heron* (p. 94): lacks red crown patch; neck is folded back over shoulders in flight.
**Best Sites:** Braddock Bay; Derby Hill; Montezuma NWR.

# BLACK-BELLIED PLOVER
*Pluvialis squatarola*

nonbreeding

During the last days of May, flocks of Black-bellied Plovers in black-and-white breeding plumage stand out against the drab soil of plowed fields. Small groups of these arctic breeders pass through our region for a brief period in spring and for a longer period in fall. From time to time, large flocks of thousands of birds can be seen, but such occurrences are considered rare. The end of the fall passage is the best time to see these birds, with the adults in their worn-out breeding plumage appearing first, followed by the plain gray, immature birds. • Black-bellied Plovers forage for small invertebrates with a robinlike run-and-stop technique, frequently pausing to lift their heads for a reassuring scan of their surroundings. • Most plovers have three toes, but the Black-belly has a fourth toe higher on its leg, like a sandpiper. The largest North American plover, the Black-bellied Plover is the most widespread of the larger plovers and is found in the greatest variety of habitats.

breeding

**ID:** short, black bill; long, black legs. *Breeding:* black face, breast, belly and flanks; white undertail coverts; white stripe leads from crown down to "collar," neck and sides of breast; mottled, black-and-white back. *Nonbreeding:* mottled, gray brown upperparts; lightly streaked, pale underparts. *In flight:* black "wing pits"; whitish rump; white wing linings.
**Size:** *L* 10½–13 in; *W* 29 in.
**Status:** very common migrant in May and from September to October; regularly seen in winter on the coast.

**Habitat:** plowed fields, sod farms, meadows, lakeshores and mudflats along the edges of reservoirs, marshes and sewage lagoons; also coastal beaches and mudflats.
**Nesting:** does not nest in NY.
**Feeding:** run-and-stop foraging technique; eats insects, mollusks and crustaceans.
**Voice:** rich, plaintive, 3-syllable whistle: *pee-oo-ee.*
**Similar Species:** *American Golden-Plover* (p. 127): gold-mottled upperparts; black undertail coverts in breeding plumage; lacks black "wing pits."
**Best Sites:** Hamlin Beach SP; Selkirk Shores SP; Jamaica Bay Wildlife Refuge; Jones Beach SP; Shinnecock Inlet–Dune Rd.

# AMERICAN GOLDEN-PLOVER

*Pluvialis dominica*

A mere 150 years ago, the American Golden-Plover population was among the largest of any bird in the world, but in the late 1800s, market gunners mercilessly culled the great flocks—a single day's shooting often yielded tens of thousands of birds. Populations have recovered somewhat, but they will likely never return to their former numbers. • Because they migrate through central North America, few American Golden-Plovers are observed here, though occasionally a large flock of 100 or more may be seen. • In its breeding plumage, the gold and white speckles on the bird's upperparts give it a cryptic coloration that blends well with the mottled earth of its arctic breeding grounds. • The Eskimo Curlew *(Numenius borealis)*, now possibly extinct, once migrated with this bird between the Canadian Arctic and South America. If the Eskimo Curlew does still exist, it may be found traveling alongside the American Golden-Plover.

*nonbreeding*

*nonbreeding*

**ID:** straight, black bill; long, black legs. *Breeding:* black face and underparts, including undertail coverts; S-shaped, white stripe from forehead down to shoulders; dark upperparts speckled with gold and white. *Nonbreeding:* broad, pale "eyebrow"; dark streaking on pale neck and underparts; much less gold on upperparts. *Immature:* somewhat brighter than adult; white forehead. *In flight:* gray "wing pits."
**Size:** *L* 10–11 in; *W* 26 in.
**Status:** uncommon fall migrant from September to October; rare spring migrant.
**Habitat:** cultivated fields, sod farms, meadows, lakeshores and mudflats along the edges of reservoirs, marshes and sewage lagoons.

**Nesting:** does not nest in NY.
**Feeding:** run-and-stop foraging technique; snatches insects, mollusks and crustaceans; also takes seeds and berries.
**Voice:** soft, melodious whistle: *quee, quee-dle.*
**Similar Species:** *Black-bellied Plover* (p. 126): white undertail coverts; whitish crown; lacks gold speckling on upperparts; conspicuous, black "wing pits" in flight.
**Best Sites:** Braddock Bay; Montezuma NWR; Jamaica Bay Wildlife Refuge; Shinnecock Inlet–Dune Rd.; Riverhead Sod Farms.

# SEMIPALMATED PLOVER

*Charadrius semipalmatus*

On the way to their arctic breeding grounds, small flocks of Semipalmated Plovers commonly touch down on our shorelines in late May and early June. Spring migration is a brief, hurried affair because there is tremendous pressure for these long-distance migrants to begin breeding before the end of the short northern summer. After nesting, the adults will leave the breeding grounds as early as July to enjoy a prolonged, leisurely migration to the coastlines of the southern United States and Central and South America. The young begin their journey as soon as they are strong enough to fly. • The scientific name *semipalmatus* means "half-webbed" and refers to the slight webbing between the toes of this plover. The webbing is thought to give the bird's feet more surface area when it is walking on soft substrates.

*nonbreeding*

**ID:** *Breeding:* dark brown back; white breast with 1 black, horizontal band; long, orange legs; stubby, black-tipped, orange bill; white patch above bill; white throat and "collar"; black band across forehead and through eye; small, white "eyebrow." *Nonbreeding:* duller; mostly dark bill. *Immature:* dark legs and bill; brown banding.
**Size:** *L* 7 in; *W* 19 in.
**Status:** very common migrant in May and from August to September; rare in winter at coastal sites.

**Habitat:** sandy beaches, lakeshores, river edges and mudflats.
**Nesting:** does not nest in NY.
**Feeding:** usually on shorelines and beaches; run-and-stop foraging technique; eats crustaceans, worms and insects.
**Voice:** crisp, high-pitched, 2-part, rising whistle: *tu-wee.*
**Similar Species:** *Killdeer* (p. 130): larger; 2 black bands across breast. *Piping Plover* (p. 129): lacks dark band through eye; lighter upperparts; narrower breast band, incomplete in females and most males.
**Best Sites:** Braddock Bay; Montezuma NWR; Jamaica Bay Wildlife Refuge; Jones Beach SP; Riverhead Sod Farms; Shinnecock Inlet–Dune Rd.

# PIPING PLOVER

*Charadrius melodus*

A master of illusion, the Piping Plover is hardly noticeable when it settles on shorelines and beaches. Its pale, sand-colored plumage is the perfect camouflage against a sandy beach. As well, from a distance the dark bands across its forehead and neckline resemble scattered pebbles or strips of washed-up vegetation. Often, the only way to find a Piping Plover is to watch for one of its characteristic short runs. • This plover's cryptic plumage, unfortunately, has done little to protect it from beach development, increased predation and disturbance by humans. The recreational use of beaches during summer, and an increase in human-tolerant predators such as gulls, raccoons and feral cats, has impeded the Piping Plover's ability to reproduce successfully. • On beaches with wave action, these birds often employ a foot-trembling strategy to entice invertebrates to the surface. • If threatened, Piping Plover chicks typically take to the water and swim away, while adults rarely swim at all.

breeding ♂

**ID:** pale, sandy upperparts; white underparts; orange legs. *Breeding:* black-tipped, orange bill; black forehead band; black "necklace," sometimes incomplete, especially on females. *Nonbreeding:* no breast or forehead band; all-black bill.
**Size:** *L* 7 in; *W* 19 in.
**Status:** endangered; uncommon breeder and migrant from April to September on Long I.; very rare migrant along L. Ontario shores where it once bred.
**Habitat:** sandy beaches, mudflats and open lakeshores.

**Nesting:** on bare sand along an open shoreline; in a shallow scrape sometimes lined with pebbles and tiny shells; pair incubates 4 pale buff eggs, blotched with dark brown and black, for 26–28 days.
**Feeding:** run-and-stop foraging technique; eats worms and insects; almost all food is taken from the ground.
**Voice:** clear, whistled melody: *peep peep peep-lo.*
**Similar Species:** *Semipalmated Plover* (p. 128): dark band through eye; much darker upperparts. *Killdeer* (p. 130): larger; 2 breast bands; much darker upperparts.
**Best Sites:** Jones Beach SP; Jacob Riis Park–Breezy Pt.–Ft. Tilden (NYC); Fire Island National Seashore; Smith Point CP; Shinnecock Inlet–Dune Rd.

# KILLDEER
*Charadrius vociferus*

The ubiquitous Killdeer is often the first shorebird that a birder learns to identify. Its boisterous calls rarely fail to catch the attention of people passing through its wide variety of nesting environments. The Killdeer's preference for open fields, gravel driveways, beach edges, golf courses and abandoned industrial areas has allowed it to thrive throughout our rural and suburban landscapes. • If you happen to wander too close to a Killdeer nest, the parent will try to lure you away by issuing loud alarm calls and feigning a broken wing. Most predators take the bait and are led far enough away for the parent to suddenly recover from its injury and fly off, sounding its piercing calls. Similar distraction displays are widespread phenomena in the bird world, but in our region, the Kildeer's broken wing act is by far the gold medal winner. • The scientific name *vociferus* aptly describes this vocal bird, but double-check all calls in spring, when the Killdeer is often imitated by frisky European Starlings.

**ID:** long, dark yellow legs; white upperparts with 2 black breast bands; brown back; white underparts; brown head; white "eyebrow"; white face patch above bill; black forehead band; rufous rump. *Immature:* downy; only 1 breast band.

**Size:** *L* 9–11 in; *W* 24 in.

**Status:** common, widespread breeder from April to July; very common migrant from March to April and from September to October; occasionally winters on Long I.

**Habitat:** open ground, fields, lakeshores, sandy beaches, mudflats, gravel streambeds, wet meadows and grasslands.

**Nesting:** on open ground; in a shallow, usually unlined, depression; pair incubates 4 darkly spotted, pale buff eggs for 24–28 days; occasionally raises 2 broods.

**Feeding:** run-and-stop foraging technique; eats mostly insects; also takes spiders, snails, earthworms and crayfish.

**Voice:** loud, distinctive *kill-dee kill-dee kill-deer* and variations, including *deer-deer*.

**Similar Species:** *Semipalmated Plover* (p. 128): smaller; only 1 breast band. *Piping Plover* (p. 129): smaller; paler upperparts; 1 breast band.

**Best Sites:** Iroquois NWR–Tonawanda WMA–Oak Orchard WMA; Montezuma NWR; Perch River WMA; Jamaica Bay Wildlife Refuge; Riverhead Sod Farms.

# AMERICAN OYSTERCATCHER

*Haematopus palliatus*

American Oystercatchers are large, stocky shorebirds with long, razor-sharp bills. Found exclusively in marine habitats, they specialize in prying or hammering open shellfish, including oysters, clams and mussels. When the opportunity arises, they will gladly eat a host of other intertidal invertebrates such as limpets, crabs, marine worms, sea urchins, chitons and even jellyfish. • New York is near the northern limit of the American Oystercatcher's breeding range. During the summer breeding season, watch for mating pairs performing their loud "piping" courtship display. These strident, calling performances are often given in flight. • The American Oystercatcher is one of the largest and heaviest North American shorebirds. • The species name *palliatus* comes from the Latin for "clad in a Greek mantle," referring to the bird's dark upperparts and white shoulders.

**ID:** long, laterally compressed, red orange bill; black head and neck; brown back; white wing and rump patches; white underparts. *In flight:* unique black-and-white wing pattern; broad wings.

**Size:** *L* 18¹/₂ in; *W* 32 in.

**Status:** common breeder from May to July on Long I.; common migrant from early March to April and from October to December; occasionally overwinters.

**Habitat:** coastal marine habitats including saltwater marshes, sandy beaches and tidal mudflats; will nest on dredge-spoil islands.

**Nesting:** usually on a gravel beach or a ridge in a salt marsh; both adults scrape out a depression in the sand and may line it with shells, pebbles or even beach wrack; pair incubates 3 speckled, buffy gray eggs for 27 days; may form a breeding trio of 2 females and 1 male who tend 1–2 nests.

**Feeding:** finds prey visually or by probing while walking in shallow water, on rocks or on mud; takes intertidal invertebrates, including mollusks, crustaceans and marine worms; shellfish form the bulk of the diet and are either hammered open or quickly stabbed and cut open.

**Voice:** call is a loud *wheet,* often given in series during flight; also utters a *pip* alarm call, *kleep* contact call, and a distinctive series of piping notes in courtship and territorial displays.

**Similar Species:** none.

**Best Sites:** Pt. Lookout–Jones Inlet; Jones Beach SP; Shinnecock Inlet–Dune Rd.; Orient Point SP.

# AMERICAN AVOCET
*Recurvirostra americana*

An American Avocet in full breeding plumage is a strikingly elegant bird, with its long, peachy red neck accentuating the length of its slender bill and stiltlike legs. Often by August, their peach-colored "hoods" have been replaced by more subdued winter grays, which these birds will wear for the greater part of the year. It is the only avocet in the world that undergoes a yearly color change. • The American Avocet's upturned bill looks bent out of shape, but is actually ideal for efficiently skimming aquatic vegetation and invertebrates off the surface of shallow water. Avocets will walk rapidly or run about in fairly deep water, swinging their bills from side to side along the muddy bottom. At other times, they use their webbed feet to swim and feed by tipping up like dabbling ducks. • If an American Avocet is disturbed while standing in its one-legged resting position, it will take off, switch legs in midair, and land on the rested leg.

*nonbreeding*

**ID:** long, upturned, black bill; long, pale blue legs; black wings with wide, white patches; white underparts; female has shorter, more upturned bill than male. *Breeding:* peachy red head, neck and breast. *Nonbreeding:* gray head, neck and breast. *In flight:* a "winged stick"; long, skinny legs and neck; black-and-white wings.
**Size:** *L* 17–18 in; *W* 31 in.
**Status:** rare visitor from June to October on Long I.; very rare in spring upstate.

**Habitat:** lakeshores, alkaline wetlands and exposed mudflats.
**Nesting:** does not nest in NY.
**Feeding:** sweeps its bill from side to side along the water's surface, picking up small crustaceans, aquatic insects and occasionally seeds; male sweeps lower in the water than female; occasionally swims and tips up like a duck.
**Voice:** harsh, shrill *plee-eek plee-eek*.
**Similar Species:** *Willet* (p. 136): grayish overall; straight bill.
**Best Sites:** Jamaica Bay Wildlife Refuge; Jones Beach SP; Mecox Bay.

# GREATER YELLOWLEGS

*Tringa melanoleuca*

The Greater Yellowlegs is one of the birds that performs the role of lookout among mixed flocks of shorebirds. At the first sign of danger, these large sandpipers bob their heads and call incessantly. If forced to, the Greater Yellowlegs will usually retreat into deeper water, becoming airborne only as a last resort. • During migration, many shorebirds, including the Greater Yellowlegs, often stand or hop around beachflats on one leg. These stubborn "one-leggers" may be mistaken for crippled individuals, but this stance may be an adaptation that conserves body heat. • Despite its long bill, the Greater Yellowlegs does not probe for its food, but instead picks it off the water's surface or swings its bill from side to side in the water like an avocet. This sweeping behavior may be a clue that you are looking at a Greater Yellowlegs and not its Lesser relative, which uses this technique far less often.

*nonbreeding*

*nonbreeding*

**ID:** long, bright yellow legs; slightly upturned, dark bill is noticeably longer than head length. *Breeding:* brown black back and upperwing; fine, dense, dark streaking on head and neck; dark barring on breast often extends onto belly; subtle, dark eye line; light lores. *Nonbreeding:* gray overall; fine streaks on breast; clear belly.
**Size:** *L* 13–15 in; *W* 28 in.
**Status:** very common migrant from April to May and August to October; uncommon and irregular in winter on Long I.
**Habitat:** almost all wetlands, including lakeshores, marshes, flooded fields and river shorelines.
**Nesting:** does not nest in NY.

**Feeding:** wades in water, sometimes sweeping its bill from side to side; primarily eats aquatic invertebrates, but will also eat small fish; occasionally snatches prey from the water's surface.
**Voice:** quick, whistled series of *tew-tew-tew*, usually 3 notes.
**Similar Species:** *Lesser Yellowlegs* (p. 134): smaller; straight bill is not noticeably longer than head length; call is generally a pair of higher notes: *tew-tew*. *Willet* (p. 136): black-and-white wings; heavier, straighter bill; dark, greenish legs.
**Best Sites:** Braddock Bay; Montezuma NWR; Jamaica Bay Wildlife Refuge; Jones Beach SP; Mecox Bay.

# LESSER YELLOWLEGS

*Tringa flavipes*

With a series of continuous, rapid-fire *tew-tew* calls, Lesser Yellowlegs streak across the surface of wetlands and lakeshores. Visits by yellowlegs are relatively brief in spring, but the fall migration period is lengthy, and these birds can be seen from mid-July to mid-October. • Many birders find it a challenge to separate Lesser Yellowlegs and Greater Yellowlegs in the field. However, with practice you will notice that the Lesser's bill is finer, straighter and not noticeably longer than the length of its head, that the Greaters will stray into deeper water and even swim at times, and that the birds' calls are different. • The Lesser Yellowlegs was a popular game bird in the late 1800s. The birds were easy targets because of this species' tendency to return and hover above wounded flockmates. • The scientific name *flavipes* is derived from Latin words meaning "yellow foot."

*nonbreeding*

*nonbreeding*

**ID:** bright yellow legs; all-dark bill is not noticeably longer than length of head; brown black back and upperwing; fine, dense, dark streaking on head, neck and breast; lacks barring on belly; subtle, dark eye line; light lores. *Nonbreeding:* similar, but gray overall.
**Size:** *L* 10–11 in; *W* 24 in.
**Status:** common migrant from April to May and from August to September.
**Habitat:** shorelines of lakes, rivers, marshes and ponds.
**Nesting:** does not nest in NY.

**Feeding:** snatches prey from the water's surface; frequently wades in shallow water; primarily eats aquatic invertebrates, but also takes small fish and tadpoles.
**Voice:** typically a pair of high-pitched *tew* notes.
**Similar Species:** *Greater Yellowlegs* (p. 133): larger; bill is slightly upturned and noticeably longer than length of head; *tew* call is usually given in a series of 3 notes. *Solitary Sandpiper* (p. 135): white eye ring; darker upperparts; greenish legs. *Willet* (p. 136): much bulkier; black-and-white wings; heavier bill; dark, greenish legs.
**Best Sites:** Braddock Bay; Montezuma NWR; Jamaica Bay Wildlife Refuge; Jones Beach SP; Shinnecock Inlet–Dune Rd.

# SOLITARY SANDPIPER

*Tringa solitaria*

True to its name, the Solitary Sandpiper is usually seen alone, bobbing its body like a spirited dancer as it forages for insects in our wetlands. In addition, Solitary Sandpipers are very aggressive when protecting a nest site or feeding, so breeding pairs are rarely in close proximity to one another. Every so often, a lucky observer may happen upon a small group of these birds during spring or fall. • A favorite foraging method of the Solitary Sandpiper is to wade in shallow water, slowly advancing and vibrating the leading foot, thus stirring the bottom sufficiently to disturb prey. In this way it captures aquatic insects and their larvae, including water boatmen and small crustaceans. • Shorebirds lay very large eggs and incubate them for comparatively long periods of time. Once sandpiper chicks break out of their eggs, they are ready to run, hide and feed on their own. The highly developed hatchlings, known as precocial young, are immediately able to fend for themselves in a dangerous world.

*breeding*

**ID:** white eye ring; short, green legs; dark, yellowish bill with black tip; spotted, gray brown back; white lores; fine, white streaks on gray brown head, neck and breast; dark upper tail feathers with black-and-white barring on sides. *In flight:* dark underwings.
**Size:** *L* 7½–9 in; *W* 22 in.
**Status:** common migrant in May and in August.
**Habitat:** wet meadows, sewage lagoons, muddy ponds, sedge wetlands, beaver ponds and wooded streams.
**Nesting:** does not nest in NY.

**Feeding:** stalks shorelines, picking up aquatic invertebrates such as water boatmen and damselfly nymphs; also gleans for terrestrial invertebrates; occasionally stirs the water with its foot to spook out prey.
**Voice:** high, thin *peet-wheet* or *wheat wheat wheat.*
**Similar Species:** *Lesser Yellowlegs* (p. 134): no eye ring; longer, bright yellow legs. *Spotted Sandpiper* (p. 137): incomplete eye ring; spotted breast in breeding plumage; black-tipped, orange bill. *Other sandpipers* (pp. 133–54): black bills and legs; lack white eye ring.
**Best Sites:** Braddock Bay; Montezuma NWR; Jamaica Bay Wildlife Refuge; Jones Beach SP; Marshlands Conservancy–Playland CP.

# WILLET
*Catoptrophorus semipalmatus*

A resting Willet cuts a rather dull figure. The moment it takes flight or displays, however, its black-and-white wings add sudden contrast while it calls out a loud, rhythmic *will-will-willet, will-will-willet!* The bright, bold flashes of the Willet's wings may alert other shorebirds to imminent danger and may also double as a means of intimidating predators during the bird's dive-bombing defense of its young. If you look closely, you may notice that the white markings across the Willet's wingspan form a rough "W" as it flies away. • In spring, most Willets establish territories that are fiercely defended throughout early summer. Where there are several pairs, they parcel out the area and take turns scolding and dive-bombing potential predators of all sizes. Once young are out of the nest, the aggressive tendencies subside and feeding parties form.

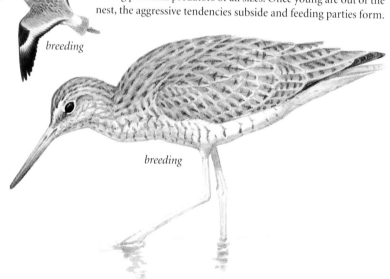

*breeding*

*breeding*

**ID:** plump; mottled gray brown overall; heavy, straight, black bill; light throat and belly. *Breeding:* dark steaking and barring overall. *In flight:* black-and-white wing pattern.
**Size:** *L* 14–16 in; *W* 26 in.
**Status:** common breeder from May to June; common migrant from April to May and from July to September on Long I.; rare migrant upstate.
**Habitat:** wet fields; shorelines of marshes, lakes and ponds.
**Nesting:** nest is a shallow scrape in short grass lined with grass; pair incubates 4 heavily spotted, olive to buff eggs for

24–26 days; precocial young leave the nest within a day.
**Feeding:** feeds by probing muddy areas for small crustaceans, worms, mollusks, aquatic insects and small fish; also gleans the ground for insects; occasionally eats shoots and seeds.
**Voice:** loud, rolling *will-will willet, will-will-willet.*
**Similar Species:** *Marbled Godwit* (p. 141) and *Hudsonian Godwit* (p. 140): larger bodies; much longer, pinkish yellow bills with dark, slightly upturned tips; lack black-and-white wing pattern. *Greater Yellowlegs* (p.133): long, yellow legs; slightly upturned bill; lacks black-and-white wing pattern.
**Best Sites:** Jamaica Bay Wildlife Refuge; Jones Beach SP; Fire Island National Seashore; Smith Point CP; Shinnecock Inlet–Dune Rd.

# SPOTTED SANDPIPER

*Actitis macularius*

This diminutive shorebird is a widespread breeder here—during summer it is the most frequently encountered sandpiper throughout much of New York. • It wasn't until 1972 that the unexpected truth about the Spotted Sandpiper's breeding activities were realized. The female Spotted Sandpiper defends a territory and mates with more than one male in a single breeding season, leaving the males to tend the nests and eggs. This unusual nesting behavior, known as polyandry, is found in about one percent of all bird species. • Even though its breast spots are not noticeable from a distance, the Spotted Sandpiper's stiff-winged, quivering flight pattern and tendency to burst from the shore are easily recognizable. This shorebird is also known for its continuous "teetering" behavior as it forages. • The scientific name *macularia* is Latin for "spot," referring to the spots on this bird's underparts in breeding plumage.

*breeding*

**ID:** teeters almost continuously. *Breeding:* white underparts are heavily spotted with black; yellow orange legs; black-tipped, yellow orange bill; white "eyebrow." *Nonbreeding* and *juvenile:* pure white breast, foreneck and throat; brown bill; dull yellow legs. *In flight:* flies close to the water's surface with very rapid, shallow wingbeats; white upperwing stripe.

**Size:** *L* 7–8 in; *W* 15 in.

**Status:** very common breeder from May to July; common migrant from April to May and in September.

**Habitat:** shorelines, gravel beaches, ponds, marshes, alluvial wetlands, rivers, streams, swamps and sewage lagoons; occasionally seen in cultivated fields.

**Nesting:** usually near water; often under overhanging vegetation among logs or under bushes; in a shallow depression lined with grass; almost exclusively the male incubates 4 darkly blotched, creamy buff eggs for 20–24 days and tends the young alone.

**Feeding:** picks and gleans along shorelines for terrestrial and aquatic invertebrates; also snatches flying insects from the air.

**Voice:** sharp, crisp *eat-wheat, eat-wheat, wheat-wheat-wheat-wheat.*

**Similar Species:** *Solitary Sandpiper* (p. 135): complete eye ring; lacks spotting on breast; yellowish bill with dark tip. *Other sandpipers* (pp. 133–54): black bills; most have dark legs; lack breast spotting.

**Best Sites:** Hamlin Beach SP; Montezuma NWR; Jamaica Bay Wildlife Refuge; Jones Beach SP; Shinnecock Inlet–Dune Rd.

# UPLAND SANDPIPER

*Bartramia longicauda*

In spring, Upland Sandpipers are sometimes seen perched atop fence posts, belting out airy, "wolf-whistle" courtship tunes. Excited males will even launch into the air to perform courtship flight displays, combining song with shallow, fluttering wingbeats. At the height of the breeding season, however, these large-eyed, inland shorebirds are rarely seen, remaining hidden in the tall grass of abandoned fields and ungrazed pastures. • Twice each year, these wide-ranging shorebirds make the incredible journey between their North American breeding grounds and South American wintering grounds without jet propulsion or inflight movies. • During the late 1800s, high market demand for this bird's meat led to severe over-harvesting and catastrophic declines in its population over much of North America. Its numbers have since improved in our region, but recent loss of grassland habitat again threatens its welfare.

**Habitat:** hayfields, ungrazed pastures, grassy meadows, abandoned fields, natural grasslands and airports.

**Nesting:** in dense grass or along a wetland; in a depression, usually with grass arching over the top; pair incubates 4 lightly spotted, pale buff eggs for 22–27 days; both adults tend the young.

**Feeding:** gleans the ground for insects, especially grasshoppers and beetles.

**Voice:** courtship song is an airy, whistled *whip-whee-ee you;* alarm call is *quip-ip-ip.*

**Similar Species:** *Willet* (p. 136): longer, heavier bill; dark greenish legs; black-and-white wings in flight. *Buff-breasted Sandpiper* (p. 154): shorter neck; larger head; daintier bill; lacks streaking on "cheek" and foreneck. *Pectoral Sandpiper* (p. 150): streaking on breast ends abruptly; smaller eyes; shorter neck; usually seen in larger numbers.

**ID:** small head; long, streaked neck; large, dark eyes; yellow legs; mottled, brownish upperparts; lightly streaked breast, sides and flanks; white belly and undertail coverts; bill is about same length as head.

**Size:** *L* 11–12½ in; *W* 26 in.

**Status:** threatened; uncommon but widespread breeder from April to June; rare to uncommon migrant; arrives in mid-April and leaves by mid-September; declining.

**Best Sites:** Nation's Road Grassland; Cape Vincent–Pt. Peninsula; Ft. Edward Grassland; Shawangunk Grasslands NWR; Riverhead Sod Farms.

# WHIMBREL

*Numenius phaeopus*

Whimbrels often travel in long lines or in V-formation, calling with four short whistles and sailing for short periods on set wings. Local birders are most likely to see Whimbrels during migration, as the birds pass along Atlantic shores. These shorebirds travel in flocks, so expect to see either sizeable groups of them or none at all. • The Whimbrel enjoys a widespread distribution, nesting across northern North America and Eurasia, and spending its winters on the shores of six continents. In migration, this bird is primarily coastal and oceanic, though some fly overland. • Both the Whimbrel and the Eskimo Curlew (*N. borealis*) suffered devastating losses to their populations during the commercial hunts of the late 1800s. While the Whimbrel population slowly recovered, the Eskimo Curlew seemed to vanish into thin air—the last confirmed sighting of this bird was in 1963. Occasional, though unconfirmed, reports offer a glimmer of hope that a few still remain. • *Numenius*, from the Greek for "new moon," refers to the curved shape of this bird's bill.

**ID:** long, down-curved bill; striped crown; dark eye line; mottled brown body; paler underparts; long legs. *In flight:* dark underwings.

**Size:** *L* 18 in; *W* 32 in.

**Status:** rare coastal migrant and common inland migrant in May; common coastal migrant, but uncommon inland migrant, in August and September.

**Habitat:** mudflats, sandy beaches, farmlands, grassy lakeshores, airports and flooded agricultural fields.

**Nesting:** does not nest in NY.

**Feeding:** probes and pecks for invertebrates in mud or vegetation; also eats berries in fall.

**Voice:** incoming flocks utter a distinctive, rippling *bibibibibibibi*.

**Similar Species:** *Upland Sandpiper* (p. 138): smaller; straight bill; lacks head markings; yellowish legs. *Willet* (p. 136): straight, heavy bill; plain, unmarked crown; gray brown plumage; black-and-white wing pattern.

**Best Sites:** Braddock Bay; Jamaica Bay Wildlife Refuge; Jones Beach SP; Smith Point CP; Shinnecock Inlet–Dune Rd.

# HUDSONIAN GODWIT

*Limosa haemastica*

Each fall, large numbers of Hudsonian Godwits gather on the shores of Hudson Bay in Canada and embark on a nonstop journey to southern South America. Their voyage is fueled solely by fat reserves that are built up on these birds' northern staging grounds before departure. This migration marathon means that Hudsonian Godwits are not often seen at typical stopover sites in New York. Fortunately, not all godwits fly directly south in early fall, so birders who are scouting the shores of the Great Lakes—even as late as November—may be able to enjoy their presence. • Hudsonian Godwits forage by probing shorelines and wetlands for worms, mollusks and crustaceans, sometimes with their bills buried up to their eyes! • The Hudsonian Godwit is smaller than the Marbled Godwit, and has distinct, black underwings that are easily seen in flight.

*nonbreeding*

**ID:** long, yellow orange bill with dark, slightly upturned tip; white rump; black tail; long, blue black legs. *Breeding:* heavily barred, chestnut red underparts; dark grayish upperparts; male is more brightly colored. *Nonbreeding:* grayish upperparts; whitish underparts may show a few short, black bars. *Juvenile:* dark, gray brown upperparts; pale underparts. *In flight:* black "wing pits" and wing linings.
**Size:** *L* 14–15½ in; *W* 29 in.
**Status:** uncommon migrant from July to September.
**Habitat:** flooded fields, marshes, mudflats and lakeshores.
**Nesting:** does not nest in NY.

**Feeding:** probes deeply into water, sand or mud; walks into deeper water than most shorebirds, but rarely swims; eats mollusks, crustaceans, insects and other invertebrates; also picks earthworms from plowed fields.
**Voice:** usually quiet in migration; sometimes a sharp, rising *god-WIT!*
**Similar Species:** *Marbled Godwit* (p. 141): larger; mottled brown overall; lacks white rump and black wing linings. *Greater Yellowlegs* (p. 133): shorter, all-dark bill; bright yellow legs; lacks white rump. *Long-billed Dowitcher* (p. 156) and *Short-billed Dowitcher* (p. 155): smaller; straight, all-dark bills; yellow green legs; mottled, rust brown upperparts in breeding plumage.
**Best Sites:** Montezuma NWR; Jamaica Bay Wildlife Refuge; Jones Beach SP; Smith Point CP; Shinnecock Inlet–Dune Rd.

# MARBLED GODWIT

*Limosa fedoa*

The Marbled Godwit's bill looks long enough to reach buried prey, but this bird doesn't seem content with its reach. It is frequently seen with its head submerged beneath the water or with its face pressed into a mudflat. These deep probings seem to pay off for this large, resourceful shorebird, and a godwit looks genuinely pleased with a freshly extracted meal and a face covered in mud. • Unlike Hudsonian Godwits, which undertake long migrations from the Arctic to South America, Marbled Godwits migrate relatively short distances to coastal wintering areas in the southern United States and Central America. Still, sightings of Marbled Godwits are rare in New York. • The genus name *Limosa*, meaning "muddy," refers to this bird's preference for muddy foraging habitats.

*nonbreeding*

**ID:** long, yellow orange bill with dark, slightly upturned tip; long neck and legs; mottled, buff brown plumage is darkest on upperparts; long, black blue legs. *In flight:* cinnamon wing linings.

**Size:** *L* 16–20 in; *W* 30 in.

**Status:** uncommon migrant from July to September on the coast; very rare migrant inland.

**Habitat:** flooded fields, wet meadows, marshes, mudflats and lakeshores.

**Nesting:** does not nest in NY.

**Feeding:** probes deeply in soft substrates for worms, insect larvae, crustaceans and mollusks; picks insects from grass; may also eat the tubers and seeds of aquatic vegetation.

**Voice:** loud, ducklike, 2-syllable squawks: *co-rect co-rect* or *god-wit god-wit*.

**Similar Species:** *Hudsonian Godwit* (p. 140): smaller; chestnut red neck and underparts; white rump; black wing linings. *Greater Yellowlegs* (p. 133): shorter, all-dark bill; bright yellow legs. *Long-billed Dowitcher* (p. 156) and *Short-billed Dowitcher* (p. 155): smaller; straight, all-dark bills; white rump wedge; yellow green legs.

**Best Sites:** Jamaica Bay Wildlife Refuge; Jones Beach SP; Shinnecock Inlet–Dune Rd.; Mecox Bay.

# RUDDY TURNSTONE

*Arenaria interpres*

During late May and early June, small flocks of boldly patterned Ruddy Turnstones settle on fields and along the shores of the Great Lakes to mingle and forage among the other shorebird migrants. These birds' painted faces and eye-catching, black-and-red backs set them apart from the multitudes of little brown-and-white sandpipers. Stocky and with heavier bills than most of their companions, Ruddies walk with a comical, rolling gait and sometimes tilt sideways to counteract the influence of strong winds. • Ruddy Turnstones are truly long-distance migrants. Individuals that nest along the shores of Canada's Arctic routinely fly to South America or western Europe to avoid frosty winters. • The name "turnstone" is appropriate for this bird, which uses its bill to flip over pebbles, shells and washed-up vegetation to expose hidden invertebrates. Its short, stubby, slightly upturned bill is ideally suited to this unusual foraging style.

*nonbreeding*

*nonbreeding*

**ID:** white belly; black "bib" curves up to shoulder; stout, black, slightly upturned bill; red orange legs. *Breeding:* ruddy upperparts (female is slightly paler); white face; black "collar"; dark, streaky crown. *Nonbreeding:* brownish upperparts and face.
**Size:** *L* 9½ in; *W* 21 in.
**Status:** common migrant in May and from July to September on the coast; fairly common fall migrant near the Great Lakes; a few winter on Long I.
**Habitat:** shores of lakes, reservoirs, marshes and sewage lagoons; also in cultivated fields.

**Nesting:** does not nest in NY.
**Feeding:** probes under and flips rocks, weeds and shells for food items; picks, digs and probes for invertebrates in soil or mud; also eats berries, seeds, spiders and carrion.
**Voice:** low, repeated contact notes; also a sharp *cut-a-cut* alarm call.
**Similar Species:** *Other sandpipers* (pp. 133–54): all lack the Ruddy Turnstone's bold patterning and flashy wing markings in flight. *Plovers* (pp. 126–30): equally bold plumage but in significantly different patterns.
**Best Sites:** Hamlin Beach SP; Braddock Bay; Jamaica Bay Wildlife Refuge; Jones Beach SP; Shinnecock Inlet–Dune Rd.

# RED KNOT

*Calidris canutus*

Small flocks of Red Knots appear in New York for a brief period, usually around the last week of May. These tubby, red-bellied knots are distinguished from the masses of migrating plovers and sandpipers by their bright rufous spring plumage. • During the breeding season, their red plumage serves to attract mates and camouflage the birds against the sea of grasses and colorful wildflowers on their arctic nesting grounds. In fall and winter, drab, gray-and-white Red Knots are difficult to distinguish from other migrating and overwintering shorebirds, and they blend in perfectly with the open sandy beaches that they inhabit at this time of year. • The Red Knot is another migratory champion, flying up to 19,000 miles in a single year. Some of these birds fly from their arctic breeding grounds to winter on the southern tip of South America, while others migrate to western Europe.

*breeding*

**ID:** chunky, round body; greenish legs. *Breeding:* rusty face, breast and underparts; brown, black and buff upperparts. *Nonbreeding:* pale gray upperparts; white underparts; some faint streaking on upper breast; faint barring on rump. *Juvenile:* buff wash on breast; scaly-looking back. *In flight:* white wing stripe.
**Size:** *L* 10½ in; *W* 23 in.
**Status:** common coastal migrant in May and from July to August; uncommon migrant from July to August on the Great Lakes.
**Habitat:** lakeshores, marshes and plowed fields.

**Nesting:** does not nest in NY.
**Feeding:** gleans shorelines for insects, crustaceans and mollusks; probes soft substrates, creating lines of small holes.
**Voice:** soft, melodious *ker ek* in flight.
**Similar Species:** *Long-billed Dowitcher* (p. 156) and *Short-billed Dowitcher* (p. 155): much longer bills; barring under tails and on flanks; white "V" on rumps and tails. *Buff-breasted Sandpiper* (p. 154): light buff plumage; finer, shorter bill; dark flecking on sides. *Other peeps* (pp. 144–53): smaller; most have black legs; only *Sanderling* (p. 144) and *Curlew Sandpiper* (p. 359) show reddish coloration on undersides in breeding plumage.
**Best Sites:** Jamaica Bay Wildlife Refuge; Jones Beach SP; Smith Point CP; Shinnecock Inlet–Dune Rd.

# SANDERLING

*Calidris alba*

A stroll along Long Island beaches is often punctuated by the sight of tiny Sanderlings running and playing in the waves. Their well-known habit of chasing waves has a simple purpose: to snatch washed-up aquatic invertebrates before the next wave rolls onto shore. Sprinting along the beach while foraging, Sanderlings move so fast on their dark legs that they appear to be gliding across the sand. • When resting, Sanderlings often tuck one leg up to preserve body heat. • This sandpiper is one of the world's most widespread birds. It breeds across the Arctic in Alaska, Canada and Russia, and it spends the winter running up and down sandy shorelines in North America, South America, Asia, Africa and Australia. The Sanderling is classified as a sandpiper but has many characteristics of a plover: three toes, a small body and a run-and-snatch foraging technique. • This common sandpiper is the symbol of the Fire Island National Seashore.

*nonbreeding*

*nonbreeding*

**ID:** straight, black bill; black legs; white underparts; white wing bar; pale rump. *Breeding:* dark spotting or mottling on rufous head and breast. *Nonbreeding:* pale gray upperparts; black shoulder patch (often concealed).

**Size:** *L* 7–8½ in; *W* 17 in.

**Status:** common migrant in May and from July to October on all coasts; somewhat less common on the Great Lakes in spring; fairly common on Atlantic beaches in winter.

**Habitat:** shores of lakes, marshes and reservoirs; also Atlantic beaches.

**Nesting:** does not nest in NY.

**Feeding:** gleans shorelines for insects, crustaceans and mollusks; probes repeatedly, creating a line of small holes in the sand.

**Voice:** flight call is a sharp *kip*.

**Similar Species:** *Least Sandpiper* (p. 147): smaller and darker; yellowish legs; lacks rufous breast in breeding plumage. *Dunlin* (p. 152): larger and darker; slightly downcurved bill. *Red Knot* (p. 143): larger; gray-barred, whitish rump; breeding adult has unstreaked, reddish belly. *Western Sandpiper* (p. 146) and *Semipalmated Sandpiper* (p. 145): lack rufous breast in breeding plumage; sandy upperparts in nonbreeding plumage.

**Best Sites:** Dunkirk Harbor; Hamlin Beach SP; Jones Beach SP; Fire Island National Seashore; Shinnecock Inlet–Dune Rd.

# SEMIPALMATED SANDPIPER

*Calidris pusilla*

The small, plain Semipalmated Sandpiper can be difficult to identify among the swarms of similar-looking *Calidris* sandpipers that appear along the shores of the southern Great Lakes each spring. Known collectively as "peeps" because of the similarity of their high-pitched calls, these strikingly similar "miniatures," which include the Semipalmated, Least, Western, White-rumped and Baird's sandpipers, can make shorebird identification either a complete nightmare or an uplifting challenge. • Each spring and fall, large numbers of Semipalmated Sandpipers touch down on our shorelines, pecking and probing in mechanized fury to replenish their body fat for the remainder of their long migratory journey. Semipalmated Sandpipers fly almost the entire length of the Americas during migration, so their staging sites must provide ample food sources. These highly efficient birds raise up to four young in just a few weeks of arctic summer, then fly 2000 non-stop miles back to their wintering grounds.

*nonbreeding*

*nonbreeding*

**ID:** short, straight, black bill; black legs. *Breeding:* mottled upperparts; slight rufous tinge on ear patch, crown and scapulars; faint streaks on upper breast and flanks. *Nonbreeding:* white "eyebrow"; gray brown upperparts; white underparts with light brown wash on sides of upper breast. *In flight:* narrow, white wing stripe; black line through white rump.
**Size:** *L* 5½–7 in; *W* 14 in.
**Status:** the most abundant fall and spring migrant shorebird in NY; migration peaks occur in May and from July to September.
**Habitat:** mudflats and the shores of ponds and lakes.

**Nesting:** does not nest in NY.
**Feeding:** probes soft substrates and gleans for aquatic insects and crustaceans.
**Voice:** flight call is a harsh *cherk;* sometimes a longer *chirrup* or a chittering alarm call.
**Similar Species:** *Least Sandpiper* (p. 147): yellowish legs; darker upperparts. *Western Sandpiper* (p. 146): longer, slightly down-curved bill; rufous crown, ear patch and scapulars. *Sanderling* (p. 144): pale gray upperparts and blackish trailing edge on flight feathers in nonbreeding plumage. *White-rumped Sandpiper* (p. 148): larger; white rump; folded wings extend beyond tail. *Baird's Sandpiper* (p. 149): larger; longer bill; folded wings extend beyond tail.
**Best Sites:** Braddock Bay; Montezuma NWR; Jamaica Bay Wildlife Refuge; Jones Beach SP; Shinnecock Inlet–Dune Rd.

145

# WESTERN SANDPIPER

*Calidris mauri*

Most Western Sandpipers are seen only along the Pacific Coast, but some adventurous individuals traverse the continent, flying to the Atlantic Coast for the winter. • Many identification guides will tell you to look for this bird's downcurved bill, and on paper this seems like a sensible plan. In the field, however, as angles and lighting change, the bills of "peeps" can look downcurved one moment, straight the next, and anything in between when double-checked. It is a good idea to spend some time getting to know the peeps before trying to identity them. The Western Sandpiper can be easily confused with other peeps, in particular the Semipalmated Sandpiper. • To track down the rare Western Sandpiper, try calling local birding hotlines to find out the locations of the most recent local sightings.

*juvenile*

**ID:** black, slightly downcurved bill; black legs. *Breeding:* rufous crown, ear patch and scapulars; V-shaped markings on upper breast and flanks; pale underparts. *Nonbreeding:* white "eyebrow"; gray brown upperparts; white underparts; streaky, light brown wash on upper breast. *Juvenile:* bright rufous edge on upper scapulars; gray lower scapulars with black "anchor" mark; lightly streaked, pinkish buff sides of breast. *In flight:* narrow, white wing stripe; black line through white rump.
**Size:** *L* 6–7 in; *W* 14 in.
**Status:** rare migrant in spring; common migrant from August to September on the coast.
**Habitat:** pond edges, lakeshores, mudflats and coastlines.
**Nesting:** does not nest in NY.

**Feeding:** gleans and probes mud and shallow water; occasionally submerges its head; primarily eats aquatic insects, worms and crustaceans.
**Voice:** flight call is a high-pitched *cheep*.
**Similar Species:** *Semipalmated Sandpiper* (p. 145): shorter, straight bill; less rufous on crown, ear patch and scapulars. *Least Sandpiper* (p. 147): smaller; yellowish legs; darker breast wash in all plumages; lacks rufous patches. *White-rumped Sandpiper* (p. 148): larger; white rump; folded wings extend beyond tail; lacks rufous patches. *Baird's Sandpiper* (p. 149): larger; folded wings extend beyond tail; lacks rufous patches. *Dunlin* (p. 152): larger; longer bill is thicker at base and droops at tip; black belly in breeding plumage; grayer, unstreaked back in nonbreeding plumage. *Sanderling* (p. 144): nonbreeding plumage shows pale gray upperparts, blackish trailing edge on flight feathers and bold, white upperwing stripe in flight.
**Best Sites:** Jamaica Bay Wildlife Refuge; Jones Beach SP; Smith Point CP; Shinnecock Inlet–Dune Rd.

# LEAST SANDPIPER
*Calidris minutilla*

The Least Sandpiper is the smallest North American shorebird, but its size does not deter it from performing migratory feats. Like most other "peeps," the Least Sandpiper migrates almost the entire length of the globe twice each year, from the Arctic to the southern tip of South America and back. • Arctic summers are incredibly short, so shorebirds must maximize their breeding efforts. Least Sandpipers lay large eggs relative to those of other sandpipers, and the entire clutch can weigh over half the weight of the female! The young hatch in an advanced state of development, getting an early start on preparations for the fall migration. These tiny shorebirds begin moving south as early as the first week of July, so they are some of the first fall migrants to arrive in New York. • This species' light-colored legs are a good field mark, though bad lighting or mud can confuse matters. • The scientific name *minutilla* is Latin for "very small"—apt for the littlest sandpiper.

*nonbreeding*

**ID:** *Breeding:* black bill; yellowish legs; dark, mottled back; buff brown breast, head and nape; light breast streaking; prominent white "V" on back. *Nonbreeding:* much duller; often lacks back stripes; prominent, streaked breast band. *Juvenile:* similar to breeding adult, but with faintly streaked breast. *In flight:* short, dark wings; indistinct wing stripe; black border to underwing; dark rump and center of tail; stiff, rapid wingbeats.

**Size:** *L* 5–6½ in; *W* 13 in.

**Status:** very common migrant from May to June and from July to September; rare in winter in small numbers.

**Habitat:** sandy beaches, lakeshores, ditches, sewage lagoons, mudflats and wetland edges.

**Nesting:** does not nest in NY.

**Feeding:** probes or pecks for insects, crustaceans, small mollusks and occasionally seeds.

**Voice:** high-pitched *kreee*.

**Similar Species:** *Semipalmated Sandpiper* (p. 145): black legs; lighter upperparts; rufous tinge on crown, ear patch and scapulars. *Western Sandpiper* (p. 146): slightly larger; black legs; lighter breast wash in all plumages; rufous patches on crown, ear and scapulars in breeding plumage. *Other peeps* (pp. 143–53): larger; most have dark legs.

**Best Sites:** Braddock Bay; Montezuma NWR; Jamaica Bay Wildlife Refuge; Jones Beach SP; Shinnecock Inlet–Dune Rd.

147

# WHITE-RUMPED SANDPIPER

*Calidris fuscicollis*

Just as a die-hard shorebird watcher is about to go into a peep-induced stupor, small brownish heads emerge from hiding, back feathers are ruffled, wings are stretched and, almost without warning, the birds take flight and flash pure white rumps. There is no doubt that the beautiful White-rumped Sandpiper has been identified. • This sandpiper's white rump may serve the same purpose as the tail of a white-tailed deer—to alert other birds when danger threatens. • When flocks of White-rumps and other sandpipers take to the air, they often defecate in unison. This spontaneous evacuation may benefit the birds by reducing their weight for takeoff. Flocks of White-rumped Sandpipers have also been known to collectively rush at a predator and then suddenly scatter in its face. • In fall, White-rumped Sandpipers migrate to the southern reaches of South America, a journey that these birds make in a few long, nonstop flights, sometimes flying for stretches of 60 hours at a time.

*breeding*

*breeding*

**ID:** black legs; black bill; wings extend well beyond tail. *Breeding:* mottled brown and rufous upperparts; streaked breast, sides and flanks. *Nonbreeding:* mottled gray upperparts; white "eyebrow." *Juvenile:* black upperparts edged with white, chestnut and buff. *In flight:* clean white rump; dark tail; indistinct wing bar.
**Size:** *L* 7–8 in; *W* 17 in.
**Status:** common migrant in May and from August to October on the coast; less common inland.

**Habitat:** shores of lakes, marshes, sewage lagoons and reservoirs; flooded and cultivated fields.
**Nesting:** does not nest in NY.
**Feeding:** gleans the ground and shorelines for insects, crustaceans and mollusks.
**Voice:** flight call is a characteristic, squealing *tzeet,* higher than any other peep.
**Similar Species:** *Other peeps* (pp. 143–53): all have dark line through rump. *Baird's Sandpiper* (p. 149): lacks clean white rump; breast streaking does not extend onto flanks. *Stilt Sandpiper* (p. 153) and *Curlew Sandpiper* (p. 359): much longer legs trail beyond tail in flight.
**Best Sites:** Hamlin Beach SP; Montezuma NWR; Jamaica Bay Wildlife Refuge; Shinnecock Inlet–Dune Rd.; Mecox Bay.

# BAIRD'S SANDPIPER

*Calidris bairdii*

The Baird's Sandpiper is one of the most difficult sandpipers to identify correctly. One clue is that while it often migrates with other sandpipers, it leaves them upon landing and feeds alone. • Like all of its *Calidris* relatives, this modest-looking shorebird has extraordinary migratory habits—it flies twice annually between South America and the Arctic. • Baird's Sandpipers remain on their northern breeding grounds for only a short time. Soon after the chicks hatch and are able to fend for themselves, the adults flock together to begin their southward migration. After a few weeks of accumulating fat reserves, the young gather in a second wave of southbound migrants. They arrive in fresh plumage and are readily identified by their long wings and the "scaly" appearance of their backs. • This bird's name honors Spencer Fullerton Baird, an early director of the Smithsonian Institute who organized several natural history expeditions across North America.

*juvenile*

**ID:** black legs and bill; faint, buff brown speckles on breast; folded wings extend beyond tail. *Breeding:* streaked, gray buff breast; black, diamondlike pattern on back and wing coverts. *Juvenile:* brighter and browner; "scaly" back. *In flight:* faint, white wing stripe.

**Size:** *L* 7–7½ in; *W* 17 in.

**Status:** uncommon migrant from August to October.

**Habitat:** sandy beaches, mudflats and wetland edges.

**Nesting:** does not nest in NY.

**Feeding:** gleans aquatic invertebrates, especially larval flies; also eats beetles and grasshoppers; rarely probes.

**Voice:** soft, rolling *kriit kriit.*

**Similar Species:** "scaly" back is distinctive. *White-rumped Sandpiper* (p. 148): clean white rump; breast streaking extends onto flanks; head and back are more streaked. *Pectoral Sandpiper* (p. 150): dark breast ends abruptly at edge of white belly. *Least Sandpiper* (p. 147): smaller; yellowish legs. *Western Sandpiper* (p. 146) and *Sanderling* (p. 144): lack streaked, gray buff breast. *Semipalmated Sandpiper* (p. 145): smaller; shorter bill; lacks streaked breast in non-breeding plumage.

**Best Sites:** Montezuma NWR; Jamaica Bay Wildlife Refuge; Jones Beach SP; Shinnecock Inlet–Dune Rd.; Riverhead Sod Farms.

# PECTORAL SANDPIPER

*Calidris melanotos*

This widespread traveler may be found in Siberia as well as the Canadian Arctic, and its epic annual migrations include destinations such as South America, Australia and New Zealand. In spring and fall, Pectoral Sandpipers are conspicuous along the shores of the lower Great Lakes and in wet, grassy fields, often in large flocks of over 1000 birds. Peak numbers occur from late August to late October. • Unlike most sandpipers, the Pectoral exhibits sexual dimorphism—the female is only two-thirds the size of the male. • The name "pectoral" refers to the location of the male's prominent air sacs. When displaying on their arctic breeding grounds, the male will inflate these air sacs, causing his feathers to rise. • If threatened, flocks of Pectoral Sandpipers suddenly launch into the air and converge into a single, swirling mass. • These sandpipers are sometimes referred to as "Grass Snipes" because of their preference for wet meadows and grassy marshes.

*nonbreeding*

**ID:** brown breast streaks end abruptly at edge of white belly; white undertail coverts; black bill has slightly down-curved tip; long, yellow legs; mottled upperparts; may have faintly rusty, dark crown and back; folded wings extend beyond tail. *Juvenile:* less spotting on breast; broader white feather edges on back form 2 white "V"s.
**Size:** *L* 9 in; *W* 18 in (female is noticeably smaller).
**Status:** common migrant in May and from August to October.

**Habitat:** lakeshores, marshes, mudflats and flooded fields or pastures.
**Nesting:** does not nest in NY.
**Feeding:** probes and pecks for small insects; eats mainly flies, but also takes beetles and some grasshoppers; may eat small mollusks, crustaceans, berries, seeds, moss, algae and some plant material.
**Voice:** sharp, short, low *krrick krrick.*
**Similar Species:** *Other peeps* (pp. 143–53): all lack well-defined, dark "bib" and yellow legs.
**Best Sites:** Braddock Bay; Montezuma NWR; Jamaica Bay Wildlife Refuge; Jones Beach SP; Riverhead Sod Farms.

# PURPLE SANDPIPER
*Calidris maritima*

You have to admire the Purple Sandpiper for choosing to live on the edge. Unlike most shorebirds, which prefer shallow marshy areas, sandy beaches or mudflats, Purple Sandpipers forage perilously close to crashing waves along rocky headlands, piers and breakwaters. These birds expertly navigate their way across rugged, slippery rocks while foraging for crustaceans, mollusks and insect larvae. In fact, they are rarely seen associated with any beach that is not near a rocky area. • Purple Sandpipers winter along the Atlantic Coast and breed in coastal regions of the High Arctic, so few grace our shores each year. No other shorebird winters as far north along the Atlantic Coast as the Purple Sandpiper. • The name "purple" was given to this sandpiper for the purplish iridescence that is occasionally observed on its shoulders.

*nonbreeding*

**ID:** long, slightly drooping, black-tipped bill with yellow orange base; yellow orange legs; dull streaking on breast and flanks. *Breeding:* streaked neck; buff crown with dark streaks; dark back feathers with tawny to rusty brown edges. *Nonbreeding:* unstreaked, gray head, neck and upper breast form "hood"; gray-spotted, white belly. *Juvenile:* streaked head; chestnut, white and buff feather edgings on upperparts.
**Size:** *L* 9 in; *W* 17 in.
**Status:** common winter visitor from November to March on the coast; less common in winter on the Great Lakes.

**Habitat:** sandy beaches, rocky shorelines, piers and breakwaters.
**Nesting:** does not nest in NY.
**Feeding:** food is found visually and is snatched while moving over rocks and sand; eats mostly mollusks, insects, crustaceans and other invertebrates; also eats a variety of plant material.
**Voice:** call is a soft *prrt-prrt*.
**Similar Species:** *Other peeps* (pp. 143–53): all lack bicolored bill, yellow orange legs and unstreaked, gray "hood" in nonbreeding plumage.
**Best Sites:** Niagara River Corridor; Marshlands Conservancy–Playland CP; Pt. Lookout–Jones Inlet; Shinnecock Inlet–Dune Rd.; Montauk Point SP.

# DUNLIN
*Calidris alpina*

Outside the breeding season, Dunlins form dynamic, synchronous flocks. These tight flocks are generally more exclusive than other shorebird troupes and rarely include other species. Sometimes hundreds of these birds are seen flying wing tip to wing tip. Unlike many of their shorebird relatives, Dunlins overwinter in North America, mostly in coastal areas—few ever cross the equator. They gather in flocks that can number in the tens of thousands. • Dunlins are fairly distinctive in their breeding attire: their black bellies and legs make them look as though they have been wading belly-deep in puddles of ink. • This bird was originally called "Dunling," meaning "little dark one," but with the passage of time, the "g" was dropped. It was also known as the "Red-backed Sandpiper" because of its rufous back in breeding plumage.

*nonbreeding*

*nonbreeding*

**ID:** slightly down-curved, black bill; black legs. *Breeding:* black belly; streaked, white neck and underparts; rufous wings, back and crown. *Nonbreeding:* pale gray underparts; brownish gray upperparts; light brown streaking on breast and nape. *Juvenile:* streaking on head; chestnut brown, white and buff feather edgings on upperparts. *In flight:* white wing stripe.
**Size:** *L* 7½–9 in; *W* 17 in.
**Status:** common migrant in May and from September to November; locally common on the coast in winter.
**Habitat:** mudflats and the shores of ponds, marshes and lakes; occasionally seen in pastures or sewage lagoons.

**Nesting:** does not nest in NY.
**Feeding:** gleans and probes for aquatic crustaceans, worms, mollusks and insects.
**Voice:** flight call is a grating *cheezp* or *treezp*.
**Similar Species:** black belly in breeding plumage is distinctive. *Western Sandpiper* (p. 146) and *Semipalmated Sandpiper* (p. 145): smaller; bill tips are less downcurved; nonbreeding plumage is browner overall. *Least Sandpiper* (p. 147): smaller; darker upperparts; yellowish legs. *Sanderling* (p. 144): paler; straight bill; usually seen running in the surf.
**Best Sites:** Hamlin Beach SP; Jamaica Bay Wildlife Refuge; Montezuma NWR; Shinnecock Inlet–Dune Rd.; Jones Beach SP.

# STILT SANDPIPER

*Calidris himantopus*

With the silhouette of a small Lesser Yellowlegs and the foraging behavior of a dowitcher—two birds with which the Stilt Sandpiper often associates—this bird is easily overlooked by most birders. Named for its relatively long legs, this shorebird prefers to feed in shallow water, where it probes with its bill, often dunking its head completely underwater. Because its bill is shorter than a dowitcher's, however, it has to lean farther forward than its larger cousin—a characteristice that can aid in identification. Moving on tall, stiltlike legs, this sandpiper will also wade into deep water up to its breast in search of a meal. • Unlike many of their *Calidris* relatives, Stilt Sandpipers never gather in large flocks. At most, you may see a gathering of 50 or so Stilts between mid-August and the end of September.

*nonbreeding*

*nonbreeding*

**ID:** long, greenish legs; long bill droops slightly at tip. *Breeding:* chestnut red ear patch; white "eyebrow"; striped crown; streaked neck; barred underparts. *Nonbreeding:* less conspicuous, white "eyebrow"; dirty white neck and breast; white belly; dark brownish gray upperparts. *Juvenile:* dark brown upperparts, fringed rufous or light buff; buff wash on throat and breast; faintly streaked, white belly. *In flight:* white rump; legs trail behind tail; no wing stripe.
**Size:** *L* 8–9 in; *W* 18 in.
**Status:** rare migrant in spring; common migrant from July to October.
**Habitat:** shores of lakes, reservoirs and marshes.

**Nesting:** does not nest in NY.
**Feeding:** probes deeply in shallow water; eats mostly invertebrates; occasionally picks insects from the water's surface or the ground; also eats seeds, roots and leaves.
**Voice:** simple, sharp *querp* or *kirr* in flight; also a clearer *whu*.
**Similar Species:** *Greater Yellowlegs* (p. 133) and *Lesser Yellowlegs* (p. 134): yellow legs; straight bills; lack red ear patch of breeding adult, blotchy back feathers of nonbreeding adult or brown mantle of immature. *Curlew Sandpiper* (p. 359): bill has more obvious curve; black legs; paler gray upperparts in nonbreeding plumage. *Dunlin* (p. 152): shorter, black legs; dark rump; whitish wing bar.
**Best Sites:** Montezuma NWR; Jamaica Bay Wildlife Refuge; Jones Beach SP; Shinnecock Inlet–Dune Rd.; Mecox Bay.

# BUFF-BREASTED SANDPIPER

*Tryngites subruficollis*

Shy in behavior and humble in appearance, the Buff-breasted Sandpiper is a rare visitor to New York. • Buff-breasts prefer drier habitats than most other sandpipers, and the best time to look for the bird is in fall, especially on sod farms. When feeding, this subtly colored bird stands motionless, blending beautifully into a backdrop of mudflats, cultivated fields or cured, grassy pastures. Only when it catches sight of moving prey does it become visible, making a short, forward sprint to snatch a fresh meal. • Buff-breasted Sandpipers, like many shorebirds, breed in the Arctic and make long-distance migrations to southern wintering grounds, in this case Argentina, Uruguay and Paraguay. Most adult Buff-breasted Sandpipers migrate through the center of the continent, so the individuals that we see here are mainly dispersing juveniles heading south in fall for the first time.

*juvenile*

**ID:** buffy, unpatterned face and foreneck; large, dark eyes; very thin, straight, black bill; buff underparts; small spots on crown, nape, breast, sides and flanks; "scaly" look to back and upperwings; yellow legs. *Juvenile:* similar to adult; wider, paler edges and darker centers to feathers on back and upperwings give more "scaly" appearance. *In flight:* pure white underwings; no wing stripe.
**Size:** *L* 7½–8 in; *W* 18 in.
**Status:** rare migrant from late August to September.

**Habitat:** shores of lakes, reservoirs and marshes; also sod farms and cultivated and flooded fields.
**Nesting:** does not nest in NY.
**Feeding:** gleans the ground and shorelines for insects, spiders and small crustaceans; may eat seeds.
**Voice:** usually silent; calls include *chup* or *tick* notes; *preet* flight call.
**Similar Species:** *Upland Sandpiper* (p. 138): bolder streaking on breast; longer neck; smaller head; larger bill; streaking on "cheek" and foreneck. *Pectoral Sandpiper* (p. 150): grayer brown on back and breast; white on belly; white undertail coverts.
**Best Sites:** Montezuma NWR; Jamaica Bay Wildlife Refuge; Riverhead Sod Farms.

# SHORT-BILLED DOWITCHER

*Limnodromus griseus*

Long before deciduous trees burst into their brilliant fall colors, Short-billed Dowitchers from northern locales arrive on our mudflats, marshes and beaches. These plump shorebirds are seen in good numbers during spring migration, but the largest concentrations usually occur during the protracted fall migration, which begins as early as mid-July. • While foraging along shorelines, these birds use their bills to "stitch" up and down into the mud with a rhythm like a sewing machine. This drilling motion liquefies the mud or sand, allowing the dowitchers to reach their hidden prey. • The best way to distinguish between Short-billed Dowitchers and the very similar Long-billed Dowitchers is by their flight calls or by listening to them feeding—Long-bills chatter softly while feeding; Short-bills feed silently.

*nonbreeding*

*nonbreeding*

**ID:** straight, long, dark bill; white "eyebrow"; chunky body; yellow green legs. *Breeding:* white belly; dark spots or bars on reddish buff neck and upper breast; prominent dark barring on white sides and flanks. *Nonbreeding:* dirty gray upperparts; dirty white underparts. *Juvenile:* chestnut-edged crown and back; barred or striped tertials; no streaking or spotting on underparts. *In flight:* white wedge on rump and lower back.
**Size:** *L* 11–12 in; *W* 19 in.
**Status:** common migrant in May and from July to September on the coast; less common migrant inland.
**Habitat:** shores of lakes, reservoirs and marshes.
**Nesting:** does not nest in NY.
**Feeding:** wades in shallow water or mud, probing deeply into substrate with a rapid, up-down bill motion; eats aquatic invertebrates, including insects, mollusks, crustaceans and worms; may feed on seeds, aquatic plants and grasses.
**Voice:** generally silent; flight call is a mellow, repeated *tututu, toodulu* or *toodu.*
**Similar Species:** *Long-billed Dowitcher* (p. 156): very little white on belly; black-and-white barring on red flanks in breeding plumage. *Red Knot* (p. 143): much shorter bill; unmarked, red breast in breeding plumage; nonbreeding birds lack barring on tail and white wedge on back in flight. *Wilson's Snipe* (p. 157): heavily striped head, back, neck and breast; bicolored bill; shorter legs. *Stilt Sandpiper* (p. 153): shorter, slightly downcurved bill; white on rump does not extend onto back.
**Best Sites:** Montezuma NWR; Jamaica Bay Wildlife Refuge; Jones Beach SP; Shinnecock Inlet–Dune Rd.; Mecox Bay.

155

# LONG-BILLED DOWITCHER

*Limnodromus scolopaceus*

Each spring and fall, mudflats and marshes host small numbers of enthusiastic Long-billed Dowitchers. These chunky, sword-billed shorebirds diligently forage up and down through shallow water and mud in a quest for invertebrate sustenance. A diet of insects, freshwater shrimp, mussels, clams and snails provides migrating Long-bills with plenty of fuel for flight and essential calcium for bone and egg development. • Dowitchers have shorter wings than most shorebirds that migrate long distances, making it more practical for them to take flight from shallow water, where a series of hops helps the birds to become airborne. • Mixed flocks of shorebirds demonstrate a variety of foraging styles: some species probe deeply, while others pick at the water's surface or glean the shorelines. It is thought that large numbers of shorebird species are able to coexist because of their different foraging styles and specialized diets.

*nonbreeding*

*nonbreeding*

**ID:** very long, straight, dark bill; dark eye line; white "eyebrow"; chunky body; yellow green legs. *Breeding:* black-and-white barring on reddish underparts; some white on belly; dark, mottled upperparts. *Nonbreeding:* gray overall; dirty white underparts. *Juvenile:* dull gray breast; narrow, rusty edges on tertials. *In flight:* white wedge on rump and lower back.
**Size:** *L* 11–12½ in; *W* 19 in.
**Status:** common migrant from September to October on the coast; uncommon migrant on the Great Lakes.
**Habitat:** lakeshores, shallow marshes and mudflats.
**Nesting:** does not nest in NY.
**Feeding:** probes in shallow water and on mudflats with a repeated, up-down bill

motion; frequently plunges its head underwater; eats shrimps, snails, worms, larval flies and other soft-bodied invertebrates.
**Voice:** alarm call is a loud, high-pitched *keek,* occasionally given in series.
**Similar Species:** *Short-billed Dowitcher* (p. 155): white sides, flanks and belly; more spots than bars on reddish sides and flanks; brighter feather edges on upperparts. *Red Knot* (p. 143): much shorter bill; unmarked, red breast in breeding plumage; nonbreeding birds lack barring on tail and white wedge on back in flight. *Wilson's Snipe* (p. 157): shorter legs; heavily striped head, back, neck and breast; bicolored bill. *Stilt Sandpiper* (p. 153): unmarked, buff underparts; yellow bill; pale bars on black crown and nape.
**Best Sites:** Jamaica Bay Wildlife Refuge; Jones Beach SP; Shinnecock Inlet–Dune Rd.; Mecox Bay.

# WILSON'S SNIPE

*Gallinago delicata*

Visit almost any open wetland in spring or early summer and you will hear the eerie, hollow, winnowing sound of courting male Wilson's Snipes. The sound is made by specialized outer tail feathers that vibrate rapidly in the air as the birds perform daring, headfirst dives high above their marshland habitat. Snipes display most actively in the early morning, but evening performances are not uncommon. • Outside the courtship season, this well-camouflaged bird remains concealed in vegetation. Only when an intruder approaches too closely will a snipe flush from cover, performing a series of aerial zigzags—an evasive maneuver designed to confuse predators. Because of this habit, hunters who were skilled enough to shoot a snipe came to be known as "snipers," a term later adopted by the military. • The snipe's eyes are placed far back on its head, allowing the bird to see both forward and backward.

**ID:** long, sturdy, bicolored bill; relatively short legs; heavily striped head, back, neck and breast; dark eye stripe; dark barring on sides and flanks; unmarked white belly. *In flight:* red orange tail; quick zigzags on takeoff.
**Size:** *L* 10½–11½ in; *W* 18 in.
**Status:** common breeder from April to June throughout northern and western NY; fall migrants depart by October; less common on the coast; occasional in winter.
**Habitat:** cattail and bulrush marshes, sedge meadows, poorly drained floodplains, bogs and fens; also willow and red-osier dogwood tangles.
**Nesting:** usually in dry grass, often under vegetation; nest is made of grass, moss and leaves; female incubates 4 darkly marked, olive buff to brown eggs for 18–20 days; both parents raise the young, often splitting the brood.

**Feeding:** probes soft substrates for larvae, earthworms and other soft-bodied invertebrates; also eats mollusks, crustaceans, spiders, small amphibians and some seeds.
**Voice:** eerie, accelerating courtship song in flight: *woo-woo-woo-woo-woo-woo;* often sings *wheat wheat wheat* from an elevated perch; alarm call is a nasal *scaip.*
**Similar Species:** *Short-billed Dowitcher* (p. 155) and *Long-billed Dowitcher* (p. 156): longer legs; all-dark bills; lack heavy striping on head, back, neck and breast; usually seen in flocks. *Marbled Godwit* (p. 141): much larger; slightly upturned bill; much longer legs. *American Woodcock* (p. 158): unmarked, buff underparts; yellowish bill; light-colored bars on black crown and nape.
**Best Sites:** Iroquois NWR–Tonawanda WMA–Oak Orchard WMA; Braddock Bay; Montezuma NWR; Perch River WMA; Black Creek Marsh WMA.

# AMERICAN WOODCOCK

*Scolopax minor*

This denizen of moist woodlands and damp thickets normally goes about its business in a quiet and reclusive manner, but during courtship the male American Woodcock reveals another side of his character. Just before dawn or just after sunset, the male struts provocatively in an open woodland clearing or a brushy, abandoned field while calling out a series of loud *peeent* notes. He then launches into the air, twittering upward in a circular flight display until, with wings partly folded, he plummets to the ground in the zigzag pattern of a falling leaf, chirping at every turn. At the end of this stunning "sky dance," he lands precisely where he started. • The clearing of forests and draining of woodland swamps has degraded or eliminated large tracts of American Woodcock habitat, resulting in a decline in this bird's populations.

**ID:** very long, sturdy bill; very short legs; large head; short neck; chunky body; large, dark eyes; unmarked, buff underparts; light-colored bars on black crown and nape. *In flight:* rounded wings; modified wing feathers make a twittering sound when the bird is flushed from cover.

**Size:** *L* 11 in; *W* 18 in.

**Status:** widespread, locally common breeder from March to June; fall migrants depart by October; rare in winter.

**Habitat:** moist woodlands and brushy thickets adjacent to grassy clearings or abandoned fields.

**Nesting:** on the ground in woods or in an overgrown field; female digs a scrape and lines it with dead leaves and other debris;

female incubates 4 buff to olive eggs, blotched with brown and gray, for 20–22 days; female tends the young.

**Feeding:** probes in soft, moist or wet soil for earthworms and insect larvae; also takes spiders, snails, millipedes and some plant material, including seeds, sedges and grasses.

**Voice:** nasal *peent;* during courtship dance male produces high-pitched, twittering, whistling sounds, made by modified wing feathers.

**Similar Species:** *Wilson's Snipe* (p. 157): heavily striped head, back, neck and breast; dark barring on sides and flanks. *Long-billed Dowitcher* (p. 156) and *Short-billed Dowitcher* (p. 155): all-dark bills; longer legs; lack pale barring on dark crown and nape; usually seen in flocks.

**Best Sites:** Iroquois NWR–Tonawanda WMA–Oak Orchard WMA; Connecticut Hill WMA; Nation's Road Grassland; Heckscher SP.

# WILSON'S PHALAROPE

*Phalaropus tricolor*

Not only are phalaropes among the most colorful of shorebirds, they are also among the most unusual. Phalaropes practice an uncommon mating strategy known as polyandry: each female mates with several males, often producing a clutch of eggs with each mate. After laying a clutch, the female usually abandons her mate, leaving him to incubate the eggs and tend the precocial young. This reversal of gender roles includes a reversal of plumage characteristics—the female is more brightly colored than her male counterpart. Even John James Audubon was fooled by the phalarope's strange breeding habits and unique coloration: he mislabeled the male and female birds in all of his phalarope illustrations. • Most phalaropes have lobed, or individually webbed, feet for swimming in the shallows of wetlands, but the Wilson's Phalarope is more terrestrial than its relatives and lacks this characteristic.

*breeding*

**ID:** dark, needle-like bill; white "eyebrow," throat and nape; light underparts; black legs. *Breeding female:* gray "cap"; chestnut brown on sides of neck; black eye line extends down side of neck and onto back. *Breeding male:* duller overall; dark "cap." *Nonbreeding:* gray upperparts; white "eyebrow"; gray eye line; white underparts; dark yellowish or greenish legs.

**Size:** *L* 9–9½ in; *W* 17 in.

**Status:** recent breeding in 1 locality in extreme northeastern NY; rare migrant in May; uncommon migrant from July to September.

**Habitat:** *Breeding:* cattail marshes and grass or sedge margins of sewage lagoons. *In migration:* lakeshores, marshes and sewage lagoons.

**Nesting:** often near water; well concealed in a depression lined with grass and other vegetation; male incubates 4 brown-blotched, buff eggs for 18–27 days; male rears the young.

**Feeding:** swims in tight, spinning circles to stir up prey, then picks aquatic insects, worms and small crustaceans from the water's surface or just below it; on land, makes short jabs to pick up invertebrates.

**Voice:** deep, grunting *work work* or *wu wu wu*, usually given on the breeding grounds.

**Similar Species:** *Red-necked Phalarope* (p. 160): rufous stripe down side of neck in breeding plumage; dark nape and line behind eye in nonbreeding plumage. *Red Phalarope* (p. 161): reddish neck, breast and underparts in breeding plumage; dark nape and broad, dark line behind eye in nonbreeding plumage; rarely seen inland. *Lesser Yellowlegs* (p. 134): larger; yellow legs; streaked neck; mottled upperparts.

**Best Sites:** Iroquois NWR–Tonawanda WMA–Oak Orchard WMA; Montezuma NWR; Jamaica Bay Wildlife Refuge; Mecox Bay.

159

# RED-NECKED PHALAROPE

*Phalaropus lobatus*

A pilgrimage to a local sewage lagoon may not be your idea of an aesthetically pleasing birding experience, but these areas are often the best places to meet many species of birds, including the Red-necked Phalarope. • One of the world's smallest seabirds, the Red-necked Phalarope is also the smallest of the three phalarope species. Most of these phalaropes migrate to and from their arctic wintering grounds via the Atlantic Coast, to the delight of local birders. • When foraging on the water with other shorebirds, phalaropes can usually be singled out by their unusual behavior—they spin and whirl about in tight circles, stirring up tiny crustaceans, mollusks and other aquatic invertebrates. As prey funnels toward the surface, these birds daintily pluck it from the water with their needlelike bills. • "Phalarope" comes from the Greek word for "coot's foot." Like coots and grebes, Red-necked Phalaropes have individually webbed, or "lobed," toes, a feature that makes them proficient swimmers.

*nonbreeding*

**ID:** thin, black bill; long, dark gray legs. *Breeding female:* chestnut brown stripe on neck and throat; white "chin"; blue black head; incomplete, white eye ring; white belly; 2 rusty buff stripes on each upperwing. *Breeding male:* white "eyebrow"; less intense colors than female. *Nonbreeding:* blue gray upperparts; white underparts; black "cap"; broad, dark band from eye to ear; white upperwing stripes.
**Size:** *L* 7 in; *W* 15 in.
**Status:** common migrant from April to May and from September to October.
**Habitat:** open ocean; open water bodies, including ponds, lakes, marshes and sewage lagoons.

**Nesting:** does not nest in NY.
**Feeding:** swims in tight, spinning circles to stir up prey, then picks insects, mollusks and small crustaceans from the water; on land, makes short jabs to pick up invertebrates.
**Voice:** often noisy in migration; soft *krit krit krit.*
**Similar Species:** *Wilson's Phalarope* (p. 159): female has gray "cap" and black eye line extending down side of neck and onto back in breeding plumage. *Red Phalarope* (p. 161): reddish neck, breast and underparts in breeding plumage; lacks white stripes on upperwing in nonbreeding plumage.
**Best Sites:** Montezuma NWR; Derby Hill; Jamaica Bay Wildlife Refuge; Mecox Bay.

# RED PHALAROPE

*Phalaropus fulicarius*

The Red Phalarope sports its reddish breeding plumage for only a short period in spring. Unfortunately, at this time, most birds are far from land or are heading to their arctic breeding grounds. This bird's dull fall wardrobe reveals why it is known as the "Gray Phalarope" in other parts of the world. Outside the breeding season, there is little to make this bird stand out from its similar-looking relative, the Red-necked Phalarope. Still, the Red Phalarope's heavier bill, larger size and plain, blue gray upperwings usually provide sufficient clues for sharp-eyed birders to distinguish between these two species in the field. • Phalaropes are the most aquatic of the shorebirds. They spend most of the nonbreeding season floating on open ocean waters, feeding on plankton, small fish, jellyfish and crustaceans. • From mid-May to early June, and again from early July to late September, huge numbers of these birds are occasionally seen offshore in the Atlantic Ocean.

*nonbreeding*

**ID:** *Breeding female:* chestnut red throat, neck and underparts; white face; black crown and forehead; black-tipped, yellow bill. *Breeding male:* mottled brown crown; duller face and underparts. *Nonbreeding:* white head, neck and underparts; blue gray upperparts; mostly dark bill; black nape; broad, dark patch extends from eye to ear. *Juvenile:* similar to nonbreeding adult, but buff-colored overall, with dark streaking on upperparts.

**Size:** *L* 8½ in; *W* 17 in.

**Status:** fairly common migrant from April to May and September to October on the Atlantic; less common but regular migrant on Great Lakes and L. Champlain.

**Habitat:** open ocean; lakes, large wetlands and sewage lagoons.

**Nesting:** does not nest in NY.

**Feeding:** gleans from the water's surface, usually while swimming in tight, spinning circles; eats small crustaceans, mollusks, insects and other invertebrates; rarely takes vegetation or small fish.

**Voice:** calls include a shrill, high-pitched *wit* or *creep* and a low *clink clink*.

**Similar Species:** *Red-necked Phalarope* (p. 160): smaller; thinner, dark bill; breeding birds lack all-red underparts; nonbreeding birds have white upperwing stripes. *Wilson's Phalarope* (p. 159): breeding birds lack all-red underparts; nonbreeding birds lack dark "mask." *Peeps* (pp. 143–53): less conspicuous facial markings; most have streaked underparts.

**Best Sites:** Dunkirk Harbor; Derby Hill; Mecox Bay; Montauk Point SP.

# POMARINE JAEGER

*Stercorarius pomarinus*

Jaegers are powerful, swift predators and notorious pirates of the vast, open oceans, and the Pomarine Jaeger is the largest of the three jaeger species. These birds spend most of their lives in the air, occasionally resting on the ocean's surface, only seeking the solid footing of land during the nesting season. • Fall and early winter appear to be the best seasons for observing the small number of Pomarine Jaegers that make regular appearances in New York. Keen fall birders patrolling piers or beaches along the coast probably have the best chance of meeting a migrant Pomarine. • Most novice birders differentiate the three jaeger species based on the shape and length of their central tail feathers. This would seem to be an easy task, but this comparison only applies to adult jaegers. Pomarines appear larger and heavier than other jaegers, and light morph birds usually have broader pectoral "collars" and duskier sides.

*light morph nonbreeding*

**ID:** long, blunt, twisted central tail feathers in breeding plumage. *Light morph:* dark brown upperparts; black "cap"; white underparts and "collar"; yellow wash on sides of neck; dark, mottled breast band, sides and flanks; dark undertail coverts. *Dark morph:* all-dark body except for white in wing. *Juvenile:* central tail feathers extend just past tail; white at base of upperwing primaries; variable, dark barring on underwings and underparts; lacks black "cap." *In flight:* white patch at base of underwing primaries; powerful, steady wingbeats.
**Size:** *L* 20–23 in; *W* 4 ft.
**Status:** uncommon migrant in June off Long I.; fairly common migrant off Long I. and rare migrant on L. Ontario from September to October.

**Habitat:** Great Lakes shorelines; Atlantic Coast.
**Nesting:** does not nest in NY.
**Feeding:** snatches fish from the water's surface while in flight; chases down small birds; pirates food from gulls.
**Voice:** generally silent; may give a sharp *which-yew,* a squealing *weak-weak* or a squeaky, whistled note during migration.
**Similar Species:** *Parasitic Jaeger* (p. 163): smaller and more slender; long, thin, pointed tail; lacks mottled sides and flanks; less white on upperwing primaries; short, sharp tail streamers; juvenile has barred underparts. *Long-tailed Jaeger* (p. 360): very long, thin, pointed tail; very little white on upperwing primaries; lacks white on base of underwing primaries; very dark vent; dark, mottled breast band, sides and flanks; juvenile has stubby, spoon-shaped tail streamers and pale belly.
**Best Sites:** Hamlin Beach SP; Derby Hill; Jones Beach SP; Montauk Point SP.

# PARASITIC JAEGER

*Stercorarius parasiticus*

Although "jaeger" means "hunter" in German, "parasitic" more aptly describes this bird's foraging tactics. "Kleptoparasitism" is the scientific term for this jaeger's pirating ways, and these birds are truly relentless. Parasitic Jaegers will harass and intimidate terns and gulls until the victims regurgitate their partially digested meals. As soon as the food is ejected, these aerial pirates snatch it out of midair or pick it from the water's surface in a swooping dive. Less than 25 percent of these encounters are successful, and many Parasitic Jaegers are forced to find their own food. • Jaegers, the most numerous predatory birds in the Arctic, fill the same niche over ocean waters and arctic tundra as raptors do on land. • On their arctic breeding grounds, adults defend their eggs and young aggressively. Both adults will attack an intruder with stooping, parabolic dives or aggressive, blazing pursuits. • The Parasitic Jaeger is the most abundant jaeger in the world and the most commonly seen in our region.

*immature
light morph
nonbreeding*

**ID:** long, dark, pointed wings; long, pointed central tail feathers; brown upperparts; dark "cap"; light underwing tips. *Light morph:* white underparts; white to cream-colored "collar"; brown neck band. *Dark morph:* all-brown underparts and "collar." *Juvenile:* barred underparts; central tail feather extends just past tail.
**Size:** *L* 15–20 in; *W* 3½–4 ft.
**Status:** uncommon migrant from May to June off Long I.; uncommon migrant off Long I. and fairly common migrant on L. Ontario from August to October.

**Habitat:** Great Lakes shorelines; Atlantic Coast.
**Nesting:** does not nest in NY.
**Feeding:** pirates, scavenges and hunts for fish, eggs, large insects and small birds and mammals; often pirates food from other birds; may scavenge at landfills.
**Voice:** generally silent; may make shrill calls in migration.
**Similar Species:** *Pomarine Jaeger* (p. 162): shorter, blunt, twisted central tail feathers; dark, mottled sides and flanks; white on upperwing primaries. *Long-tailed Jaeger* (p. 360): much smaller; much longer, pointed central tail feathers; lacks dark neck band.
**Best Sites:** Hamlin Beach SP; Derby Hill; Jones Beach SP; Fire Island National Seashore; Montauk Point SP.

# LAUGHING GULL

*Larus atricilla*

The black-hooded Laughing Gull's beautiful plumage and lilting laugh are readily accepted by humans today, but life has not always been so easy for this bird. In the late 19th century, high commercial demand for egg collections and feathers for use in women's hats resulted in the extirpation of this gull as a breeding species in many parts of its Atlantic Coast range. Today, East Coast populations are gradually assuming their former abundance. Although this gull may appear in any month of the year in our state, May, June, August and September support the most sightings. • The Laughing Gull's breeding range is primarily along the Atlantic and Gulf coasts of North America and in the Caribbean. It winters in Mexico and Central and South America. • While the laughing call explains this bird's common name, the Latin name *atricilla* refers to a black band present only on the tails of immature birds.

*breeding*

**Nesting:** colonial; pair builds a grass-lined nest of debris, sticks and grass on the ground; pair incubates 2–4 brown-blotched, buff-colored eggs for 20 days; both adults care for the young.

**Feeding:** omnivorous; gleans insects, small mollusks, crustaceans, spiders and small fish from the ground or water; may steal food from other birds; may eat the eggs and nestlings of other birds; often scavenges at landfills.

**Voice:** loud, high-pitched, laughing call: *ha-ha-ha-ha-ha-ha.*

**Similar Species:** *Franklin's Gull* (p. 360): smaller; shorter, slimmer bill; nonbreeding has black "mask." *Black-headed Gull* (p. 166) and *Bonaparte's Gull* (p. 167): orange or reddish legs; slimmer bill (Bonaparte's has black bill); lighter mantle; white wedge on upper leading edge of wing; black "hood" on breeding adult does not extend over nape; white head with black ear spot in nonbreeding plumage. *Little Gull* (p. 165): much smaller; paler mantle; reddish legs; dainty, black bill; no eye ring; lacks black wing tips.

**ID:** white neck and underparts; dark gray back; black wing tips; black legs. *Breeding:* black head; bold, white eye crescents; red bill. *Nonbreeding:* white head with some pale gray bands; black bill. *Immature:* variable plumage; brown to gray and white overall; broad, black subterminal tail band. *In flight:* white trailing edge to wing; flies with pointed wings swept back.

**Size:** *L* 15–17 in; *W* 3¼ ft.

**Status:** common breeder in May and June on Long I.; common migrant from April to May and from August to September.

**Habitat:** shorelines of lakes, bays and rivers; open water; also landfills.

**Best Sites:** Jamaica Bay Wildlife Refuge; Jones Beach SP; Pt. Lookout–Jones Inlet.

# LITTLE GULL

*Larus minutus*

This common Eurasian gull was first identified in North America around 1820 as a specimen collected on the first expediton of the 19th-century explorer John Franklin. It was considered an exceptionally rare vagrant until 1962, when the first documented nest in the New World was discovered in Ontario, Canada. In the 1980s, a breeding population was found in the Hudson Bay Lowlands in Canada, and some speculate that this bird may have been nesting there long before the first nest was discovered. As nesting in neighboring Canada increases, more Little Gulls are being seen throughout New York, most often in flocks of Bonaparte's Gulls. Look for the Little Gull's dark underwings when it is in flight to distinguish it from the masses of white-underwinged Bonaparte's Gulls. • The Little Gull, true to its name, is the smallest of all gulls.

*nonbreeding*

*nonbreeding*

**ID:** white neck, rump, tail and underparts; gray back and wings; orange red feet and legs. *Breeding:* black head; dark red bill. *Nonbreeding:* black bill; dark ear spot and "cap." *Immature:* pinkish legs; brown and black on wings and tail. *In flight:* white wing tips and trailing edge of wing; dark underwings.

**Size:** *L* 10–11 in; *W* 24 in.

**Status:** fairly regular visitor in small numbers; most frequently seen from September to April.

**Habitat:** freshwater marshes, ponds and beaches.

**Nesting:** does not nest in NY.

**Feeding:** gleans insects from the ground or from the water's surface; may also take small mollusks, fish, crustaceans, marine worms and spiders.

**Voice:** repeated *kay-ee*; low *kek-kek-kek*.

**Similar Species:** *Bonaparte's Gull* (p. 167): black-tipped primary feathers; breeding has broken, white eye ring, larger, black bill and white nape; nonbreeding has white "cap." *Black-headed Gull* (p. 166): black-tipped primary feathers; breeding has broken, white eye ring, larger bill and white nape; nonbreeding has white "cap" and red bill. *Franklin's Gull* (p. 360): larger; black wing tips; darker mantle; breeding has broken, white eye ring, white nape and brighter red bill; nonbreeding has black "mask." *Laughing Gull* (p. 164): larger; black wing tips; darker mantle; black legs; breeding has broken, white eye ring and much larger bill.

**Best Sites:** Dunkirk Harbor; Niagara River Corridor, Braddock Bay; Pt. Lookout–Jones Inlet; Jones Beach SP.

# BLACK-HEADED GULL

*Larus ridibundus*

Black-headed Gulls are a regular and increasing attraction for birders in New York. Several of these birds can usually be found among large gatherings of Bonaparte's Gulls in winter, and the often raucous concentrations of gulls in the Niagara River frequently have a small number of these wanderers. • The Black-headed Gull is a relative newcomer to North America—the first sighting was recorded in the 1920s. Small nesting colonies are now established on islands off the coast of Atlantic Canada, and there has been at least one unsuccessful nesting attempt in Massachusetts. • In North America, there are many gulls with black heads. Ironically, the Black-headed Gull has a chocolate-brown head in breeding plumage, which can easily be mistaken for black in the usually harsh seacoast conditions.

*nonbreeding*

*nonbreeding*

**ID:** white neck, rump, tail and underparts; gray mantle; red feet and legs. *Breeding:* red bill; dark brown "hood" appears blackish and does not extend onto nape; broken, white eye ring. *Nonbreeding:* dark ear patch; white "cap"; red bill. *Immature:* pale pinkish orange legs; dark tail band; black-tipped, yellow bill; dusky "cap"; white mottling on "hood" in summer; brown on wings in winter. *In flight:* white upper forewing wedge; black wing tips; dark underwing primaries.
**Size:** *L* 16 in; *W* 3¼ ft.
**Status:** rare migrant and winter visitor from November to March on the Atlantic Coast and Great Lakes shores.
**Habitat:** lakeshores, inlets and coastlines.
**Nesting:** does not nest in NY.
**Feeding:** gleans insects, small mollusks, crustaceans, spiders and small fish from the ground or the water's surface; often catches insects in flight; may also take some seeds and berries; may steal food from other birds.
**Voice:** high-pitched *craah;* flocks utter high-pitched, laughing notes.
**Similar Species:** *Bonaparte's Gull* (p. 167): smaller overall; daintier, black bill; mostly white underwing primaries; orange legs; black "hood" on breeding extends onto upper nape. *Little Gull* (p. 165): dark underwings; primary feathers lack black tips; breeding has all-black head, smaller bill and no eye ring; nonbreeding has dark "cap" and black bill. *Franklin's Gull* (p. 360) and *Laughing Gull* (p. 164): black crescent on wing tips; lack white triangle on upper leading edge of wing; black "hood" on breeding extends over nape; nonbreeding Franklin's has black "mask" and bill.
**Best Sites:** Niagara River Corridor; Durand-Eastman Park (Rochester); Pt. Lookout–Jones Inlet; Jacob Riis Park–Breezy Pt.–Ft. Tilden(NYC).

# BONAPARTE'S GULL

*Larus philadelphia*

Many people feel great disdain for gulls, but they might change their minds when they meet the Bonaparte's Gull. This graceful, reserved gull is nothing like its contentious, aggressive relatives. Delicate in plumage and behavior, this small gull avoids landfills, preferring to dine on insects caught in midair or plucked from the water's surface. This engaging bird sometimes even tips up like a dabbling duck to catch small invertebrates in the shallows. Only when a flock of Bonaparte's spies a school of fish or an intruder do these birds raise their soft, scratchy voices in excitement. • During cold winters, most Bonaparte's Gulls move south to the Atlantic Coast by December. • This gull was named after Charles-Lucien Bonaparte, a nephew of Napoleon and a naturalist who made significant contributions to the study of ornithology in the 1800s.

*nonbreeding*

*nonbreeding*

**ID:** black bill; gray mantle; white underparts. *Breeding:* black head; white eye ring; orange legs. *Nonbreeding:* white head; dark ear patch. *In flight:* white upper forewing wedge; black wing tips.

**Size:** *L* 11½–14 in; *W* 33 in.

**Status:** common migrant and winter visitor from October to April.

**Habitat:** large lakes, rivers and marshes; also coastal inlets and open ocean.

**Nesting:** does not nest in NY.

**Feeding:** dabbles and tips up for aquatic invertebrates, small fish and tadpoles; gleans the ground for terrestrial invertebrates; also captures insects in the air.

**Voice:** scratchy, soft *ear ear* while feeding.

**Similar Species:** *Franklin's Gull* (p. 360): larger; lacks white upper forewing wedge; breeding has orange bill; nonbreeding has black "mask." *Little Gull* (p. 165): smaller; daintier bill; white wing tips; black "hood" of breeding adult lacks white eye ring and extends over nape; nonbreeding has black "cap." *Black-headed Gull* (p. 166): larger overall; larger, red bill; dark underwing primaries; more red than orange on legs; breeding has brownish "hood."

**Best Sites:** Dunkirk Harbor; Niagara River Corridor; Braddock Bay; Pt. Lookout–Jones Inlet; Montauk Point SP.

# RING-BILLED GULL
*Larus delawarensis*

Ring-billed Gulls wander almost everywhere and tend to pick up many of the bad habits associated with their larger relatives. This gull's numbers have greatly increased in recent years, and its tolerance for humans has practically made it a part of our everyday lives. Ring-bills readily join Herring Gulls to scavenge our litter and even foul the windshields of our automobiles in parking lots. • In the early 1900s, Ring-bill populations were small, but by the 1960s, this gull's numbers had grown to the hundreds of thousands. Some people feel that Ring-billed Gulls have become pests—many parks, beaches, golf courses and even fast-food restaurant parking lots are inundated with marauding gulls looking for handouts. Few species, however, have fared as well as the Ring-billed Gull in the face of human development, which, in itself, is something to appreciate.

*nonbreeding*

*breeding*

**ID:** white head; yellow bill and legs; black ring around bill tip; pale gray mantle; yellow eyes; white underparts. *Immature:* gray back; brown wings and breast. *In flight:* black wing tips with a few white spots.
**Size:** *L* 18–20 in; *W* 4 ft.
**Status:** abundant year-round resident on the Great Lakes and Atlantic Coast; local and common breeder from May to July in western NY and on eastern L. Ontario islands; fairly common in winter.
**Habitat:** *Breeding:* sparsely vegetated islands, open beaches, breakwaters and dredge-spoil areas. *In migration and*

*winter:* lakes, rivers, landfills, golf courses, fields and parks; also bays and ocean.
**Nesting:** colonial; in a shallow scrape on the ground lined with plants, debris, grass and sticks; pair incubates 2–4 brown-blotched, gray to olive eggs for 23–28 days.
**Feeding:** gleans the ground for human food waste, spiders, insects, rodents, earthworms, grubs and some waste grain; scavenges for carrion; surface-tips for aquatic invertebrates and fish.
**Voice:** high-pitched *kakakaka-akakaka;* also a low, laughing *yook-yook-yook.*
**Similar Species:** *Herring* (p. 169), *Glaucous* (p. 172) and *Iceland* (p. 170) *gulls:* larger; pinkish legs; yellow bills with red spot near tip of lower mandible; lack bill ring. *Lesser Black-backed Gull* (p. 171): larger; much darker mantle; much less white on wing tips; lacks bill ring.
**Best Sites:** Niagara River Corridor; Cape Vincent–Pt. Peninsula; Verona Beach SP–Sylvan Beach; Pt. Lookout–Jones Inlet; Montauk Point SP.

# HERRING GULL

*Larus argentatus*

Although Herring Gulls are as adept as their smaller Ring-billed relatives at scrounging for handouts on the beach, they are as likely to be found in wilderness areas as urban settings. Settling on lakes and large rivers where Ring-billed Gulls would usually not be found, Herring Gulls nest comfortably in large colonies, though a pair may choose a nest site miles from any other gulls. • Herring Gulls are skilled hunters, but they are also opportunistic birds that scavenge at landfills and in fast-food restaurant parking lots. Their foraging habits might seem unsanitary, but these birds have thrived by adopting the task of finishing off leftovers. • Like many gulls, Herring Gulls have a small red spot on the lower mandible that serves as a target for nestling young. When a downy chick pecks at the lower mandible, the parent recognizes the cue and regurgitates its meal.

*breeding*

*nonbreeding*

**ID:** large gull; yellow bill; red spot on lower mandible; light eyes; pale gray mantle; pink legs. *Breeding:* white head; white underparts. *Nonbreeding:* white head and nape are washed with brown. *Immature:* mottled brown overall. *In flight:* black wing tips with white spots.

**Size:** *L* 23–26 in; *W* 4½–5 ft.

**Status:** present year-round; common breeder from April to July on Long I. and in northern NY; abundant throughout most of the state in winter.

**Habitat:** large lakes, wetlands, rivers, landfills and urban areas; also bays and ocean.

**Nesting:** singly or colonially; on an open beach or island; on the ground in a shallow scrape lined with plants and sticks; pair incubates 3 darkly blotched, olive to buff eggs for 31–32 days.

**Feeding:** surface-tips for aquatic invertebrates and fish; gleans the ground for insects and worms; scavenges dead fish and human food waste; eats other birds' eggs and young.

**Voice:** loud, buglelike *kleew-kleew;* also an alarmed *kak-kak-kak.*

**Similar Species:** *Ring-billed Gull* (p. 168): smaller; black bill ring; yellow legs. *Thayer's* (p. 361), *Glaucous* (p. 172) and *Iceland* (p. 170) *gulls:* paler mantles; all lack black on wings. *Lesser Black-backed Gull* (p. 171): much darker mantle.

**Best Sites:** Niagara River Corridor; Robert Moses SP; Cohoes–Crescent–Peebles Island SP; Pt. Lookout–Jones Inlet; Montauk Point SP.

# ICELAND GULL

*Larus glaucoides*

Like its close relatives the Thayer's Gull and the Glaucous Gull, the pale Iceland Gull can be seen each winter in small numbers, usually among larger flocks of more common wintering gulls. This graceful glider spends much of its time searching for schools of fish over icy, open waters. When fishing proves unrewarding, this opportunistic gull has no qualms about digging through a landfill in search of food. Human onlookers might think that the Iceland Gull's dirty brown head and breast streaking are a result of its filthy scavenging habits, but in truth, these are the natural markings of its nonbreeding plumage. • The Iceland Gull appears in two well-recognized forms in our region. The more common is the "Kumlein's" form, which has gray on its wing tips. On Baffin Island in Canada, the Kumlein's subspecies interbreeds with the Thayer's Gull, producing fertile hybrids that are also seen here occasionally. Debate continues on the status of these gulls, and some scientists believe that the Thayer's Gull is really just a subspecies of the Iceland Gull.

*nonbreeding*

**ID:** *Breeding:* relatively short, yellow bill; red spot on lower mandible; rounded head; yellow eyes; dark eye ring; white wing tips with some dark gray; pink legs; white underparts; pale gray mantle. *Nonbreeding:* brown-streaked head and breast. *Immature:* dark eyes; black bill; varying amounts of gray on upperparts and brown flecking over entire body. *In flight:* fairly wide, pointed wings; variable amounts of gray spotting on white primaries.
**Size:** *L* 22 in; *W* 4½ ft.
**Status:** common winter visitor from November to April in northern NY, less common on the Atlantic Coast.

**Habitat:** landfills; open water on large lakes and rivers.
**Nesting:** does not nest in NY.
**Feeding:** eats mostly fish; may also take crustaceans, mollusks, carrion, seeds and human food waste; scavenges at landfills.
**Voice:** high, screechy calls, much less bugling than other large gulls.
**Similar Species:** *Herring Gull* (p. 169): black wing tips; darker mantle. *Thayer's Gull* (p. 361): more dark gray than white on wing tips; dark eyes. *Glaucous Gull* (p. 172): larger; longer, heavier bill; pure white wing tips. *Ring-billed Gull* (p. 168): smaller; dark ring on yellow bill; yellow legs. *Lesser Black-backed Gull* (p. 171): darker mantle; black wing tips; yellow legs.
**Best Sites:** Dunkirk Harbor; Niagara River Corridor; Robert Moses SP; Pt. Lookout–Jones Inlet; Montauk Point SP.

# LESSER BLACK-BACKED GULL

*Larus fuscus*

Equipped with long wings for long-distance flights, small numbers of Lesser Black-backed Gulls leave their familiar European and Icelandic surroundings each fall to make their way to North America. Most of these gulls settle along the Atlantic Coast during winter, where it is often challenging to pick them out in a huge roosting flock of gulls. Birders are advised to keep a close eye on Great Lakes shores and landfills—the most likely locations in which to find Lesser Black-backed Gulls. • The Lesser Black-backed Gull is a strictly European nesting species, with the closest colonies located in Iceland. The increasing number of sightings outside the winter months suggests that this immigrant may soon be applying for American status, much like some of its smaller relatives have already done. Some Lesser Black-backed Gulls have already been found paired with Herring Gulls, which suggests that we could someday be seeing some puzzling hybrids.

*nonbreeding*

*nonbreeding*

**ID:** *Breeding:* dark gray mantle; mostly black wing tips; yellow bill has red spot on lower mandible; yellow eyes and legs; white head and underparts. *Nonbreeding:* brown-streaked head and neck. *Juvenile:* varying amounts of gray on upperparts and brown flecking over entire body; black bill or pale bill with black tip; eyes may be dark or light. *In flight:* long, slender wings; dark slate gray upperparts with contrasting black primaries; single, white primary spot; juvenile has plain gray underwings.

**Size:** *L* 21 in; *W* 4½ ft.

**Status:** rare but increasing winter visitor from November to April.

**Habitat:** landfills and open water on large lakes and rivers.

**Nesting:** does not nest in NY.

**Feeding:** eats mostly fish, crustaceans, mollusks, insects, small rodents, seeds, carrion and human food waste; scavenges at landfills.

**Voice:** screechy call is like a lower-pitched version of the Herring Gull's.

**Similar Species:** *Herring Gull* (p. 169): lighter mantle; pink legs. *Thayer's* (p. 361), *Glaucous* (p. 172) and *Iceland* (p. 170) *gulls:* pale gray mantles; white or gray wing tips; pink legs. *Ring-billed Gull* (p. 168): smaller; dark ring on yellow bill; paler mantle. *Slaty-backed Gull:* larger; more white on trailing edge of wing; pink legs. *Great Black-backed Gull* (p. 173): much larger; black mantle; pale pinkish legs.

**Best Sites:** Niagara River Corridor; Robert Moses SP; Cohoes–Crescent–Peebles Island SP; Pt. Lookout–Jones Inlet; Shinnecock Inlet–Dune Rd.

# GLAUCOUS GULL

*Larus hyperboreus*

The Glaucous Gull's white underparts and pale gray mantle camouflage it against the cloud-filled winter skies as it scans the open waters of the Great Lakes. Its pale plumage also helps birders to distinguish its ghostly figure from other, more numerous, overwintering gull species. • Glaucous Gulls are among the largest gulls in the region, and traditionally fished for their meals or stole food from smaller gulls. More recently, many wintering birds have traded the rigors of hunting for the job of defending plots of garbage at various landfills. • In summer, while other gulls are strolling along local beaches or hanging out in fast-food restaurant parking lots, the Glaucous Gull is far away in the arctic wilderness, though some immature birds may linger well into the summer before drifting back north. The scientific name *hyperboreus* means "of the Far North."

*nonbreeding*

*nonbreeding*

**ID:** *Breeding:* relatively long, heavy, yellow bill has red spot on lower mandible; flattened crown profile; yellow eyes; pink legs; white underparts; very pale gray mantle. *Nonbreeding:* brown-streaked head, neck and breast. *Immature:* dark eyes; pale, black-tipped bill; various plumages have varying amounts of brown flecking on body. *In flight:* larger and paler than all other eastern gulls; tips of primaries are always white.
**Size:** *L* 27 in; *W* 5 ft.
**Status:** uncommon winter visitor from November to April.

**Habitat:** landfills; open water on large lakes and rivers; also bays and ocean.
**Nesting:** does not nest in NY.
**Feeding:** predator, pirate and scavenger; eats mostly fish, crustaceans, mollusks and some seeds; feeds on carrion and at landfills.
**Voice:** high, screechy *kak-kak-kak* calls, similar to Herring Gull's.
**Similar Species:** *Thayer's Gull* (p. 361) and *Iceland Gull* (p. 170): smaller; slightly darker mantle; gray on wing tips. *Herring Gull* (p. 169): slightly smaller; black wing tips; much darker mantle. *Great Black-backed Gull* (p. 173): darker in all plumages.
**Best Sites:** Niagara River Corridor; Robert Moses SP; Cohoes–Crescent–Peebles Island SP; Pt. Lookout–Jones Inlet; Montauk Point SP.

# GREAT BLACK-BACKED GULL

*Larus marinus*

The Great Black-backed Gull's commanding size and bold, aggressive disposition enable it to dominate other gulls, ensuring that it has first dibs at food, whether it is fresh fish or a meal from a landfill. • In recent years, Great Black-backed Gulls have greatly expanded their breeding range to Long Island and southward. In fall and winter, good numbers of these gulls can be found at landfills and in areas of open water. • Like many other North American gulls, the Great Black-backed Gull is a "four-year gull," which means that it goes through various plumage stages until its fourth winter, when it develops its full adult plumage. Most immature gulls have dark streaking, spotting or mottling, which allows them to blend into their surroundings and avoid detection by predators.

*breeding*

**ID:** very large gull. *Breeding:* white overall except for gray underwings and black mantle; pale pinkish legs; light-colored eyes; large, yellow bill has red spot on lower mandible. *Nonbreeding:* may have faintly streaked nape. *Immature:* variable plumage; mottled gray brown, white and black; black bill or pale bill with black tip. *In flight:* large, white spots on tips of primaries; narrow white trailing edge to wings; immature has marbled underwings and dark, narrow tail band.
**Size:** *L* 30 in; *W* 5–5½ ft.
**Status:** present year-round; common breeder from April to June on the Atlantic Coast and in a few places in northern NY; common in winter throughout the state.

**Habitat:** landfills and open water on large lakes and rivers.
**Nesting:** in colonies or isolated pairs; on an island or beach; pair builds a mound of vegetation and debris on the ground, often near rocks; pair incubates 2–3 brown-blotched, olive to buff eggs for 27–28 days.
**Feeding:** opportunistic feeder; finds food by flying, swimming or walking; eats fish, eggs, birds, small mammals, berries, carrion, mollusks, crustaceans, insects and other invertebrates, as well as human food waste; scavenges at landfills.
**Voice:** a harsh *kyow*.
**Similar Species:** *Other gulls* (pp 164–75): smaller; most lack black mantle.
**Best Sites:** Niagara River Corridor; Robert Moses SP; Cohoes–Crescent–Peebles Island SP; Pt. Lookout–Jones Inlet; Montauk Point SP.

# SABINE'S GULL

*Xema sabini*

It is unfortunate that only a few people in New York will ever see this attractive, ternlike gull—the Sabine's Gull is a truly stunning bird. A rarity in our state, this gull can best be observed in fall, when small numbers trickle southward from the Arctic on their way to South Africa and other wintering sites. • The Sabine's Gull shares the same size, shape and head color pattern as the common, black-headed gulls of the genus *Larus*. Like the terns of the genus *Sterna*, it has a buoyant, dipping flight pattern and a forked tail. • Sabine's Gulls feed while in flight, gently dipping down to the water's surface to snatch up prey without landing. • Sir Edward Sabine was a distinguished military man whose primary interests were astronomy and terrestrial magnetism. He joined an expedition to explore the Arctic in 1818, and it was off the west coast of Greenland that he collected a specimen of the gull that was to be named in his honor.

*nonbreeding*

*nonbreeding*

**ID:** yellow-tipped, black bill; dark gray mantle; black feet. *Breeding:* dark, slate gray "hood" trimmed with black. *Nonbreeding:* white head; dark gray nape. *In flight:* distinctive, tricolored, upperwing pattern is gray at base, then white, then black at tip; shallowly forked tail.
**Size:** *L* 13–14 in; *W* 33 in.
**Status:** rare but regular migrant from September to October.

**Habitat:** lakes and large rivers; Atlantic waters.
**Nesting:** does not nest in NY.
**Feeding:** gleans the water's surface while swimming or flying; eats mostly insects, fish and crustaceans.
**Voice:** ternlike *kee-kee;* not frequently heard in migration.
**Similar Species:** *Bonaparte's* (p. 167), *Laughing* (p. 164) and *Black-headed* (p. 166) *gulls:* all lack bold wing pattern, forked tail and yellow-tipped bill.
**Best Sites:** Dunkirk Harbor; Niagara River Corridor; Hamlin Beach SP; Derby Hill; Montauk Point SP.

# BLACK-LEGGED KITTIWAKE

*Rissa tridactyla*

The Black-legged Kittiwake is more closely associated with the marine environment than any other North American gull. The only true gull that is commonly seen at sea, it comes ashore only to breed in noisy, cliff-ledge colonies. This gull is a migrant and winter visitor to New York, and most of the Black-legged Kittiwakes that move through the state migrate well offshore. Even during the most violent storms, these birds remain in open water, floating among massive swells. • Because they spend most of their lives in saltwater environments, Black-legged Kittiwakes have evolved glands above their eyes that enable them to extract and secrete excess salt from the water. • Unlike the majority of gulls, the Black-legged Kittiwake makes its living by fishing rather than by foraging in landfills or near fast-food restaurants. • The name "kittiwake" comes from the call that these gulls make at nesting colonies.

*breeding*

*1st winter*

*nonbreeding*

**ID:** *Breeding:* black legs; gray mantle; white underparts; white head; yellow bill. *Nonbreeding:* gray nape; dark gray smudge behind eye. *Immature:* black bill; wide, black "half-collar"; dark ear patch. *In flight:* black triangle on wing tips; immature has black "M" on upper forewing from wing tip to wing tip and black terminal tail band.

**Size:** *L* 16–18 in; *W* 3 ft.

**Status:** common winter visitor from November to March.

**Habitat:** open water on Great Lakes and Atlantic Ocean.

**Nesting:** does not nest in NY.

**Feeding:** dips to the water's surface to snatch prey; gleans the water's surface or plunges underwater while swimming; prefers small fish; also takes crustaceans, insects and mollusks.

**Voice:** calls are *kittewake* and *kekekek*, given mostly on breeding grounds.

**Similar Species:** *Laughing* (p. 164), *Bonaparte's* (p. 167), *Black-headed* (p. 166) and *Little* (p. 165) *gulls:* all lack the combination of black legs, yellow bill, gray nape and black triangle on wing tips. *Sabine's Gull* (p. 174): immature has gray brown wash on sides and head and lacks dark "M" on wings and mantle.

**Best Sites:** Niagara River Corridor; Derby Hill; Shinnecock Inlet–Dune Rd.; Montauk Point SP; Robert Moses SP.

175

# GULL-BILLED TERN

*Sterna nilotica*

Unlike most members of the tern family, whose diets consist primarily of fish and aquatic invertebrates, the Gull-billed Tern seldom dives for fish and is typically seen flying into the wind, scooping up struggling flying insects in its path. Although it feeds primarily on insects, the heavy, gull-like bill for which this bird is named allows it to capture and consume a wide variety of nontraditional tern foods such as frogs and mice. • In defiance of the persecution once shown to it by humans in some of its traditional saltmarsh nesting sites, this bird has learned to find more secluded nesting areas on islands and even on out-of-reach gravel rooftops. In the late 1800s, it was one of the species most affected by hunters seeking birds and feathers for the millinery trade. The most serious conservation threats today are habitat destruction and disturbance by humans, including recreational activity and beach development. • A cosmopolitan species, the Gull-billed Tern is a widespread though not numerous bird that is found in North and South America, Eurasia, Africa and Australia.

*breeding*

**ID:** heavy, black bill; shallowly forked tail. *Breeding:* black legs, "cap" and nape; pale gray upperparts; white underparts; *Nonbreeding:* white head; dark ear patch; grayish nape patch. *Immature:* similar to nonbreeding adult, but with dark mottling on head and mantle.
**Size:** *L* 14 in; *W* 34 in.
**Status:** rare and local breeder from May to June on Long I.; has only recently begun breeding in NY in very small numbers.
**Habitat:** saltwater marshes, coastal bays, farmlands and open country close to ocean coast; nests on beaches and islands.

**Nesting:** colonial; pair lines a shallow depression in soil, sand or gravel with vegetation, shells or other debris; pair incubates 2–3 darkly spotted, pale buff eggs for 22 days.
**Feeding:** catches insects on the wing, on the ground and on the water's surface; may also eat crustaceans, mollusks, other invertebrates, small amphibians, reptiles and mammals; rarely makes plunging dives.
**Voice:** call is a raspy *kay-weck* or *zah zah zah.*
**Similar Species:** *Other terns* (pp. 177–84): orange or yellow bills; more deeply forked tails.
**Best Sites:** Jamaica Bay Wildlife Refuge; Jones Beach SP; Shinnecock Inlet–Dune Rd.

# CASPIAN TERN

*Sterna caspia*

In size and habits, the mighty Caspian Tern bridges the gulf between the smaller terns and the larger, raucous gulls. It is the largest tern in North America, and its wingbeats are slower and more gull-like than those of most other terns—a trait that can lead birders to confuse it with a gull. However, this tern's distinctive, heavy, red orange bill and forked tail usually reveal its true identity. • Caspian Terns are often seen together with gulls on shoreline sandbars and mudflats in migration or during the breeding season, when they nest in colonies on exposed islands and protected beaches. • The sight of a Caspian Tern foraging for small, schooling fish is impressive. Flying high over open waters, the tern hovers, then suddenly folds its wings and plunges headfirst toward its target. • This species was first collected from the Caspian Sea, hence its name. Caspian Terns are found nesting the world over, in Eurasia, Africa and even Australia.

*breeding*

**ID:** black "cap"; heavy, red orange bill has faint black tip; light gray mantle; black legs; shallowly forked tail; white underparts; long, frosty, pointed wings; dark gray patch on underside of outer primaries. *Nonbreeding:* black "cap" streaked with white.

**Size:** *L* 19–23 in; *W* 4–4½ ft.

**Status:** common breeder in June and July in eastern L. Ontario region; uncommon migrant from April to May and from August to September along the coast; more common migrant on inland lakes.

**Habitat:** *Breeding:* islands in the Great Lakes. *In migration:* wetlands and shorelines of large lakes and rivers.

**Nesting:** in a shallow scrape on bare sand, lightly vegetated soil or gravel; nest is sparsely lined with vegetation, rocks or twigs; pair incubates 1–3 darkly spotted, pale buff eggs for 20–22 days.

**Feeding:** hovers over water and plunges headfirst after small fish, tadpoles and aquatic invertebrates; also feeds by swimming and gleaning at the water's surface.

**Voice:** low, harsh *ca-arr;* loud *kraa-uh.*

**Similar Species:** *Common* (p. 180), *Arctic* (p. 181) and *Forster's* (p. 182) *terns:* much smaller; daintier bills; lack dark underwing patch. *Royal Tern* (p. 178): yellow orange bill; less black on wing tips; unstreaked, white forehead in nonbreeding plumage.

**Best Sites:** Montezuma NWR; Selkirk Shores SP; Cape Vincent–Pt. Peninsula; Verona Beach SP–Sylvan Beach; Shinnecock Inlet–Dune Rd.

# ROYAL TERN

*Sterna maxima*

Fifty years ago, this tern was a casual vagrant to Long Island waters, and its occurrence was almost always the result of birds being blown or carried north by the hurricanes of late summer and fall. Since then, this species has expanded its range northward and sightings are more common. • Royal Terns once nested in very large colonies on the beaches of the southeastern states. Commercial egg collectors took enormous numbers of eggs from these colonies for market and seriously depleted tern populations. By the early 1900s, bird protection laws were passed and governments began preserving some of our coastal beaches. Tern populations rebounded and the Royal Tern now nests in good numbers as far north as Maryland. Every summer, they are seen along Long Island's south shore beaches, with some arriving as early as June, though most arrive later. Sightings of adults feeding juveniles tantalize birders looking for the first New York breeding of this species, but these terns are noted for feeding juveniles well into fall and far away from nesting colonies.

*nonbreeding*

**ID:** pale gray upperparts; white underparts; long, yellow orange bill; dark wedge on tip of upperwing; deeply forked tail; black legs. *Breeding:* black "cap" is frayed at back of head. *Nonbreeding:* lacks black "cap," but has frayed black fringe at back of head. *Juvenile:* dusky version of nonbreeding adult with dusky tail tip; legs may be yellow orange. *In flight:* narrow, dark edge on outer underwing primaries.
**Size:** *L* 20 in; *W* 3½ ft.
**Status:** fairly common coastal visitor from July to September.

**Habitat:** coastal habitats, including sandy beaches, estuaries, saltwater marshes, islands, bays and lagoons.
**Nesting:** does not nest in NY.
**Feeding:** primarily eats small fish and crabs; may also take shrimp, squid and other crustaceans; typically plunges into water from hovering flight; may snatch items from the ground or from the water's surface; may forage at night and far out from shore.
**Voice:** bleating call is a high-pitched *kee-er;* also gives a whistling *turreee.*
**Similar Species:** *Caspian Tern* (p. 177): thick, red orange bill; dark, streaked "cap" in nonbreeding plumage; lacks frayed crest and deeply forked tail; harsh *ka-raa* call.
**Best Sites:** Fire Island National Seashore; Smith Point CP; Shinnecock Inlet–Dune Rd.; Mecox Bay.

# ROSEATE TERN

*Sterna dougallii*

The Roseate Tern can be found worldwide, but outside the tropics it is uncommon or only found locally. In New York, it is considered an endangered species, though there are a couple of breeding colonies on Long Island. • The Roseate Tern often nests in colonies with other terns. It scrapes out a shallow depression for a nest, usually in dense vegetation, but it may build its nest in such human-made structures as tires or wooden boxes. • If you think that you see three terns looking after the same brood, this just may be the case. Unmated birds sometimes try to help out with the parental duties of a nesting pair. Quite often these helpers are driven off by the parents, but occasionally they are welcomed with open wings to form trios or quartets. • This tern is named for the very faint pink blush on its breast in breeding plumage.

*breeding*

**ID:** *Breeding:* black crown and nape; pale gray upperparts; white underparts; faint pink wash on breast; black bill with red base; red orange legs. *Nonbreeding:* white breast; black "cap" extends forward only to eye. *In flight:* long, deeply forked tail; relatively short, straight, narrow wings; quick, stiff wingbeats.

**Size:** *L* 12–13 in; *W* 29 in.

**Status:** endangered; uncommon breeder from May to July on eastern Long I.; migrates in May and from August to September.

**Habitat:** sandy or rocky islands; often in protected bays and estuaries; usually close to shallow water for foraging.

**Nesting:** colonially with other terns; on the ground under cover of vegetation, rocks, driftwood or human-made objects such as tires and wooden boxes; in a shallow scrape; pair incubates 1–4 brown-blotched, creamy white eggs for 21–26 days.

**Feeding:** flies low over water and dives to capture prey; takes mostly small fish and sometimes crustaceans, mollusks and insects.

**Voice:** sharp *keek* or soft, ploverlike *chi-vik* given in flight.

**Similar Species:** *Caspian Tern* (p. 177) and *Royal Tern* (p. 178): larger; long, thick, all-red bills; black legs. *Forster's* (p. 181) and *Common* (p. 180) *terns:* dark wing tips visible in flight; lack rosy wash on breast. *Gulls* (pp. 164–75): either lack black "cap" or black "cap" extends below eye.

**Best Sites:** Jones Beach SP; Fire Island National Seashore; Shinnecock Inlet–Dune Rd.; Orient Point SP.

# COMMON TERN

*Sterna hirundo*

Common Terns patrol the shorelines of lakes and rivers during spring and fall, and settle in large nesting colonies over the summer months, usually on islands. Both males and females perform aerial courtship dances, and for most pairs the nesting season commences when the female accepts her suitor's gracious fish offerings. • Tern colonies are noisy and chaotic, and are often associated with even noisier gull colonies. The most successful colonies seem to be the larger ones, which can number well into the thousands. Should an intruder approach a tern nest, the parent will dive repeatedly, often defecating on the offender. Needless to say, it is best to keep a respectful distance from nesting terns, and from all nesting birds, for that matter. • Terns are effortless fliers, as well as being some of the most impressive long-distance migrants. Once, a Common Tern banded in Great Britain was recovered in Australia.

*breeding*

*breeding*

**Nesting:** colonial; usually on an island with nonvegetated, open areas; in a small scrape lined sparsely with pebbles, vegetation or shells; pair incubates 1–3 variably marked eggs for 20–23 days.

**Feeding:** hovers over water and plunges headfirst after small fish and aquatic invertebrates.

**Voice:** high-pitched, drawn-out *keee-are*, most commonly heard at colonies, but also in foraging flights.

**Similar Species:** *Forster's Tern* (p. 182): gray tail with white outer edges; upper primaries have silvery look; broad, black eye band in nonbreeding plumage. *Arctic Tern* (p. 181): all-red bill; deeply forked tail; grayer underparts; upper primaries lack dark gray wedge; rare in migration. *Caspian Tern* (p. 177): much larger overall; much heavier, red orange bill; dark primary underwing patch.

**Best Sites:** Niagara River Corridor; Verona Beach SP–Sylvan Beach; Montezuma NWR; Jones Beach SP; Shinnecock Inlet–Dune Rd.

**ID:** *Breeding:* black "cap"; thin, red, black-tipped bill; red legs; white rump; white tail with gray outer edges; white underparts. *Nonbreeding:* black nape; lacks black "cap." *In flight:* shallowly forked tail; long, pointed wings; dark gray wedge near lighter gray upperwing tips.

**Size:** *L* 13–16 in; *W* 30 in.

**Status:** threatened; locally common breeder from May to August on Long I. and in western and northern NY; common migrant from April to May and from August to September.

**Habitat:** *Breeding:* islands, breakwaters and beaches. *In migration:* large lakes, open wetlands and slowly moving rivers.

# ARCTIC TERN

*Sterna paradisaea*

Arctic Terns make annual, round-trip migrations from northern breeding grounds to foreign lands and oceans that include South America, Antarctica, Europe, Africa and the Indian Ocean. In some years, an Arctic Tern might fly a distance of 20,000 miles! Because they experience long hours of daylight while on their northern nesting grounds, and long days of sunlight on their wintering grounds, Arctic Terns probably experience more daylight in an average year than most living creatures. • Nesting in the High Arctic, this tern migrates east toward Europe, then flies south down the mid-Atlantic to Antarctica. A few are blown into New York waters by late summer storms. Small numbers breed in New England, though, so there is speculation that New Yorkers should be seeing more Arctic Terns than are reported. Confusion with Common Terns may be a factor.

*nonbreeding*

**ID:** *Breeding:* blood red bill and legs; black "cap" and nape; short neck; white "cheek"; gray underparts; long, white, forked tail extends to wing tips when perched. *Nonbreeding* and *immature:* white underparts; black band through eye and across nape; black bill. *In flight:* appears neckless; deeply forked tail; gray wings with thin, dark trailing edge to underwing.
**Size:** *L* 12 in; *W* 31 in.
**Status:** rare migrant from May to June and from September to October in Atlantic waters.

**Habitat:** open ocean.
**Nesting:** does not nest in NY.
**Feeding:** dives into the water from a stationary hover; preys on small fish and aquatic invertebrates.
**Voice:** harsh, high-pitched, down-slurred *kee kahr;* also utters short, single *kip* notes and rough, agitated call notes.
**Similar Species:** *Common Tern* (p. 180): black-tipped, red orange bill; dark gray wedge on upper primaries; whiter underparts. *Roseate Tern* (p. 179): all-black bill; pure white wings; sometimes light rosy tinge on breast.
**Best Sites:** Montauk Point SP; Orient Point SP.

# FORSTER'S TERN

*Sterna forsteri*

The Forster's Tern so closely resembles the Common Tern that the two often seem indistinguishable to the eyes of many observers. It is usually not until these terns acquire their distinct fall plumages that birders begin to note the Forster's presence. • Most terns are known for their extraordinary ability to catch fish in dramatic headfirst dives, but the Forster's excels at gracefully snatching flying insects in midair. • The Forster's Tern is the only tern that has an exclusively North American breeding distribution. In New York, it is found nesting in colonies in salt-marsh habitat. • In 1834, taxonomist Thomas Nuttall named this species in honor of German naturalist Johann Reinhold Forster, who lived and worked in England and accompanied Captain Cook on his 1772 voyage.

*breeding*

**ID:** *Breeding:* black "cap" and nape; thin, black-tipped, orange bill; orange legs; light gray mantle; pure white underparts; white rump; gray tail with white outer edges. *Nonbreeding:* black band through eye; lacks black "cap." *In flight:* forked, gray tail; long, pointed wings.
**Size:** *L* 14–16 in; *W* 31 in.
**Status:** recent breeder in June in Long I. salt marshes; rare migrant from April to May; common coastal migrant from August to October.
**Habitat:** *Breeding:* salt marshes. *In migration:* lakes and marshes.
**Nesting:** colonial; in a salt marsh atop dense vegetation; occasionally on a muskrat lodge; pair incubates 3 brown-marked, buff to olive eggs for 23–25 days.
**Feeding:** hovers above the water and plunges headfirst after small fish and aquatic invertebrates; catches flying insects and snatches prey from the water's surface.
**Voice:** flight call is a nasal, short *keer keer;* also a grating *tzaap.*
**Similar Species:** *Common Tern* (p. 180): darker red bill and legs; mostly white tail; gray wash on underparts; dark wedge near tip of primaries. *Arctic Tern* (p. 181): lacks black-tipped bill; short, red legs; gray underparts; white tail with gray outer edges. *Caspian Tern* (p. 177): much larger overall; much heavier, red orange bill.
**Best Sites:** Jamaica Bay Wildlife Refuge; Jones Beach SP; Shinnecock Inlet–Dune Rd.; Mecox Bay.

# LEAST TERN

*Sterna antillarum*

Though the Least Tern persists today at scattered sites on Long Island, its plight dramatizes the impact that human activities can have upon birds of the estuarine beaches. Plume hunters harvested huge numbers of these birds in the late 1800s, and human disturbance and recreational, industrial and residential development have since further diminished their breeding habitat. The Least Tern is a protected species in much of its North American range, and numbers have remained stable along the Atlantic Coast and have actually increased in some areas. • As is true for many colonial waterbirds, breeding success varies annually in response to food supply, weather, predation and disturbance. Most colonies are small, with only a couple of dozen birds, and are usually in open, vegetation-free areas of beach. Predation is a significant problem, and feral house cats appear to be a growing issue in the management of these endangered birds.

*breeding*

**ID:** *Breeding:* black "cap" and nape; white forehead; black-tipped, yellow orange bill; yellow orange legs; gray upperparts; white underparts; black wedge on upper side of outer primaries. *Immature:* black eye line; white forehead; dark "cap"; yellow bill and feet. *In flight:* rapid, dashing wingstrokes.

**Size:** *L* 9 in; *W* 20 in.

**Status:** threatened; common and local breeder and migrant from May to September on Long I.

**Habitat:** waters and shores of Long I.

**Nesting:** colonial; on undisturbed flat ground near water; nest is a shallow scraped-out depression often lined with pebbles, grasses or debris; pair incubates 1–3 pale olive to buff eggs, marked with brown and gray, for 20–22 days and raises the young together.

**Feeding:** plunges to or below the water's surface from hovering flight; eats mostly fish, crustaceans and insects; may eat mollusks and other invertebrates; will take insects on the wing, from the ground or from the water's surface.

**Voice:** call is a loud, high-pitched *chirreek!* and *kip kip kip.*

**Similar Species:** *Common Tern* (p. 180) and *Forster's Tern* (p. 182): larger; breeding birds lack white forehead and black-tipped, yellow bill.

**Best Sites:** Jamaica Bay Wildlife Refuge; Jones Beach SP; Caumsett SP; Smith Point CP; Montauk Point SP.

# BLACK TERN

*Chlidonias niger*

*breeding*

Wheeling about in foraging flights, Black Terns pick small minnows from the water's surface or catch flying insects in midair. Black Terns have dominion over the winds and these acrobats slice through the sky with grace even in a stiff wind. When these terns leave our region in August and September, they head for the warmer climes of Central and South America. • Black Terns are finicky nesters and refuse to return to nesting areas that show even slight changes in water level or in the density of emergent vegetation. This selectiveness, coupled with the degradation of marshes across North America, has contributed to a significant decline in populations of this bird over recent decades. Commitment to restoring and protecting valuable wetland habitats may eventually help this bird to reclaim its once-prominent place in New York. • In order to spell this tern's genus name correctly, one must misspell *chelidonias*, the Greek word for "swallow." This bird is named for its swallowlike, darting flight as it pursues insects.

*breeding*

**ID:** *Breeding:* black head and underparts; gray back, tail and wings; white undertail coverts; black bill; reddish black legs.
*Nonbreeding:* white underparts and forehead; molting fall birds may be mottled with brown. *In flight:* long, pointed wings; shallowly forked tail.
**Size:** *L* 9–10 in; *W* 24 in.
**Status:** endangered; local breeder from May to July on the Great Lakes; fairly common migrant in May and from August to September on Long I., large interior lakes and the Great Lakes.

**Habitat:** shallow, freshwater cattail marshes, wetlands, lake edges and sewage ponds with emergent vegetation.
**Nesting:** loosely colonial; pair builds a flimsy nest of dead plant material on floating vegetation, a muddy mound or a muskrat house; pair incubates 3 darkly blotched, olive to pale buff eggs for 21–22 days.
**Feeding:** snatches insects from the air, tall grass and the water's surface; also eats small fish.
**Voice:** greeting call is a shrill, metallic *kik-kik-kik-kik-kik;* typical alarm call is *kreea.*
**Similar Species:** *Other terns* (pp. 176–83): all are light in color, not dark.
**Best Sites:** Braddock Bay; Montezuma NWR; Upper and Lower Lakes WMA; Perch River WMA; Selkirk Shores SP.

# BLACK SKIMMER

*Rynchops niger*

The amazing Black Skimmer is a unique and wonderful bird to observe. Propelling itself through the air on long, swept-back wings, this bird forages by plowing the water just below the surface with its longer lower mandible, patiently waiting for contact with its prey. As soon as a fish touches its submerged scoop, the skimmer's upper mandible slams down on the slippery body, clamping the meal securely within the grasp of the bill. It is the only bird in North America that is equipped with a lower mandible that is longer than its upper mandible. The Black Skimmer also has a vertical pupil like a cat or rattlesnake, designed to reduce the blinding glare of sun-drenched, sandy beaches and reflective ocean water. • The squawking of young skimmers contributes to the loud, chaotic atmosphere of typical breeding colonies. Nestling skimmers caught out in the open will attempt to lie flat or even burrow underneath the sand to elude predatory gulls and crows.

*breeding*

**ID:** black upperparts; white underparts; long, thick, red bill with black tip; lower mandible is longer than upper mandible. *Nonbreeding:* white collar; duller upperparts. *Immature:* dull, mottled brown upperparts. *In flight:* light, graceful flight with head down and wings held above body.

**Size:** *L* 18 in; *W* 3½ ft.

**Status:** special concern; common breeder from May to August on the south shore of Long I.; migrants arrive in April and May and depart in September and October.

**Habitat:** coastal marine habitats including estuaries, lagoons, sheltered bays and inlets.

**Nesting:** colonial; on a beach or sandy island; in a shallow, scraped-out depression in the open; pair, mainly the male, incubates 3–5 darkly blotched, creamy white to buff eggs for 23–25 days; both adults feed the young by regurgitation; family sometimes remains together through winter.

**Feeding:** catches small fish by flying close to the water's surface and skimming the water with its lower mandible; may eat some crustaceans and aquatic invertebrates; feeds mostly in twilight or at night when fish are more active.

**Voice:** call is a quick, croaking, barking *yep*, often repeated; alarm call is a fast, roughly trilled, descending *aaaaw*; begging juveniles utter high-pitched, yipping notes.

**Similar Species:** none.

**Best Sites:** Jamaica Bay Wildlife Refuge; Jones Beach SP; Fire Island National Seashore; Smith Point CP; Shinnecock Inlet–Dune Rd.

# RAZORBILL

*Alca torda*

This bird's name refers to its sharp bill, which is well-adapted to capturing slippery fish. As the Razorbill "flies" underwater with its powerful wings, it may catch several fish in its large mouth in a single dive. One of the larger species of alcids, the Razorbill also routinely supplements its captures with fish pirated from other birds. • Like other alcids, the Razorbill molts all of its feathers at once, rendering it flightless at sea for a few weeks following the breeding season. • Razorbills, as well as Common Murres and Thick-billed Murres, are unique in that each pair raises only a single chick, which leaves the nest before its flight feathers have developed. The chick completes its growth on the water, fed by the male parent only. These flightless adult-chick pairs usually remain alone at sea for several weeks until the chick can fly. • The Razorbill is believed to be the closest living relative of the extinct Great Auk *(Penguinus impennis)*, a very large alcid that was formerly found in New York waters in winter.

breeding

first winter

**ID:** black upperparts; white underparts; tall, laterally compressed bill with 1 vertical, white line; horizontal white line along top of bill; white trailing edge on wings. *Breeding:* black extends down neck. *Nonbreeding:* white "cheek" and throat.
**Size:** *L* 17 in; *W* 26 in.
**Status:** uncommon winter visitor from December to March in Atlantic coastal waters.
**Habitat:** concentrates over offshore shoals and ledges.

**Nesting:** does not nest in NY.
**Feeding:** dives for small fish, small crustaceans and marine worms; dives are usually to depths of 30 ft, but may be to over 300 ft when food is scarce; may steal fish from other birds.
**Voice:** generally silent; sometimes produces a grunting *urrr* call.
**Similar Species:** *Thick-billed Murre* (p. 362), *Common Murre* and *Black Guillemot* (p. 187): thinner bills lack vertical white line. *Dovekie* (p. 362): much smaller; short bill.
**Best Sites:** Pt. Lookout–Jones Inlet; Shinnecock Inlet–Dune Rd.; Montauk Point SP.

# BLACK GUILLEMOT

*Cepphus grylle*

Very rare in New York, the Black Guillemot prefers to feed in shallower water than many other alcids. It makes shallow foraging dives, sometimes turning over rocks along the sea floor in search of prey. • The Black Guillemot has a nearly circumpolar distribution and, in eastern North America, breeds from the Canadian Arctic south to the coast of Maine. Some alcids nest on open ledges on cliffs, but Black Guillemots prefer to nest in holes and cavities in rocky cliff faces. Unlike most alcids, which lay single egg clutches, Black Guillemots sometimes lay two eggs. • The Black Guillemot's common name is appropriate only during the breeding season—in winter this bird's plumage is primarily white. In most of its North American range, this alcid is also known as "Sea Pigeon" because of its white winter plumage and pigeonlike flight.

*nonbreeding*

*nonbreeding*

**ID:** thin, black bill; reddish legs and feet. *Breeding:* black overall with large, white wing patch. *Nonbreeding:* white overall with some black on back, wings and tail. *In flight:* very broad, rounded wings; white underwings; feet trail behind tail.
**Size:** *L* 13 in; *W* 21 in.
**Status:** very rare winter visitor from December to February off eastern Long I.; 1 seen on L. Champlain.

**Habitat:** usually close to shore in relatively shallow water; sometimes far offshore.
**Nesting:** does not nest in NY.
**Feeding:** dives for fish and crustaceans, but also takes mollusks, insects and marine worms; most dives are to depths of about 30 ft, but may dive to 100 ft.
**Voice:** a drawn-out, high-pitched *see-oo* or *swweeeeeer.*
**Similar Species:** *Razorbill* (p. 186): darker upperparts in nonbreeding plumage; lacks distinctive white wing patch.
**Best Sites:** Shinnecock Inlet–Dune Rd.; Montauk Point SP.

187

# ROCK PIGEON

*Columba livia*

Though now feral, Rock Pigeons began as domestic pigeons that were brought to North America from Europe in the early 17th century. Never found far from human habitation, these birds have settled wherever there are cities, towns and farms. • Rock Pigeons are believed to have been domesticated from Eurasian birds in about 4500 BC as a source of meat. Since their domestication, they have been used as message couriers (both Caesar and Napoleon used them), as scientific subjects and even as pets. One of the most intensively studied birds, much of our understanding of bird migration, avian flight mechanics, endocrinology, navigation and sensory perception derives from experiments involving Rock Pigeons. • All members of the pigeon family, including doves, feed "milk" to their young. Because birds lack mammary glands, it is not true milk, but a nutritious liquid produced by glands in the bird's crop. The chicks insert their bills down the adult's throat to eat the thick, protein-rich fluid. • Until 2003, this bird was known as "Rock Dove."

**ID:** color is highly variable (iridescent blue gray, red, white or tan); usually has white rump and orange feet; dark-tipped tail. *In flight:* holds wings in deep "V" while gliding.
**Size:** *L* 12–13 in; *W* 28 in.
**Status:** abundant year-round resident, except in mountains and heavily forested areas.
**Habitat:** urban areas, railroad yards and agricultural areas; high cliffs provide a more natural habitat for some.

**Nesting:** on a ledge in a barn or on a cliff, bridge, building or tower; flimsy nest is built from sticks, grass and assorted vegetation; pair incubates 2 white eggs for 16–19 days; pair feeds the young "pigeon milk"; may raise broods year-round.
**Feeding:** gleans the ground for waste grain, seeds and fruits; occasionally eats insects.
**Voice:** soft, cooing *coorrr-coorrr-coorrr*.
**Similar Species:** *Mourning Dove* (p. 189): smaller; slimmer; pale brown plumage; long wings and tail.
**Best Sites:** widespread; Durand-Eastman Park (Rochester); Cohoes–Crescent–Peebles Island SP; Central Park (NYC); Prospect Park (NYC).

# MOURNING DOVE

*Zenaida macroura*

The soft cooing of the Mourning Dove that filters through our broken woodlands, farmlands and suburban parks and gardens is often confused with the muted sounds of a hooting owl. Tracking down the source of these calls, however, usually reveals one or two doves perched upon a fence, tree branch or utility wire. • The Mourning Dove is one of the most abundant and widespread native birds in North America and one of the most popular game birds. This species has benefited from human-induced changes to the landscape, and its numbers and distribution have increased since the continent was settled. It is encountered in both rural and urban habitats, but avoids heavily forested areas. • Despite its fragile look, the Mourning Dove is a swift, direct flier whose wings often whistle as the bird cuts through the air at high speed. When it bursts into flight, the dove's wings clap above and below its body. • This bird's common name reflects its sad, cooing song.

**ID:** buffy, gray brown plumage; small head; long, white-trimmed, tapering tail; sleek body; dark, shiny patch below ear; dull red legs; dark bill; pale rosy underparts; black spots on upperwing.
**Size:** *L* 11–13 in; *W* 18 in.
**Status:** common year-round resident; breeds from March to October.

**Habitat:** open woodlands, riparian woodlands, woodlots, forest edges, agricultural and suburban areas and open parks.
**Nesting:** in a shrub or tree, occasionally on the ground; female builds a fragile, shallow platform nest from twigs supplied by the male; pair incubates 2 white eggs for 14 days; young are fed "pigeon milk."
**Feeding:** gleans the ground and vegetation for seeds; visits feeders.
**Voice:** mournful, soft, slow *oh-woe-woe-woe*.
**Similar Species:** *Rock Pigeon* (p. 188): stockier; white rump; shorter tail; iridescent neck.
**Best Sites:** Durand-Eastman Park (Rochester); Stewart Park–Cayuga L.; Saratoga National Historical Park; Central Park (NYC).

# MONK PARAKEET

*Myiopsitta monachus*

Originally from South America, the Monk Parakeet has been introduced throughout the world, mostly by irresponsible pet owners. The boom of the exotic pet industry in the late 1960s led to the introduction of this bird to North American urban parks, and it appeared in New York in about 1968. Unlike most parrots, this bird originated in the more temperate regions of South America, and therefore can survive in the North American climate. It is considered an agricultural pest in its native regions, and fears that it would devastate crops in the U.S. led to attempts to eradicate the species in the 1970s. These attempts failed, and in 1996 the Monk Parakeet was added to the New York State checklist. • The Monk Parakeet is the only species in the parrot family to nest communally. Other parrots use nest cavities, but Monk Parakeets build complex structures of sticks and grass in trees or atop utility poles. These structures sometimes house as many as 20 pairs of birds and are used year-round. • In the pet world, these birds are known as "Quaker Parakeets."

**ID:** green upperparts; grayish white underparts and forehead; greenish yellow belly band; blue outer wings; pink bill; long, green tail; gray legs and feet.
**Size:** *L* 11–12 in; *W* 19–20 in.
**Status:** localized year-round resident in New York City and on Long I.; escapes occasionally reported elsewhere.

**Habitat:** treed parks and backyards; visits feeders in winter.
**Nesting:** on a pole or high up in a tree; a group of parakeets builds a large, multi-compartment, communal nest of twigs, sticks and grass; each pair has an "apartment"; pair incubates 6–8 white eggs for 25–30 days; raises 2 broods each year; juveniles may stay to help with new broods.
**Voice:** rough chattering and shrieking.
**Similar Species:** none.
**Best Sites:** Brooklyn College Campus and the south end of Whitestone Bridge (NYC).

# BLACK-BILLED CUCKOO

*Coccyzus erythropthalmus*

Shrubby field edges, hedgerows, tangled riparian thickets and abandoned, overgrown fields provide the elusive Black-billed Cuckoo with its preferred nesting haunts. Though this bird is not particularly rare in New York, it remains an enigma to many would-be observers. Arriving in mid-May, this cuckoo quietly hops, flits and skulks through low, dense, deciduous vegetation in its secretive search for sustenance. Only when vegetation is in full bloom will males issue their loud, long, irregular calls, advertising to females that it is time to nest. After a brief courtship, newly joined Black-billed Cuckoo pairs construct a makeshift nest, incubate the eggs and raise their young, after which they promptly return to their covert lives. • The Black-billed Cuckoo is one of only a few birds that thrive on hairy caterpillars, particularly tent caterpillars. There is even evidence to suggest that populations of this bird increase when a caterpillar infestation occurs. • This cuckoo is reluctant to fly more than a short distance during nesting, but it will migrate as far as northwestern South America to avoid North American winters.

**ID:** brown upperparts; white underparts; long, white-spotted undertail; dark, downcurved bill; reddish eye ring; gray legs and feet.

**Size:** *L* 11–13 in; *W* 18 in.

**Status:** common breeder from May to August; migrants arrive in May and leave by October.

**Habitat:** dense second-growth woodlands, shrubby areas and thickets; often in tangled riparian areas and abandoned farmlands with low deciduous vegetation and adjacent open areas.

**Nesting:** in a shrub or small deciduous tree; flimsy nest of twigs is lined with grass and other vegetation; occasionally lays eggs in other birds' nests; pair incubates 2–5 pale blue green eggs for 10–14 days.

**Feeding:** gleans hairy caterpillars from leaves, branches and trunks; also eats other insects and berries.

**Voice:** fast, repeated *cu-cu-cu* or *cu-cu-cu-cu-cu;* also a series of *ca, cow* and *coo* notes.

**Similar Species:** *Yellow-billed Cuckoo* (p. 192): yellow bill; rufous tinge to primaries; larger, more prominent, white undertail spots; lacks red eye ring. *Mourning Dove* (p. 189): short, straight bill; pointed, triangular tail; buffy, gray brown plumage; black spots on upperwing.

**Best Sites:** Letchworth SP; Howland Island WMA; Saratoga SP; Bashakill WMA; Caumsett SP.

# YELLOW-BILLED CUCKOO

*Coccyzus americanus*

Most of the time, the Yellow-billed Cuckoo skillfully negotiates its tangled home within impenetrable, deciduous undergrowth in silence, relying on obscurity for survival. However, for a short period during nesting, the male cuckoo tempts fate by issuing a barrage of loud, rhythmic courtship calls. Some people have suggested that the cuckoo has a propensity for calling on dark, cloudy days in late spring and early summer. It is even called "Rain Crow" in some parts of its North American range. • The Yellow-billed Cuckoo's diet is varied. In addition to consuming large quantities of hairy caterpillars, these birds feast on wild berries, young frogs and newts, small bird eggs and a variety of insects, including beetles, grasshoppers and cicadas. • Unlike distantly related Eurasian cuckoos, which lay their eggs only in other birds' nests, neither of the North American cuckoos is considered to be a "nest parasite." • Some Yellow-billed Cuckoos migrate as far south as Argentina for the winter.

**Nesting:** in a deciduous shrub or small tree, within 7 ft of the ground; flimsy platform of twigs is lined with roots and grass; pair incubates 3–4 pale bluish green eggs for 9–11 days.

**Feeding:** gleans insect larvae, especially hairy caterpillars, from deciduous vegetation; also eats berries, small fruits, small amphibians and occasionally the eggs of small birds.

**Voice:** long series of deep, hollow *kuks,* slowing near the end: *kuk-kuk-kuk-kuk kuk kop kow kowlp kowlp.*

**Similar Species:** *Black-billed Cuckoo* (p. 191): all-black bill; lacks rufous tinge on primaries; less prominent, white undertail spots; red eye ring. *Mourning Dove* (p. 189): short, straight bill; pointed, triangular tail; buffy, gray brown plumage; black spots on upperwing.

**Best Sites:** Michigan Hollow–Spencer Marsh; Saratoga National Historical Park; Bashakill WMA; Sterling Forest SP; Heckscher SP.

**ID:** olive brown upperparts; white underparts; downcurved bill with black upper mandible and yellow lower mandible; yellow eye ring; long tail with large, white spots on underside; rufous tinge on primaries.
**Size:** *L* 11–13 in; *W* 18 in.
**Status:** localized breeder from May to August in central and southern NY; migrants arrive in May and leave by October.
**Habitat:** semi-open deciduous habitats; dense tangles and thickets at the edges of orchards, urban parks, agricultural fields and roadways; sometimes woodlots.

# BARN OWL

*Tyto alba*

The haunting look of this nocturnal hunter has long inspired superstitions. In truth, the dedicated hunting efforts of these owls help to keep farmlands and even city yards free from undesirable rodents. • Like the House Sparrow and Rock Pigeon, the Barn Owl has found success by associating with urban and agricultural areas. Its nocturnal habits, taste for small rodents and general tolerance of humans has allowed this adaptable bird to prosper on six continents. It is the most widespread of all the owl species and one of the most widespread of all land birds. • At the northern end of its range in New York, the Barn Owl is not common here. As well, modern farming practices have diminished the Barn Owl's foraging habitat locally. • Though some owls hunt by day as well as by night, the Barn Owl is almost entirely nocturnal and is thought to have the most accurate hearing of any animal.

**Habitat:** roosts and nests in cliffs, hollow trees, caves, barns and other unoccupied structures; hunts in open areas, including agricultural fields, pastures, lawns, marshy meadows, open beach edges or open streamsides.

**Nesting:** in a natural or artificial cavity, often in a sheltered hollow of a building; may use an artificial nest box; no actual nest is built; female incubates 4–7 whitish eggs for 32–34 days; male feeds female during incubation.

**Feeding:** forages mainly at night in low flight or from a perch; eats mostly small mammals, especially rodents; also takes small numbers of snakes, birds and large insects; rarely takes frogs and fish; can locate prey by sound alone.

**Voice:** calls include harsh, raspy screeches and hisses; also makes metallic, bill-snapping sounds.

**ID:** white, heart-shaped facial disc; dark eyes; pale bill; golden brown upperparts spotted with black and gray; black spotting on creamy white underparts; long legs; white undertail and underwings; females are darker and have more spotting on underparts. *In flight:* buoyant, somewhat uneven flight; deep, rather slow wingbeats.

**Size:** *L* 16 in; *W* 3½ ft.

**Status:** rare year-round resident upstate; more common in southern NY and Long I.; breeds mainly from April to June, but there are records in all months.

**Similar Species:** *Short-eared Owl* (p. 199): yellow eyes set in black sockets; vertical streaks on breast and belly; black "wrist" patches; erratic flight pattern. *Barred Owl* (p. 197): horizontal barring on neck and upper breast; vertical belly streaking; darker facial disc.

**Best Sites:** Shawangunk Grasslands NWR; Jamaica Bay Wildlife Refuge; Jones Beach SP.

# EASTERN SCREECH-OWL
*Megascops asio*

The diminutive Eastern Screech-Owl is a year-round resident of deciduous woodlands, but its presence is rarely detected. Most screech-owls sleep away the daylight hours snuggled safely inside a tree cavity or an artificial nest box. An encounter with a screech-owl is usually the result of a sound cue—the noise of mobbing hordes of chickadees or squawking gangs of Blue Jays may alert you to an owl's presence during daylight hours. Smaller birds that mob a screech-owl during the day often do so after losing a family member during the night. More commonly, you will find this owl by listening for the male's eerie, "horse-whinny" courtship calls and loud, spooky, nocturnal trills. • Despite its small size, the Eastern Screech-Owl is an adaptable hunter. It has a varied diet that ranges from insects, small rodents, earthworms and fish to birds larger than itself. • Unique among the owls found in our region, Eastern Screech-Owls are polychromatic: they show red or gray color morphs. Mixed-color pairs may produce young that are an intermediate buff brown.

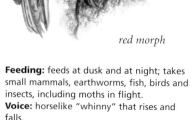

*red morph*

**ID:** short "ear" tufts; reddish or grayish overall; dark, vertical breast streaking; yellow eyes; pale grayish bill; large feet.

**Size:** *L* 8–9 in; *W* 20–22 in.

**Status:** fairly common year-round resident; absent at higher elevations of the Catskills and Adirondacks; breeds from March to June.

**Habitat:** mature deciduous forests, open deciduous woodlands, riparian woodlands, orchards and shade trees with natural cavities; also city parks and cemeteries.

**Nesting:** in a natural cavity or artificial nest box; no nest material is added; female incubates 4–5 white eggs for about 26 days; male brings food to the female during incubation.

**Feeding:** feeds at dusk and at night; takes small mammals, earthworms, fish, birds and insects, including moths in flight.

**Voice:** horselike "whinny" that rises and falls.

**Similar Species:** *Northern Saw-whet Owl* (p. 200): lacks "ear" tufts; long, reddish streaks on white underparts. *Long-eared Owl* (p. 198): much longer, slimmer body; longer, close-set "ear" tufts; rusty facial disc; mottled brown plumage. *Great Horned Owl* (p. 195): much larger; lacks vertical breast streaks.

**Best Sites:** Braddock Bay; Stewart Park–Cayuga L.; Five Rivers Environmental Education Center; Pelham Bay Park (NYC); Heckscher SP.

# GREAT HORNED OWL

*Bubo virginianus*

The familiar *hoo-hoo-hoooo hoo-hoo* that resounds through campgrounds, suburban parks and farmyards is the call of the adaptable and superbly camouflaged Great Horned Owl. These owls often begin their courtship as early as January, at which time their hooting calls make them quite conspicuous. By February and March, females are already incubating their eggs.

The pair continues to feed the young, both in and out of the nest, well into autumn. • This formidable, primarily nocturnal hunter uses its acute hearing and powerful vision to hunt a wide variety of prey. Almost any small creature that moves is fair game for the Great Horned Owl. However, it apparently has a poorly developed sense of smell, which might explain why it is the only consistent predator of skunks. • The large eyes of an owl are fixed in place, so to look up, down or to the side, the bird must move its entire head. As an adaptation to this situation, an owl can swivel its neck 270 degrees to either side and 90 degrees up and down!

**Habitat:** fragmented forests, agricultural areas, woodlots, meadows, riparian woodlands, wooded suburban parks and the wooded edges of landfills and town dumps.

**Nesting:** in the abandoned stick nest of another bird; may also nest on a cliff; adds little or no material to the nest; mostly the female incubates 2–3 dull whitish eggs for 28–35 days.

**Feeding:** mostly nocturnal; may hunt at dusk or by day in winter; usually swoops from a perch; eats small mammals, birds, snakes, amphibians and even fish.

**Voice:** call during the breeding season is 4–6 deep hoots: *hoo-hoo-hoooo hoo-hoo* or *eat-my-food, I'll-eat-you;* male also gives higher-pitched hoots.

**Similar Species:** *Long-eared Owl* (p. 198): smaller; thinner; vertical breast streaks; "ear" tufts are close together. *Eastern Screech-Owl* (p. 194): much smaller; vertical breast streaks. *Short-eared Owl* (p. 199) and *Barred Owl* (p. 197): no "ear" tufts.

**Best Sites:** Iroquois NWR–Tonawanda WMA–Oak Orchard WMA; Montezuma NWR; Saratoga National Historical Park; Partridge Run WMA; Connetquot River SP.

**ID:** yellow eyes; tall "ear" tufts set wide apart; fine, horizontal barring on breast; facial disc is outlined in black and is often rusty orange in color; white "chin"; heavily mottled, gray, brown and black upperparts; overall plumage varies from light gray to dark brown.

**Size:** *L* 18–25 in; *W* 3½–4 ft.

**Status:** locally common year-round resident; breeds from late January to May; numbers are augmented by winter visitors.

# SNOWY OWL

*Bubo scandiacus*

When the mercury drops and the landscape hardens in winter's icy grip, ghostly white Snowy Owls appear on fence posts, utility poles, fields and lakeshores throughout the region. These birds blend in perfectly against almost any flat, open, snow-covered landscape. Snow cover is not a prerequisite for a Snowy Owl visit—many of these birds perch conspicuously on earth-tone fields in snowless portions of our region each winter. • Feathered to the toes, a Snowy Owl can remain active at cold temperatures that often send other owls to the woods for shelter. • As Snowy Owls age, their plumage becomes lighter in color—older males are often pure white. • When lemming and vole populations in the Arctic crash, large numbers of Snowy Owls venture south in search of food. • Snowy Owls are recognizable in the oldest prehistoric cave art and may have inspired the first bird painting.

**ID:** predominantly white; yellow eyes; black bill and talons; no "ear" tufts. *Male:* almost entirely white with very little dark flecking. *Female:* prominent dark barring or flecking on breast and upperparts. *Immature:* heavier barring than adult female.
**Size:** *L* 20–27 in; *W* 4½–6 ft (female is noticeably larger).
**Status:** irruptive winter visitor, mostly from November to March; absent some years, present in good numbers in others.

**Habitat:** open country, including croplands, meadows, airports and lakeshores; often perches on fence posts, buildings and utility poles.
**Nesting:** does not nest in NY.
**Feeding:** swoops from a perch, often punching through the snow to take mice, voles, grouse, hares, weasels and, rarely, songbirds and waterbirds.
**Voice:** quiet in winter.
**Similar Species:** no other owl in the region is largely white and lacks "ear" tufts.
**Best Sites:** Montezuma NWR; Cape Vincent–Pt. Peninsula; Essex-Westport; Jones Beach SP; Shinnecock Inlet–Dune Rd.

# BARRED OWL

*Strix varia*

Each spring, the memorable sound of courting Barred Owls echoes through our forests: *Who cooks for you? Who cooks for you all?* The escalating laughs, hoots and gargling howls reinforce the bond between pairs. At the height of courtship and when raising young, a pair of Barred Owls may continue their calls well into daylight hours, and they may hunt actively day and night. They also tend to be more vocal during early evening or early morning when the moon is full and the air is calm. • Barred Owls are usually most active between midnight and 4 AM, when the forest floor rustles with the movements of mice, voles and shrews. These owls have relatively weak talons, so they prey on smaller animals such as voles. They may also take small birds and even smaller owls. • Barred Owls were once inhabitants of the moist, deciduous woodlands and swamps that covered our region, but their numbers have declined with the destruction of these habitats.

**ID:** dark eyes; horizontal barring on neck and upper breast; vertical streaking on belly; pale bill; no "ear" tufts; mottled, dark gray brown plumage.

**Size:** *L* 17–24 in; *W* 3½–4 ft.

**Status:** locally common year-round resident; breeds from March to May; very rare on Long I.

**Habitat:** mature deciduous and mixedwood forests, especially in dense stands near swamps, streams and lakes.

**Nesting:** in a natural tree cavity, broken treetop or abandoned stick nest; adds very little material to the nest; female incubates 2–3 white eggs for 28–33 days; male feeds the female during incubation.

**Feeding:** nocturnal; swoops down on prey from a perch; eats mice, voles and squirrels; also takes amphibians and small birds.

**Voice:** most characteristic of all the owls; loud, hooting, rhythmic, laughing call is heard mostly in spring but also throughout the year: *Who cooks for you? Who cooks for you all?*; frequently called "Old Eight-Hooter."

**Similar Species:** *Great Horned Owl* (p. 195): "ear" tufts; yellow eyes. *Short-eared Owl* (p. 199): yellow eyes; lacks horizontal barring on upper breast.

**Best Sites:** Howland Island WMA; Whetstone Gulf SP; Ferd's Bog; Saratoga National Historical Park; Partridge Run WMA.

# LONG-EARED OWL
*Asio otus*

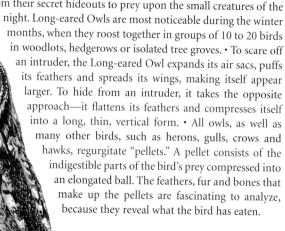

Long-eared Owls are widespread throughout the state, but are easily overlooked because of their cryptic plumage and reclusive habits. Only at dusk do these owls emerge from their secret hideouts to prey upon the small creatures of the night. Long-eared Owls are most noticeable during the winter months, when they roost together in groups of 10 to 20 birds in woodlots, hedgerows or isolated tree groves. • To scare off an intruder, the Long-eared Owl expands its air sacs, puffs its feathers and spreads its wings, making itself appear larger. To hide from an intruder, it takes the opposite approach—it flattens its feathers and compresses itself into a long, thin, vertical form. • All owls, as well as many other birds, such as herons, gulls, crows and hawks, regurgitate "pellets." A pellet consists of the indigestible parts of the bird's prey compressed into an elongated ball. The feathers, fur and bones that make up the pellets are fascinating to analyze, because they reveal what the bird has eaten.

**ID:** long, relatively close-set "ear" tufts; slim body; vertical belly markings; rusty brown facial disc; mottled brown plumage; yellow eyes; white around bill.

**Size:** *L* 13–16 in; *W* 3 ft.

**Status:** rare and local breeder from March to May; fairly common migrant and winter resident from November to March.

**Habitat:** *Breeding:* dense coniferous, mixed and riparian forests and areas with tall shrubs. *Winter:* woodlots, dense riparian woodlands, hedgerows and isolated tree groves in meadows, fields, cemeteries, farmyards and parks.

**Nesting:** often in an abandoned hawk or crow nest; female incubates 2–6 white eggs for 26–28 days; male feeds the female during incubation.

**Feeding:** nocturnal; flies low, pouncing on prey from the air; eats mostly voles and mice; occasionally takes shrews, moles, small rabbits, small birds and amphibians.

**Voice:** breeding call is a low, soft, ghostly *quoo-quoo;* alarm call is *weck-weck-weck;* also issues various shrieks, hisses, whistles, barks, hoots and dovelike coos.

**Similar Species:** *Great Horned Owl* (p. 195): much larger; wider-set "ear" tufts; stout body; rounder face. *Short-eared Owl* (p. 199): lacks long "ear" tufts. *Eastern Screech-Owl* (p. 194): much shorter, stout body; shorter, wider-set "ear" tufts.

**Best Sites:** Braddock Bay; Cape Vincent–Pt. Peninsula; Pelham Bay Park (NYC); Jones Beach SP; Napeague Bay–Hither Hills SP.

# SHORT-EARED OWL

*Asio flammeus*

Like the Snowy Owl of the Arctic, the Short-eared Owl lacks conspicuous "ear" tufts and fills a niche in open country that has been left unoccupied by forest-dwelling owls. In New York, the Short-eared Owl occupies habitats such as wet meadows, marshes, fields and bogs. • In spring, pairs perform visually dramatic courtship dances. Courting pairs fly together, and the male claps his wings together on each downstroke as he periodically performs short dives. Short-eared Owls do not "hoot" like forest-dwelling owls, perhaps because visual displays are a more effective means of communication in open environments. • As with many other predators, Short-eared Owl populations grow and decline over a period of years in response to dramatic fluctuations in prey availability. Cold weather and decreases in small mammal populations occasionally force large numbers of these owls, especially immature birds, to become temporary nomads, often sending them to areas well outside their usual range.

**ID:** yellow eyes set in black sockets; heavy, vertical streaking on buff belly; dark streaks on tawny upperparts; short, inconspicuous "ear" tufts. *In flight:* dark "wrist" crescents; deep wingbeats; long wings.

**Size:** *L* 13–17 in; *W* 3–4 ft.

**Status:** endangered; rare and local breeder from April to May; fairly common migrant and winter visitor from November to March.

**Habitat:** open areas, including grasslands, wet meadows, marshes, fields, airports and forest clearings.

**Nesting:** on wet ground in an open area; a slight depression is sparsely lined with grass; female incubates 4–7 white eggs for 24–28 days; male feeds the female during incubation.

**Feeding:** forages in low flights over marshes, wet meadows and tall vegetation; pounces on prey from the air; eats mostly voles and other small rodents; also takes insects, small birds and amphibians.

**Voice:** generally quiet; produces a soft *toot-toot-toot* during the breeding season; also squeals and barks like a small dog.

**Similar Species:** *Long-eared Owl* (p. 198) and *Great Horned Owl* (p. 195): long "ear" tufts; rarely hunt during the day. *Barred Owl* (p. 197): dark eyes; horizontal barring on upper breast; nocturnal hunter.

**Best Sites:** Nation's Road Grassland; Cape Vincent–Pt. Peninsula; Ft. Edward Grassland; Shawangunk Grasslands NWR; Jones Beach SP.

# NORTHERN SAW-WHET OWL

*Aegolius acadicus*

The tiny Northern Saw-whet Owl is an opportunistic hunter, taking whatever it can, whenever it can. If temperatures are below freezing and prey is abundant, this small owl may choose to catch more than it can eat in a single sitting.

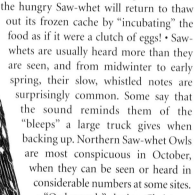

The extra food is usually stored in a tree, where it quickly freezes. When hunting efforts fail, the hungry Saw-whet will return to thaw out its frozen cache by "incubating" the food as if it were a clutch of eggs! • Saw-whets are usually heard more than they are seen, and from midwinter to early spring, their slow, whistled notes are surprisingly common. Some say that the sound reminds them of the "bleeps" a large truck gives when backing up. Northern Saw-whet Owls are most conspicuous in October, when they can be seen or heard in considerable numbers at some sites. • "Owl prowls" during Christmas Bird Counts frequently concentrate much energy on Northern Saw-whets.

**ID:** small body; large, rounded head; pale, unbordered facial disc; dark bill; vertical, rusty streaks on underparts; white-spotted, brown upperparts; white-streaked forehead; short tail. *Juvenile:* white patch between eyes; rich brown head and breast; buff brown belly.

**Size:** *L* 7–9 in; *W* 17–22 in.

**Status:** uncommon and local breeder from March to June; fairly common migrant and winter visitor from October to March.

**Habitat:** pure and mixed coniferous and deciduous forests; wooded city parks and ravines.

**Nesting:** in an abandoned woodpecker cavity, natural tree hollow or artificial nest box; female incubates 5–6 white eggs for 27–29 days; male feeds the female during incubation.

**Feeding:** swoops down on prey from a perch; eats mostly mice and voles; also takes larger insects, songbirds, shrews, moles and occasionally amphibians; may cache food.

**Voice:** whistled, evenly spaced notes repeated about 100 times per minute: *whew-whew-whew-whew.*

**Similar Species:** *Boreal Owl:* pale bill; white spotting on black forehead; dark, vertical "eyebrow"; dark border to facial disc; juvenile has chocolate brown breast. *Eastern Screech-Owl* (p. 194): "ear" tufts.

**Best Sites:** Braddock Bay; Cape Vincent–Pt. Peninsula; Pelham Bay Park (NYC); Jones Beach SP; Napeague Bay–Hither Hills SP.

# COMMON NIGHTHAWK

*Chordeiles minor*

Each May and June, the male Common Nighthawk flies high above forest clearings, lakeshores and townsites, gaining elevation in preparation for the climax of his noisy aerial dance. From a great height, the male dives swiftly, then thrusts his wings forward in a final braking action as he strains to pull out of the steep dive. This quick thrust of the wings produces a deep, hollow *vroom* that attracts female nighthawks. • Like other members of the nightjar family, the Common Nighthawk is adapted for catching insects in midair: its gaping mouth is surrounded by feather shafts that funnel insects into its mouth. • Common Nighthawks generally less nocturnal than other nightjars, but they still spend most of the daylight hours resting on a tree limb or on the ground. These birds have very short legs and small feet, and sit along the length of a tree branch, rather than across the branch as do most perching birds.

**ID:** cryptic, mottled plumage; barred underparts. *Male:* white throat. *Female:* buff throat. *In flight:* bold, white "wrist" patches on long, pointed wings; shallowly forked, barred tail; erratic flight.
**Size:** *L* 8½–10 in; *W* 24 in.
**Status:** special concern; widespread but local breeder from May to July; spring migrants arrive in May; common fall migrant from August to September.
**Habitat:** *Breeding:* forest openings, burns, bogs, rocky outcroppings, gravel rooftops and sometimes fields with sparse cover or bare patches. *In migration:* anywhere large numbers of flying insects can be found; usually roosts in trees, often near water.
**Nesting:** on bare ground; no nest is built; female incubates 2 heavily speckled, creamy white eggs for about 19 days; both adults feed the young.
**Feeding:** primarily at dawn and dusk; catches insects in flight, often high in the air; may fly around street lights at night to catch prey attracted to the light; eats mosquitoes, blackflies, midges, beetles, flying ants, moths and other flying insects.
**Voice:** frequently repeated, nasal *peent peent.*
**Similar Species:** *Whip-poor-will* (p. 203) and *Chuck-will's-widow* (p. 202): less common; found in forests; shorter, rounder wings; rounded tails; lack white "wrist" patches.
**Best Sites:** *Breeding:* best found over cities, such as Rochester, Syracuse and Binghampton. *In migration:* Cape Vincent–Pt. Peninsula; Saratoga Natural Historical Park; Five Rivers Environmental Education Center; Shawangunk Grasslands NWR.

# CHUCK-WILL'S-WIDOW
*Caprimulgus carolinensis*

During daylight, you would be lucky to see this perfectly camouflaged bird roosting on the furrowed bark of a horizontal tree limb or sitting among scattered leaves on the ground. Even during nesting it is virtually undetectable: this bird incubates its eggs and raises its young on the forest floor. At dusk, however, the Chuck-will's-widow is easily detected as it calls its own name while it patrols the evening skies for flying insects. • Since the mid-1800s, the Chuck-will's-widow has expanded its range northward and eastward. This bird's core range is in the hot, humid southeastern U.S., and it is at the northern limit of its range in southern New York. Only a few pairs currently nest in the state, mostly in and around Long Island's pine barrens. • The Chuck-will's-widow is the largest North American nightjar.

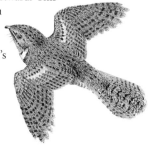

**ID:** mottled, brown-and-buff body with overall reddish tinge; pale brown to buff throat; whitish "necklace"; dark breast; long, rounded tail. *Male:* outer tail feathers have white inner webs.
**Size:** *L* 12 in; *W* 26 in.
**Status:** rare and local breeder from May to June on Long I.; migrants arrive in May and depart in August and September.
**Habitat:** riparian woodlands, swamp edges and deciduous and pine woodlands.

**Nesting:** on bare ground; no nest is built; female incubates 2 heavily blotched, creamy white or pinkish eggs for about 21 days and raises the young alone.
**Feeding:** catches insects on the wing or by hawking; eats beetles, moths and other large flying insects.
**Voice:** 4 loud, whistled notes, often paraphrased as *chuck-will's-widow.*
**Similar Species:** *Whip-poor-will* (p. 203): smaller; grayer overall; "necklace" contrasts with black throat; male shows much more white in tail feathers; female's dark tail feathers are bordered with buff on outer tips. *Common Nighthawk* (p. 201): forked tail; white "wrist" patches on wings; male has white throat; female has buff throat.
**Best Sites:** Jones Beach SP; Connetquot River SP.

# WHIP-POOR-WILL

*Caprimulgus vociferus*

This nocturnal hunter fills the late evening with calls of its own name: *whip-poor-will*. Although the Whip-poor-will is heard throughout many of the open woodlands in New York, this cryptic bird is rarely seen. Because of its camouflaged plumage, nocturnal habits and secretive nesting behavior, a hopeful observer must literally stumble upon a Whip-poor-will to see it. Only occasionally is this bird seen roosting on an exposed tree branch or alongside a quiet road. • The Whip-poor-will is one of three members of the nightjar, or "goatsucker," family found in the state. Birds in this family were named "goatsuckers" during the days of Aristotle because there was a widely believed superstition that they would suck milk from the udders of female goats, causing the goats to go blind! • Within days of hatching, young Whip-poor-wills scurry away from their nest in search of protective cover. For the first 20 days after hatching, until the young are able to fly, the parents feed them regurgitated insects.

**ID:** mottled, gray brown overall with black flecking; reddish tinge on rounded wings; black throat; long, rounded tail. *Male:* white "necklace"; white outer tail feathers. *Female:* buff "necklace."

**Size:** *L* 9–10 in; *W* 16–20 in.
**Status:** special concern; fairly common but local breeder from May to June on the coastal plain and in the Adirondacks and Catskills; migrants arrive in May and depart in August and September.
**Habitat:** open deciduous and pine woodlands; often along forest edges.
**Nesting:** on the ground, often in leaf or pine needle litter; no nest is built; female incubates 2 gray-blotched, whitish eggs for 19–21 days; both adults raise the young.
**Feeding:** almost entirely nocturnal; catches insects in flight, often high in the air; eats mosquitoes, blackflies, midges, beetles and other flying insects; particularly partial to moths; some grasshoppers are taken and swallowed whole.
**Voice:** loud, whistled *whip-poor-will*, with emphasis on the *will*.
**Similar Species:** *Chuck-will's-widow* (p. 202): larger; pale brown to buff throat; darker breast; more reddish overall; much less white on male's tail; different call. *Common Nighthawk* (p. 201): shallowly forked, barred tail; longer, pointed wings with white "wrist" patches; male has white throat; female has buff throat.
**Best Sites:** Perch River WMA; Saratoga L.; Connetquot River SP; Southaven CP–Wertheim NWR.

# CHIMNEY SWIFT

*Chaetura pelagica*

Chimney Swifts are the "frequent fliers" of the bird world—they feed, drink, bathe, collect nesting material and even mate while in flight! They spend much of their time scooping up flying insects high above urban neighborhoods, and only nesting and sleep keep these birds off their wings. • Chimney Swifts are most conspicuous as they forage on warm summer evenings and also during fall migration, when huge flocks migrate south alongside large numbers of Common Nighthawks. • Chimney Swifts once relied on natural tree cavities and woodpecker excavations for roosting and nesting, but in recent times they have adapted to living in brick chimneys. • The legs of Chimney Swifts are so weak and small that if one of these birds lands on the ground, it may not be able to gain flight again. Swifts do have strong claws, though, which allow them to cling to vertical surfaces. • Chimney Swift populations appear to be declining throughout eastern North America, but the cause is unclear. The answer may lie on their wintering grounds in the remote forests of Peru.

**Habitat:** forages over cities and towns; roosts and nests in chimneys; may nest in tree cavities in more remote areas.
**Nesting:** often colonial; nests deep in the interior of a chimney or tree cavity, or in the attic of an abandoned building; pair uses saliva to attach a half-saucer nest of short, dead twigs to a vertical wall; pair incubates 4–5 white eggs for 19–21 days; both adults feed the young.
**Feeding:** swallows flying insects whole during continuous flight.
**Voice:** call is a rapid *chitter-chitter-chitter,* given in flight; also a rapid series of *chip* notes.
**Similar Species:** *Swallows* (pp. 240–45): broader, shorter wings; smoother flight pattern; most have forked or notched tails.
**Best Sites:** Niagara River Corridor; Stewart Park–Cayuga L.; Cohoes–Crescent–Peebles Island SP; Ward Pound Ridge Reservation; Central Park (NYC).

**ID:** brown overall; slim body and long, thin, pointed wings; squared tail. *In flight:* rapid wingbeats; boomerang-shaped profile; erratic flight pattern.
**Size:** *L* 4½–5½ in; *W* 12–13 in.
**Status:** common breeder from May to June; migrants arrive in late April and May and depart in August and September.

# RUBY-THROATED HUMMINGBIRD

*Archilochus colubris*

Ruby-throated Hummingbirds span the ecological gap between birds and bees—they feed on the sweet, energy-rich nectar that flowers provide and pollinate the flowers in the process. Many avid gardeners and birders have long understood this interdependence and cultivate native, nectar-producing plants in their yards to attract these delightful birds. Even nongardeners can attract hummingbirds by maintaining a clean sugarwater feeder in a safe location. • Weighing about as much as a nickel, a hummingbird is capable of briefly achieving speeds of up to 60 miles per hour. It is also among the few birds that are able to fly vertically and in reverse. In straight-ahead flight, a hummingbird beats its wings up to 80 times per second, and its heart beats up to 1200 times per minute! • Each year, Ruby-throated Hummingbirds migrate across the Gulf of Mexico—an incredible, nonstop journey of more than 500 miles. In order to accomplish this feat, these tiny birds first double their body mass by fattening up on insects and nectar before departing.

**ID:** long bill; iridescent, green back; light underparts; dark tail. *Male:* ruby red throat; black "chin." *Female* and *immature:* fine, dark throat streaking.

**Size:** *L* 3½–4 in; *W* 4½ in.

**Status:** widespread breeder from May to August; common migrant, arriving in May and departing in October.

**Habitat:** open, mixed woodlands, wetlands, orchards, tree-lined meadows, flower gardens and backyards with trees and feeders.

**Nesting:** on a horizontal tree limb; tiny, deep cup nest of plant down and fibers is held together with spider silk; lichens and leaves are pasted on the exterior wall of the nest; female incubates 2 white eggs for 13–16 days; female feeds the young.

**Feeding:** uses its long bill and tongue to probe blooming flowers and sweetened water from feeders; also eats small insects and spiders.

**Voice:** most noticeable is the soft buzzing of the wings while in flight; also produces a loud *chick* and other high squeaks.

**Similar Species:** none; hawk moths hovering at flowers are sometimes mistaken for hummingbirds.

**Best Sites:** Roger Tory Peterson Nature Center; Beaver Meadow Nature Center; Paul Smiths Visitor Interpretive Center (Adirondack Park); John Boyd Thacher SP.

# BELTED KINGFISHER

*Ceryle alcyon*

The boisterous Belted Kingfisher closely monitors many of our lakes, rivers, streams, marshes and beaver ponds. Never far from water, this bird is often found uttering its distinctive, rattling call while perched on a bare branch that extends out over a productive pool. With a precise headfirst dive, the kingfisher can catch fish at depths of up to 2 feet, or snag a frog immersed in only a few inches of water. The kingfisher has even been observed diving into water to elude avian predators. • During the breeding season, a pair of kingfishers typically takes turns excavating the nest burrow. The birds use their bills to chip away at an exposed sandbank and then kick loose material out of the tunnel with their feet. The female kingfisher has the traditional female reproductive role for birds, but is more colorful than her mate—she has an extra red band across her belly. • In Greek mythology, Alcyon (Halcyone), the daughter of the wind god, grieved so deeply for her drowned husband that the gods transformed them both into kingfishers.

**ID:** bluish upperparts; shaggy crest; blue gray breast band; white "collar"; long, straight bill; short legs; white underwings; small, white patch near eye. *Male:* no "belt." *Female:* rust-colored "belt" (may be incomplete).
**Size:** *L* 11–14 in; *W* 20 in.
**Status:** widespread, common breeder and migrant from mid-March to November; rare in winter along larger rivers and bays.
**Habitat:** rivers, large streams, lakes, marshes and beaver ponds, especially near exposed soil banks, gravel pits or bluffs.

**Nesting:** in a cavity at the end of an earth burrow, often up to 6 ft long, dug by the pair with their bills and claws; pair incubates 6–7 white eggs for 22–24 days; both adults feed the young.
**Feeding:** dives headfirst into water, either from a perch or from hovering flight; eats mostly small fish, aquatic invertebrates and tadpoles.
**Voice:** fast, repetitive, cackling rattle.
**Similar Species:** *Blue Jay* (p. 235): more intense blue color; smaller bill and head; behaves in a completely different fashion.
**Best Sites:** Allegany SP; Braddock Bay; Black Creek Marsh WMA; Perch River WMA; Marshlands Conservancy–Playland CP.

# RED-HEADED WOODPECKER

*Melanerpes erythrocephalus*

Easily recognized by its all-red head, white underparts and black-and-white patterned upperparts, the adult Red-headed Woodpecker is a favorite visitor to feeders, although the brown-and-white juveniles are seen more often. • Red-headed Woodpeckers were once common throughout their range, but their numbers have declined dramatically over the past century. Since the introduction of the European Starling, Red-headed Woodpeckers have been largely outcompeted for nesting cavities. As well, these birds frequently become traffic fatalities, often struck by vehicles when the birds dart from their perches and over road-ways to catch flying insects. • The Red-headed Woodpecker is one of only four woodpecker species that regularly caches food. • This bird's scientific name *erythrocephalus* means "red head" in Greek.

**ID:** bright red head, "chin," throat and "bib" with black border; black back, wings and tail; white breast, belly, rump, lower back and inner wing patches. *Juvenile:* brown head, back, wings and tail; slight brown streaking on white underparts.

**Size:** *L* 9–9½ in; *W* 17 in.

**Status:** special concern; uncommon year-round resident in central and western NY; sparse migrant from March to April and in September in the rest of the state.

**Habitat:** open deciduous woodlands (especially oak), urban parks, river edges and roadsides with groves of scattered trees.

**Nesting:** male excavates a nest cavity in a dead tree or limb; pair incubates 4–5 white eggs for 12–13 days; both adults feed the young.

**Feeding:** flycatches for insects; hammers dead and decaying wood for grubs; eats mostly insects, earthworms, spiders, nuts, berries, seeds and fruit; may also eat some young birds and eggs.

**Voice:** loud series of *kweer* or *kwrring* notes; occasionally a chattering *kerr-r-ruck;* also drums softly in short bursts.

**Similar Species:** adult is distinctive. *Red-bellied Woodpecker* (p. 208): whitish face and underparts; black-and-white barring on back. *Yellow-bellied Sapsucker* (p. 209): large, white wing patch.

**Best Sites:** Iroquois NWR–Tonawanda WMA–Oak Orchard WMA; Nation's Road Grassland; Verona Beach SP–Sylvan Beach; Shawangunk Grasslands NWR.

# RED-BELLIED WOODPECKER
*Melanerpes carolinus*

These birds often issue noisy, rolling *churr* calls as they poke around wooded landscapes in search of seeds, fruit and a variety of insects. Unlike most woodpeckers, which eat primarily insects, Red-bellies consume large amounts of plant material, seldom excavating wood. • The Red-bellied Woodpecker is a year-round resident in most of its range and does well in suburban areas as well as in more remote wilderness regions. In the southeastern U.S., where it is more common, this woodpecker is often considered a pest because it feeds on commercial fruit crops. • The Red-bellied Woodpecker's namesake, its red belly, is only a small reddish area that is difficult to see in the field.

**ID:** black-and-white barring on back; white patches on rump and topside base of primaries; reddish tinge on belly. *Male:* red forehead, crown and nape. *Female:* red on nape only. *Juvenile:* dark gray crown; streaked breast.

**Size:** *L* 9–10½ in; *W* 16 in.

**Status:** common year-round resident, localized in the Genesee Valley–Finger Lakes region and southern NY; breeds from April to June.

**Habitat:** mature deciduous woodlands; occasionally in wooded residential areas.

**Nesting:** in a cavity; female selects one of several nest sites excavated by the male; pair may use a natural cavity or the abandoned cavity of another woodpecker; pair incubates 4–5 white eggs for 12–14 days; both adults raise the young.

**Feeding:** forages in trees, on the ground or occasionally on the wing; eats mostly insects, seeds, nuts and fruit; may also eat tree sap, small amphibians, bird eggs or small fish.

**Voice:** call is a soft, rolling *churr;* drums in second-long bursts.

**Similar Species:** *Northern Flicker* (p. 214): yellow underwings; gray crown; brown back with dark barring; black "bib"; large, dark spots on underparts. *Red-headed Woodpecker* (p. 207): all-red head; unbarred, black back and wings; white patch on trailing edge of wing.

**Best Sites:** Iroquois NWR–Tonawanda WMA–Oak Orchard WMA; Braddock Bay; Stewart Park–Cayuga L.; Vischer Ferry Nature and Historic Preserve; Caleb Smith State Park Preserve–Nissequogue River SP.

# YELLOW-BELLIED SAPSUCKER

*Sphyrapicus varius*

Yellow-bellied Sapsuckers are conspicuous in May, when they perform their courting rituals throughout our woodlands. The drumming of sapsuckers differs from that of other woodpeckers in our region—it consists of a loud roll with clearly separated taps at the end, like a motor running out of gas. • Lines of parallel, freshly drilled "wells" in tree bark are a sure sign that sapsuckers are nearby. A pair of sapsuckers may drill a number of sites within their forest territory. The wells fill with sweet, sticky sap that attracts insects, then the sapsuckers make their rounds, eating both the trapped bugs and the pooled sap. A sapsucker does not actually suck sap—the bird laps it up with a tongue that resembles a paintbrush. • Other species such as hummingbirds, kinglets, warblers and waxwings benefit from the wells made by Yellow-bellied Sapsuckers, especially early in the season when flying insects, fruits and nectar are rare.

**ID:** black "bib"; red forecrown; black-and-white face, back, wings and tail; large, white wing patch; yellow wash on lower breast and belly. *Male:* red "chin." *Female:* white "chin." *Juvenile:* brownish overall; large, clearly defined wing patches.
**Size:** *L* 7–9 in; *W* 16 in.
**Status:** common breeder from April to June at higher elevations; common migrant in April and from September to October.
**Habitat:** deciduous and mixed forests, especially dry, second-growth woodlands.
**Nesting:** in a cavity; usually in a live poplar or birch tree with heart rot; often lines the cavity with wood chips; pair incubates 5–6 white eggs for 12–13 days.
**Feeding:** hammers trees for insects; drills "wells" in live trees to collect sap and trap insects; also flycatches for insects.

**Voice:** nasal, catlike *meow*; soft *vee-ooo* when alarmed; territorial and courtship hammering has a distinctive, 2-speed quality.
**Similar Species:** *Red-headed Woodpecker* (p. 207): juvenile lacks white wing patch. *Downy Woodpecker* (p. 210) and *Hairy Woodpecker* (p. 211): red napes; white backs; lack large, white wing patch and red forecrown. *Black-backed Woodpecker* (p. 213) and *American Three-toed Woodpecker* (p. 212): yellow forecrowns; predominantly black heads; lack white wing patch.
**Best Sites:** Allegany SP; Ferd's Bog–Moose River Plains; Cherry Plain SP; John Boyd Thacher SP; Sterling Forest SP.

# DOWNY WOODPECKER

*Picoides pubescens*

A regular patron of backyard suet feeders, the small and widely common Downy Woodpecker is often the first woodpecker a novice birder will identify with confidence. It is generally more approachable and tolerant of human activities than most birds, and once you become familiar with its dainty appearance, it won't be long before you recognize it by its soft taps and brisk staccato calls. These encounters are not all free of confusion, however, because the closely related Hairy Woodpecker looks remarkably similar. • Like other members of the woodpecker family, the Downy has evolved a number of features that help to cushion the repeated shocks of a lifetime of hammering. These characteristics include a strong bill, strong neck muscles, a flexible, reinforced skull and a brain that is tightly packed in its protective cranium. Another feature that Downies share with other woodpeckers is feathered nostrils, which serve to filter out the sawdust it produces when hammering.

**Nesting:** pair excavates a cavity in a dying or decaying trunk or limb and lines it with wood chips; pair incubates 4–5 white eggs for 11–13 days; both adults feed the young.

**Feeding:** forages on trunks and branches, often in saplings and shrubs; chips and probes for insects and their eggs, cocoons and larvae; also eats nuts and seeds; attracted to suet feeders.

**Voice:** long, unbroken trill; calls are a sharp *pik* or *ki-ki-ki* or whiny *queek queek;* drums more than Hairy Woodpecker and at a higher pitch, usually on smaller trees and dead branches.

**Similar Species:** *Hairy Woodpecker* (p. 211): larger; no spots on white outer tail feathers. *Yellow-bellied Sapsucker* (p. 209): large, white wing patch; red forecrown; lacks red nape and clean white back. *Black-backed Woodpecker* (p. 213) and *American Three-toed Woodpecker* (p. 212): larger; yellow forecrown; predominantly black head; black barring on sides.

**Best Sites:** Roger Tory Peterson Nature Center; Beaver Meadow Nature Center; Sapsucker Woods (Cornell Laboratory of Ornithology); Five Rivers Environmental Education Center; Connetquot River SP.

**ID:** clear white belly and back; white bars on black wings; black eye line and crown; short, stubby bill; mostly black tail; black spots on white outer tail feathers. *Male:* small, red patch on back of head. *Female:* no red patch. *Juvenile:* red patch on forehead.

**Size:** *L* 6–7 in; *W* 12 in.

**Status:** common year-round resident; breeds in May and June.

**Habitat:** all wooded environments, especially deciduous and mixed forests and areas with tall, deciduous shrubs.

# HAIRY WOODPECKER

*Picoides villosus*

A second or third look is often required to confirm the identity of the Hairy Woodpecker, because it is so similar in appearance to its smaller cousin, the Downy Woodpecker. A convenient way to learn to distinguish one bird from the other is by watching these woodpeckers at a backyard feeder. It is not uncommon to see both of these birds vying for food, and the Hairy Woodpecker is the larger and more aggressive of the two. • The secret to woodpeckers' feeding success is hidden in their skulls. Most woodpeckers have very long tongues—in some cases more than four times the length of the bill—made possible by twin structures that wrap around the perimeter of the skull. These structures store the tongue in much the same way that a measuring tape is stored in its case.

**ID:** pure white belly; white spots on black wings; black "cheek" and crown; black tail with white outer feathers. *Male:* small, red patch on back of head. *Female:* no red patch. *Juvenile:* more indistinct patterning, with brown instead of black.
**Size:** *L* 8–9½ in; *W* 15 in.
**Status:** common year-round resident; breeds in May and June.
**Habitat:** deciduous and mixed forests.
**Nesting:** pair excavates a nest site in a tree trunk or limb; cavity is lined with wood chips; pair incubates 4–5 white eggs for 12–14 days; both adults feed the young.
**Feeding:** forages on tree trunks and branches; chips, hammers and probes bark for insects and their eggs, cocoons and larvae; also eats nuts, fruit and seeds; attracted to feeders with suet, especially in winter.
**Voice:** call is a loud, sharp *peek peek;* also issues a long, unbroken trill: *keek-ik-ik-ik-ik;* drums less regularly and at a lower pitch than Downy Woodpecker, always on tree trunks and large branches.

**Similar Species:** *Downy Woodpecker* (p. 210): smaller; shorter bill; dark spots on white outer tail feathers. *Yellow-bellied Sapsucker* (p. 209): large, white wing patch; red forecrown; lacks red nape and clean white back. *Black-backed Woodpecker* (p. 213) and *American Three-toed Woodpecker* (p. 212): yellow forecrowns; predominantly black heads; black barring on sides.
**Best Sites:** Roger Tory Peterson Nature Center; Beaver Meadow Nature Center; Beaver Lake CP; Paul Smiths Visitor Interpretive Center (Adirondack Park); Five Rivers Environmental Education Center; John Boyd Thacher SP.

211

# AMERICAN THREE-TOED WOODPECKER

*Picoides dorsalis*

The American Three-toed Woodpecker is a very rare, quiet resident of our coniferous forests and is found in areas with standing dead trees infested with wood-boring beetle larvae. Burned-over areas and soggy bogs are also favorite haunts of this elusive bird. • The American Three-toed Woodpecker does not drill holes while foraging for food. Instead, it chisels off large flakes of bark from old or dying conifers, exposing the red inner surface of the trunk. Eventually the trees take on a distinct reddish look and are skirted with fragments of bark. • This species breeds farther north than any other woodpecker in North America, being found as far north as trees grow in Canada and Alaska. Its small New York population in the Adirondacks is geographically isolated from its Canadian stronghold.

**ID:** black-and-white barring down center of back; white underparts; black barring on sides; mostly black head with 2 narrow, white stripes; black tail with black-spotted, white outer tail feathers; 3 toes. *Male:* yellow crown. *Female:* black crown with occasional white spotting. *Juvenile:* yellow on forecrown.
**Size:** *L* 8–9 in; *W* 15 in.
**Status:** rare year-round resident in Adirondack forests; breeds in May and June.
**Habitat:** spruce and fir forests, bogs and disturbed areas; also forest burns, which traditionally attract this species and the Black-backed Woodpecker in succeeding years owing to beetle destruction.
**Nesting:** excavates a cavity, usually in a dead or dying conifer trunk; pair incubates 3–4 white eggs for 12–14 days; both adults feed the young.
**Feeding:** chips away bark to expose larval and adult wood-boring insects; occasionally eats berries and sap.
**Voice:** call is a low *pik* or *teek;* drumming is a prolonged series of short bursts.
**Similar Species:** *Black-backed Woodpecker* (p. 213): solid black back; unspotted, white outer tail feathers. *Hairy Woodpecker* (p. 211): clean white back; lacks dark barring on sides. *Yellow-bellied Sapsucker* (p. 209): large, white wing patch; red forecrown; black "bib"; yellow-tinged underparts.
**Best Sites:** Ferd's Bog–Moose River Plains; Chubb River Swamp.

# BLACK-BACKED WOODPECKER

*Picoides arcticus*

The Black-backed Woodpecker is a regular resident in northern New York, but is uncommon in the rest of the state. This generally quiet woodpecker prefers a secretive life in remote, uninhabited tracts of coniferous forest. Only during the brief courtship season does the male Black-backed Woodpecker advertise his presence by drumming on the top of a broken, standing dead tree or "snag." • This reclusive bird is most active in recently burned forest patches where wood-boring beetles thrive under the charred bark of spruce, pine and fir trees. When it forages on blackened tree trunks, this bird's black-backed form can be difficult to spot, especially from a distance. • Large, irruptive invasions of Black-backed Wood-peckers and American Three-toed Wood-peckers seem to occur at six- to eight-year intervals.

**ID:** solid black back; white under-parts; black barring on sides; predominantly black head with white line below eye; black "mustache" stripe; 3 toes; black tail with pure white outer tail feathers. *Male:* yellow crown. *Female:* black crown. *Juvenile:* yellow crown; smaller bill.

**Size:** *L* 9–10 in; *W* 16 in.

**Status:** uncommon year-round resident in the Adirondacks; breeds in May and June.

**Habitat:** coniferous forests, especially burned-over sites with many snags.

**Nesting:** excavates a cavity in a dead or dying conifer trunk or limb; pair incubates 4 white eggs for 12–14 days; both adults feed the young.

**Feeding:** chisels away bark flakes to expose larval and adult wood-boring insects; may eat some nuts and fruits.

**Voice:** call is a low *kik;* drumming is a prolonged series of short bursts.

**Similar Species:** *American Three-toed Woodpecker* (p. 212): white back with black, horizontal barring; black spots on white outer tail feathers. *Hairy Woodpecker* (p. 211): clean white back; lacks dark barring on sides. *Yellow-bellied Sapsucker* (p. 209): black-and-white back; large, white wing patch; red forecrown; black "bib"; yellow-tinged underparts.

**Best Sites:** Ferd's Bog–Moose River Plains; Chubb River Swamp; Paul Smiths Visitor Interpretive Center (Adirondack Park); Bloomingdale Bog; Elk L.

# NORTHERN FLICKER

*Colaptes auratus*

The Northern Flicker is one of our most common woodpeckers. Unlike most other woodpeckers, this species spends much of its time on the ground, feeding mostly on ants. It appears almost robinlike as it hops about on anthills and in grassy meadows, fields and along forest clearings. • Flickers are often seen bathing in dusty depressions. The dust particles absorb oils and bacteria that are harmful to the birds' feathers. To clean even more thoroughly, flickers will crush captured ants and then preen themselves with the remains. Ants contain formic acid, which kills small parasites on the flickers' skin and feathers. • Like many woodpeckers, the Northern Flicker has zygodactyl feet—each foot has two toes facing forward and two toes pointing back- ward—which allow the bird to move vertically up and down tree trunks. As well, stiff tail feathers help to prop up woodpeckers' bodies while they scale trees and excavate cavities.

**ID:** brown, barred back and wings; spotted, buff to whitish under- parts; black "bib"; yellow underwings and undertail; white rump; long bill; brownish to buff face; gray crown. *Male:* black "mustache" stripe; red nape crescent. *Female:* no "mustache."
**Size:** *L* 12½–13 in; *W* 20 in.
**Status:** common, widespread breeder and migrant from March to November; regu- larly seen in winter, particularly on Long I.
**Habitat:** open deciduous, mixed and conif- erous woodlands and forest edges, fields,

meadows, beaver ponds and other wet- lands.
**Nesting:** pair excavates a cavity in a dead or dying deciduous tree; may also use a nest box; cavity is lined with wood chips; pair incubates 5–8 white eggs for 11–16 days; both adults feed the young.
**Feeding:** forages on the ground for ants and other terrestrial insects; probes bark; also eats berries and nuts; occasionally fly- catches.
**Voice:** loud, laughing, rapid *kick-kick-kick- kick-kick-kick;* courtship call is *woika-woika- woika.*
**Similar Species:** *Red-bellied Woodpecker* (p. 208): black-and-white pattern on back; more red on head; dark underwings.
**Best Sites:** Tifft Nature Preserve; Braddock Bay; Beaver Lake CP; Five Rivers Environ- mental Education Center; Caumsett SP.

# PILEATED WOODPECKER

*Dryocopus pileatus*

With its flaming red crest, swooping flight and maniacal call, this impressive deep-forest dweller can stop hikers in their tracks. Using its powerful, dagger-shaped bill and stubborn determination, the Pileated Woodpecker chisels out uniquely shaped rectangular cavities in its unending search for grubs and ants. These cavities are often the first indication that a breeding pair is resident in an area. • Because they require large home territories, these magnificent birds are not encountered with much frequency. A pair of breeding Pileated Woodpeckers generally needs more than 100 acres of mature forest in which to settle. • As a primary cavity nester, the Pileated Woodpecker plays an important role in forest ecosystems. Other birds and even mammals depend on the activities of this woodpecker—ducks, small falcons, owls and even flying squirrels are frequent nesters in abandoned Pileated Woodpecker cavities. • Not surprisingly, a woodpecker's bill becomes shorter as the bird ages.

**ID:** predominantly black; white wing linings; bright red crest; yellow eyes; stout, dark bill; white stripe runs from bill to shoulder; white "chin." *Male:* red "mustache"; red crest (red extends from bill to nape). *Female:* red on crest only; gray brown forehead; lacks red "mustache."

**Size:** *L* 16–19 in; *W* 29 in.

**Status:** common year-round resident, except on the coastal plain where it is a very rare visitor; breeds in April and May.

**Habitat:** extensive tracts of mature deciduous, mixed or coniferous forest; some occur in riparian woodlands or woodlots in suburban and agricultural areas.

**Nesting:** pair excavates a cavity in a dead or dying tree trunk and lines it with wood chips; pair incubates 4 white eggs for 15–18 days; both adults feed the young.

**Feeding:** often hammers the base of rotting trees, creating fist-sized or larger rectangular holes; eats carpenter ants, wood-boring beetle larvae, berries and nuts.

**Voice:** loud, fast, laughing, rolling *woika-woika-woika-woika;* long series of *kuk* notes; loud resonant drumming.

**Similar Species:** *Other woodpeckers* (pp. 207–14): much smaller. *American Crow* (p. 236) and *Common Raven* (p. 238): lack white underwings and bright red crest.

**Best Sites:** Allegany SP; Michigan Hollow–Spencer Marsh; Partridge Run WMA; Bear Mountain SP; Sterling Forest SP.

# PASSERINES

Passerines are also commonly known as songbirds or perching birds. Although these terms are easier to comprehend, they are not as strictly accurate, because some passerines neither sing nor perch, and many nonpasserines do sing and perch. In a general sense, however, these terms represent passerines adequately: they are among the best singers, and they are typically seen perched on a branch or wire.

It is believed that passerines, which all belong to the order Passeriformes, make up the most recent evolutionary group of birds. Theirs is the most numerous of all orders, representing about 28 percent of the bird species in New York, and nearly three-fifths of all living birds worldwide.

Passerines are grouped together based on the sum total of many morphological and molecular similarities, including such things as the number of tail and flight feathers and reproductive characteristics. All passerines share the same foot shape: three toes face forward and one faces backward, and no passerines have webbed toes. Also, all passerines have a tendon that runs along the back side of the bird's knee and tightens when the bird perches, giving it a firm grip.

Some of our most common and easily identified birds are passerines, such as the Black-capped Chickadee, American Robin and House Sparrow, but the passerines also include some of the most challenging and frustrating birds to identify, until their distinct songs and call are learned.

*Flycatchers*

*Shrikes & Vireos*

*Jays & Crows*

*Larks & Swallows*

*Chickadees, Nuthatches & Wrens*

*Kinglets, Bluebirds & Thrushes*

*Mimics, Starlings & Waxwings*

*Wood-Warblers & Tanagers*

*Sparrows, Grosbeaks & Buntings*

*Blackbirds & Orioles*

*Finchlike Birds*

# OLIVE-SIDED FLYCATCHER
*Contopus cooperi*

An early morning hike through a coniferous forest often reveals a most curious and incessant wild call: *quick-three-beers! quick-three-beers!* This interpretation of the male Olive-sided Flycatcher's courtship song may seem silly, but it is surprisingly accurate. Once nesting has begun, this flycatcher quickly changes its tune to an equally enthusiastic, but less memorable, territorial *pip-pip-pip*. Like other "tyrant flycatchers," the Olive-sided Flycatcher is a fierce defender of its nest and will harass and chase off squirrels and other predators. • From their perches high among towering conifer spires, Olive-sided Flycatchers have easy access to an abundance of flying insects that inhabit the sunny forest heights. These feisty birds are difficult to spot, so look for a big-headed silhouette perched at the tip of a mature conifer or dead branch. • Like all flycatchers, this olive-vested songbird perches with a distinctive, upright, attentive profile. Its ready-and-waiting stance allows it to quickly launch out and snatch flying insects in midair.

**Habitat:** semi-open mixed and coniferous forests near water; prefers burned areas and wetlands.

**Nesting:** high in a conifer, usually far from the trunk; nest of twigs and plant fibers is bound with spider silk; female incubates 3 darkly spotted, white to pinkish buff eggs for 14–17 days.

**Feeding:** flycatches insects from a perch.

**Voice:** *Male:* song is a chipper and lively *quick-three-beers!*, with the 2nd note highest in pitch; descending *pip-pip-pip* when excited.

**Similar Species:** *Eastern Wood-Pewee* (p. 218): smaller; gray breast; 2 faint wing bars; lacks white rump tufts. *Eastern Phoebe* (p. 224): all-dark bill; lacks white rump tufts; often wags tail. *Eastern Kingbird* (p. 226): all-dark bill; white-tipped tail; lacks white rump tufts.

**ID:** dark olive gray "vest"; pale throat and belly; olive gray to olive brown upperparts; white tufts on sides of rump; dark upper mandible; dull yellow orange base to lower mandible; inconspicuous eye ring.

**Size:** *L* 7–8 in; *W* 13 in.

**Status:** uncommon breeder and migrant in the Adirondacks and Tug Hill area from late May to September; rare breeder in the Catskills.

**Best Sites:** Ferd's Bog–Moose River Plains; Paul Smiths Visitor Interpretive Center (Adirondack Park); Bloomingdale Bog; Elk L.

217

# EASTERN WOOD-PEWEE

*Contopus virens*

Perched on an exposed tree branch in a suburban park, woodlot edge or neighborhood yard, the male Eastern Wood-Pewee whistles his plaintive *pee-ah-wee pee-oh* song all day long throughout the summer. Some of the keenest suitors will even sing their charms late into the evening, long after most birds have silenced their weary courtship songs. • Like other flycatchers, the Eastern Wood-Pewee loops out from an exposed perch to snatch flying insects in midair, a technique often referred to as "flycatching" or "hawking." • Many insects have evolved defense mechanisms to avert potential predators such as the Eastern Wood-Pewee and its flycatching relatives. Some flying insects are camouflaged, while others are distasteful or poisonous and flaunt their foul nature with vivid colors. Interestingly, some insects even mimic their poisonous allies, displaying warning colors even though they are perfectly tasty.

**ID:** olive gray to olive brown upperparts; 2 narrow, white wing bars; whitish throat; gray breast and sides; whitish or pale yellow belly, flanks and undertail coverts; dark upper mandible; dull yellow orange base to lower mandible; no eye ring.
**Size:** *L* 6–6½ in; *W* 10 in.
**Status:** common breeder and migrant from May to September.
**Habitat:** open mixed and deciduous woodlands with a sparse understory, especially woodland openings and edges; rarely in open coniferous woodlands.
**Nesting:** in a deciduous tree; open cup of grass, plant fibers and lichen is bound with spider silk; female incubates 3 creamy white eggs, wreathed with dark blotches, for 12–13 days.
**Feeding:** flycatches insects from a perch; may also glean insects from foliage, especially while hovering.

**Voice:** *Male:* song is a clear, slow, plaintive *pee-ah-wee*, with the 2nd note lower, followed by a downslurred *pee-oh*, given with or without pauses; also a *chip* call.
**Similar Species:** *Olive-sided Flycatcher* (p. 217): larger; white rump tufts; olive gray "vest"; lacks white wing bars. *Eastern Phoebe* (p. 224): all-dark bill; lacks white wing bars; often pumps its tail. *Eastern Kingbird* (p. 226): larger; white-tipped tail; brighter white underparts; all-dark bill. *Empidonax flycatchers* (pp. 219–23): smaller; more conspicuous wing bars; eye rings.
**Best Sites:** Allegany SP; Letchworth SP; John Boyd Thacher SP; Bear Mountain SP; Alley Pond Park (NYC).

# YELLOW-BELLIED FLYCATCHER

*Empidonax flaviventris*

You can expect to find the reclusive Yellow-bellied Flycatcher deep within soggy, mosquito-infested bogs and fens in the Adirondack Mountains. In late spring and early summer, the male spends much of his time singing plain, soft, liquidy *che-lek* songs and occasionally zipping out from inconspicuous perches to help reduce the insect population. Once nesting has begun, the male changes his tune to a slow, rising *per-wee* and focuses his attention on defending his nesting territory and supplying food to his growing young.

• There are fine opportunities in New York for birders to develop their *Empidonax* flycatcher identification skills— the state boasts a large assemblage of these nearly indistinguishable flycatchers. The Yellow-bellied Flycatcher is the most elusive and secretive of this confusing genus. It does not habitually perch in the open but, in the breeding season, it distinguishes itself from other flycatchers by its yellow underparts and by nesting on the ground.

**Size:** *L* 5–6 in; *W* 8 in.

**Status:** fairly common breeder and migrant from May to September in the Adirondacks and Catskills.

**Habitat:** coniferous bogs and fens and shady spruce and pine forests with a dense shrub understory.

**Nesting:** on the ground in dense sphagnum moss or among the upturned roots of

**ID:** olive green upperparts; 2 whitish wing bars; yellowish eye ring; white throat; yellow underparts; pale olive breast; bicolored bill.

a fallen tree; small cup nest of moss, rootlets and weeds is lined with grass, sedges and fine rootlets; female incubates 3–4 lightly spotted, whitish eggs for 12–14 days.

**Feeding:** flycatches for insects at low to middle levels of the forest; also gleans vegetation for larval and adult invertebrates while hovering.

**Voice:** *Male:* song is a soft *che-luk* or *che-lek* (2nd syllable is lower pitched); calls include a chipper *pe-wheep, preee, pur-wee* or *killik*.

**Similar Species:** *Acadian* (p. 220), *Willow* (p. 222), *Alder* (p. 221) and *Least* (p. 223) *flycatchers:* all lack extensive yellow wash from throat to belly; white eye rings; different songs; all but Acadian have browner upperparts.

**Best Sites:** Ferd's Bog–Moose River Plains; Bloomingdale Bog; Chubb River Swamp; Elk L.; Paul Smiths Visitor Interpretive Center (Adirondack Park).

# ACADIAN FLYCATCHER

*Empidonax virescens*

As most experienced birders will tell you, one of the keys to identifying a flycatcher is to listen for its distinctive song. The Acadian Flycatcher's signature song is a quick, forceful *peet-sa*. • Learning to identify this bird is only half the fun. Its speedy, aerial courtship chases and the male's hovering flight displays are sights to behold—that is if you can survive the swarming hordes of bloodsucking mosquitoes deep within the swampy woodlands of southern New York where this flycatcher is primarily found. • Maple and beech trees provide preferred nesting sites for the Acadian Flycatcher. The nest is built on a horizontal branch up to 20 feet above the ground, and can be quite conspicuous because loose material often dangles from the nest, giving it a sloppy appearance. • Flycatchers are members of the family Tyrannidae, or "Tyrant Flycatchers," so named because of their feisty, aggressive behavior.

**ID:** narrow, yellowish eye ring; 2 buff to yellowish wing bars; large bill has dark upper mandible and pinkish yellow lower mandible; white throat; faint olive yellow breast; yellow belly and undertail coverts; olive green upperparts; very long primaries.
**Size:** *L* 5½–6 in; *W* 9 in.
**Status:** local breeder and migrant from May to September; reinvading and expanding into former range in southern NY.
**Habitat:** fairly mature deciduous woodlands, riparian woodlands and wooded swamps.
**Nesting:** in a beech or maple, 8–20 ft above the ground; female builds a loose, sloppy-looking cup nest from bark strips, catkins, fine twigs and grasses held together with spider silk; female incubates 3 lightly spotted, creamy white eggs for 13–15 days; both parents raise the young.
**Feeding:** forages primarily by hawking or by gleaning from foliage while hovering; takes insects and insect larvae, including wasps, bees, spiders and ants; may also eat berries and small fruits.
**Voice:** *Male:* song is a forceful *peet-sa;* call is a softer *peet;* may issue a loud *ti-ti-ti-ti-ti* during the breeding season.
**Similar Species:** *Alder Flycatcher* (p. 221): narrower, white eye ring is often inconspicuous; browner overall; smaller head relative to its body; song is *fee-bee-o. Willow Flycatcher* (p. 222): browner overall; smaller head; very faint eye ring; song is an explosive *fitz-bew. Least Flycatcher* (p. 223): bold, white eye ring; rounded head; shorter wings; song is a clear *che-bek. Yellow-bellied Flycatcher* (p. 219): yellow wash from throat to belly; song is a liquid *che-lek.*
**Best Sites:** Allegany SP; Letchworth SP; Iroquois NWR–Tonawanda WMA–Oak Orchard WMA; Bashakill WMA; Bear Mountain SP.

# ALDER FLYCATCHER

*Empidonax alnorum*

The nondescript Alder Flycatcher is well named because it is often found in alder and willow shrubs—a fact that can help in its identification. This flycatcher frequently competes against the Willow Flycatcher for control over dense, riparian alder and willow thickets. • The Alder Flycatcher is often indistinguishable from other *Empidonax* flycatchers until it opens its small, bicolored beak and reveals its identity with a hearty *fee-bee-o* or *free beer*. Once this aggressive bird has been spotted, its feisty behavior can often be observed without distraction as it drives away rivals and pursues flying insects. • Many birds have to learn their songs and calls, but Alder Flycatchers instinctively know the simple phrase of their species. Even if a young bird is isolated from the sounds of other Alder Flycatchers, it can produce a perfectly acceptable *fee-bee-o* when it matures. • The Willow Flycatcher is a close relative of the Alder Flycatcher, and until 1973, these two species were grouped together as a single species known as "Traill's Flycatcher."

grass and other plant materials; female incubates 3–4 darkly spotted, white eggs for 12–14 days; both adults feed the young.
**Feeding:** flycatches from a perch for beetles, bees, wasps and other flying insects; also eats berries and occasionally seeds.
**Voice:** *Male:* song is a snappy *fee-bee-o* or *free beer;* call is a *wheep* or *peep.*
**Similar Species:** *Eastern Wood-Pewee* (p. 218): larger; narrower wing bars; lacks eye ring. *Willow Flycatcher* (p. 222): song is an explosive *fitz-bew;* mostly found in drier areas. *Least Flycatcher* (p. 223): bolder white eye ring; greener upperparts; pale gray white underparts; song is a clear *che-bek. Acadian Flycatcher* (p. 220): yellowish eye ring; greener upperparts; yellower underparts; song is a forceful *peet-sa. Yellow-bellied Flycatcher* (p. 219): yellowish eye ring; greener upperparts; yellower underparts; song is a liquid *che-lek.*
**Best Sites:** Hanging Bog WMA; Whetstone Gulf SP; Ferd's Bog–Moose River Plains; Partridge Run WMA.

**ID:** olive brown upperparts; 2 dull white to buff wing bars; faint, whitish eye ring; dark upper mandible; orange lower mandible; long tail; white throat; pale olive breast; pale yellowish belly.
**Size:** *L* 5½–6 in; *W* 8½ in.
**Status:** common breeder and migrant from May to September in northern and western New York.
**Habitat:** alder or willow thickets bordering lakes or streams.
**Nesting:** near the ground in a dense bush or shrub; small cup nest is loosely woven of

# WILLOW FLYCATCHER

*Empidonax traillii*

When warm spring winds flood our region with migrant songbirds, the characteristic, sneezy *fitz-bew* call of the Willow Flycatcher occasionally rises above the sounds of the crowd. Upon arriving in a suitable shrubby area of thick willows and tangled dogwood, male Willow Flycatchers swing energetically on advantageous perches to do vocal battle over preferred territories. Once the boundaries are drawn and the business of nesting begins, these flycatchers become shy, inconspicuous birds that prefer to remain out of sight. Only when an avian intruder violates an established boundary does the resident Willow Flycatcher aggressively reveal itself. • After raising their young and fattening themselves up in late summer and early fall, Willow Flycatchers begin their migratory journey to Central and South America. • The Willow Flycatcher is the most widely distributed North American *Empidonax* flycatcher.

**ID:** olive brown upperparts; 2 whitish wing bars; indistinct eye ring; white throat; yellowish belly; pale olive brown breast band.

**Size:** *L* 5½–6 in; *W* 8½ in.

**Status:** fairly common breeder and migrant from May to September at lower elevations.

**Habitat:** shrubby areas of hawthorn, apple, red-osier dogwood, willow or other low growth on abandoned farmlands and in riparian corridors.

**Nesting:** in a dense shrub, usually 3–7 ft above the ground; female builds an open cup nest of grass, bark strips and plant fibers and lines it with down; female incubates 3–4 brown-spotted, whitish to pale buff eggs for 12–15 days.

**Feeding:** flycatches insects; also gleans insects from vegetation, usually while hovering.

**Voice:** *Male:* song is a quick, sneezy *fitz-bew* that drops off at the end, repeated up to 30 times a minute; call is a quick *whit*.

**Similar Species:** *Eastern Wood-Pewee* (p. 218): larger; narrower wing bars; lacks eye ring. *Alder Flycatcher* (p. 221): song is *fee-bee-o;* usually found in wetter areas. *Least Flycatcher* (p. 223): bolder white eye ring; pale gray white underparts; song is a clear *che-bek. Acadian Flycatcher* (p. 220): yellowish eye ring; greener upperparts; yellower underparts; song is a forceful *peet-sa. Yellow-bellied Flycatcher* (p. 219): yellowish eye ring; greener upperparts; yellower underparts; song is a liquid *che-lek.*

**Best Sites:** Iroquois NWR–Tonawanda WMA–Oak Orchard WMA; Montezuma NWR; Five Rivers Environmental Education Center; Jones Beach SP; Caumsett SP.

# LEAST FLYCATCHER

*Empidonax minimus*

Though it is not as colorful and glamorous as other birds in New York, the Least Flycatcher is the most common and widespread *Empidonax* flycatcher in our region, and you should have no problem meeting one in these parts. • Though it might not look like a bully, the Least Flycatcher is one of the boldest and most pugnacious songbirds of our deciduous woodlands. During the nesting season, it is noisy and conspicuous, forcefully repeating its simple, two-part *che-bek* call throughout much of the day. Intense song battles normally eliminate the need for physical aggression, but feathers fly in fights that are occasionally required to settle disputes over territory and courtship privileges. • These birds often fall victim to nest parasitism by the Brown-headed Cowbird, whose hatched young often smother the much smaller Least Flycatcher nestlings. • *Empidonax* flycatchers are aptly named: the literal translation is "mosquito king" and refers to their insect-hunting prowess.

**ID:** olive brown upperparts; 2 white wing bars; bold, white eye ring; fairly long, narrow tail; mostly dark bill has yellow orange lower base; white throat; gray breast; grayish white to yellowish belly and undertail coverts.

**Size:** L 4½–6 in; W 8 in.

**Status:** common, widespread breeder and migrant from late April to September, except rare on Long I.

**Habitat:** open deciduous or mixed woodlands; forest openings and edges; often in second-growth woodlands; occasionally near human habitation.

**Nesting:** in a small tree or shrub; female builds a small cup nest of plant fibers and bark; female incubates 4 creamy white eggs for 13–15 days; both adults feed the young.

**Feeding:** flycatches insects; also gleans trees and shrubs for insects while hovering; may eat some fruit and seeds.

**Voice:** *Male:* song is a constantly repeated, dry *che-bek che-bek*.

**Similar Species:** *Eastern Wood-Pewee* (p. 218): larger; narrower wing bars; lacks eye ring. *Alder Flycatcher* (p. 221): faint eye ring; song is *fee-bee-o;* usually found in wetter areas. *Willow Flycatcher* (p. 222): indistinct eye ring; greener upperparts; yellower underparts; song is an explosive *fitz-bew. Acadian Flycatcher* (p. 220) yellowish eye ring; greener upperparts; yellower underparts; song is a forceful *peet-sa. Yellow-bellied Flycatcher* (p. 219): yellowish eye ring; greener upperparts; yellower underparts; song is a liquid *che-lek. Ruby-crowned Kinglet* (p. 258): broken eye ring; much daintier bill; shorter tail.

**Best Sites:** Allegany SP; Beaver Meadow Nature Center; Sapsucker Woods (Cornell Laboratory of Ornithology); Saratoga National Historical Park; John Boyd Thacher SP.

# EASTERN PHOEBE

*Sayornis phoebe*

Whether you are poking around your summer cottage, a campground picnic shelter or your backyard shed, there is a very good chance you will stumble upon an Eastern Phoebe family and its marvelous mud nest. The Eastern Phoebe's nest building and territorial defense is normally well underway by the time most other songbirds arrive in our region in mid-May. Once limited to nesting on natural cliffs and fallen riparian trees, this adaptive flycatcher has gradually found success in nesting on buildings and bridges, although it prefers sites near water. • The Eastern Phoebe sometimes reuses a nest site for many years and, too often, people unnecessarily destroy the phoebe's mud nests. Some people have caught on to the benefits of having phoebe tenants, because these birds can be effective at controlling insect pests. • Some other birds pump their tails while perched, but few species can match the zest and frequency of the Eastern Phoebe's tail pumping.

**ID:** gray brown upperparts; white underparts with gray wash on breast and sides; belly may be washed with yellow in fall; no eye ring; no obvious wing bars; all-black bill; dark legs.

**Size:** *L* 6½–7 in; *W* 10½ in.

**Status:** common breeder from April to August; common migrant from late March to April and from September to October; rare in winter.

**Habitat:** open deciduous woodlands, forest edges and clearings; usually near water.

**Nesting:** under the ledge of a building, picnic shelter, culvert, bridge, cliff or well; cup-shaped mud nest is lined with moss, grass, fur and feathers; female incubates 4–5 sparsely spotted, white eggs for 14–16 days; both adults feed the young.

**Feeding:** flycatches beetles, flies, wasps, grasshoppers, mayflies and other insects; occasionally plucks aquatic invertebrates and small fish from the water's surface.

**Voice:** *Male:* song is a hearty, snappy *fee-bee,* delivered frequently; call is a sharp *chip*.

**Similar Species:** *Eastern Wood-Pewee* (p. 218): smaller; pale wing bars; bicolored bill; does not pump its tail. *Olive-sided Flycatcher* (p. 217): dark "vest"; fluffy, white patches border rump. Empidonax *flycatchers* (pp. 219–23): most have eye rings and conspicuous wing bars. *Eastern Kingbird* (p. 226): white-tipped tail; black upperparts.

**Best Sites:** Tifft Nature Preserve; Letchworth SP; Stewart Park–Cayuga L.; John Boyd Thacher SP; Connetquot River SP.

# GREAT CRESTED FLYCATCHER

*Myiarchus crinitus*

The Great Crested Flycatcher's nesting habits are unusual for a flycatcher: it is a cavity nester, and although it prefers to nest in a natural tree cavity or abandoned woodpecker nest, it will occasionally use a nest box intended for a bluebird. Often, the Great Crested Flycatcher will decorate the entrance of its nest with a shed snakeskin. The purpose of this practice is not fully understood, though it might make any would-be predators think twice! In some instances, this versatile bird has even been known to substitute translucent plastic wrap for genuine reptilian skin.
• Songbirds such as the Great Crested Flycatcher are often thought of as birds that fly south for the winter. In reality, it would be more correct to say that they fly north for the summer. This flycatcher, as well as many other migrants, are subtropical or tropical birds of Central and South America that visit our country only briefly to raise their young before returning home.

**Nesting:** in a tree cavity, nest box or other artificial cavity; nest is lined with grass, bark strips and feathers; may hang a shed snakeskin or plastic wrap from the entrance hole; female incubates 4–5 heavily marked, creamy white to pale buff eggs for 13–15 days.

**Feeding:** flycatches for insects, often in the upper branches of deciduous trees; may also glean caterpillars and occasionally fruit.

**Voice:** loud, whistled *wheep!* and a rolling *prrrrreet!*

**Similar Species:** *Yellow-bellied Flycatcher* (p. 219): much smaller; yellow throat; lacks reddish brown tail and large, all-black bill.

**Best Sites:** Roger Tory Peterson Nature Center; Sapsucker Woods (Cornell Laboratory of Ornithology); Bear Mountain SP; Caumsett SP; Heckscher SP.

**ID:** bright yellow belly and undertail coverts; gray throat and upper breast; reddish brown tail; peaked, "crested" head; dark olive brown upperparts; heavy black bill.

**Size:** *L* 8–9 in; *W* 13 in.

**Status:** common, widespread breeder and migrant from May to September.

**Habitat:** deciduous and mixed woodlands, usually near openings or edges.

225

# EASTERN KINGBIRD

*Tyrannus tyrannus*

When you think of a tyrant, images of an oppressive dictator or a large, carnivorous dinosaur are much more likely to come to mind than a little bird. True as that may be, no one familiar with the pugnacity of the Eastern Kingbird is likely to refute its scientific name, *Tyrannus tyrannus*. This bird is a brawler, and it will fearlessly attack crows, hawks and even humans that pass through its territory. Intruders are often vigorously pursued, pecked and plucked for some distance until the kingbird is satisfied that there is no further threat. In contrast, its butterfly-like courtship flight, which is characterized by shallow, quivering wingbeats, reveals a gentler side of this bird. • Eastern Kingbirds are common and widespread in New York, so during a drive in the country it is likely you will spot at least one of these birds sitting on a fenceline or utility wire along a roadside. • Eastern Kingbirds rarely walk or hop on the ground—they prefer to fly, even for very short distances.

**ID:** dark gray to black upperparts; white underparts; white-tipped tail; black bill; small head crest; thin, orange red crown (rarely seen); no eye ring; black legs.

**Size:** *L* 8½ in; *W* 15 in.

**Status:** common, widespread breeder and migrant from May to September.

**Habitat:** rural fields with scattered trees or hedgerows, clearings in fragmented forests, open roadsides, burned areas; also near human settlements.

**Nesting:** in a tree or shrub, on a standing stump or in an upturned tree root; pair builds a deep, bulky cup nest of weeds, twigs and grass; female incubates 3–4 darkly blotched, white to pinkish white eggs for 14–18 days.

**Feeding:** flycatches insects; infrequently eats berries.

**Voice:** call is a quick, loud, chattering *kit-kit-kitter-kitter*; also a buzzy *dzee-dzee-dzee*.

**Similar Species:** *Tree Swallow* (p. 241): iridescent, dark blue back; more streamlined body; smaller bill; lacks white-tipped tail. *Olive-sided Flycatcher* (p. 217): 2 white tufts border rump; lacks white-tipped tail and all-white underparts. *Eastern Wood-Pewee* (p. 218): smaller; bicolored bill; lacks white-tipped tail and all-white underparts.

**Best Sites:** Beaver Meadow Nature Center; Beaver Lake CP; Saratoga National Historical Park; Ward Pound Ridge Reservation; Caumsett SP.

# NORTHERN SHRIKE

*Lanius excubitor*

Northern Shrikes are carnivorous songbirds that appear in our region each winter in unpredictable and highly variable numbers. During their winter visits, they are typically seen perched like hawks on exposed treetops, from which they survey open and semi-open hunting grounds. Winter feeding stations also tempt many shrikes to test their hunting skills on the feeding birds. • An adult Northern Shrike looks somewhat like a gray robin with the bill of a small hawk, and it specializes in catching and killing small birds and rodents. When this bird strikes a target, it relies on its sharp, hooked beak to dispatch its quarry, though it may use its feet to help. Shrikes are the world's only true carnivorous songbirds and the greatest diversity of shrikes occurs in Africa and Eurasia. • The Northern Shrike's habit of impaling its kills on thorns and barbs has earned it the names "Butcher Bird" and "Nine-Killer." Its scientific name *Lanius excubitor* translates as "watchful butcher," an appropriate description of the Northern Shrike's foraging behavior.

**ID:** black tail and wings; pale gray upperparts; finely barred, light underparts; black "mask" does not extend above hooked bill. *Immature:* faint "mask"; light brown upperparts; brown or gray barring on underparts. *In flight:* white wing patches; white tail edges.
**Size:** *L* 10 in; *W* 14½ in.
**Status:** irruptive winter visitor from November to March; uncommon some winters, almost absent in others.
**Habitat:** open country, including fields, shrubby areas, forest clearings and roadsides.

**Nesting:** does not nest in NY.
**Feeding:** swoops down on prey from a perch or chases prey through the air; regularly eats small birds, shrews and rodents; prey may be impaled on a thorn or barb for later consumption.
**Voice:** usually silent; infrequently gives a long grating laugh: *raa-raa-raa-raa.*
**Similar Species:** *Loggerhead Shrike* (p. 364): generally absent in winter; black "mask" extends above bill onto forehead; lacks barring on underparts. *Northern Mockingbird* (p. 269): slimmer overall; slim bill; no "mask"; paler wings and tail.
**Best Sites:** Nation's Road Grassland; Cape Vincent–Pt. Peninsula; Essex-Westport; Ft. Edward Grasslands; Five Rivers Environmental Education Center.

# WHITE-EYED VIREO

*Vireo griseus*

Proclaiming its spring arrival, the White-eyed Vireo sings *chick-ticha-wheeyou, chick-ticha-wheeyou-chick* among vibrant, early spring blossoms in local scrub. Like most vireos, the White-eyed Vireo can be a challenge to spot as it sneaks through dense tangles of branches and foliage in search of insects. • Even more secretive than the bird itself is the location of its precious nest. Intricately woven from grass, twigs, bark, lichens, moss, plant down, leaves and the fibrous paper from a wasp nest, the nest of the White-eyed Vireo is hung between the forking branches of a tree or shrub. • White-eyed Vireos are renowned for their complex vocalizations. A single bird may have a repertoire of a dozen or more songs. This vireo is also an excellent vocal mimic and may incorporate the calls of other bird species into its own songs! • As this bird's name implies, adult birds have white eyes, though the eyes of immature birds are brown.

**ID:** yellow "spectacles"; olive gray upperparts; white underparts with yellow sides and flanks; 2 whitish wing bars; dark wings and tail; pale eyes; dark bill; blue gray legs.
**Size:** *L* 5 in; *W* 7½ in.
**Status:** local breeder and migrant from May to September in southeastern NY and on Long I.
**Habitat:** dense, shrubby undergrowth and thickets in open, swampy, deciduous woodlands, overgrown fields, young second-growth woodlands, woodland clearings and along woodlot edges.

**Nesting:** in a deciduous shrub or small tree; deep, hanging cup nest is suspended from a horizontal fork; pair incubates 4 lightly speckled, white eggs for 13–15 days; both adults feed the young.
**Feeding:** gleans insects from branches and foliage during very active foraging; often hovers while gleaning.
**Voice:** loud, snappy, 3–9-note song, usually beginning and ending with "chick": *chick-ticha-wheeyou, chick-ticha-wheeyou-chick!*
**Similar Species:** *Pine Warbler* (p. 290) and *Yellow-throated Vireo* (p. 229): yellow throats. *Blue-headed Vireo* (p. 230): white "spectacles"; dark eyes; yellow highlights on wings and tail.
**Best Sites:** Bashakill WMA; Ward Pound Ridge Reservation; Marshlands Conservancy–Playland CP; Jamaica Bay Wildlife Refuge; Caumsett SP.

# YELLOW-THROATED VIREO

*Vireo flavifrons*

The Yellow-throated Vireo is usually found in mature deciduous woodlands with little or no understory and particularly likes tall oaks and maples. Like its treetop neighbor the Cerulean Warbler, the Yellow-throated Vireo forages high above the forest floor, making it a difficult bird to observe. • An unmated male will sing tirelessly as he searches for nest sites, often placing a few pieces of nest material in several locations. When a female appears, the male dazzles her with his displays and leads her on a tour of potential nesting sites within his large territory. If a bond is established, they will mate and build an intricately woven, hanging nest in the forking branches of a deciduous tree. The male is a devoted helper, assisting the female to build the nest, incubate the eggs and rear the young. • The Yellow-throat is North America's most colorful vireo. It is the only vireo with a bright yellow throat and breast and a white belly.

**ID:** bright yellow "spectacles," "chin," throat and breast; olive upperparts, except for gray rump and dark wings and tail; 2 white wing bars; white belly and undertail coverts.
**Size:** *L* 5½ in; *W* 9½ in.
**Status:** locally common breeder and migrant from May to September.
**Habitat:** mature deciduous woodlands with minimal understory.
**Nesting:** in a deciduous tree; pair builds a deep cup nest of plant fibers and spider silk; pair incubates 4 darkly spotted, creamy white to pinkish eggs for 14–15 days; each parent takes on guardianship of half the fledged young.

**Feeding:** forages by inspecting branches and foliage in the upper canopy; eats mostly insects, but also feeds on seasonally available berries.
**Voice:** song is a slowly repeated series of hoarse phrases with long pauses in between: *ahweeo, eeoway, away;* calls include a throaty *heh heh heh.*
**Similar Species:** *Pine Warbler* (p. 290): olive yellow rump; thinner bill; faint, darkish streaking along sides; yellow belly; faint "spectacles." *White-eyed Vireo* (p. 228): white "chin" and throat; grayer head and back; white eyes. *Blue-headed Vireo* (p. 230): white "spectacles" and throat; yellow highlights on wings and tail.
**Best Sites:** Howland Island WMA; Stewart Park–Cayuga L.; Five Rivers Environmental Education Center; Sterling Forest SP; Bear Mountain SP.

# BLUE-HEADED VIREO

*Vireo solitarius*

From the canopies of shady woodlands, the purposeful, liquid notes of the Blue-headed Vireo penetrate the dense foliage. This vireo prefers different habitat than many of its relatives, which favor broadleaf trees or immature stands. Though this bird is also found in deciduous habitats, it is the only vireo that commonly occupies coniferous forests. • During courtship, male Blue-headed Vireos fluff out their yellowish flanks and bob ceremoniously to their prospective mates. When mating is complete and the eggs are in the nest, the parents become extremely quiet. Once the young hatch, however, Blue-headed parents will readily scold an intruder long before it gets close to the nest. • The distinctive "spectacles" that frame this bird's eyes provide a good field mark. They are among the boldest of the eye rings seen on our songbirds. • Until 1997, the Blue-headed, Cassin's *(V. cassinii)* and Plumbeous *(V. plumbeus)* vireos were lumped together as a single species, the "Solitary Vireo."

**ID:** bold, white "spectacles"; blue gray head; 2 white wing bars; olive green upperparts; white underparts; yellow sides and flanks; yellow highlights on dark wings and tail; stout bill; dark legs.

**Size:** *L* 5–6 in; *W* 9½ in.

**Status:** common breeder and migrant from May to October at higher elevations of the Adirondacks, Catskills and Allegany Plateau.

**Habitat:** primarily remote, mixed coniferous-deciduous forests; also pure coniferous forests and pine plantations.

**Nesting:** in a coniferous tree or tall shrub; hanging, basketlike cup nest is made of grass, roots, bark strips and spider silk; pair incubates 3–5 lightly spotted, whitish eggs for 12–14 days.

**Feeding:** gleans branches for insects; frequently hovers to pluck insects from vegetation.

**Voice:** *Male:* slow, purposeful, slurred, robinlike notes with moderate pauses in between: *chu-wee, taweeto, toowip, chee-rio, teeyay; churr* call.

**Similar Species:** *White-eyed Vireo* (p. 228): yellow "spectacles"; light-colored eyes. *Yellow-throated Vireo* (p. 229): yellow "spectacles" and throat.

**Best Sites:** Allegany SP; Letchworth SP; Ferd's Bog–Moose River Plains; John Boyd Thacher SP; Cherry Plain SP.

# WARBLING VIREO
*Vireo gilvus*

The charming Warbling Vireo is a common summer resident of sparsely wooded areas, and by early May, its wondrous voice fills many local parks and backyards. Because this vireo often settles close to urban areas, its bubbly, warbling songs should be familiar to most people. • The Warbling Vireo lacks splashy field marks and is only readily observed when it moves from one leaf-hidden stage to another. During its stay in our region, this bird prefers old maples and cottonwoods as foraging and nesting sites. Searching treetops for this generally inconspicuous vireo may literally be a "pain in the neck," but the satisfaction of visually confirming its identity is exceptionally rewarding. • The hanging nests of vireos are usually much harder to find than the birds themselves. In winter, however, nests are revealed as they swing precariously from bare deciduous branches.

**ID:** partial, dark eye line borders white "eyebrow"; no wing bars; olive gray upper-parts; greenish flanks; white to pale gray under-parts; gray crown.
**Size:** *L* 5–5½ in; *W* 8½ in.
**Status:** common breeder and migrant from May to September; uncommon on coastal plain and absent at higher elevations.
**Habitat:** open deciduous woodlands; parks and gardens with deciduous trees; prefers mature maples and cottonwoods.
**Nesting:** in a deciduous tree or shrub; hanging, basketlike cup nest is made of grass, roots, plant down and spider silk; pair incubates 4 lightly speckled, white eggs for 12–14 days.
**Feeding:** gleans foliage for insects; may hover to glean insects from vegetation.

**Voice:** *Male:* song is a long, husky, musical warble of slurred whistles; calls include a querulous, 2-syllable *eeeah* and a quick *twip*.
**Similar Species:** *Philadelphia Vireo* (p. 232): yellow breast, sides and flanks; full, dark eye line borders white "eyebrow." *Red-eyed Vireo* (p. 233): black eye line extends to bill; blue gray crown; red eyes. *Tennessee Warbler* (p. 277): blue gray "cap" and nape; olive green back; slimmer bill.
**Best Sites:** Iroquois NWR–Tonawanda WMA–Oak Orchard WMA; Montezuma NWR; Beaver Lake CP; Saratoga National Historical; Sterling Forest SP.

# PHILADELPHIA VIREO

*Vireo philadelphicus*

Although many similar-looking birds sound quite different, the Philadelphia Vireo and Red-eyed Vireo are two species that sound very similar but are easy to tell apart once you locate them with your binoculars. Most forest songbirds are initially identified by voice, however, so the Philadelphia Vireo is often overlooked because its song is almost identical to that of the more abundant Red-eyed Vireo. • The Philadelphia Vireo nests in mixed boreal forests where it fills a niche left unoccupied by the strictly deciduous-dwelling Warbling Vireo. • The Philadelphia Vireo breeds farther north than any other vireo. In migration, it often travels in the company of other warblers and vireos. • This bird bears the name of the city in which the first scientific specimen of this species was collected. Philadelphia was the center of America's budding scientific community in the early 1800s, and much of the study of birds and other natural sciences originated in Pennsylvania.

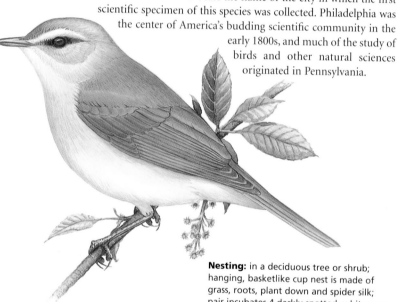

**ID:** gray "cap"; full, dark eye line borders bold, white "eyebrow"; dark olive green upperparts; pale yellow breast, sides and flanks; white belly (underparts may be completely yellow in fall); robust bill; pale eyes.

**Size:** L 4½–5 in; W 8 in.

**Status:** rare breeder in the Adirondacks in June and July; uncommon migrant, arriving in May and leaving in September; more common as a migrant in western NY.

**Habitat:** open broadleaf and mixed woodlands with aspen, willow and alder components; also in second-growth on burns and cutovers; occasionally in gardens and parks.

**Nesting:** in a deciduous tree or shrub; hanging, basketlike cup nest is made of grass, roots, plant down and spider silk; pair incubates 4 darkly spotted, white eggs for about 14 days.

**Feeding:** gleans vegetation for insects; frequently hovers to glean food from foliage.

**Voice:** *Male:* song is similar to that of the Red-eyed Vireo, but is usually slower, slightly higher pitched and not as variable: *look-up way-up tree-top see-me.*

**Similar Species:** *Red-eyed Vireo* (p. 233): blue gray crown with black border; red eyes; lacks yellow breast; similar song. *Warbling Vireo* (p. 231): partial, dark eye line (mostly behind eye); lacks yellow breast. *Tennessee Warbler* (p. 277): blue gray "cap" and nape; olive green back; slimmer bill; lacks yellow breast.

**Best Sites:** Whiteface Mt.; Crown Point SP; Saratoga National Historical Park; Cohoes–Crescent–Peebles Island SP; Jones Beach SP.

# RED-EYED VIREO

*Vireo olivaceus*

The Red-eyed Vireo is the undisputed champion of vocal endurance in our region. In spring and early summer, males sing continuously through the day, carrying on long after most songbirds have curtailed their courtship melodies. One particularly vigorous Red-eyed Vireo male holds the record for most songs delivered in a single day: approximately 21,000!
• The Red-eyed Vireo adopts a particular stance when it hops up and along branches. It tends to be more hunched over than other songbirds, and hops with its body diagonal to the direction of travel. • There is no firm agreement about the reason for this vireo's red eye color. Red eyes are very unusual among songbirds and tend to be more prevalent in nonpasserines, such as accipiters, grebes and some herons. • Red-eyed Vireos sound a lot like American Robins, and beginning birders are often delighted to discover these shy birds hiding behind a familiar song.

**ID:** dark eye line; white "eyebrow"; blue gray crown with black border; olive green upperparts; olive "cheek"; white to pale gray underparts; may have yellow wash on sides, flanks and undertail coverts, especially in fall; no wing bars; red eyes (seen only at close range).
**Size:** *L* 6 in; *W* 10 in.
**Status:** very common, widespread breeder and migrant from May to October.
**Habitat:** deciduous woodlands with a shrubby understory.

**Nesting:** in a deciduous tree or shrub; hanging, basketlike cup nest is made of grass, roots, spider silk and cocoons; female incubates 4 darkly spotted, white eggs for 11–14 days.
**Feeding:** gleans foliage for insects, especially caterpillars; often hovers; also eats berries.
**Voice:** call is a short, scolding *neeah. Male:* song is a continuous, variable, robinlike run of quick, short phrases with distinct pauses in between: *look-up, way-up, tree-top, see-me, here-I-am!*
**Similar Species:** *Philadelphia Vireo* (p. 232): yellow breast; lacks black border to blue gray "cap"; song is very similar, but slightly higher pitched. *Warbling Vireo* (p. 231): dusky eye line does not extend to bill; lacks black border on gray "cap." *Tennessee Warbler* (p. 277): blue gray "cap" and nape; olive green back; slimmer bill.
**Best Sites:** Letchworth SP; Allegany SP; Stewart Park–Cayuga L.; John Boyd Thacher SP; Caumsett SP.

233

# GRAY JAY

*Perisoreus canadensis*

Few other birds rival the mischievous Gray Jay for curiosity and boldness. Attracted by any foreign sound or potential feeding opportunity, small family groups glide gently and unexpectedly out of spruce, pine and fir stands. These mooching marauders are often encountered by winter campers, when these jays approach for handouts. • Gray Jays lay their eggs and begin incubation as early as mid-March. Their nests are well insulated to conserve heat, and getting an early start on nesting means that young jays will learn how to forage efficiently and store food before the next cold season approaches. • In preparation for the winter months, Gray Jays often store food. Their specialized salivary glands coat the food with a sticky mucus that helps to preserve it. • This common bird has some interesting alternate names: "Whiskey Jack" is derived from the Algonquin name for this bird, *wis-kat-jon;* others affectionately call this bird "Camp Robber."

**ID:** fluffy, pale gray plumage; fairly long tail; white forehead, "cheek," throat and undertail coverts; dark gray nape and upperparts; light gray breast and belly; dark bill. *Immature:* dark sooty gray overall; pale bill with dark tip.

**Size:** *L* 11–13 in; *W* 18 in.

**Status:** fairly common year-round resident in the Adirondacks; breeds from March to May.

**Habitat:** dense and open coniferous and mixed forests, bogs and fens.

**Nesting:** in a coniferous tree; bulky, well-insulated nest of plant fibers, roots, moss and twigs is lined with plant down, feathers and fur; female incubates 3–4 speckled and blotched, pale gray to greenish eggs for 16–18 days.

**Feeding:** searches the ground and vegetation for insects, fruit, seeds, fungi, bird eggs and nestlings, carrion and berries; stores food items at scattered cache sites.

**Voice:** complex vocal repertoire includes a soft, whistled *quee-oo,* a chuckled *cla-cla-cla* and a *churr;* also imitates other birds.

**Similar Species:** *Northern Shrike* (p. 227): black "mask"; black-and-white wings and tail; hooked bill. *Northern Mockingbird* (p. 269): darker wings and tail; white wing patch; white outer tail feathers; longer, slimmer bill.

**Best Sites:** Ferd's Bog–Moose River Plains; Bloomingdale Bog; Paul Smiths Visitor Interpretive Center (Adirondack Park); Chubb River Swamp; Elk L.

# BLUE JAY

*Cyanocitta cristata*

The large trees and bushy ornamental shrubs of our suburban neighborhoods and rural communities are perfect habitat for the adaptable Blue Jay. Common wherever there are fruit-bearing plants and backyard feeding stations that are maintained with a generous supply of sunflower seeds and peanuts, this jay is one of the most recognizable songbirds. Blue Jays can appear a bit "piggish" at the feeder, but they are often only storing the food in caches strategically placed around the neighborhood. • The Blue Jay embodies all the admirable traits and aggressive qualities of the corvid family, which also includes crows and ravens. Beautiful, resourceful and vocally diverse, the Blue Jay occasionally raids nests and bullies other feeder occupants. • Whether on its own or gathered in a mob, the Blue Jay will rarely hesitate to drive away smaller birds, squirrels or even cats when threatened. It seems that there is no predator, not even the Great Horned Owl, that is too formidable for this bird to cajole or harass.

**ID:** blue crest; black "necklace"; blue upperparts; white underparts; white bar and flecking on wings; dark bars and white corners on blue tail; black bill.

**Size:** *L* 11–12½ in; *W* 16 in.

**Status:** common year-round resident; breeds from April to June.

**Habitat:** mixed deciduous forests, agricultural areas, scrubby fields and townsites.

**Nesting:** in a tree or tall shrub; pair builds a bulky stick nest and incubates 4–5 darkly spotted, greenish, buff or pale blue eggs for 16–18 days.

**Feeding:** forages on the ground and among vegetation for nuts, berries, eggs, nestlings and birdseed; also eats insects and carrion; visits feeders for peanuts and sunflower seeds; caches food.

**Voice:** noisy, screaming *jay-jay-jay;* nasal *queedle queedle queedle-queedle* sounds a little like a muted trumpet; often imitates sounds.

**Similar Species:** none.

**Best Sites:** Roger Tory Peterson Nature Center; Beaver Lake CP; Durand-Eastman Park (Rochester); Five Rivers Environmental Education Center; Pelham Bay Park (NYC).

# AMERICAN CROW

*Corvus brachyrhynchos*

American Crows are wary and intelligent birds that have flourished despite considerable human effort, over many generations, to reduce their numbers. These birds are ecological generalists, and much of their strength lies in their ability to adapt to a variety of habitats. • American Crows are common throughout much of our region in both summer and winter. In fall, crows group together in flocks numbering in the hundreds or thousands. In some places, many thousands of crows may roost together on any given winter night. Aggregations of crows are known as "murders." • Crows are impressive mimics, able to whine like a dog, cry like a child, squawk like a hen, and laugh like a human. Some crows in captivity are able to mimic simple spoken words. • The American Crow's cumbersome-sounding scientific name *Corvus brachyrhynchos* is Latin for "raven with the small nose."

**ID:** glossy, purple black plumage; slim, sleek head and throat; black bill and legs; square-shaped tail. **Size:** *L* 17–21 in; *W* 3–3½ ft.

**Status:** common year-round resident; breeds from March to June.

**Habitat:** urban areas, agricultural fields and other open areas with scattered woodlands; also among clearings, marshes, lakes and rivers in densely forested areas.

**Nesting:** in a coniferous or deciduous tree or on a utility pole; large stick-and-branch nest is lined with fur and soft plant materials; female incubates 4–6 darkly blotched,

gray green to blue green eggs for about 18 days.

**Feeding:** very opportunistic; feeds on carrion, small vertebrates, other birds' eggs and nestlings, berries, seeds, invertebrates and human food waste; also visits feeders.

**Voice:** distinctive, far-carrying, repetitive *caw-caw-caw*.

**Similar Species:** *Common Raven* (p. 238): larger; wedge-shaped tail; shaggy throat; heavier bill. *Fish Crow* (p. 237): slightly smaller; distinguished by more nasal call: *cah-cah-cah*.

**Best Sites:** Nation's Road Grassland; Montezuma NWR; Essex-Westport; Cohoes–Crescent–Peebles Island SP; Caumsett SP.

# FISH CROW
*Corvus ossifragus*

Most people who encounter this ebony bird quickly dismiss it as just another one of those seemingly omnipresent American Crows, not realizing that it possesses a unique identity separate from that of its larger relative. Best identified by its more nasal, two-note call, the Fish Crow has adapted to survive in association with aquatic environments and seems to be expanding its range inland along large rivers and their tributaries. A large part of its success can be attributed to its ability to eat a diverse array of foods including carrion, insects, crustaceans, fish, seeds and fruits. Other food sources such as the carefully guarded eggs and young of other birds, or the odorous food waste left behind by humans in awkward, concealing containers, often require this crafty bird to employ more intelligent strategies characteristic of all the members of the corvid family. Its effective combination of a nimble bill, strong, dexterous feet and the ability to learn allow this bird to solve most foraging problems.

**ID:** virtually identical to American Crow, but with marginally shorter legs; black plumage with purplish gloss; heavy, black bill; best identified by voice.

**Size:** *L* 15½ in; *W* 3 ft.

**Status:** common year-round resident on Long I., in New York City and on tidal Hudson R. to Albany; increasing in central NY; breeds from March to June.

**Habitat:** river valleys and coastal habitats, including tidal saltwater marshes, swamps, beaches, estuaries, riparian woodlands, fields and dumps near water.

**Nesting:** in a loose colony; in the topmost crotch of a tree, usually a conifer, or shrub; pair builds a bulky nest of sticks and twigs; female incubates 4–5 heavily marked, pale bluish to greenish eggs for 16–18 days.

**Feeding:** omnivorous scavenger; feeds on a wide variety of foods including carrion, fish, crustaceans and other aquatic invertebrates, insects, eggs, seeds, nestling birds and human food waste; typically forages by walking along shorelines, in shallow water and on fields in small flocks.

**Voice:** calls are a nasal *cah-cah-cah* or 2-note *eh-eh*, hoarser and higher-pitched than calls of other corvids.

**Similar Species:** *American Crow* (p. 236): slightly larger, but otherwise identical; call is a single or repeated *caw*.

**Best Sites:** Stewart Park–Cayuga L.; Cohoes–Crescent–Peebles Island SP; Marshlands Conservancy–Playland CP; Jamaica Bay Wildlife Refuge; Connetquot River SP.

# COMMON RAVEN

*Corvus corax*

Whether stealing food from a flock of gulls, harassing a soaring hawk in midair, dining from a roadside carcass or confidently strutting among campers at a park, the Common Raven is worthy of its reputation as a bold and clever bird. It is glorified in native cultures across the Northern Hemisphere as the avian embodiment of humankind. From its complex vocalizations to its occasional playful bouts of sliding down a snowbank, this raucous bird exhibits behaviors that many people once thought of as exclusively human. • Ravens maintain loyal, life-long pair bonds that are reinforced each winter in courtship chases consisting of drag races, barrel rolls, dives and tumbles. • Distributed throughout the Northern Hemisphere, the Common Raven is found along coastlines, in deserts, on mountaintops and even on arctic tundra. Ravens once inhabited every corner of our region, but deforestation of the state for agriculture and lumber led to great declines in their population. • The Common Raven is the largest passerine, or perching, bird.

**ID:** glossy, black plumage; heavy, black bill; wedge-shaped tail; shaggy throat; rounded wings.
**Size:** *L* 17–21 in; *W* 4 ft.

**Status:** common year-round resident in the Adirondacks; increasing in the Catskills and Appalachian Plateau; breeds in March and April; startling population increases in the past decade.

**Habitat:** coniferous and mixed forests and woodlands; also townsites, campgrounds and landfills.

**Nesting:** on a ledge, bluff or utility pole or in a tall coniferous tree; large stick-and-branch nest is lined with fur and soft plant materials; female incubates 4–6 darkly blotched, greenish eggs for 18–21 days.

**Feeding:** very opportunistic; feeds on carrion, small vertebrates, other birds' eggs and nestlings, berries, invertebrates and human food waste; may forage along roads.

**Voice:** deep, guttural, far-carrying, repetitive *craww-craww* or *quork quork;* also many other vocalizations.

**Similar Species:** *American Crow* (p. 236): smaller; square-shaped tail; slim throat; slimmer bill; call is a higher-pitched *caw-caw-caw.*

**Best Sites:** Ferd's Bog–Moose River Plains; Bloomingdale Bog; Elk L.; John Boyd Thacher SP; Thompson Pond–Stissing Mt.

# HORNED LARK

*Eremophila alpestris*

The tinkling sounds of Horned Larks flying over pastures and fields are a sure sign that another spring has arrived. Horned Larks are among the earliest breeding birds to arrive in our region, settling on farm fields long before the snow is gone. • The male Horned Lark performs an elaborate song-flight courtship display. Flying and gliding in circles as high up as 800 feet, the male issues his sweet, tinkling song before he closes his wings and plummets in a dramatic, high-speed dive that he aborts at the last second, just before hitting the ground. • These open-country inhabitants are most common during spring and fall migration and in early winter as they congregate in flocks on farm fields, beaches and airfields, often in the company of Snow Buntings and Lapland Longspurs. Horned Larks are commonly found along the shoulders of gravel roads, where they search for seeds. These birds are easy to see but often tough to identify because they fly off into adjacent fields or open ground at the approach of any vehicle.

**ID:** *Male:* small black "horns" (rarely raised); black line under eye extends from bill to "cheek"; light yellow to white face; dull brown upperparts; black breast band; dark tail with white outer tail feathers; pale throat. *Female:* less distinctively patterned; duller plumage overall.

**Size:** *L* 7 in; *W* 12 in.

**Status:** special concern; locally common breeder from late February to July; common migrant and winter visitor from November to March.

**Habitat:** *Breeding:* open areas, including pastures, croplands, sparsely vegetated fields, weedy meadows and airfields. *In migration* and *winter:* croplands, fields and roadside ditches.

**Nesting:** on the ground; in a shallow scrape lined with grass, plant fibers and roots; female incubates 3–4 brown speckled, pale gray to greenish white eggs for 10–12 days.

**Feeding:** gleans the ground for seeds; sometimes chases insects; eats more insects during migration and mostly seeds in winter.

**Voice:** call is a tinkling *tsee-titi* or *zoot;* flight song is a long series of tinkling, twittered whistles.

**Similar Species:** *Sparrows* (pp. 312–21), *Lapland Longspur* (p. 330) and *American Pipit* (p. 272): all lack distinctive facial pattern, "horns" and solid black breast band.

**Best Sites:** Nation's Road Grassland; Montezuma NWR; Cape Vincent–Pt. Peninsula; Essex-Westport; Jones Beach SP.

# PURPLE MARTIN

*Progne subis*

Purple Martins once nested in natural tree hollows and in cliff crevices, but as early as 1831, John James Audubon reported nests in boxes above tavern signs. With today's martin "apartment" complexes, these birds have all but abandoned natural nest sites. • To be successful in attracting these large swallows to your backyard, place a martin house high on a pole in a large, open area, preferably near water. Cavity openings must be the correct size and the house must be cleaned out each winter. Unfortunately, there is always the chance that aggressive House Sparrows and European Starlings will chase away any Purple Martins that dare to move in. If all goes well, however, each spring will bring the return of a Purple Martin colony. The result will be an endlessly entertaining summer spectacle as the adult martins spiral around the house in pursuit of flying insects, and the young perch clumsily at the opening of their apartment cavity. • The Purple Martin is the largest North American swallow.

**ID:** glossy, dark blue body; slightly forked tail; pointed wings; small bill. *Male:* dark underparts. *Female:* sooty gray underparts.

**Size:** *L* 7–8 in; *W* 18 in.

**Status:** locally common breeder and migrant from May to September, especially near the shores of lakes Erie, Ontario, Oneida and Champlain, the Finger Lakes and Long I.

**Habitat:** semi-open areas, often near water.

**Nesting:** communal; usually in a human-made, apartment-style birdhouse; rarely in a tree cavity or cliff crevice; nest materials include feathers, grass, mud and vegetation; female incubates 4–5 white eggs for 15–18 days.

**Feeding:** mostly while in flight; usually eats flies, ants, bugs, dragonflies and mosquitoes; may also walk on the ground, taking insects and rarely berries.

**Voice:** rich, fluty, robinlike *pew-pew,* often heard in flight.

**Similar Species:** *European Starling* (p. 271): longer bill (yellow in summer); lacks forked tail. *Barn Swallow* (p. 245): deeply forked tail; buff orange to reddish brown throat; whitish to cinnamon underparts. *Tree Swallow* (p. 241): white underparts.

**Best Sites:** Dunkirk Harbor; Braddock Bay; Montezuma NWR; Saratoga L.; Marshlands Conservancy–Playland CP.

# TREE SWALLOW
*Tachycineta bicolor*

Tree Swallows, our most common summer swallows, are often seen perched beside their fence-post nest boxes. When conditions are favorable, these busy birds are known to return to their young 10 to 20 times per hour, providing observers with numerous opportunities to watch the birds in action. • Tree Swallows prefer to nest in natural tree hollows or woodpecker cavities in standing dead trees, but where cavities are scarce, nest boxes may be used as temporary sites. Increasingly, landowners, park managers and forestry companies are realizing the value of dead trees as homes for wildlife and are choosing to leave them standing. • In bright spring sunshine, the iridescent back of the Tree Swallow appears dark blue; prior to fall migration, it appears green. Unlike other North American swallows, female Tree Swallows do not acquire their full adult plumage until their second or third year. • The scientific name *bicolor* is Latin for "two colors" and refers to the contrast between the bird's dark upperparts and white underparts.

**ID:** iridescent, dark blue or green head and upper-parts; white underparts; no white on "cheek"; dark rump; small bill; long, pointed wings; shallowly forked tail. *Female:* slightly duller plumage.
**Size:** *L* 5½ in; *W* 14½ in.
**Status:** common breeder from May to July; sometimes abundant migrant from March to April and from September to November; very rare in winter on the coast.
**Habitat:** open areas, such as beaver ponds, marshes, lakeshores, field fencelines, town-sites and open woodlands.
**Nesting:** in a tree cavity or nest box lined with weeds, grass and feathers; female incubates 4–6 white eggs for 13–16 days.

**Feeding:** catches flies, midges, mosquitoes, beetles and ants on the wing; also takes stoneflies, mayflies and caddisflies over water; may eat some berries and seeds.
**Voice:** alarm call is a metallic, buzzy *klweet*. *Male:* song is a liquid, chattering twitter.
**Similar Species:** *Purple Martin* (p. 240): male is dark blue overall; female has sooty gray underparts. *Eastern Kingbird* (p. 226): larger; white-tipped tail; longer bill; dark gray to blackish upperparts. *Bank Swallow* (p. 243) and *Northern Rough-winged Swallow* (p. 242): brown upperparts. *Barn Swallow* (p. 245): buff orange to reddish brown throat; deeply forked tail.
**Best Sites:** Dunkirk Harbor; Braddock Bay; Essex-Westport; Jamaica Bay Wildlife Refuge; Jones Beach SP.

# NORTHERN ROUGH-WINGED SWALLOW

*Stelgidopteryx serripennis*

Northern Rough-winged Swallows typically nest on their own in sandy banks along rivers and streams, enjoying their own private piece of waterfront. Once in a while, a pair may nest among a large colony of Bank Swallows, but most are happy with the company of their own species. In a wheeling flock of feeding swallows, Northern Rough-wings are often completely overlooked among their similar-looking cousins. The Rough-wing is most likely to be feeding over water, picking off insects on or near the water's surface. • Unlike other swallows, male Northern Rough-wings have curved barbs along the outer edge of their primary wing feathers. The purpose of this saw-toothed edge remains a mystery, but it may be used to produce sound during courtship displays. The ornithologist who initially named this bird must have been very impressed with its wings: *Stelgidopteryx* means "scraper wing" and *serripennis* means "saw feather."

**ID:** brown upperparts; creamy white underparts; gray brown wash on breast and sides; small bill; dark "cheek"; dark rump; long, pointed wings; notched tail.

**Size:** *L* 5½ in; *W* 14 in.

**Status:** fairly common breeder and migrant from April to September.

**Habitat:** open and semi-open areas, including fields and open woodlands, usually near water; also gravel pits.

**Nesting:** occasionally in small colonies; pair excavates a long burrow in a steep, earthen bank and lines the end of the burrow with leaves and dry grass; may reuse a kingfisher burrow, rodent burrow or other land crevice; mostly the female incubates 4–8 white eggs for 12–16 days.

**Feeding:** catches flying insects on the wing; occasionally eats insects from the ground; drinks while flying.

**Voice:** generally quiet; occasionally a quick, short, squeaky *brrrtt*.

**Similar Species:** *Bank Swallow* (p. 243): dark breast band. *Tree Swallow* (p. 241): iridescent, dark bluish to greenish upperparts; clean white underparts. *Cliff Swallow* (p. 244): blue gray upperparts; buff forehead; orangy rump.

**Best Sites:** Braddock Bay; Montezuma NWR; Cape Vincent–Pt. Peninsula; Bashakill WMA; Caumsett SP.

# BANK SWALLOW

*Riparia riparia*

A colony of Bank Swallows can be a constant flurry of activity as eager parents pop in and out of their earthen burrows with mouthfuls of insects for their insatiable young. Parents can quickly distinguish their own nestlings' demanding squeaks among the thousands of cries for food in the colony's bankside chambers. All this activity tends to attract attention, but few predators are able to catch these swift and agile birds. • Bank Swallows usually excavate their own nest burrows, first using their small bills and later digging with their feet. Most nestlings are safe from predators within their nest chamber, which is typically at the end of a burrow that is 2 to 3 feet in length. • In medieval Europe, it was believed that swallows spent the winter in the mud at the bottom of swamps because they were not seen at that time of year. In those days, it was beyond imagination that these birds might fly south for the winter. • *Riparia* is from the Latin for "riverbank," which is a common nesting site for this bird.

**ID:** brown upperparts; light underparts; brown breast band; long, pointed wings; shallowly forked tail; white throat; dark "cheek"; small bill and feet.

**Size:** *L* 5½ in; *W* 13 in.

**Status:** common, widespread breeder and migrant from April to September.

**Habitat:** steep banks, lakeshore bluffs and gravel pits.

**Nesting:** colonial; pair excavates or reuses a long burrow in a steep earthen bank; the end of the burrow is lined with grass, rootlets, weeds, straw and feathers; pair incubates 4–5 white eggs for 14–16 days.

**Feeding:** catches flying insects; drinks on the wing.

**Voice:** twittering chatter: *speed-zeet speed-zeet.*

**Similar Species:** *Northern Rough-winged Swallow* (p. 242): lacks dark, defined breast band. *Tree Swallow* (p. 241): iridescent, dark bluish to greenish upperparts; lacks dark breast band. *Cliff Swallow* (p. 244): blue gray upperparts; buff forehead; orangy rump; lacks dark breast band.

**Best Sites:** Dunkirk Harbor; Braddock Bay; Cape Vincent–Pt. Peninsula; Saratoga L.; Caumsett SP.

# CLIFF SWALLOW

*Petrochelidon pyrrhonota*

If the Cliff Swallow were to be renamed in the 20th century, it would probably be called "Bridge Swallow," because so many bridges over rivers in eastern North America have a colony living under them. If you stop to inspect the underside of a bridge, you may see hundreds of gourd-shaped mud nests stuck to the pillars and structural beams. • Master mud masons, Cliff Swallows roll mud into balls with their bills and press the pellets together to form their characteristic nests. Brooding parents peer out of the circular neck of the nest, their gleaming eyes watching the world go by and white forehead patches warning intruders that somebody is home. These swallows are known to observe the feeding habitats of neighbors to find the best spots for foraging. • Cliff Swallows are brood parasites—females often lay one or more eggs in the temporarily vacant nests of neighboring Cliff Swallows. The owners of parasitized nests accept the foreign eggs and care for them as if they were their own.

**ID:** orangy rump; buff forehead; blue gray head and wings; rusty "cheek," nape and throat; buff breast; white belly; spotted undertail coverts; nearly square tail.
**Size:** *L* 5½ in; *W* 13½ in.
**Status:** locally common breeder from May to July upstate; common migrant from April to May and from August to September throughout the state.
**Habitat:** steep banks, cliffs, bridges and buildings, often near watercourses.
**Nesting:** colonial; under a bridge, on a cliff or building or under the eaves of a barn; pair builds a gourd-shaped mud nest with a small opening near the bottom; pair incubates 4–5 brown-spotted, white to pinkish eggs for 14–16 days.

**Feeding:** forages over water, fields and marshes; catches flying insects in midair; occasionally eats berries; drinks on the wing.
**Voice:** twittering chatter: *churrr-churrr;* also *nyew* alarm call.
**Similar Species:** *Barn Swallow* (p. 245): deeply forked tail; dark rump; usually has rust-colored underparts and forehead.
*Other swallows* (pp. 240–43): lack buff forehead and orangy rump.
**Best Sites:** Allegany SP; Braddock Bay; Verona Beach SP–Sylvan Beach; Saratoga L.; Bashakill WMA.

# BARN SWALLOW

*Hirundo rustica*

Although Barn Swallows do not occur in mass colonies, they are very familiar birds because they usually build their nests on human-made structures. Barn Swallows once nested on cliffs and in the entrances to caves, but their cup-shaped mud nests are now found under house eaves, in barns and boathouses, under bridges or on any other structure that provides shelter. • Unfortunately, not everyone appreciates nesting Barn Swallows—the young can be very messy—and people often scrape nests off buildings just as the nesting season begins. However, these graceful birds are natural pest controllers, and their close association with urban areas and tolerance for human activity affords us the wondrous opportunity to observe and study the normally secretive reproductive cycle of birds. • In New York, the Barn Swallow is the only swallow that has a deeply forked tail. • The most widely distributed swallow in the world, the Barn Swallow breeds over much of North America, Europe, Asia and Africa, and winters throughout the Southern Hemisphere.

**ID:** long, deeply forked tail; rufous throat and forehead; blue black upperparts; rust-to buff-colored underparts; long, pointed wings.

**Size:** *L* 7 in; *W* 15 in.

**Status:** common breeder and migrant from April to October.

**Habitat:** open rural and urban areas where bridges, culverts and buildings are found near rivers, lakes, marshes or ponds.

**Nesting:** singly or in small, loose colonies; on a vertical or horizontal building structure under a suitable overhang; half or full cup nest is made of mud and grass or straw; pair incubates 4–7 brown-spotted, white eggs for 13–17 days.

**Feeding:** catches flying insects on the wing.

**Voice:** continuous, twittering chatter: *zip-zip-zip;* also *kvick-kvick.*

**Similar Species:** *Cliff Swallow* (p. 244): squared tail; buff forehead; orangy rump; pale underparts. *Purple Martin* (p. 240): shallowly forked tail; male is entirely blue black; female has sooty gray underparts. *Tree Swallow* (p. 241): clean white underparts; notched tail.

**Best Sites:** Roger Tory Peterson Nature Center; Braddock Bay; Stewart Park–Cayuga L.; Bashakill WMA; Jones Beach SP.

# BLACK-CAPPED CHICKADEE

*Poecile atricapillus*

Flocks of energetic Black-capped Chickadees can be seen year-round as they flit from tree to tree, scouring branches and shriveled leaves for insects and sometimes hanging upside down to catch the fleeing bugs. In winter, all other residents seem to fall into step with the lively, active chickadees, and these engaging birds are common visitors to well-stocked feeders. They can even occasionally be enticed to land on an outstretched hand offering a sunflower seed. In spring and fall, migrants rely on the local knowledge of Black-caps to find the best food areas. In summer, the best place to look for Black-capped Chickadees is wherever there are birch stands—they like to feast on the many insect pests found in these trees. • Most songbirds, including the Black-capped Chickadee, have both songs and calls. The chickadee's *swee-tee* song is heard primarily during spring courtship, and its *chick-a-dee-dee-dee* call maintains contact among flock members and keeps flocks together. • The scientific name *atricapilla* is Latin for "black crown."

**ID:** black "cap" and "bib"; white "cheek"; gray back and wings; white underparts; light buff sides and flanks; dark legs; white edging on wing feathers.

**Size:** *L* 5–6 in; *W* 8 in.

**Status:** common, widespread year-round resident; breeds from April to August.

**Habitat:** deciduous and mixed forests, woodlots, riparian woodlands, wooded urban parks and backyards with bird feeders.

**Nesting:** excavates a cavity in a soft, rotting stump or tree; cavity is lined with fur, feathers, moss and grass; will often use a birdhouse; female incubates 6–8 finely dotted, white eggs for 12–13 days.

**Feeding:** gleans vegetation, branches and the ground for small insects and spiders; often visits backyard feeders; also eats conifer seeds and invertebrate eggs.

**Voice:** call is a chipper, whistled *chick-a-dee-dee-dee*; song is a slow, whistled *swee-tee* or *fee-bee*.

**Similar Species:** *Boreal Chickadee* (p. 247): gray brown "cap," sides and flanks. *Blackpoll Warbler* (p. 294): breeding male has 2 white wing bars, dark streaking on white underparts, orangy legs and longer, paler bill.

**Best Sites:** Roger Tory Peterson Nature Center; Beaver Meadow Nature Center; Sapsucker Woods (Cornell Laboratory of Ornithology); Five Rivers Environmental Education Center; Caumsett SP.

# BOREAL CHICKADEE
*Poecile hudsonica*

**B**irders generally love chickadees, and the Boreal Chickadee is especially sought after as the northern representative of this endearing family. As its name suggests, the Boreal Chickadee resides primarily in boreal forests. Unlike the more common and familiar Black-capped Chickadee, the Boreal Chickadee prefers the seclusion of coniferous forests and tends to be softer spoken. • Chickadees burn so much energy that they must replenish their stores daily to survive winter—they have insufficient fat reserves to endure a prolonged stretch of cold weather. Chickadees store food in holes and bark crevices where it will be easy to find once the snow falls. During a cold night, a chickadee enters a state of torpor, slowing down its metabolism so that it uses less energy. A chickadee can lower its body temperature at night by as much as 22° F. • The scientific name *hudsonica* refers to the Hudson Bay region of Canada, the Boreal Chickadee's primary range.

**ID:** gray brown "cap," back, sides and flanks; black "bib"; whitish to light gray breast and belly; whitish "cheek" patch; gray wings and tail; small, black bill.

**Size:** *L* 5–5½ in; *W* 8 in.

**Status:** fairly common year-round resident in the Adirondacks; breeds from June to August; very rarely irruptive to other parts of the state.

**Habitat:** spruce, fir and pine forests; occasionally in mixed coniferous forests with a small deciduous component.

**Nesting:** excavates a cavity in soft, rotting wood or uses a natural cavity or abandoned woodpecker nest in a conifer; female lines the nest with fur, feathers, moss and grass; female incubates 5–8 finely dotted, white eggs for 11–16 days.

**Feeding:** gleans vegetation, branches and infrequently the ground for spiders and small, tree-infesting insects, including their pupae and eggs; also eats conifer seeds.

**Voice:** soft, nasal, wheezy *scick-a day day day,* slower and wheezier than the Black-capped Chickadee.

**Similar Species:** *Black-capped Chickadee* (p. 246): black "cap"; buffy flanks; more grayish than brownish overall.

**Best Sites:** Ferd's Bog–Moose River Plains; Paul Smiths Visitor Interpretive Center (Adirondack Park); Bloomingdale Bog; Chubb River Swamp; Elk L.

# TUFTED TITMOUSE

*Baeolophus bicolor*

This bird's amusing feeding antics keep curious observers entertained at bird feeders. Grasping an acorn or sunflower seed with its tiny feet, the dexterous Tufted Titmouse will strike its sharp bill repeatedly against the hard outer coating, eventually exposing the inner core. • A breeding pair of Tufted Titmice will maintain their bond throughout the year, even when joining small, multispecies flocks for the cold winter months. The titmouse family bond is so strong that the young from one breeding season will often stay with their parents long enough to help them with nesting and feeding duties the following year. In late winter, mated pairs break away from their flocks to search for nesting cavities and soft lining material. If you are fortunate enough to have titmice living in your area, you might be able to attract nesting pairs by setting out your own hair that has accumulated in a hairbrush. There is a good chance that these curious birds will gladly incorporate your offering into the construction of their nest.

**ID:** gray crest and upperparts; black forehead patch; white underparts; buffy flanks.
**Size:** *L* 6–6½ in; *W* 10 in.
**Status:** fairly common year-round resident in southeastern and central NY; breeds in April and May; expanding its range northward into lower elevations.
**Habitat:** deciduous woodlands, groves and suburban parks with large, mature trees.
**Nesting:** in a natural or woodpecker cavity lined with soft vegetation and animal hair; female may be fed by the male from courtship to time of hatching; female incubates 5–6 finely dotted, white eggs for 12–14 days; both adults and occasionally a "helper" raise the young.
**Feeding:** forages on the ground and in trees, often hanging upside down like a chickadee; eats insects, supplemented with seeds, nuts and fruits; will eat seeds and suet from feeders.
**Voice:** noisy, scolding call, like that of a chickadee; song is a whistled *peter peter* or *peter peter peter*.
**Similar Species:** no other small gray bird has a crest.
**Best Sites:** Durand-Eastman Park (Rochester); Stewart Park–Cayuga L.; Five Rivers Environmental Education Center; Clarence Fahnestock SP; Caumsett SP.

# RED-BREASTED NUTHATCH

*Sitta canadensis*

The Red-breasted Nuthatch looks like a red rocket as it streaks toward a neighborhood bird feeder from the cover of a coniferous tree. The nuthatch ejects empty shells left behind by other birds and then selects its own meal before speeding off, never lingering longer than it takes to pick up a seed. • Red-breasted Nuthatches frequently join in on bird waves—groups of warblers, chickadees, kinglets, titmice and small woodpeckers that often forage together through woodlands in winter or during migration. Nuthatches stand out from other songbirds because of their unusual body form and their habit of moving headfirst down tree trunks. • This bird smears the entrance of its nesting cavity with resin from pine or spruce trees. This sticky doormat may prevent ants and other animals from entering the nest chamber. Invertebrates can be the most serious threat to nesting success because they can transmit fungal infections or parasitize nestlings.

**ID:** rusty underparts; gray blue upperparts; white "eyebrow"; black eye line; black "cap"; straight bill; short tail; white "cheek."
*Male:* deeper rust on breast; black crown.
*Female:* light red wash on breast; dark gray crown.
**Size:** *L* 4½ in; *W* 8½ in.
**Status:** common breeder from April to June in the Adirondacks; uncommon to rare breeder elsewhere; fairly common migrant from March to April and from September to October; fairly common winter visitor.
**Habitat:** *Breeding:* spruce-fir and pine forests; pine plantations. *In migration* and *winter:* mixed woodlands, especially those near bird feeders.
**Nesting:** excavates a cavity or uses an abandoned woodpecker nest; usually smears the entrance with resin; nest is made of bark shreds, grass and fur; female incubates 5–6 brown-speckled, white eggs for about 12 days.
**Feeding:** forages headfirst down trees, probing under loose bark for larval and adult invertebrates; eats pine and spruce seeds in winter; often seen at feeders.
**Voice:** call is a slow, continually repeated, nasal *yank-yank-yank* or *rah-rah-rah-rah;* also a short *tsip.*
**Similar Species:** *White-breasted Nuthatch* (p. 250): larger; lacks black eye line and red underparts.
**Best Sites:** Braddock Bay; Ferd's Bog– Moose River Plains; Cherry Plain SP; Jones Beach SP; Montauk Point SP.

# WHITE-BREASTED NUTHATCH

*Sitta carolinensis*

To a novice birder, seeing a White-breasted Nuthatch call repeatedly while clinging to the underside of a branch is an odd sight. To the nuthatch, however, this gravity-defying act is completely natural. Moving headfirst down a tree trunk, the White-breasted Nuthatch forages for invertebrates while pausing to survey its surroundings and occasionally issuing a noisy call. Unlike woodpeckers and creepers, nuthatches do not use their tails to brace themselves against tree trunks—nuthatches grasp the tree with their feet alone. • Although the White-breasted Nuthatch is a regular visitor to most backyard feeders, it only sticks around long enough to grab a seed and then dash off. Only an offering of suet can persuade this small bird to remain in a single spot for any length of time. • The name "nuthatch" probably derives from the birds' habit of wedging seeds and nuts in crevices and hacking them open with their bills.

**ID:** white underparts; white face; gray blue back; rusty undertail coverts; short tail; straight bill; short legs. *Male:* black "cap." *Female:* dark gray "cap."

**Size:** *L* 5½–6 in; *W* 11 in.

**Status:** common year-round resident; breeds from April to June.

**Habitat:** mixedwood forests, woodlots and backyards.

**Nesting:** in a natural cavity or abandoned woodpecker nest in a large deciduous tree; female lines the cavity with bark, grass, fur and feathers; female incubates 5–8 brown-speckled, white eggs for 12–14 days.

**Feeding:** forages headfirst down trees in search of larval and adult invertebrates; also eats nuts and seeds; regularly visits feeders.

**Voice:** song is a frequently repeated *werwerwerwerwer;* calls include *ha-ha-ha ha-ha-ha, ank ank* and *ip.*

**Similar Species:** *Red-breasted Nuthatch* (p. 249): black eye line; rusty underparts. *Black-capped Chickadee* (p. 246): black "bib."

**Best Sites:** Roger Tory Peterson Nature Center; Stewart Park–Cayuga L.; Letchworth SP; John Boyd Thacher SP; Caumsett SP.

# BROWN CREEPER

*Certhia americana*

The cryptic Brown Creeper is never easy to find, often going unnoticed until a flake of bark suddenly takes the shape of a bird. If a creeper is frightened, it will freeze and flatten itself against a tree trunk, becoming even more difficult to see. • The Brown Creeper feeds by slowly spiraling up a tree trunk, searching for hidden invertebrates. When it reaches the upper branches, the creeper floats down to the base of a neighboring tree to begin another foraging ascent. Its long, stiff tail feathers prop it up against vertical tree trunks as it hitches its way skyward. • The thin whistle of the Brown Creeper is so high-pitched that birders often fail to hear it. To increase the confusion, the creeper's song often takes on the boisterous, warbling quality of a wood-warbler song. • There are many species of creepers in Europe and Asia, but the Brown Creeper is the only member of its family found in North America.

**ID:** brown back heavily streaked with buff white; white "eyebrow"; white underparts; downcurved bill; long, pointed tail feathers; rusty rump; buffy wing stripe in flight.

**Size:** *L* 5–5½ in; *W* 7½ in.

**Status:** common breeder and migrant from April to October at higher elevations; becoming more common in woodlands throughout the state; fairly common in winter.

**Habitat:** mature deciduous, coniferous and mixed forests and woodlands, especially in wet areas with large, dead trees; also found near bogs.

**Nesting:** under loose bark or in a tree crevice; nest of grass, roots, moss and twigs is lined with feathers and finer materials;

female incubates 5–6 finely speckled, whitish eggs for 14–17 days.

**Feeding:** hops up tree trunks and large limbs, probing loose bark for adult and larval invertebrates.

**Voice:** song is a faint, high-pitched *trees-trees-trees see the trees;* call is a high *tseee.*

**Similar Species:** *Red-breasted Nuthatch* (p. 249) and *White-breasted Nuthatch* (p. 250): gray blue backs; straight or slightly upturned bills. *Woodpeckers* (pp. 207–15): straight bills; all lack brown back streaking.

**Best Sites:** Allegany SP; Letchworth SP; Cherry Plain SP; John Boyd Thacher SP; Connetquot River SP.

# CAROLINA WREN

*Thryothorus ludovicianus*

The energetic and cheerful Carolina Wren can also be shy and retiring, often hiding deep inside dense shubbery. The best opportunity for viewing this large wren is when it sits on a conspicuous perch while unleashing its impressive song. Pairs perform lively "duets" at any time of day and in any season. The duet often begins with introductory chatter by the female, followed by innumerable ringing variations of *tea-kettle tea-kettle tea-kettle tea* from her mate. • In years of mild winter weather, Carolina Wren populations remain stable, but a winter of frigid temperatures with ice and snow can decimate an otherwise healthy population. Fortunately, the effects of such disasters are only temporary and populations recover within a few years. • Carolina Wrens will readily nest in the brushy thickets of an overgrown backyard or in an obscure nook or crevice in a house or barn. If conditions are favorable, two broods may be raised in a single season.

**ID:** long, prominent, white "eyebrow"; rusty brown upperparts; rich buff-colored underparts; white throat; slightly downcurved bill.

**Size:** *L* 5½ in; *W* 7½ in.

**Status:** locally common year-round resident in southern and central NY; breeds from April to August; increasing at lower elevations along major river valleys.

**Habitat:** dense forest undergrowth, especially shrubby tangles and thickets.

**Nesting:** in a nest box or natural or artificial cavity; pair fills the cavity with twigs and vegetation and lines it with finer materials; nest cup may be domed and may include a snakeskin; female incubates 4–5 brown-blotched, white eggs for 12–16 days; both adults feed the young.

**Feeding:** usually forages in pairs on the ground and among vegetation; eats mostly insects and other invertebrates; also takes berries, fruits and seeds; will visit feeders for peanuts and suet.

**Voice:** loud, repetitious *tea-kettle tea-kettle tea-kettle* may be heard at any time of day or year; female often chatters while male sings.

**Similar Species:** *House Wren* (p. 253) and *Winter Wren* (p. 254): lack white "eyebrow." *Marsh Wren* (p. 256): black, triangular back patch is streaked with white; prefers marsh habitat. *Sedge Wren* (p. 255): white streaking on dark crown and back; indistinct, pale "eyebrow."

**Best Sites:** Stewart Park–Cayuga L.; Five Rivers Environmental Education Center; Bear Mountain SP; Caumsett SP; Connetquot River SP.

# HOUSE WREN

*Troglodytes aedon*

The House Wren's bubbly song and energetic demeanor make it a welcome addition to any neighborhood. A small cavity in a standing dead tree or a custom-made nest box is usually all it takes to attract this joyful bird to most backyards. Sometimes even an empty flowerpot or vacant drainpipe is deemed a suitable nest site, provided there is a local abundance of insect prey. Occasionally, you may find that your nest site offering is packed full of twigs and left abandoned without any nesting birds in sight. Male wrens often build numerous nests, which later serve as decoys or "dummy" nests. In such a case, you should just clean out the cavity and hope that another pair of wrens will find your real estate more appealing.

• This bird is sometimes called "Jenny Wren," a name which originally referred to the Wren (*T. troglodytes*) of Europe, our Winter Wren.

**ID:** brown upperparts; fine, dark barring on upperwings, lower back and short, upraised tail; faint, pale "eyebrow" and eye ring; whitish throat; whitish to buff underparts; faintly barred flanks.

**Size:** *L* 4½–5 in; *W* 6 in.

**Status:** common breeder and migrant from April to September, except in higher elevations of the Adirondacks.

**Habitat:** thickets and shrubby openings along the edges of deciduous or mixed woodlands; often in shrubs and thickets near buildings.

**Nesting:** in a natural cavity or abandoned woodpecker nest; also in a nest box or other artificial cavity; nest of sticks and grass is lined with feathers, fur and other soft materials; female incubates 6–8 heavily speckled, white to pinkish buff eggs for 12–15 days.

**Feeding:** gleans the ground and vegetation for insects, especially beetles, caterpillars, grasshoppers and spiders.

**Voice:** call is a harsh, scolding rattle; song is a smooth, running, bubbly warble: *tsi-tsi-tsi-tsi oodle-oodle-oodle-oodle,* lasting about 2–3 seconds.

**Similar Species:** *Winter Wren* (p. 254): smaller; darker overall; much shorter, stubby tail; prominent, dark barring on flanks. *Sedge Wren* (p. 255): faint white streaking on dark crown and back. *Carolina Wren* (p. 252): richer brown plumage; long, bold, white "eyebrow."

**Best Sites:** Roger Tory Peterson Nature Center; Sapsucker Woods (Cornell Laboratory of Ornithology); Five Rivers Environmental Education Center; Marshlands Conservancy–Playland CP; Connetquot River SP.

# WINTER WREN

*Troglodytes troglodytes*

Winter Wrens boldly announce their claims to patches of moist coniferous woodland, where they often make their homes in the green moss and gnarled, upturned roots of decomposing tree trunks. • The song of the Winter Wren is distinguished by its explosive delivery, melodious, bubbly tone and extended duration. Few other singers in our region can sustain their songs for up to 10 music-packed seconds. When the Winter Wren is not singing or nesting, it skulks through the forest understory, quietly probing the myriad nooks and crannies for invertebrates. • While the female raises the young, the male wren brings food to the nest and defends the territory through song. At night, the male sleeps away from his family in an unfinished nest. • The Winter Wren is the only North American wren that is also found across Europe and Asia, where it is a common garden bird known simply as a "Wren."

**ID:** very short, upraised tail; fine, pale buff "eyebrow"; dark brown upperparts; lighter brown underparts; dark barring on flanks.

**Size:** *L* 4 in; *W* 5½ in.

**Status:** fairly common breeder and migrant from April to November at higher elevations; rare in winter at lower elevations.

**Habitat:** *Breeding:* moist boreal forests, spruce bogs, cedar swamps and mixed forests dominated by mature pine and hemlock; often near water. *In migration:* woodland thickets.

**Nesting:** in a natural cavity, under bark or among upturned tree roots; bulky nest is made of twigs, moss, grass and fur; male frequently builds up to 4 "dummy" nests prior to egg laying; female incubates 5–7 sparsely speckled, white eggs for 14–16 days.

**Feeding:** forages on the ground and in trees for beetles, wood-boring insects and other invertebrates.

**Voice:** *Male:* song is a warbled, tinkling series of quick trills and twitters, often more than 8 seconds long; call is a sharp *chip-chip.*

**Similar Species:** *House Wren* (p. 253): tail is longer than leg; paler overall; less conspicuous barring on flanks. *Carolina Wren* (p. 252): much larger; long, bold, white "eyebrow"; long tail. *Marsh Wren* (p. 256): white streaking on black back; bold, white "eyebrow." *Sedge Wren* (p. 255): white streaking on black back and crown; longer tail; paler underparts.

**Best Sites:** Ferd's Bog–Moose River Plains; Bloomingdale Bog; Chubb River Swamp; John Boyd Thacher SP; Slide Mt.

# SEDGE WREN

*Cistothorus platensis*

L ike most wrens, the Sedge Wren is secretive and difficult to observe. It is the least familiar of all our wrens because it keeps itself well concealed in dense stands of sedges and tall, wet grass. These wrens are also less loyal to specific sites than other wrens, and may totally disappear from an area after a few years for no apparent reason. • Sedge Wrens are feverish nest builders, and construction begins immediately after they settle on a nesting territory. Each energetic male may build several incomplete nests throughout his territory before the females arrive. The decoys or "dummy" nests are not wasted: they often serve as dormitories for young and adult birds later in the season. • The scientific name *platensis* refers to the Rio de la Plata in Argentina, where an isolated population of this wren is found. • Until 1983, this bird was known as "Short-billed Marsh Wren."

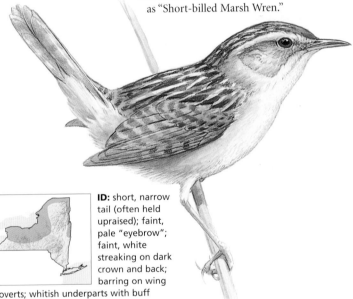

**ID:** short, narrow tail (often held upraised); faint, pale "eyebrow"; faint, white streaking on dark crown and back; barring on wing coverts; whitish underparts with buff orange sides, flanks and undertail coverts.
**Size:** *L* 4–4½ in; *W* 5½ in.
**Status:** threatened; rare and local breeder and migrant from May to September.
**Habitat:** wet sedge meadows, wet grassy fields, alfalfa fields, marshes, bogs and beaver ponds; often in abandoned, wet fields with low, shrubby willows and alders.
**Nesting:** near the ground in sedges or grasses; well-built globe nest with a side entrance is woven from sedges and grasses; female incubates 4–8 unmarked, white eggs for 12–16 days.
**Feeding:** forages low in dense vegetation, picking and probing for adult and larval insects and spiders; occasionally catches flying insects.

**Voice:** song is a few short, staccato notes followed by a rattling trill: *chap-chap-chap-chap, chap, churr-r-r-r-r;* call is a sharp *chat* or *chep.*
**Similar Species:** *Marsh Wren* (p. 256): bold, white "eyebrow"; prominent white streaking on black back; unstreaked crown; prefers cattail marshes. *Winter Wren* (p. 254): darker overall; shorter, stubby tail; unstreaked crown. *House Wren* (p. 253): unstreaked, dark brown crown and back.
**Best Sites:** Montezuma NWR; Cape Vincent–Pt. Peninsula; Perch River WMA; Ft. Edward Grasslands.

# MARSH WREN

*Cistothorus palustris*

Fueled by newly emerged aquatic insects, the Marsh Wren zips about in short bursts through tall stands of cattails and bulrushes. This expert hunter catches flying insects with lightning speed, but don't expect to see the Marsh Wren in action—it is a reclusive bird that prefers to remain hidden deep within its dense marshland habitat. A patient observer might be rewarded with a brief glimpse of a Marsh Wren, but it is more likely that this bird's distinctive song, reminiscent of an old-fashioned treadle sewing machine, will inform you of its presence. • Marsh Wrens occasionally destroy the nests and eggs of other Marsh Wrens as well as those of other marsh-nesting songbirds such as the Red-winged Blackbird. Other birds are usually prevented from doing the same, because the Marsh Wren's globe nest keeps the eggs well hidden, and several decoy nests help to divert predators from the real nest. • This bird was formerly known as "Long-billed Marsh Wren."

**ID:** white "chin" and belly; rufous brown upperparts; black triangle on upper back is streaked with white; bold, white "eyebrow"; unstreaked brown crown; long, thin, downcurved bill.
**Size:** *L* 5 in; *W* 6 in.
**Status:** common breeder and migrant from April to October in larger marshes; rare at higher elevatons; rare in winter in Long I. marshes.

**Habitat:** large cattail and bulrush marshes interspersed with open water; occasionally in tall grass–sedge marshes.
**Nesting:** in a marsh among cattails or tall emergent vegetation; globelike nest is woven from cattails, bulrushes, weeds and grass and lined with cattail down; female incubates 4–6 heavily dotted, chocolate brown eggs for 12–16 days.
**Feeding:** gleans vegetation and flycatches for adult aquatic invertebrates, especially dragonflies and damselflies.
**Voice:** *Male:* rapid, rattling, staccato warble; call is a harsh *chek*.
**Similar Species:** *Sedge Wren* (p. 255): smaller; streaked crown. *House Wren* (p. 253): faint "eyebrow"; black back lacks white streaking. *Carolina Wren* (p. 252): larger; buff underparts; black back lacks white streaking.
**Best Sites:** Braddock Bay; Montezuma NWR; Perch River WMA; Black Creek Marsh WMA; Jones Beach SP.

# GOLDEN-CROWNED KINGLET

*Regulus satrapa*

As they refuel on insects and berries, Golden-crowned Kinglets use tree branches as swings and trapezes, flashing their regal crowns and constantly flicking their tiny wings. During summer, these dainty forest sprites are often too busy to make an appearance for admiring observers. Not much larger than hummingbirds, Golden-crowned Kinglets can be difficult to spot as they flit and hover among coniferous treetops. • In winter, Golden-crowned Kinglets are commonly seen and heard among multispecies flocks that often include chickadees, Red-breasted Nuthatches and Brown Creepers. Kinglets manage to survive cold winter temperatures by roosting together in groups or in empty squirrel nests. Like chickadees, these birds can lower their body temperature at night to conserve energy. • The Golden-crowned Kinglet's extremely high-pitched call is very faint and is often lost in the slightest woodland breeze.

**ID:** olive back; darker wings and tail; light underparts; dark "cheek"; 2 white wing bars; black eye line; white "eyebrow"; crown has black border. *Male:* crown is reddish orange and yellow. *Female:* yellow crown.
**Size:** *L* 4 in; *W* 7 in.
**Status:** common breeder from May to July at higher elevations; becoming more common as a breeder in conifer plantations at lower elevations; common migrant and winter visitor from October to April.
**Habitat:** *Breeding:* mixed and pure mature coniferous forests, especially those dominated by spruce; also conifer plantations. *In migration* and *winter:* coniferous, deciduous and mixed forests and woodlands.

**Nesting:** usually in a spruce or other conifer; hanging nest is made of moss, lichens, twigs and leaves; female incubates 8–9 speckled, whitish to pale buff eggs for 14–15 days.
**Feeding:** gleans and hovers among the forest canopy for insects, berries and occasionally sap.
**Voice:** call is a very high-pitched *tsee tsee tsee;* song is a faint, high-pitched, accelerating *tsee-tsee-tsee-tsee, why do you shilly-shally?*
**Similar Species:** *Ruby-crowned Kinglet* (p. 258): bold, broken, white eye ring; crown lacks black border. *Black-capped Chickadee* (p. 246) and *Boreal Chickadee* (p. 247): grayish plumage; lack bright, colorful crown.
**Best Sites:** Pharsalia WMA; Whetstone Gulf SP; Ferd's Bog–Moose River Plains; Bloomingdale Bog; Cherry Plain SP.

# RUBY-CROWNED KINGLET
*Regulus calendula*

The loud, rolling song of the Ruby-crowned Kinglet is a familiar tune that echoes through our coniferous forests in May and June, though its loudness and exuberance are somewhat unexpected from such a small bird. • The male kinglet erects his brilliant, red crown and sings to impress prospective mates during courtship. Throughout most of the year, though, the crown remains hidden among dull gray feathers on the bird's head and is impossible to see even through binoculars. • In migration, Ruby-crowned Kinglets are regularly seen flitting among treetops, mingling with a colorful assortment of warblers and vireos. This kinglet might be mistaken for an *Empidonax* flycatcher, but its frequent hovering and energetic wing-flicking behavior set it apart from look-alikes. The wing flicking is thought to startle insects into movement, allowing the kinglet to spot them and pounce.

**ID:** bold, broken eye ring; 2 bold, white wing bars; olive green upperparts; dark wings; whitish to yellowish underparts; short, dark tail; flicks its wings. *Male:* small, red crown (usually hidden). *Female:* no red crown.
**Size:** *L* 4 in; *W* 7½ in.
**Status:** common breeder in May and June in the Adirondacks; common migrant from late April to May and from September to October throughout the state; rare in winter.
**Habitat:** mixed woodlands and pure coniferous forests, especially those dominated by spruce; often found near wet forest openings and edges.

**Nesting:** usually in a spruce or other conifer; female builds a hanging nest of moss, lichen, twigs and leaves; female incubates 7–8 brown-spotted, whitish to pale buff eggs for 13–14 days.
**Feeding:** gleans and hovers for insects and spiders; also eats seeds and berries.
**Voice:** *Male:* song is an accelerating and rising *tea-tea-tea-tew-tew-tew look-at-Me, look-at-Me, look-at-Me.*
**Similar Species:** *Golden-crowned Kinglet* (p. 257): dark "cheek"; black border around crown; male's crown is orange and yellow; female has yellow crown. *Orange-crowned Warbler* (p. 278): no eye ring or wing bars. Empidonax *flycatchers* (pp. 219–23): complete eye ring or no eye ring at all; larger bills; longer tails; all lack red crown.
**Best Sites:** Ferd's Bog–Moose River Plains; Bloomingdale Bog; Chubb River Swamp; Jones Beach SP.

# BLUE-GRAY GNATCATCHER
*Polioptila caerulea*

The most widespread of its genus and the only gnatcatcher found in cooler, temperate regions, the tiny, long-tailed Blue-gray Gnatcatcher is also the only truly migratory gnatcatcher. Populations have been expanding northward on both coasts since the 1960s, and the species is now regularly found across the northern U.S. from coast to coast. • Gnatcatchers inhabit woodlands and brushy areas, restlessly flitting from shrub to shrub with their long tails cocked in the air and moving from side to side. Their scratchy, banjolike, twanging calls announce progress and keep pairs close together. During courtship, which may start early as late April, a male gnatcatcher follows his prospective mate around his territory. Once a bond is established, the paired birds are inseparable and males take a greater part in nesting and raising the young than in other, closely related species. • Although these birds undoubtedly eat gnats, this food item is not a major part of the gnatcatcher's varied diet.

*breeding*
♂

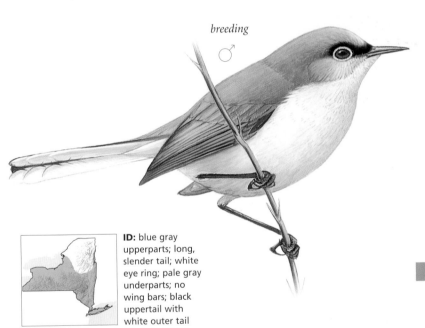

**ID:** blue gray upperparts; long, slender tail; white eye ring; pale gray underparts; no wing bars; black uppertail with white outer tail feathers. *Breeding male:* black forehead.
**Size:** *L* 4½ in; *W* 6 in.
**Status:** uncommon breeder and migrant from April to August at lower elevations; expanding range.
**Habitat:** deciduous woodlands along streams, ponds, lakes and swamps; also in orchards, shrubby tangles along woodland edges and oak savannas.
**Nesting:** on a branch, usually halfway to the trunk; cup nest is made of plant fibers and bark chips and decorated with lichens; female incubates 3–5 brown-speckled, pale bluish white eggs for 11–15 days; male feeds female and young.
**Feeding:** gleans vegetation and flycatches for insects, spiders and other invertebrates.
**Voice:** *Male:* song is a faint, airy *puree;* call is a high-pitched, banjolike twang: *chee.*
**Similar Species:** *Golden-crowned Kinglet* (p. 257) and *Ruby-crowned Kinglet* (p. 258): olive green overall; short tails; wing bars.
**Best Sites:** Montezuma NWR; Stewart Park–Cayuga L.; Black Creek Marsh WMA; Bear Mountain SP; Connetquot River SP.

# EASTERN BLUEBIRD

*Sialia sialis*

With the colors of the cool sky on its back and the warm setting sun on its breast, the male Eastern Bluebird looks like a piece of pure sky come to life. Like the feathers of all blue birds, Eastern Bluebird feathers are not actually pigmented blue. The blue color is a result of each feather's microscopic structure—shiny blues are produced by iridescence and dull blues are a result of the same process that produces the blue of the sky. • When House Sparrows and European Starlings were introduced to North America, Eastern Bluebirds were forced to compete with them for nest sites, and bluebird numbers began to decline. The development of "bluebird trails," with nest boxes mounted on fence posts along rural roads, has aided in this species' recovery in much of eastern North America—these boxes exclude competing European Starlings because the entrance is too small for them, but perfect for bluebirds.

♂

**ID:** chestnut red "chin," throat, breast and sides; white belly and undertail coverts; dark bill and legs. *Male:* deep blue upperparts. *Female:* thin, white eye ring; gray brown head and back tinged with blue; blue wings and tail; paler chestnut on underparts.
**Size:** *L* 7 in; *W* 13 in.
**Status:** fairly common and widespread breeder and migrant from late March to October; locally common during mild winters.
**Habitat:** cropland fencelines, meadows, fallow and abandoned fields, pastures, forest clearings and edges; also golf courses, large lawns and cemeteries.
**Nesting:** in an abandoned woodpecker cavity, natural cavity or nest box; female builds a cup nest of grass, weed stems and small twigs; mostly the female incubates 4–5 pale blue eggs for 13–16 days.
**Feeding:** swoops from a perch to pursue flying insects; also forages on the ground for invertebrates.
**Voice:** song is a rich, warbling *turr, turr-lee, turr-lee;* call is a chittering *pew.*
**Similar Species:** *Indigo Bunting* (p. 335): blue overall.
**Best Sites:** Beaver Meadow Nature Center; Nation's Road Grassland; Saratoga National Historical Park; Five Rivers Environmental Education Center; Caumsett SP.

# VEERY

*Catharus fuscescens*

Navigating its way across the forest floor, the Veery travels in short, springy hops, flipping leaves and scattering leaf litter in search of worms and grubs. This shy, well-camouflaged bird is always attuned to the sounds of wiggling prey or approaching danger. The Veery is the most terrestrial of the North American thrushes and is often difficult to find. Listen for it in spring and early summer when its fluty, cascading song is easily detected. • When startled by an intruder, the Veery either flushes or faces the threat with its faintly streaked, buffy breast exposed, hoping for concealment. • The Veery's name is an imitation of its airy song. • These birds migrate to South America each winter, so there's a very good chance that the Veery pairs nesting in your local ravine might soon be traveling to the rainforests of the Amazon!

**ID:** reddish brown or tawny upperparts; very thin, grayish eye ring; faintly streaked, buff throat and upper breast; pale underparts; gray flanks and face patch.

**Size:** *L* 6½–7½ in; *W* 12 in.

**Status:** common and widespread breeder in May and June; common migrant in May and from August to September.

**Habitat:** *Breeding:* cool, moist deciduous and mixed forests and woodlands with a dense understory of shrubs and ferns; often in disturbed woodlands. *In migration:* a variety of forested areas, parks and backyards.

**Nesting:** on the ground or in a shrub; female builds a bulky nest of leaves, weeds, bark strips and rootlets; female incubates 3–4 pale greenish blue eggs for 10–15 days.

**Feeding:** gleans the ground and lower vegetation for invertebrates and berries.

**Voice:** *Male:* song is a fluty, descending *da-vee-ur, vee-ur, vee-ur, veer, veer, veer;* call is a high, whistled *feeyou.*

**Similar Species:** *Swainson's Thrush* (p. 264): bold eye ring; olive brown upperparts; darker spotting on throat and upper breast. *Hermit Thrush* (p. 265): reddish rump and tail; brownish back; bold eye ring; buff brown flanks; large, dark spots on throat and breast. *Gray-cheeked Thrush* (p. 262): gray brown upperparts; dark breast spots; brownish gray flanks.

**Best Sites:** Allegany SP; Montezuma NWR; Black Creek Marsh WMA; Bashakill WMA; Bear Mountain SP.

# GRAY-CHEEKED THRUSH

*Catharus minimus*

Few people have ever heard of the Gray-cheeked Thrush, but keen birders find this inconspicuous bird a source of great interest. A champion migrant, this thrush winters as far south as Peru and regularly summers in the Arctic, farther north than any other North American thrush. Each spring the Gray-cheeked Thrush migrates through our region to the Hudson Bay Lowlands in Canada, where it nests among willows and stunted black spruce. Unfortunately, the inaccessibility of this remote northern region has prevented most birders and ornithologists from documenting more than a few nesting records for this elusive bird. • In migration, the Gray-cheeked Thrush travels primarily at night, so it is most often seen or heard rustling through shrub-covered leaf litter early in the morning. • Until 1995, the Gray-cheeked Thrush and the very similar-looking Bicknell's Thrush (*C. bicknelli*) were classified as a single species.

**ID:** gray brown upperparts; gray face; inconspicuous eye ring may not be visible; heavily spotted breast; pale underparts; brownish gray flanks.
**Size:** *L* 7–8 in; *W* 13 in.
**Status:** fairly common migrant in May and from September to October.
**Habitat:** woodlands and thickets at lower elevations, including riparian woodlands, city parks and coastal thickets.
**Nesting:** does not nest in NY.

**Feeding:** hops along the ground, picking up insects and other invertebrates; may also feed on berries during migration.
**Voice:** distinctive, high-pitched, nasal song, heard mostly at dusk or dawn, ends with a clear, descending whistle *wee-a, wee-o, wee-a, titi, wheeeee;* call is a downslurred *wee-o.*
**Similar Species:** *Swainson's Thrush* (p. 264): prominent eye ring; buff "cheek" and upper breast. *Hermit Thrush* (p. 265): reddish tail; olive brown upperparts; lacks gray "cheek." *Veery* (p. 261): reddish brown upperparts; very light breast streaking. *Bicknell's Thrush* (p. 263): slightly warmer brown; pale base to lower mandible.
**Best Sites:** Hamlin Beach SP; Braddock Bay; Howland Island WMA; Stewart Park–Cayuga L.; Central Park (NYC).

# BICKNELL'S THRUSH
*Catharus bicknelli*

Long classified as a subspecies of the Gray-cheeked Thrush, Bicknell's Thrush was given full species status in 1995. The two species are very difficult to tell apart, and both thrushes may be seen in migration in New York. Gray-cheeked Thrushes from Newfoundland, Canada, are browner, which compounds the identification problem. The best way to distinguish the two species is not by appearance, but by song, although even this may be challenging. The Bicknell's Thrush has a higher-pitched, more nasal song, with the last note rising. • On both its breeding and wintering grounds this bird is vulnerable to habitat loss from timber harvesting and forest fragmentation. It has a small breeding range that extends from eastern Canada south to New York State. This thrush's wintering range is even smaller—it is regularly found only on islands in the Greater Antilles. • This thrush was named for Eugene P. Bicknell, an amateur ornithologist who obtained the first specimen in 1881 in the Catskill Mountains.

**ID:** warm brown upperparts; gray brown "cheek"; partial, whitish eye ring; buff breast is heavily spotted with brown; white belly; reddish tinge on wings and tail.
**Size:** *L* 6–7 in; *W* 11–12 in.
**Status:** special concern; breeds in June at elevations above 3000 ft in the Adirondacks and Catskills; uncommon migrant in May and from September to October.
**Habitat:** *Breeding:* coniferous, sometimes mixed, forests with dense undergrowth, usually in the timberline zone at upper elevations of mountains. *In migration:* mainly coastal scrub; occasionally second-growth and thickets at lower elevations, including riparian woodlands and city parks.
**Nesting:** in a short, stunted conifer; female builds a cup nest of grass, leaves, bark, mud and moss; female incubates 3–6 brown-spotted, bluish green eggs for 13–14 days.

**Feeding:** forages on the ground and gleans vegetation; eats mostly insects and their larvae, spiders and earthworms.
**Voice:** a high-pitched, nasal *ch-ch zree p-zreeeew p-p-zreeee* with the last note rising; call note is a buzzy, descending *vee-ah.*
**Similar Species:** *Gray-cheeked Thrush* (p. 262): slightly larger; upperparts more gray brown (except Newfoundland *minimus* race); darker lower mandible; grayish face. *Swainson's Thrush* (p. 264): buffy lores; more buff on face and breast; more grayish upperparts. *Hermit Thrush* (p. 265): distinct white eye ring; buff rump; only obviously rufous coloration is in tail. *Wood Thrush* (p. 266): very reddish upperparts; dark spots extend onto belly. *Veery* (p. 261): reddish upperparts; finer, reddish spotting on breast.
**Best Sites:** Whiteface Mt.; Slide Mt.

# SWAINSON'S THRUSH

*Catharus ustulatus*

The upward spiral of this thrush's song lifts the soul of any listener with each rising note. The Swainson's Thrush is an integral part of the morning chorus, and its inspiring song can also be heard at dusk. In fact, this bird is routinely the last of the forest singers to be silenced by nightfall. • Most thrushes feed on the ground, but the Swainson's Thrush is also adept at gleaning food from the airy heights of trees, sometimes briefly hover-gleaning like a warbler or vireo. • On its breeding grounds, this thrush is most often seen perched high in a treetop, cast in silhouette against the sky. In migration, the Swainson's Thrush skulks low on the ground under shrubs and tangles, occasionally visiting backyards and neighborhood parks. A wary bird, this thrush does not allow many viewing opportunities, and it often gives a sharp warning call from some distance. • William Swainson was an English zoologist and illustrator in the early 19th century. His name also graces the Swainson's Hawk.

**ID:** olive brown upperparts; conspicuous buff eye ring; buff wash on "cheek" and upper breast; spots arranged in streaks on throat and breast; white belly and undertail coverts; brownish gray flanks.

**Size:** L 7 in; W 12 in.

**Status:** common breeder from May to July in the Adirondacks, Catskills and Tug Hill area; common migrant in May and September, often heard calling from overhead at night.

**Habitat:** *Breeding:* edges and openings of coniferous and mixed boreal forests; prefers moist areas with spruce and fir.

*In migration:* a variety of forested areas, parks and backyards.

**Nesting:** usually in a shrub or small tree; small cup nest of grass, moss, leaves, roots and lichen is lined with fur and soft fibers; female incubates 3–4 brown-spotted, pale blue eggs for 12–14 days.

**Feeding:** gleans vegetation and forages on the ground for invertebrates; also eats berries.

**Voice:** song is a slow, rolling, rising spiral: *Oh, Aurelia will-ya, will-ya will-yeee;* call is a sharp *wick* or *prit*.

**Similar Species:** *Gray-cheeked Thrush* (p. 262) and *Bicknell's Thrush* (p. 263): gray brown upperparts; gray "cheeks"; lack obvious eye ring. *Hermit Thrush* (p. 265): reddish tail and rump; grayish brown upperparts; darker breast spotting on whiter breast. *Veery* (p. 261): more reddish upperparts; finer breast spotting; lacks bold eye ring.

**Best Sites:** Allegany SP; Ferd's Bog–Moose River Plains; Bloomingdale Bog; Whiteface Mt.; Slide Mt.

# HERMIT THRUSH

*Catharus guttatus*

True to its name, the Hermit Thrush is generally a very quiet and unobtrusive bird. It remains hidden much of the time in the lower branches of the undergrowth or on the forest floor. This reclusive behavior changes in spring and early summer when the male Hermit Thrush takes up a prominent perch and sings his beautiful, flutelike song in the dawn and dusk choruses. Similar to the song of the Swainson's Thrush, the song of the Hermit Thrush is almost always preceded by a single questioning note, as if this bird's hermitlike behavior prompts it to ask if the coast is clear. • For the first two days after arriving in a male's territory, a female Hermit Thrush will be attacked and chased. If the female still remains after these two days, the male gradually accepts her and a union is formed. • The Hermit Thrush is a ground nester, often hiding its cryptic cup nest in a natural hollow between raised, mossy hummocks under the low branches of a spruce or fir.

**ID:** reddish brown tail and rump; grayish brown upperparts; black-spotted throat and breast; pale under-parts; buff flanks; thin, pale eye ring.

**Size:** *L* 7 in; *W* 11½ in.

**Status:** common but local breeder from May to August; common migrant in April and October; occasionally winters in southern NY.

**Habitat:** deciduous, mixed or coniferous woodlands; wet coniferous bogs bordered by trees.

**Nesting:** usually on the ground; occasionally in a small tree or shrub; female builds a bulky cup nest of grass, twigs, moss and bark strips; female incubates 4 pale blue to greenish blue eggs for 11–13 days.

**Feeding:** forages on the ground and gleans vegetation for insects and other invertebrates; also eats berries.

**Voice:** song is a series of beautiful flutelike notes, both rising and falling in pitch; a small questioning note may precede the song; calls include a faint *chuck* and a fluty *treee*.

**Similar Species:** *Swainson's Thrush* (p. 264): buff "cheek" and wash on breast; olive brown upperparts. *Veery* (p. 261): lightly streaked upper breast; reddish brown upperparts and tail. *Gray-cheeked Thrush* (p. 262) and *Bicknell's Thrush* (p. 263): gray "cheek"; lack conspicuous eye ring. *Fox Sparrow* (p. 323): stockier; conical bill; brown breast spots.

**Best Sites:** Allegany SP; Ferd's Bog–Moose River Plains; Cherry Plain SP; John Boyd Thacher SP.

# WOOD THRUSH

*Hylocichla mustelina*

The loud, warbled notes of the Wood Thrush once resounded through our woodlands, but forest fragmentation and urban sprawl have reduced this bird's nesting habitat. Broken forests and diminutive woodlots have allowed the invasion of common, open-area predators and parasites, such as raccoons, skunks, crows, jays and cowbirds, which traditionally had little access to nests that were insulated deep within vast stands of hardwood forest. Many tracts of forest that have been urbanized or developed for agriculture now host families of American Robins rather than the once-prominent Wood Thrush. • The Wood Thrush's wintering grounds extend from southeastern Mexico down to Panama. It makes its way northward each spring, breeding primarily in the eastern U.S., from the Gulf Coast to southern Canada. • Naturalist and author Henry David Thoreau considered the Wood Thrush's song to be the most beautiful of avian sounds. The male Wood Thrush can even sing two notes at once!

**ID:** plump body; rusty head and back; brown wings, rump and tail; large, black spots on white breast, sides and flanks; bold, white eye ring.

**Size:** *L* 8 in; *W* 13 in.

**Status:** widespread, common breeder and migrant from May to September; less common in northern NY.

**Habitat:** moist, mature and preferably undisturbed deciduous woodlands and mixed forests.

**Nesting:** low in a deciduous tree; female builds a bulky cup nest of grass, twigs, moss, bark strips and mud; female incubates 3–4 pale, greenish blue eggs for 13–14 days.

**Feeding:** forages on the ground and gleans vegetation for insects and other invertebrates; also eats berries.

**Voice:** *Male:* bell-like phrases of 3–5 notes, with each note at a different pitch and followed by a trill: *Will you live with me? Way up high in a tree, I'll come right down and...seeee!;* calls include a *pit pit* and *bweebeebeep.*

**Similar Species:** *Other thrushes* (pp. 260–67): smaller spots on underparts; most have colored wash on sides and flanks; all lack bold, white eye ring and rusty "cap" and back.

**Best Sites:** Roger Tory Peterson Nature Center; Sapsucker Woods (Cornell Laboratory of Ornithology); Beaver Lake Nature Center; Five Rivers Environmental Education Center; Caumsett SP.

# AMERICAN ROBIN

*Turdus migratorius*

American Robins are widely recognized as harbingers of spring, often arriving in early March. These birds are widespread and abundant in many of our natural habitats, but they are familiar to most of us because they commonly inhabit residential lawns, gardens and parks. • A hunting robin may appear to be listening for prey, but it is actually looking for movements in the soil—it tilts its head because its eyes are placed on the sides of its head. The robin's habit of stamping is designed to get earthworms to betray their presence by moving. • Robins are occasionally seen hunting with their bills stuffed full of earthworms and grubs, a sign that hungry young are somewhere close at hand. Young robins are easily distinguished from their parents by their disheveled appearance and heavily spotted underparts. • The American Robin was named by English colonists after the Robin *(Erithacus rubecula)* of their native land. Both birds look and behave similarly, even though they are only distantly related.

**ID:** gray brown back; dark head; white throat streaked with black; white undertail coverts; incomplete, white eye ring; black-tipped, yellow bill. *Male:* black head; deep brick red breast. *Female:* dark gray head; light red orange breast. *Juvenile:* heavily spotted breast.
**Size:** *L* 10 in; *W* 17 in.
**Status:** the most common and widespread breeder in NY; breeds from March to July; very common migrant, arriving in early March and leaving by late November; fairly common in winter when there are abundant berry crops.

**Habitat:** residential lawns and gardens, pastures, urban parks, broken forests, bogs and river shorelines.
**Nesting:** in a coniferous or deciduous tree or shrub; sturdy cup nest is built of grass, moss and loose bark and cemented with mud; female incubates 4 light blue eggs for 11–16 days; may raise up to 3 broods each year.
**Feeding:** forages on the ground and among vegetation; eats larval and adult insects, earthworms, other invertebrates and berries.
**Voice:** song is an evenly spaced warble: *cheerily cheer-up cheerio;* call is a rapid *tut-tut-tut.*
**Similar Species:** none.
**Best Sites:** Tifft Nature Center; Durand-Eastman Park (Rochester); Beaver Lake CP; Five Rivers Environmental Education Center; Caumsett SP.

# GRAY CATBIRD

*Dumetella carolinensis*

Gray Catbirds are most common in summer, when nesting pairs build their loose cup nests deep within impenetrable tangles of shrubs, brambles and thorny thickets. Catbirds vigorously defend their nesting territories, and their defense tactics are so effective that the nesting success of neighboring warblers and sparrows may increase as a result of the catbirds' constant vigilance. • Gray Catbirds are less prone to parasitism by Brown-headed Cowbirds because female catbirds are very loyal to their nests. Even if a cowbird sneaks past the watchful female catbird to deposit an egg in the nest, the mother catbird often recognizes the foreign egg and immediately ejects it. • True to its name, this bird's call sounds much like the scratchy mewing of a house cat. The Gray Catbird is a member of the mockingbird family, and its characteristic call and boisterous, hectic, mimicked phrases are often the only evidence of this bird's presence.

**Nesting:** in a dense shrub or thicket; bulky cup nest is loosely built with twigs, leaves and grass; female incubates 4 greenish blue eggs for 12–15 days.

**Feeding:** forages on the ground and in vegetation for ants, beetles, grasshoppers, caterpillars, moths and spiders; also eats berries and visits feeders.

**ID:** dark gray overall; black "cap"; long tail may be dark gray to black; chestnut undertail coverts; black eyes, bill and legs; short, rounded wings.

**Size:** *L* 8½–9 in; *W* 11 in.

**Status:** widespread, common breeder and migrant from late April to October, except at higher elevations; occasional in winter on Long I.

**Habitat:** dense thickets, brambles, shrubby or brushy areas and hedgerows, often near water.

**Voice:** calls include a catlike *meoow* and a harsh *check-check*; song is a variety of warbles, squeaks and mimicked phrases repeated only once and often interspersed with a *mew* call.

**Similar Species:** *Northern Mockingbird* (p. 269): lacks black "cap" and chestnut undertail coverts; repeats each song phrase 3 times. *Brown Thrasher* (p. 270): rusty brown upperparts; streaked underparts; 2 white wing bars; repeats each song phrase twice.

**Best Sites:** Roger Tory Peterson Nature Center; Hamlin Beach SP; Beaver Lake CP; Five Rivers Environmental Education Center; Connetquot River SP.

# NORTHERN MOCKINGBIRD

*Mimus polyglottos*

The Northern Mockingbird's amazing vocal dexterity is so well known that this mockingbird has been appointed the state bird in five states. It has been known to sing more than 200 different song types and can imitate other birds, barking dogs and even musical instruments, though no one has yet determined the purpose of the mockingbird's mimicry. It can replicate sounds so accurately that even computerized auditory analysis is often unable to detect differences between the original source and the mockingbird's imitation. Both male and female mockingbirds sing, but only unmated males continue their songs into the night. • Mockingbirds form long-term pair bonds and pairs are highly territorial. A pair may establish a year-round territory or may have separate wintering and breeding territories. • Mockingbirds have clearly benefited from the colonization of North America. Residential areas provide them with ideal nesting habitat and, in winter, a bountiful supply of wild and ornamental fruits.

**ID:** gray upperparts; dark wings; 2 thin, white wing bars; long, dark tail with white outer tail feathers; light gray underparts. *Juvenile:* paler overall; spotted breast.

**Size:** *L* 10 in; *W* 14 in.

**Status:** common year-round resident on Long I. and in Hudson Valley and central NY lowlands; breeds from April to July.

**Habitat:** hedges, suburban gardens and orchard margins with an abundance of available fruit; hedgerows of multiflora roses are especially important in winter.

**Nesting:** often in a small shrub or tree; cup nest is built with twigs, grass, fur and leaves; female incubates 3–4 brown-blotched, bluish gray to greenish eggs for 12–13 days.

**Feeding:** gleans vegetation and forages on the ground for beetles, ants, wasps and grasshoppers; also eats berries and wild fruit; visits feeders for suet and raisins.

**Voice:** song is a medley of mimicked phrases, with the phrases often repeated 3 times or more; calls include a harsh *chair* and *chewk*.

**Similar Species:** *Northern Shrike* (p. 227) and *Loggerhead Shrike* (p. 364): thicker, hooked bills; black "masks." *Gray Catbird* (p. 268): gray overall; black "cap"; chestnut undertail coverts; lacks white outer tail feathers.

**Best Sites:** Braddock Bay; Stewart Park–Cayuga L.; Five Rivers Environmental Education Center; Marshlands Conservancy–Playland CP; Jones Beach SP.

# BROWN THRASHER

*Toxostoma rufum*

Amid the various chirps and warbles that rise from woodland and lakefront edges in spring and early summer, the song of the male Brown Thrasher stands alone—its lengthy, complex chorus of twice-repeated phrases is unique. This thrasher has the most extensive vocal repertoire of any North American bird, and estimates indicate it is capable of up to 3000 distinctive combinations of various phrases. • Despite its relatively large size, the Brown Thrasher generally goes unnoticed in its shrubby domain. A typical sighting of this thrasher consists of nothing more than a flash of rufous as it zips from one tangle to another. • Because this bird nests on or close to the ground, its eggs and nestlings are particularly vulnerable to predation by snakes, weasels, skunks and other animals. • Unlike other notable singers, such as the Northern Mockingbird and the similarly shaped, shrub-dwelling Gray Catbird, the Brown Thrasher prefers to live well away from urban areas.

**ID:** reddish brown upperparts; pale underparts with heavy, brown spotting and streaking; long, downcurved bill; yellow orange eyes; long, rufous tail; 2 white wing bars.

**Size:** *L* 11½ in; *W* 13 in.

**Status:** common, widespread breeder and migrant from April to October, except at higher elevations; apparently declining.

**Habitat:** dense shrubs and thickets, overgrown pastures (especially those with hawthorns), woodland edges and brushy areas; rarely close to human habitation.

**Nesting:** usually in a low shrub; often on the ground; cup nest of grass, twigs and leaves; pair incubates 4 heavily speckled, pale bluish eggs for 11–14 days.

**Feeding:** gleans the ground and vegetation for larval and adult invertebrates; occasionally tosses leaves aside with its bill; also eats seeds and berries.

**Voice:** sings a large variety of phrases, with each phrase usually repeated twice: *dig-it dig-it, hoe-it hoe-it, pull-it-up pull-it-up;* calls include a loud crackling note, a harsh *shuck,* a soft *churr* and a whistled, 3-note *pit-cher-ee.*

**Similar Species:** *Hermit Thrush* (p. 265): shorter tail; gray brown back and crown; dark eyes; pale eye ring; much shorter bill and tail; lacks wing bars.

**Best Sites:** Beaver Meadow Nature Center; Braddock Bay; Five Rivers Environmental Education Center; Jones Beach SP; Connetquot River SP.

# EUROPEAN STARLING

*Sturnus vulgaris*

The European Starling was introduced to North America in 1890 and 1891, when about 100 birds were released into New York City's Central Park as part of the local Shakespeare society's plan to introduce all the birds mentioned in their favorite author's writings. The European Starling quickly established itself in the New York landscape, then spread rapidly across the continent, often at the expense of native cavity-nesting birds such as the Tree Swallow, Eastern Bluebird and Red-headed Woodpecker. Despite many concerted efforts to control or even eradicate this species, the European Starling will no doubt continue to assert its claim in the New World. The current population of this species in North America is estimated to be over 200 million birds. • Courting European Starlings are infamous for their ability to reproduce the sounds of other birds such as Killdeers, Red-tailed Hawks, Soras and meadowlarks.

*breeding*

**ID:** short, squared tail; dark eyes. *Breeding:* iridescent, blackish plumage; yellow bill. *Nonbreeding:* blackish wings; feather tips are heavily spotted with white and buff. *Juvenile:* gray brown plumage; brown bill.
**Size:** *L* 8½ in; *W* 16 in.
**Status:** abundant year-round resident everywhere except in dense forests; breeds from April to June.
**Habitat:** agricultural areas, townsites, woodland and forest edges, landfills and roadsides.
**Nesting:** in an abandoned woodpecker cavity, natural cavity, nest box or other artificial cavity; nest is made of grass, twigs and straw; mostly the female incubates 4–6 bluish to greenish white eggs for 12–14 days.
**Feeding:** forages mostly on the ground; diverse diet includes many invertebrates, berries, seeds and human food waste.
**Voice:** variety of whistles, squeaks and gurgles; imitates other birds throughout the year.
**Similar Species:** *Rusty Blackbird* (p. 340): longer tail; black bill; lacks spotting; yellow eyes; rusty tinge on upperparts in fall. *Brown-headed Cowbird* (p. 343): lacks spotting; male has longer tail, shorter, dark bill and brown head. *Common Grackle* (p. 341): larger; much longer tail.
**Best Sites:** Niagara River Corridor; Durand-Eastman Park (Rochester); Cohoes–Crescent–Peebles Island SP; Central Park (NYC); Prospect Park (NYC).

# AMERICAN PIPIT

*Anthus rubescens*

Each fall and spring, agricultural fields and open shorelines serve as refueling stations for large concentrations of migratory American Pipits. Flocks of pipits may go unnoticed to untrained eyes, because their dull brown-and-buff plumage blends into the landscape. However, to keen observers, their plain attire, white outer tail feathers and habit of continuously wagging their tails makes them readily identifiable. The best indicator that pipits are nearby is their telltale, two-syllable call of *pip-it pip-it*, which is usually given in flight. • Although adults may already be paired upon arriving on their nesting grounds—a strategy that is thought to save valuable nesting time—a conspicuous courtship display helps each pair establish and defend the boundaries of their exclusive nesting territory. American Pipits nest in the Arctic, so few of us will ever have a chance to view this bird on its nesting grounds. • This bird was formerly known as "Water Pipit" (*A. spinoletta*).

nonbreeding

**ID:** slim bill and body; faintly streaked, gray brown upperparts; lightly streaked "necklace" on upper breast; streaked sides and flanks; dark legs; dark tail with white outer tail feathers; buff-colored underparts.
**Size:** *L* 6–7 in; *W* 10½ in.
**Status:** common to uncommon migrant from April to May and from September to November; unpredictable and erratic.
**Habitat:** agricultural fields, pastures and the shores of wetlands, lakes and rivers.

**Nesting:** does not nest in NY.
**Feeding:** gleans the ground and vegetation for terrestrial and aquatic invertebrates and for seeds.
**Voice:** familiar flight call is *pip-it pip-it*. *Male:* harsh, sharp *tsip-tsip* or *chiwee*.
**Similar Species:** *Horned Lark* (p. 239): black "horns"; distinctive facial markings. *Vesper Sparrow* (p. 317): conical bill; does not wag tail.
**Best Sites:** Braddock Bay; Montezuma NWR; Cape Vincent–Pt. Peninsula; Ft. Edward Grassland; Jamaica Bay Wildlife Refuge.

# BOHEMIAN WAXWING

*Bombycilla garrulus*

Descending upon mountain-ash and other ornamental plantings, great flocks of Bohemian Waxwings thrill us with their unpredictable appearances. Bohemian Waxwings nest in the northern forests of Alaska and western Canada, and visit only during the winter months in search of food. The faint, quavering whistles of these birds attract attentive naturalists who take pleasure in watching the birds descend on berry-filled trees. In most years, Bohemians are only seen in small groups, usually intermingled with overwintering flocks of similar-looking Cedar Waxwings. Their chestnut undertail coverts readily distinguish them from their Cedar Waxwing counterparts. • Waxwings get their name from the spots on their secondary feathers. These "waxy" spots are actually colorful enlargements of the feather shafts, whose pigments are derived from the birds' berry-filled diet. Juvenile birds have smaller pigment spots that will grow in size until the birds reach their adult plumage.

**Size:** *L* 8 in; *W* 14 in.
**Status:** erratic winter visitor from November to April; common some years, absent in others; almost annual in extreme northern NY.
**Habitat:** natural and residential areas with wild berries and fruit.
**Nesting:** does not nest in NY.
**Feeding:** gleans vegetation for insects and wild fruit; also takes flying insects on the wing; depends on berries and fruit in winter.
**Voice:** faint, high-pitched, quavering whistle.
**Similar Species:** *Cedar Waxwing* (p. 274): smaller; browner overall; slight yellow wash on belly; white undertail coverts; lacks white on wings.
**Best Sites:** Cape Vincent–Pt. Peninsula; Chazy Landing–Point au Roche SP; Ausable Pt.; Essex-Westport.

**ID:** gray-and-cinnamon crest; black "mask" and throat; soft brownish gray body; yellow terminal tail band; chestnut undertail coverts; small white, red and yellow markings on wings. *Juvenile:* gray brown upperparts; streaked underparts; pale throat; no "mask"; white wing patches.

# CEDAR WAXWING

*Bombycilla cedrorum*

Flocks of handsome Cedar Waxwings gorge on berries during late summer and fall. Waxwings have a remarkable ability to digest a wide variety of berries, some of which are inedible or even poisonous to humans. If the fruits have fermented, these birds will show definite signs of tipsiness. Native berry-producing trees and shrubs planted in your backyard can attract Cedar Waxwings and will often encourage them to nest in your area. • Cedar Waxwing pairs perform a wonderful courtship dance: the male first lands slightly away from the female, then tentatively hops toward her and offers her a berry. The female accepts the berry and hops away from the male, then she stops, hops back and offers him the berry. This gentle ritual can last for several minutes. • Cedar Waxwings are late nesters, which ensures that berry crops will be ripe when nestlings are ready to be fed.

**ID:** cinnamon crest; brown upperparts; black "mask"; yellow wash on belly; gray rump; yellow terminal tail band; white undertail coverts; small red "drops" on wings. *Juvenile:* no "mask"; streaked underparts; gray brown body.

**Size:** *L* 7 in; *W* 12 in.

**Status:** common breeder and migrant from April to October throughout the state; fairly common in winter.

**Habitat:** wooded residential parks and gardens, overgrown fields, forest edges, second-growth and riparian and open woodlands.

**Nesting:** in a coniferous or deciduous tree or shrub; cup nest of twigs, grass, moss and lichen is lined with fine grass; female incubates 3–5 sparsely spotted, pale gray to bluish gray eggs for 12–16 days.

**Feeding:** catches flying insects on the wing or gleans vegetation; eats large amounts of berries and wild fruit, especially in fall and winter.

**Voice:** faint, high-pitched, trilled whistle: *tseee-tseee-tseee.*

**Similar Species:** *Bohemian Waxwing* (p. 273): larger; chestnut undertail coverts; small white, red and yellow markings on wings; juvenile has chestnut undertail coverts and white wing patches.

**Best Sites:** Braddock Bay; Beaver Lake Nature Center; Saratoga National Historical Park; Sterling Forest SP; Caumsett SP.

# BLUE-WINGED WARBLER

*Vermivora pinus*

During the mid-1800s, the Blue-winged Warbler began expanding its range eastward and northward from its home in the central midwestern U.S., finding new breeding territories among overgrown fields and pastures near abandoned human settlements. Eventually it came into contact with the Golden-winged Warbler, a bird with completely different looks but practically identical habitat requirements and breeding biology. Where both species share the same habitat, a distinctive, fertile hybrid known as "Brewster's Warbler" may be produced. This hybrid tends to be more grayish overall, like the Golden-winged Warbler, but retains the thin, black eye line and the touch of yellow on the breast from its Blue-winged parent. In rare instances when two of these hybrids are able to reproduce successfully, a second-generation hybrid known as "Lawrence's Warbler" is produced. It is more yellowish overall, like the Blue-winged Warbler, but has the black "mask," "chin" and throat of the Golden-winged Warbler.

**ID:** bright yellow head and under-parts, except for white to yellowish undertail coverts; olive yellow upperparts; bluish gray wings and tail; black eye line; thin, dark bill; 2 white wing bars; bold, white spots on underside of tail.
**Size:** *L* 4½–5 in; *W* 7½ in.
**Status:** common breeder from May to August; fairly common migrant from late April through May and in August and September.
**Habitat:** second-growth woodlands, willow swamps, shrubby, overgrown fields, pastures and woodland edges and openings.

**Nesting:** on or near the ground, concealed by vegetation; female builds a narrow, inverted, cone-shaped nest of grass, leaves and bark strips; female incubates 5 brown-speckled, white eggs for about 11 days.
**Feeding:** gleans insects and spiders from the lower branches of trees and shrubs.
**Voice:** buzzy, 2-note song: *beee-bzzz.*
**Similar Species:** *Prothonotary Warbler* (p. 298): lacks black eye line and white wing bars. *Pine Warbler* (p. 290): darker; white belly; faint streaking on sides and breast. *Yellow Warbler* (p. 281): yellow wings; lacks black eye line. *Prairie Warbler* (p. 291): black streaking on sides and flanks; darker wings.
**Best Sites:** Iroquois NWR–Tonawanda WMA–Oak Orchard WMA; Howland Island WMA; Five Rivers Environmental Education Center; Sterling Forest SP; Connetquot River SP.

# GOLDEN-WINGED WARBLER

*Vermivora chrysoptera*

Unlike people, who are able to build fences around their property, the male Golden-winged Warbler uses song to defend his nesting territory. If song fails to repel rival males, then body language and aggression calls warn intruders to stay away. When a male's claim is seriously challenged, a warning call, a raised crown and a spread tail may be employed. The last resort is to physically remove the competitor in a high-speed chase or a winged duel. • The battle to maintain breeding territory is not confined within the species—the Golden-winged Warbler may be losing ground to its colonizing relative the Blue-winged Warbler, which seems to be outcompeting the Golden-wing through hybridization. • Blue-winged Warblers and Golden-winged Warblers have very similar songs. The former will sometimes sing the latter's primary song, which can make identification based on song very difficult.

**ID:** yellow fore-crown and wing patch; dark "chin," throat and "mask" over eye bordered by white; bluish gray upperparts and flanks; white undersides; white tail spots on underside of tail. *Female: similar to male, but duller overall; gray throat and "mask."*
**Size:** *L* 4½–5 in; *W* 7½ in.
**Status:** special concern; local breeder and migrant upstate, arriving in May and departing in September.
**Habitat:** moist shrubby fields, woodland edges and early-succession forest clearings.

**Nesting:** on the ground, concealed by vegetation; female builds an open cup nest of grasses, leaves and grapevine bark and lines it with softer materials; female incubates 5 sparsely speckled, whitish to pale cream eggs for about 11 days.
**Feeding:** gleans insects and spiders from tree and shrub canopies.
**Voice:** buzzy song begins with a higher note: *zee-bz-bz-bz;* call is a sweet *chip.*
**Similar Species:** *Yellow-rumped Warbler* (p. 286): white throat; dark breast patches; yellow sides. *Black-throated Green Warbler* (p. 287): lacks dark "mask"; 2 white wing bars; black streaking on sides.
**Best Sites:** Connecticut Hill WMA; Beaver Lake CP; Saratoga National Historical Park; Sterling Forest SP.

# TENNESSEE WARBLER

*Vermivora peregrina*

Tennessee Warblers lack the bold, bright features found on other warblers. Even so, they are difficult birds to miss because they have a loud, distinctive, three-part song. • Migrating Tennessee Warblers often sing their tunes and forage for insects high in the forest canopy. However, inclement weather or the need for food after a long flight can force these birds to lower levels in the forest. Females build their nests on the ground and usually remain close to the forest floor when foraging. • Tennessee Warblers thrive during spruce budworm outbreaks. During times of plenty, these birds may produce more than seven young in a single brood. • Alexander Wilson, an ornithologist in the early 1800s, discovered this bird along the Cumberland River in Tennessee and named it after that state. However, it is just a migrant in Tennessee, and breeds only in Canada and the northern border states.

♀ *breeding*

♂

**ID:** *Breeding male:* blue gray crown; olive green back, wings and tail edges; white "eyebrow"; black eye line; clean white underparts; thin bill. *Breeding female:* yellow wash on breast and pale "eyebrow"; olive gray crown. *Nonbreeding:* olive yellow upperparts; yellow "eyebrow"; yellow underparts except for white undertail coverts; male may have white belly.

**Size:** *L* 4½–5 in; *W* 8 in.

**Status:** rare breeder in the Adirondacks; fairly common migrant in May and September.

**Habitat:** *Breeding:* mature coniferous or mixed forests; occasionally spruce bogs. *In migration:* woodlands or areas with tall shrubs.

**Nesting:** on the ground or on a raised hummock; female builds a small cup nest of grass, moss and roots and lines it with fur; female incubates 5–6 speckled, white eggs for 11–12 days.

**Feeding:** gleans foliage and buds for small insects, caterpillars and other invertebrates; also eats berries; occasionally visits suet feeders.

**Voice:** male's song is a loud, sharp, accelerating *ticka-ticka-ticka swit-swit-swit-swit chew-chew-chew-chew-chew;* call is a sweet *chip.*

**Similar Species:** *Warbling Vireo* (p. 231): stouter overall; thicker bill; much less green on upperparts. *Philadelphia Vireo* (p. 232): stouter overall; thicker bill; yellow breast and sides. *Orange-crowned Warbler* (p. 278): lacks white "eyebrow" and blue gray crown.

**Best Sites:** Letchworth SP; Hamlin Beach SP; Five Rivers Environmental Education Center; Bear Mountain SP; Jones Beach SP.

# ORANGE-CROWNED WARBLER

*Vermivora celata*

Don't be disappointed if you can't see the Orange-crowned Warbler's telltale orange crown, because this bird's most distinguishing characteristic is its lack of field marks: wing bars, eye rings and color patches are all conspicuously absent. • When encountered, this warbler usually appears as a blurred, olive yellow bundle flitting nervously among the leaves and branches of low shrubs. In addition, its drab, olive yellow appearance makes it frustratingly similar to females of other warbler species. • Although this warbler breeds widely over most of the western and northern parts of the continent and eastward across Canada, it is seen in our region mainly as a migrant and can easily be overlooked. • The Orange-crowned Warbler is often the most common species to capitalize on the sap wells drilled by Yellow-bellied Sapsuckers.

**ID:** olive yellow to olive gray body; faintly streaked underparts; bright yellow undertail coverts; thin, faint, dark eye line; bright yellow "eyebrow" and broken eye ring; thin bill; faint orange crown patch (rarely seen).
**Size:** *L* 5 in; *W* 7 in.
**Status:** rare migrant from September to October; rare migrant in western NY in May; very rare in winter on Long I.
**Habitat:** woodlands or areas with tall shrubs.
**Nesting:** does not nest in NY.

**Feeding:** gleans foliage for invertebrates, berries, nectar and sap; often hover-gleans.
**Voice:** *Male:* song is a faint trill that breaks downward halfway through; call is a clear, sharp *chip*.
**Similar Species:** *Tennessee Warbler* (p. 277): blue gray crown; dark eye line; bold, white "eyebrow"; white underparts, including undertail coverts. *Ruby-crowned Kinglet* (p. 258): broken, white eye ring; white wing bars. *Wilson's Warbler* (p. 307): complete, bright yellow eye ring; brighter yellow underparts; pale legs; lacks breast streaks. *Yellow Warbler* (p. 281): brighter head and underparts; reddish breast streaks (faint or absent on female). *Common Yellowthroat* (p. 305): female has darker face and upperparts; lacks breast streaks.
**Best Sites:** Tifft Nature Preserve; Hamlin Beach SP; Cohoes–Crescent–Peebles Island SP; Jones Beach SP; Montauk Point SP.

# NASHVILLE WARBLER

*Vermivora ruficapilla*

The Nashville Warbler has an unusual distribution, with two widely separated breeding populations: one eastern and the other western. These populations are believed to have been created thousands of years ago when a single core population was split apart during continental glaciation. • These warblers are best found in overgrown farmland and second-growth forest as they forage low in trees and thickets, often at the edge of a dry forest or burn area. Considered a rare bird in the 1800s, Nashville Warblers have benefited from the clearing of old-growth forests for timber and agriculture. • This warbler was first described near Nashville, Tennessee, but it does not breed in that state. This misnomer is not an isolated incident: the Tennessee, Cape May and Connecticut warblers all bear names that misrepresent their breeding distributions.

**ID:** bold, white eye ring; yellow green upperparts; yellow underparts; white between legs. *Male:* blue gray head; may show small, chestnut red crown. *Female:* duller overall; light eye ring; olive gray head; blue gray nape.
**Size:** *L* 4½–5 in; *W* 7½ in.
**Status:** fairly common breeder in northern and central NY; common migrant from late April through May and in August and September.
**Habitat:** second-growth mixed woodlands; also wet coniferous forests, riparian woodlands, cedar-spruce swamps and moist, shrubby, abandoned fields.
**Nesting:** on the ground under a fern, sapling or shrubby cover; female builds a cup nest of grass, bark strips, ferns and moss; female incubates 4–5 speckled, white eggs for 11–12 days.
**Feeding:** gleans foliage for insects, such as caterpillars, flies and aphids.
**Voice:** *Male:* song begins with a thin, high-pitched *see-it see-it see-it see-it,* followed by a trilling *ti-ti-ti-ti-ti;* call is a metallic *chink.*
**Similar Species:** *Common Yellowthroat* (p. 305) and *Wilson's Warbler* (p. 307): all-yellow underparts; females lack grayish head and bold, white eye ring. *Connecticut Warbler* (p. 365) and *Mourning Warbler* (p. 304): yellow between legs; females have grayish to brownish "hoods."
**Best Sites:** Michigan Hollow–Spencer Marsh; Ferd's Bog–Moose River Plains; Bloomingdale Bog; Cherry Plain SP.

# NORTHERN PARULA

*Parula americana*

Young Northern Parulas spend the first few weeks of their lives enclosed in a fragile, socklike nest suspended from a tree branch. Once they have grown too large for the nest, the young leave their warm abode, dispersing among the surrounding trees and shrubs. As warm summer nights slip away to be replaced by cooler fall temperatures, newly fledged Northern Parulas migrate to the warmer climes of Central America, but mature birds winter in the U.S. • Nesting Northern Parulas are typically found in older forests where the lichens that they use in their nests have had a chance to mature. Males spend most of their time singing and foraging among the tops of tall coniferous spires. When the young have hatched, Northern Parulas expand their foraging areas from conifers only to include deciduous trees, or from only deciduous trees to include understory shrubs, to obtain the extra food needed for the new family.

**ID:** blue gray upperparts; olive patch on back; 2 bold, white wing bars; bold, white eye ring broken by black eye line; yellow "chin," throat and breast; white belly and flanks. *Male:* 1 black and 1 orange breast band.

**Size:** *L* 4½ in; *W* 7 in.

**Status:** fairly common breeder in the Adirondacks; rare breeder in Appalachian Uplands; common migrant in May and from September to October.

**Habitat:** *Breeding:* moist coniferous forests, humid riparian woodlands and swampy deciduous woodlands, especially where lichens hang from branches. *In migration:* woodlands or areas with tall shrubs.

**Nesting:** usually in a conifer; female weaves a small hanging nest into strands of tree lichens; may add lichens to a dense cluster of conifer boughs; pair incubates 4–5 brown-marked, whitish eggs for 12–14 days.

**Feeding:** forages for insects and other invertebrates by hovering, gleaning or hawking; feeds from the tips of branches and occasionally on the ground.

**Voice:** song is a rising, buzzy trill ending with an abrupt, lower-pitched *zip*.

**Similar Species:** *Cerulean Warbler* (p. 295): streaking on breast and sides; lacks white eye ring. *Blue-winged Warbler* (p. 275): yellow underparts. *Yellow-rumped Warbler* (p. 286): yellow rump and crown; lacks yellow throat.

**Best Sites:** Ferd's Bog–Moose River Plains; Bloomingdale Bog; Chubb River Swamp; Bear Mountain SP; Central Park (NYC).

# YELLOW WARBLER

*Dendroica petechia*

Yellow Warblers usually arrive here in early May in search of caterpillars, aphids, beetles and other invertebrates. Flitting from branch to branch among open woodland edges and riparian shrubs, these inquisitive birds seem to be in perpetual motion. • Yellow Warblers are among the most frequent victims of nest parasitism by Brown-headed Cowbirds. Unlike many birds, these warblers can recognize the foreign eggs and many pairs will either abandon their nest or build another nest overtop the old eggs. Some persistent Yellow Warblers build over and over, creating bizarre, multilayered, high-rise nests. • During fall migration, silent, plain-looking Yellow Warblers and other similar-looking warblers can cause confusion for birders who have been lulled into a false sense of familiarity with these birds. Yellow Warblers are unique, however, in having yellow patches on the sides of their tails. • Because of its bright yellow plumage, the Yellow Warbler is often mistakenly called "Wild Canary."

*breeding*

**ID:** bright yellow body; black bill and eyes; bright yellow highlights on dark yellow olive tail and wings. *Breeding male:* reddish breast streaks. *Breeding female:* faint, red breast streaks.

**Size:** *L* 5 in; *W* 8 in.

**Status:** common breeder except at higher elevations; common migrant from late April through May and in September.

**Habitat:** usually near water; moist, open woodlands with dense, low scrub; also shrubby meadows, willow tangles, shrubby fencerows and riparian woodlands.

**Nesting:** in a deciduous tree or small shrub; female builds a compact cup nest of grass, weeds and shredded bark; female incubates 4–5 heavily speckled, greenish white eggs for 11–12 days.

**Feeding:** gleans foliage and vegetation for invertebrates, especially caterpillars, inchworms, beetles, aphids and cankerworms; occasionally hover-gleans.

**Voice:** *Male:* song is a fast, frequently repeated *sweet-sweet-sweet summer sweet.*

**Similar Species:** *Orange-crowned Warbler* (p. 278): darker olive plumage overall; lacks reddish breast streaks. *American Goldfinch* (p. 354): black wings and tail; male often has black forehead. *Wilson's Warbler* (p. 307): shorter, darker tail; male has black "cap"; female has darker crown and upperparts. *Common Yellowthroat* (p. 305): darker face and upperparts; female lacks yellow highlights on wings.

**Best Sites:** Allegany SP; Braddock Bay; Montezuma NWR; Black Creek Marsh WMA; Heckscher SP.

# CHESTNUT-SIDED WARBLER

*Dendroica pensylvanica*

When colorful waves of warbler migrants flood across the landscape each May, the Chestnut-sided Warbler is consistently ranked among the most anticipated arrivals. The boldly patterned males never fail to dazzle on-lookers as they flit about at eye level. • Chestnut-sided Warblers tend to favor early-succession forests, which have become abundant over the past century. Although clear-cut logging has had a negative impact on other warbler species, it has created suitable habitat for this warbler. A good indicator of this species' success is the fact that each spring you can easily see more Chestnut-sided Warblers in a single day than John J. Audubon saw in his entire life—he saw only one! • Although other warblers lose some of their brighter colors in fall yet still look familiar, the Chestnut-sided Warbler undergoes a complete transformation, looking more like a flycatcher or kinglet in its green-and-gray coat.

*breeding*

**ID:** *Breeding male:* chestnut brown sides; white underparts; yellow "cap"; black legs; yellowish wing bars; black "mask." *Breeding female:* similar to male, but with washed-out colors; dark streaking on yellow "cap." *Nonbreeding:* yellow green crown, nape and back; white eye ring; gray face and sides; white underparts.
**Size:** *L* 5 in; *W* 8 in.
**Status:** common breeder from May to July; common migrant in May and in August and September.
**Habitat:** shrubby, deciduous second-growth woodlands, abandoned fields and orchards; especially areas that are regenerating after logging or fire.
**Nesting:** low in a shrub or sapling; small cup nest is made of bark strips, grass, roots and weed fibers; female incubates 4 brown-marked, whitish eggs for 11–12 days.
**Feeding:** gleans trees and shrubs at midlevel for insects.
**Voice:** loud, clear song: *so pleased, pleased, pleased to MEET-CHA!;* musical *chip* call.
**Similar Species:** *Bay-breasted Warbler* (p. 293): black face; dark chestnut crown, throat and flanks; buff belly and undertail coverts; white wing bars. *American Redstart* (p. 297): female has large, yellow patches on wings and tail and is more grayish overall.
**Best Sites:** Allegany SP; Braddock Bay; Saratoga National Historical Park; Bear Mountain SP; Heckscher SP.

# MAGNOLIA WARBLER

*Dendroica magnolia*

The Magnolia Warbler is widely regarded as one of the most beautiful wood-warblers. Like a customized Cadillac, the Magnolia comes fully loaded with all the fancy features: bold "eyebrows," flashy wing bars and tail patches, an elegant "necklace," a bright yellow rump and breast and a dark "mask." It frequently forages along the lower branches of trees and among shrubs, allowing for reliable, close-up observations. In the fall, the Magnolia Warbler loses the dark mask and "necklace," but is immediately identifiable by the distinctive white tail patches. • Male Magnolias flash their white wing and tail patches, snap bills, chase and use *chip* notes to discourage intruders, but competitive singing is used to settle the most intense disputes. • Many songbirds, including Magnolia Warblers, migrate at night. Unfortunately, many birds are killed each year when they collide with buildings, radio towers and tall smokestacks.

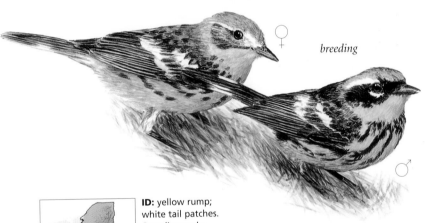

*breeding*

**ID:** yellow rump; white tail patches. *Breeding male:* bold, black streaks on yellow under-parts; black "mask"; white "eyebrow"; blue gray crown; dark upperparts; white wing bars often blend into larger patch. *Female and nonbreeding male:* duller overall; pale "mask"; 2 distinct, white wing bars; streaked, olive back.

**Size:** *L* 4½–5 in; *W* 7½ in.

**Status:** common breeder from May to July in the Adirondacks, Catskills and Appalachian Plateau; migrants arrive in May and depart by October.

**Habitat:** *Breeding:* open coniferous and mixed forests, mostly in natural openings and along edges, often near water; prefers areas with short balsam fir and white spruce. *In migration:* woodlands or areas with tall shrubs.

**Nesting:** in a conifer; loose cup nest is made of grass, twigs and weeds; female incubates 4 brown-speckled, white eggs for 11–13 days.

**Feeding:** gleans vegetation and buds; occasionally flycatches for beetles, flies, wasps, caterpillars and other insects; sometimes eats berries.

**Voice:** *Male:* song is a quick, rising *pretty pretty lady* or *wheata wheata wheet-zu;* call is a *clank.*

**Similar Species:** *Yellow-rumped Warbler* (p. 286): white throat; yellow crown patch; white belly. *Cape May Warbler* (p. 284): chestnut "cheek" patch on yellow face; lacks white tail patches. *Prairie Warbler* (p. 291): dusky jaw stripe; faint, yellowish wing bars.

**Best Sites:** Allegany SP; Connecticut Hill WMA; Whetstone Gulf SP; Ferd's Bog; Bloomingdale Bog.

283

# CAPE MAY WARBLER
*Dendroica tigrina*

Cape May Warblers require mature forests that are at least 50 years old for secure nesting habitat and an abundance of canopy-dwelling insects. You may find yourself with "a pain in the neck" as you strain your head back for a glimpse of these warblers as they forage and sing at the very tops of tall trees. • Throughout most of their breeding range, these small birds are spruce budworm specialists. In years of budworm outbreaks, Cape Mays successfully fledge more young. The harvesting of old-growth spruce adversely affects breeding populations of these warblers. • The Cape May's semi-tubular tongue is unique among wood-warblers and allows it to feed on nectar and fruit juices, both during migration and on its tropical wintering grounds. • Named after Cape May, New Jersey, where the first scientific specimen was collected in 1811, this bird was not recorded there again for over 100 years!

*breeding*

**ID:** dark streaking on yellow underparts; yellow side "collar"; dark olive green upperparts; yellow rump; clean white undertail coverts. *Breeding male:* chestnut "cheek" on yellow face; dark crown; large, white wing patch. *Female:* paler overall; 2 faint, thin, white wing bars; grayish "cheek" and crown.
**Size:** L 4½–5½ in; W 8 in.
**Status:** rare breeder in the Adirondacks; common migrant in early May and from September to October.
**Habitat:** mature coniferous and mixed forests, especially in dense old-growth stands of white spruce and balsam fir.

**Nesting:** near the top of a spruce or fir; female builds a cup nest of moss, weeds and grass; female incubates 6–7 whitish eggs, spotted with reddish brown, for about 12 days.
**Feeding:** gleans treetop branches and foliage for spruce budworms, flies, beetles, moths, wasps and other insects; occasionally hover-gleans.
**Voice:** song is a very high-pitched, weak *see see see see;* call is a very high-pitched *tsee.*
**Similar Species:** *Bay-breasted Warbler* (p. 293): male has black face, chestnut crown, throat and flanks, 2 white wing bars and lacks black streaking on buff underparts. *Black-throated Green Warbler* (p. 287): black throat or upper breast or both; white lower breast and belly; lacks chestnut "cheek" patch; 2 white wing bars. *Magnolia Warbler* (p. 283): white tail patches; less streaking on underparts; lacks chestnut "cheek" patch and yellow side "collar."
**Best Sites:** Letchworth SP; Howland Island WMA; Bloomingdale Bog; John Boyd Thacher SP; Jones Beach SP.

# BLACK-THROATED BLUE WARBLER

*Dendroica caerulescens*

Dark and handsome, the male Black-throated Blue Warbler is a treasured sight to the eyes of any bird enthusiast or casual admirer. The female looks nothing like her male counterpart, however, appearing more like a vireo or a plain-colored Tennessee Warbler. The males and females are so different in appearance that early naturalists, including John J. Audubon, initially thought that they were two different species. • This warbler forages less energetically than other wood-warblers, preferring to work methodically over a small area, snatching up insects from branches and foliage, and gleaning insects from the undersides of leaves. • Typical of warblers, the Black-throated Blue female is able to construct a highly sophisticated nest within three to five days, using cobwebs and saliva to glue strips of bark together.

**ID:** *Male:* black face, throat, upper breast and sides; dark blue upperparts; clean white underparts and wing patch. *Female:* olive brown upperparts; unmarked buff underparts; faint white "eyebrow"; small, buff to whitish wing patch (may not be visible).

**Size:** *L* 5–5½ in; *W* 7½ in.

**Status:** common breeder at higher elevations of the Adirondacks, Catskills and Appalachian Plateau; common migrant in May and from September to October.

**Habitat:** *Breeding:* upland deciduous and mixed forests with a dense understory of deciduous saplings and shrubs; second-growth woodlands and brushy clearings. *In migration:* shrubby woodlands or areas with tall shrubs.

**Nesting:** in a dense shrub or sapling, usually within 3 ft of the ground; female builds an open cup nest of weeds, bark strips and spider webs; female incubates 4 brown-marked, creamy white eggs for 12–13 days.

**Feeding:** thoroughly gleans the understory for caterpillars, moths, spiders and other insects; occasionally eats berries and seeds.

**Voice:** song is a slow, wheezy, rising *I am soo lay-zeee;* call is a short *tip.*

**Similar Species:** male is distinctive. *Tennessee Warbler* (p. 277): lighter "cheek"; greener back; lacks white wing patch. *Philadelphia Vireo* (p. 232): stouter bill; lighter "cheek"; more yellowish white on underparts; lacks white wing patch. *Cerulean Warbler* (p. 295): female has 2 white wing bars and broader, yellowish "eyebrow."

**Best Sites:** Allegany SP; Letchworth SP; Ferd's Bog–Moose River Plains; Chubb River Swamp; Bear Mountain SP.

# YELLOW-RUMPED WARBLER

*Dendroica coronata*

The Yellow-rumped Warbler is the most abundant and widespread wood-warbler in North America. The best time to look for this bird is in the first few hours after dawn, when most Yellow-rumps forage in trees along streams or lakeshores. • Adults are generally quiet when they have eggs or young to guard. When they are noisy and aggressive, it is a good sign that the young have left the nest. • In migration, Yellow-rumps are the least choosy of all warblers, spreading out and using all manner of growth. These birds are generalists and forage in a wide variety of habitats. • Sometimes known as the "Myrtle Warbler," the Yellow-rump is unique among warblers in its ability to digest the waxes in bayberries and wax myrtle. • "Audubon's Warbler," a subspecies found mainly in western North America, sometimes occurs in New York.

*breeding*

**ID:** yellow patches on foreshoulder and rump; white underparts with dark streaking; faint white wing bars; thin "eyebrow"; white throat (yellow in Audubon's). *Male:* yellow crown patch; blue gray upperparts with black streaking; black "cheek" and breast band. *Female:* gray brown upperparts with dark streaking; dark gray "cheek."

**Size:** L 5–6 in; W 9 in.

**Status:** common breeder in the Adirondacks, Catskills and Appalachian Plateau; very common migrant from mid-April through May and from September to October; fairly common in winter on Long I. and in river valleys.

**Habitat:** *Breeding:* coniferous and mixed forests; rarely in pure deciduous woodlands. *In migration:* woodlands or shrubby areas.

**Nesting:** in a conifer; female builds a compact cup nest of grass, bark strips, moss, lichens and spider silk; female incubates 4–5 brown-marked, creamy white eggs for about 12 days.

**Feeding:** hawks and hovers for beetles, flies, wasps, caterpillars, moths and other insects; also gleans vegetation; sometimes eats berries.

**Voice:** *Male:* song is a tinkling trill, often given in 2-note phrases that rise or fall at the end; call is a sharp *chip* or *check.*

**Similar Species:** *Magnolia Warbler* (p. 283): yellow throat and underparts; bold, white "eyebrow"; white tail patches; lacks yellow crown. *Chestnut-sided Warbler* (p. 282): chestnut sides on otherwise clean white underparts; lacks yellow rump. *Cape May Warbler* (p. 284): heavily streaked yellow throat, breast and sides; lacks yellow crown.

**Best Sites:** Allegany SP; Letchworth SP; Chubb River Swamp; Jones Beach SP; Montauk Point SP.

# BLACK-THROATED GREEN WARBLER

*Dendroica virens*

Before the first warm rays of dawn brighten the spires of our forests, male Black-throated Green Warblers offer up their distinctive *see-see-see SUZY!* tunes. On their breeding grounds, not only do males use song to defend their turf, but they also seem to thrive on chasing each other, and even other songbirds, from their territories. • In other parts of its range, the Black-throated Green Warbler is a denizen of old-growth coniferous forests. In our region, however, it also nests in mixed woodlands, pure deciduous forests and even conifer plantations. • When foraging among the forest canopy, males are highly conspicuous as they dart from branch to branch, chipping noisily as they go. Females often prefer to feed at lower levels among the foliage of tall shrubs and sapling trees. • Female Black-throated Green Warblers will lay one egg every day for four to five days, and will not begin to brood the eggs until the last egg is laid.

*breeding*

♀

♂

**ID:** yellow face; may show faint, dusky "cheek" or eye line; black upper breast band; streaking along sides; olive crown, back and rump; dark wings and tail; 2 bold, white wing bars; white lower breast, belly and undertail coverts. *Male:* black throat. *Female:* whitish throat.

**Size:** *L* 4½–5 in; *W* 7½ in.

**Status:** fairly common breeder at higher elevations; common migrant in May and from September to October.

**Habitat:** *Breeding:* coniferous and mixed forests; also deciduous woodlands with beech, maple or birch; may inhabit cedar swamps, hemlock ravines and conifer plantations. *In migration:* woodlands or areas with tall shrubs.

**Nesting:** usually in a conifer; compact cup nest of grass, weeds, twigs, bark, lichens and spider silk; female incubates 4–5 brown-speckled, creamy white to gray eggs for 12 days.

**Feeding:** gleans vegetation and buds for beetles, flies, wasps, caterpillars and other insects; sometimes takes berries; frequently hover-gleans.

**Voice:** fast *see-see-see SUZY!* or *zoo zee zoo zoo zee;* call is a fairly soft *tick*.

**Similar Species:** *Blackburnian Warbler* (p. 288): female has yellowish underparts and angular, dusky facial patch. *Cape May Warbler* (p. 284): heavily streaked, yellow throat, breast and sides. *Pine Warbler* (p. 290): yellowish breast and upper belly; lacks black upper breast band.

**Best Sites:** Letchworth SP; Connecticut Hill WMA; Ferd's Bog–Moose River Plains; Central Park (NYC); Jones Beach SP.

287

# BLACKBURNIAN WARBLER

*Dendroica fusca*

High among towering coniferous spires lives the colorful Blackburnian Warbler, its fiery orange throat ablaze in spring. Widely regarded as one of the most beautiful warblers, the Blackburnian Warbler stays hidden in the upper canopy for much of the summer. • Different species of wood-warblers are able to coexist through a partitioning of foraging niches and feeding strategies. This intricate partitioning reduces competition for food sources and avoids the exhaustion of particular resources. Some warblers inhabit high treetops, a few feed and nest along outer branches—some at high levels and some at lower levels—and others restrict themselves to inner branches and tree trunks. Blackburnians have found their niche predominantly in the outermost branches of the crowns of mature trees. • This bird's name is thought to honor the Blackburne family of England, whose members collected the first specimen and managed the museum in which it was housed.

*breeding*

**Habitat:** *Breeding:* mature coniferous and mixed forests. *In migration:* woodlands or areas with tall shrubs.

**Nesting:** high in a mature conifer; female builds a cup nest of bark, twigs and plant fibers; female incubates 3–5 white to greenish white, brown-blotched eggs for about 13 days.

**Feeding:** forages on the uppermost branches; gleans budworms, flies, beetles and other invertebrates; occasionally hover-gleans.

**Voice:** song is a soft, faint, high-pitched *ptoo-too-too-too tititi zeee* or *see-me see-me see-me see-me;* call is a short *tick.*

**Similar Species:** *Prairie Warbler* (p. 291): faint, yellowish wing bars; black facial stripes do not form solid angular patch. *Cape May Warbler* (p. 284): yellow underparts.

**Best Sites:** Allegany SP; Letchworth SP; Whetstone Gulf SP; Ferd's Bog–Moose River Plains; Cherry Plain SP.

**ID:** *Breeding male:* fiery reddish orange upper breast and throat; yellow orange head; angular, black "mask"; 2 broad, black crown stripes; blackish upperparts; large, white wing patch; yellowish to whitish underparts; dark streaking on sides and flanks. *Female:* brown version of male with yellower upper breast and throat.

**Size:** *L* 5–5½ in; *W* 8½ in.

**Status:** fairly common breeder above 1000 ft elevation; common migrant in May and September.

# YELLOW-THROATED WARBLER

*Dendroica dominica*

The striking Yellow-throated Warbler is a breeding bird in the southeastern U.S., but a few pioneers have expanded their traditional range and migrated into our region, with some nesting. In the 19th century, this bird nested as far north as southern Michigan and northern Ohio, but for unknown reasons it disappeared from this part of its range. Since the 1940s, the Yellow-throated Warbler has been slowly expanding its breeding range northward, reoccupying its former territory. These warblers are fond of wet, lowland forests, and show a preference for the upper canopy. • The Yellow-throated Warbler forages more like a creeper than a warbler, inserting its unusually long bill into cracks and crevices in bark and often foraging on the undersides of horizontal branches. • The odd wayward Yellow-throated Warbler is occasionally seen at a backyard feeder in fall and early winter.

**ID:** yellow throat and upper breast; triangular black "mask"; black forehead; bold, white "eyebrow" and ear patch; white underparts; bluish gray upperparts; long, dark bill; black streaking on sides; 2 white wing bars;
**Size:** *L* 5–5½ in; *W* 8 in.
**Status:** very rare breeder; rare migrant in May; very rare fall migrant; most records are from extreme southern NY and the New York City–Long I. region.
**Habitat:** riparian woodlands with tall sycamore trees; occasionally at backyard feeders in winter.
**Nesting:** high in a sycamore tree; female builds a cup nest of fine grasses, weed stems, plant down and caterpillar silk; female incubates 4 blotched and speckled, greenish white eggs for 12–13 days.
**Feeding:** gleans insects from tree trunks and foliage; often flycatches insects in

midair; wintering birds may eat suet from feeders.
**Voice:** boisterous song is a series of downslurred whistles with a final rising note: *tee-ew tee-ew tee-ew tew-wee;* call is a loud *churp.*
**Similar Species:** *Magnolia Warbler* (p. 283): black "necklace"; yellow breast, belly and rump; lacks white ear patch. *Blackburnian Warbler* (p. 288): yellow orange to orange red throat, "eyebrow," ear patch and crown stripe; blackish upperparts; often shows yellowish underparts. *Yellow-throated Vireo* (p. 229): lacks black and white on face and dark streaking on sides. *Kentucky Warbler* (p. 303): unmarked, all-yellow underparts; yellow "eyebrow"; lacks white ear patch and wing bars.
**Best Sites:** Allegany SP; Central Park (NYC); Prospect Park (NYC); Jamaica Bay Wildlife Refuge.

# PINE WARBLER

*Dendroica pinus*

These unassuming birds are perfectly named because they are bound to majestic, sheltering pines. Pine Warblers are often difficult to find because they typically forage near the tops of very tall, mature pine trees. They are particularly attracted to stands of long-needled white pine and red pine, and tend to avoid pine trees with shorter needles. Occasionally, foraging Pine Warblers can be seen smeared with patches of sticky resin. • The Pine Warbler's modest appearance, which is very similar to that of a number of immature and fall-plumaged vireos and warblers, forces birders to obtain a good, long look before making a positive identification. This warbler is most often confused with the Bay-breasted Warbler or Blackpoll Warbler in drab fall plumage. • The Pine Warbler is peculiar among the wood-warblers in that both its breeding and wintering ranges are located almost entirely within Canada and the U.S.

**Habitat:** *Breeding:* open, mature pine woodlands and mature pine plantations. *In migration:* mixed and deciduous woodlands.

**Nesting:** toward the end of a pine limb; female builds a deep, open cup nest of twigs, bark, weeds, grasses, pine needles and spider webs; pair incubates 3–5 brown-speckled, whitish eggs for about 10 days.

**Feeding:** gleans from the ground or foliage by climbing around trees and shrubs; may hang upside down on branch tips; eats mostly insects, berries and seeds.

**Voice:** song is a short, musical trill; call note is a sweet *chip*.

**ID:** *Male:* olive green head and back; dark grayish wings and tail; whitish to dusky wing bars; yellow throat and breast; faint dark streaking or dusky wash on sides of breast; white undertail coverts and belly; faint dark line through eye; pale yellow, broken eye ring. *Female:* similar to male but duller in color, especially in fall.

**Size:** *L* 5–5½ in; *W* 8½ in.

**Status:** common breeder in Long I. pine barrens; uncommon breeder in upstate pine forests; rare in winter on Long I.; migrants arrive from late March through April and depart from September to October.

**Similar Species:** *Prairie Warbler* (p. 291): distinctive, dark facial stripes; darker streaking on sides; yellowish wing bars. *Bay-breasted Warbler* (p. 293) and *Blackpoll Warbler* (p. 294): long, thin, yellow "eyebrow"; nonbreeding birds have dark streaking on head or back or both. *Yellow-throated Vireo* (p. 229): bright yellow "spectacles"; gray rump; lacks streaking on sides.

**Best Sites:** Hamlin Beach SP; Selkirk Shores SP; Connetquot River SP; Napeague Bay–Hither Hills SP; Montauk Point SP.

# PRAIRIE WARBLER

*Dendroica discolor*

Open scrublands host the summer activities of the inappropriately named Prairie Warbler. This bird prefers early successional areas with such poor soil conditions that the vegetation remains short and scattered. • It is thought that the Prairie Warbler was rare over much of its current breeding range in the early 1800s, before North America was widely colonized. As settlers cleared land, the Prairie Warbler gradually occupied what is now its current range. Because this bird uses early successional habitats, which change over time, its breeding locations change as well. A male Prairie Warbler may return each year to a favored nest site until the vegetation in that area grows too tall and dense, at which point he moves to a new area. • On their nesting territories, song wars occasionally result in physical fights between competing males. When the dust and feathers clear, the victor resumes his slow, graceful, butterfly-like courtship flight.

**ID:** *Male:* bright yellow face and underparts, except for white under-tail coverts; dark "cheek" stripe and eye line; black streaking on sides; olive gray upperparts; inconspicuous chestnut streaks on back; 2 faint, yellowish wing bars. *Female:* similar to male, but duller in color.

**Size:** *L* 4½–5 in; *W* 7 in.

**Status:** fairly common breeder on Long I. and in the Hudson Valley with range expanding northward; fairly common migrant from late April through May and from September to October.

**Habitat:** *Breeding:* dry, open scrubby sand dunes; young jack pine plains; shrubby, burned-over sites; young pine plantations with deciduous scrub. *In migration:* shrubby sites and young pine plantations.

**Nesting:** low in a shrub or small tree; female builds an open cup nest of soft vegetation and lines it with animal hair; female incubates 4 brown-spotted, whitish eggs for 11–14 days; both adults raise the young; may form small, loose nesting colonies.

**Feeding:** gleans, hover-gleans and occasionally hawks for prey; eats mainly insects; will also eat berries and tree sap exposed by sapsuckers.

**Voice:** buzzy song is an ascending series of *zee* notes; call is a sweet *chip*.

**Similar Species:** *Pine Warbler* (p. 290): lighter streaking on sides; whitish wing bars; lacks distinctive dark streaking on face. *Yellow-throated Warbler* (p. 289): white belly; bold, white wing bars, "eyebrow" and ear patch. *Bay-breasted Warbler* (p. 293) and *Blackpoll Warbler* (p. 294): nonbreeding birds have lighter upperparts with dark streaking and white bellies and wing bars.

**Best Sites:** Five Rivers Environmental Education Center; Partridge Run WMA; Ward Pound Ridge Reservation; Heckscher SP.

# PALM WARBLER

*Dendroica palmarum*

Considering this bird's subtropical wintering range, it may make sense to call it the Palm Warbler, even though it doesn't actually forage in palm trees. Based on its summer range, however, it could just as easily have been named the "Bog Warbler" because of its preference for northern bogs and fens of sphagnum moss and black spruce. Despite its name, the Palm Warbler nests farther north than all other wood-warblers except the Blackpoll Warbler. • The Palm Warbler is unusual in its preference for foraging on the ground or in low shrubs and vegetation. It nests directly on the ground in a bog, usually beneath a young conifer. • Whether the Palm Warbler is hopping on the ground or perched momentarily on an elevated limb, it incessantly bobs its tail. This trait is a prominent field mark, particularly in fall, when its distinctive chestnut crown fades to olive brown.

**ID:** chestnut brown crown (may be inconspicuous in fall); yellow "eyebrow," throat and undertail coverts; yellow breast and belly; dark streaking on breast and sides; olive brown upperparts; may show dull yellowish rump; frequently bobs tail.

**Size:** *L* 4–5½ in; *W* 8 in.

**Status:** several breeding sites in the Adirondacks; common, sometimes numerous, migrant in April and from September to October; a few winter each year on Long I.

**Habitat:** *Breeding:* edges of mature bogs with scattered black spruce; less frequently in openings of spruce-tamarack forests with sphagnum moss and shrubs; rarely jack pine plains. *In migration:* woodlands or areas with tall shrubs.

**Nesting:** on the ground, in a low shrub or stunted spruce or on a sphagnum hummock; female builds a cup nest of grass, weeds and bark; female incubates 4–5 brown-marked, creamy white eggs for about 12 days.

**Feeding:** gleans the ground and vegetation for a wide variety of insects and berries while perched or hovering; occasionally hawks for insects; may take some seeds.

**Voice:** *Male:* song is a weak, buzzy trill with a quick finish; call is a sharp *sup* or *check*.

**Similar Species:** *Yellow-rumped Warbler* (p. 286): white wing bars, throat and undertail coverts; bright yellow rump, crown patch and foreshoulder patch. *Prairie Warbler* (p. 291): dark jaw stripe; darker eye line; lacks chestnut crown and dark streaking on breast. *Chipping Sparrow* (p. 314) and *American Tree Sparrow* (p. 313): stouter bodies; unstreaked, grayish underparts; lack yellow plumage. *Pine Warbler* (p. 290): faint, whitish wing bars; white undertail coverts; lacks chestnut crown and bold, yellow "eyebrow."

**Best Sites:** Hamlin Beach SP; Montezuma NWR; Vischer Ferry Nature and Historic Preserve; Jamaica Bay Wildlife Refuge; Jones Beach SP.

# BAY-BREASTED WARBLER

*Dendroica castanea*

The handsome Bay-breasted Warbler can be difficult to spot because it typically forages deep within stands of old-growth spruce and fir, often on the inner branches of a tree. • These warblers are spruce budworm specialists, and their populations fluctuate from year to year along with the cyclical rise and fall of budworm numbers. Bay-breasted Warblers are invaluable when it comes to long-term suppression of budworm outbreaks, typically moving to where the larvae are most numerous. It is estimated that in outbreak years, one Bay-breasted Warbler can eat over 5000 budworms per acre through the breeding season. Although Bay-breasts are insectivorous on their breeding grounds, they switch to an almost all-fruit diet while they winter in Panama and Colombia. • The Bay-breasted Warbler's scientific name *castanea*, which means "chestnut" in Latin, comes from its being discovered sitting in a chestnut tree.

*breeding*

**ID:** *Breeding male:* black "mask"; chestnut crown, throat and flanks; creamy yellow belly, undertail coverts and neck patch; 2 white wing bars. *Breeding female:* paler overall; dusky face; whitish to creamy underparts and neck patch; faint chestnut "cap"; rusty wash on sides and flanks. *Nonbreeding:* yellow olive head and back; dark streaking on crown and back; whiter underparts.
**Size:** *L* 5–6 in; *W* 9 in.
**Status:** rare breeder in the Adirondacks; fairly common migrant in May and from September to October.
**Habitat:** *Breeding:* mature coniferous and mixed boreal forests; almost exclusively in stands of spruce and fir. *In migration:* woodlands or areas with tall shrubs.
**Nesting:** usually in a conifer; open cup nest is built of grass, twigs, moss, roots and lichen; female incubates 4–5 darkly marked, whitish eggs for 12–13 days.

**Feeding:** usually forages at the midlevel of trees; gleans vegetation and branches for spruce budworms, caterpillars and adult invertebrates.
**Voice:** song is an extremely high-pitched *seee-seese-seese-seee;* call is a high *see*.
**Similar Species:** *Cape May Warbler* (p. 284): chestnut "cheek" on yellow face; dark streaking on mostly yellow underparts; lacks reddish flanks and crown. *Chestnut-sided Warbler* (p. 282): yellow crown; white "cheek" and underparts; nonbreeding birds have white eye ring, unmarked, whitish face and underparts and lack bold streaking on yellow green upperparts. *Blackpoll Warbler* (p. 294): white undertail coverts; nonbreeding has dark streaking on breast and sides and lacks chestnut on sides and flanks.
**Best Sites:** Letchworth SP; Braddock Bay; Ferd's Bog–Moose River Plains; Central Park (NYC); Prospect Park (NYC).

# BLACKPOLL WARBLER

*Dendroica striata*

Blackpoll Warblers are the greatest warbler migrants: eastern migrants are known to fly south over the Atlantic, leaving land at Cape Cod and flying for 88 nonstop hours until they reach the northern coast of Venezuela. During such a trip, these small birds will cover almost 1900 miles, and in a single year, may fly up to 15,000 miles! In migration, Blackpoll Warblers adjust their flying altitude—sometimes flying at heights of 20,000 feet—to best use shifting prevailing winds to reach their destination. These warblers are truly international residents, so conservation of their habitat requires the efforts of several nations. • Blackpoll Warblers in fall plumage are easily confused with very similar-looking Bay-breasted Warblers. Most Blackpolls, however, migrate later in fall than their Bay-breasted counterparts.

*breeding*

common migrant in mid-May and from September to October.

**Habitat:** mixed woodlands.

**Nesting:** against the trunk of a spruce; female builds a bulky nest of twigs, bark and grasses; female incubates 4–5 brown-spotted, white eggs for 11–12 days.

**Feeding:** gleans buds, leaves and branches for aphids, mosquitoes, beetles, wasps, caterpillars and many other insects; often flycatches for insects.

**Voice:** song is an extremely high-pitched, uniform trill: *tsit tsit tsit;* call is a loud *chip.*

**Similar Species:** *Black-and-white Warbler* (p. 296): black-and-white-striped crown; male has black throat and "cheek." *Black-capped Chickadee* (p. 246): black "chin" and throat; lacks wing bars and black streaking on underparts. *Bay-breasted Warbler* (p. 293): chestnut sides and flanks; buff undertail coverts; nonbreeding lacks dark streaking on underparts.

**Best Sites:** Whiteface Mt.; Slide Mt.; Bear Mountain SP; Central Park (NYC); Jamaica Bay Wildlife Refuge.

**ID:** 2 white wing bars; black streaking on white underparts; white undertail coverts. *Breeding male:* black "cap" and "chin" stripe; white "cheek"; black-streaked, olive gray upperparts; orange legs. *Breeding female:* streaked, yellow olive head and back; small, dark eye line; pale "eyebrow." *Nonbreeding:* olive yellow head, back, rump, breast and sides; yellow "eyebrow."

**Size:** *L* 5–5½ in; *W* 9 in.

**Status:** fairly common breeder at higher elevations of the Adirondacks and Catskills;

# CERULEAN WARBLER

*Dendroica cerulea*

The Cerulean Warbler leads a mysterious life concealed high in the canopy of mature deciduous forests. The handsome blue-and-white male is particularly difficult to observe as he blends into the sunny summer sky while foraging among treetop foliage. Often the only evidence of a meeting with this largely unobservable canopy-dweller is the sound of the male's buzzy, trilling voice. • Only in the last few decades have ornithologists been able to document this bird's breeding behavior. Courtship, mating, nesting and the rearing of young all take place high in the canopy, well out of sight of most casual observers. Cerulean Warblers also attack each other high in the canopy: flying aggressively toward one another they collide with an audible thud, then spiral together toward the ground. Females also fight, and an aggressive female may even knock her own mate off his perch.

*breeding*

**Nesting:** high in a deciduous tree; female builds an open cup nest of bark strips, weeds, grass, lichen and spider silk; female incubates 3–5 brown-spotted, gray to creamy white eggs, for 12–13 days.

**Feeding:** gleans insects from upper canopy foliage and branches; often hawks for insects.

**Voice:** song is a rapid, accelerating sequence of buzzy notes leading into a higher trilled note; call is a sharp *chip*.

**ID:** white undertail coverts and wing bars. *Male:* blue upperparts; white throat and underparts; black "necklace" and streaking on sides.

*Female:* blue green crown, nape and back; dark eye line; yellow "eyebrow," throat and breast; pale streaking on sides.

**Size:** L 4½–5 in; W 7 in.

**Status:** special concern; locally common breeder in central NY and the Hudson Valley; migrants arrive in early May and depart by August.

**Habitat:** mature deciduous hardwood forests and extensive woodlands with a clear understory; particularly drawn to riparian stands.

**Similar Species:** *Black-throated Blue Warbler* (p. 285): lacks wing bars; male has black face, throat, upper breast and sides; female has small, white wing patch. *Blackpoll Warbler* (p. 294) and *Bay-breasted Warbler* (p. 293): similar to female Cerulean but have more yellow than green on mantle. *Pine Warbler* (p. 290): browner; similar to female Cerulean but has more yellow on mantle.

**Best Sites:** Letchworth SP; Stewart Park–Cayuga L.; Montezuma NWR; Schodack Island SP; Bear Mountain SP.

# BLACK-AND-WHITE WARBLER

*Mniotilta varia*

The foraging behavior of the Black-and-white Warbler stands in sharp contrast to that of most of its kin. Rather than zipping quickly between twig perches, Black-and-white Warblers behave more like creepers and nuthatches—a distantly related group of birds. Birders with frayed nerves and tired eyes from watching flitty warblers will be refreshed by the sight of this bird as it methodically creeps up and down tree trunks, probing bark crevices. • Novice birders can easily identify this unique, two-tone warbler, which retains its standard plumage throughout its stay in our region. Even a trip to its wintering grounds will reveal this warbler in the same black-and-white outfit. A keen ear also helps to identify this bird: its gentle oscillating song—like a wheel in need of greasing—is easily recognized and remembered.

breeding

**ID:** black-and-white-striped crown; white streaks on dark upperparts; 2 white wing bars; white underparts with black streaking on sides, flanks and undertail coverts; black legs. *Breeding male:* black "cheek" and throat. *Breeding female:* gray "cheek"; white throat.

**Size:** *L* 5–5½ in; *W* 8 in.

**Status:** common breeder; migrants occur from late April through May and from September to October.

**Habitat:** deciduous or mixed forests, often near water; also in cedar swamps and alder and willow thickets bordering muskeg and beaver ponds.

**Nesting:** usually on the ground in a shallow scrape; often among a pile of dead leaves; female builds a cup nest with grass, leaves, bark strips, rootlets and pine needles; female incubates 5 brown-flecked, creamy white eggs for 10–12 days.

**Feeding:** gleans insect eggs, larval insects, beetles, spiders and other invertebrates.

**Voice:** series of high, thin, 2-syllable notes: *weetsee weetsee weetsee weetsee weetsee weetsee;* call is a sharp *pit* and a soft, high *seat.*

**Similar Species:** *Blackpoll Warbler* (p. 294): breeding male has solid black "cap" and clean white undertail coverts.

**Best Sites:** Letchworth SP; Stewart Park–Cayuga L.; Five Rivers Environmental Education Center; Bear Mountain SP; Connetquot River SP.

# AMERICAN REDSTART

*Setophaga ruticilla*

American Redstarts are a consistent favorite among birders. These supercharged birds flit from branch to branch in dizzying pursuit of prey. Even when perched, their tails sway rhythmically back and forth. Few birds can rival a mature male redstart for his contrasting black-and-orange plumage and amusing behavior. • A common foraging technique used by the American Redstart is to flash its wings and tail patches to flush prey. If a concealed insect tries to flee, the redstart will give chase. • Although Redstarts are common here, their beautiful, trilly songs are so variable that identifying one is a challenge to birders of all levels. • On its wintering grounds, the American Redstart is called "Butterfly Bird" in the U.S. and *candelita*, meaning "little candle," in Central America.

**ID:** *Male:* black overall; red orange patches on foreshoulder, wings and tail; white belly and undertail coverts. *Female:* olive brown upperparts; gray green head; yellow patches on foreshoulder, wings and tail; clean white underparts.

**Size:** *L* 5 in; *W* 8 in.

**Status:** common breeder; common migrant in May and September.

**Habitat:** shrubby woodland edges, open and semi-open deciduous and mixed forests with a deciduous understory of shrubs and saplings; often near water.

**Nesting:** in a shrub or sapling, usually 3–23 ft above the ground; female builds an open cup nest of plant down, bark shreds, grass and rootlets and lines it with feathers; female incubates 4 brown-marked, whitish eggs for 11–12 days.

**Feeding:** actively gleans foliage and hawks for insects and spiders on leaves, buds and branches; often hover-gleans.

**Voice:** male's song is a highly variable series of *tseet* or *zee* notes, often given at different pitches; call is a sharp, sweet *chip*.

**Similar Species:** none.

**Best Sites:** Allegany SP; Letchworth SP; John Boyd Thacher SP; Bear Mountain SP; Heckscher SP.

# PROTHONOTARY WARBLER

*Protonotaria citrea*

The Prothonotary Warbler is the only eastern wood-warbler to nest in cavities. Standing dead trees and stumps riddled with natural cavities and woodpecker excavations provide perfect nesting habitat for this bird, especially if the site is near stagnant, swampy water. Much of the Prothonotary Warbler's swampy habitat is inaccessible to birders, but if you are in the right place at the right time, you might be lucky enough to come across this bird as it forages for insects along tree trunks and decaying logs, in low, tangled thickets and on debris floating on the water's surface. • The male can be very aggressive when defending his territory, and often resorts to combative aerial chases when songs and warning displays fail to intimidate an intruder. • This bird acquired its unusual name because its plumage was thought to resemble the yellow hoods worn by prothonotaries, high-ranking clerics in the Catholic Church.

*breeding*

**ID:** long bill; unmarked, yellow head; yellow undersides except for white under-tail coverts; olive green back; unmarked, bluish gray wings and tail.

**Size:** *L* 5½ in; *W* 8½ in.

**Status:** uncommon and local breeder; rare migrant in late April through May.

**Habitat:** wooded deciduous swamps and riparian woodlands.

**Nesting:** in a cavity in a standing dead tree or rotten stump; also in a birdhouse or abandoned woodpecker nest; often returns to the same nest site; mostly the male builds a cup nest of twigs, leaves, moss and plant down; female incubates 4–6 brown-spotted, creamy to pinkish eggs for 12–14 days.

**Feeding:** forages for a variety of insects and small mollusks; gleans from vegetation; may hop on floating debris or creep along tree trunks.

**Voice:** *Male:* song is a loud, ringing series of *sweet* or *zweet* notes issued on a single pitch; flight song is *chewee chewee chee chee;* call is a brisk *tink.*

**Similar Species:** *Blue-winged Warbler* (p. 275): white wing bars; black eye line; yellowish white undertail coverts. *Yellow Warbler* (p. 281): yellow highlights on dark wings and tail; yellow undertail coverts; male has reddish streaking on breast. *Hooded Warbler* (p. 306): female has yellow undertail coverts and yellow olive upperparts.

**Best Sites:** Iroquois NWR–Tonawanda WMA–Oak Orchard WMA; Montezuma NWR; Bashakill WMA; Bear Mountain SP; Caleb Smith State Park Preserve–Nissequogue R.

# WORM-EATING WARBLER

*Helmitheros vermivorum*

Those wishing to see this bird have a challenge ahead of them because the Worm-eating Warbler is rare in New York. To make things more difficult, this warbler's subdued colors allow it to blend in with the decomposing twigs, roots and leaves that litter the forest floor. It spends most of its time foraging for caterpillars, small terrestrial insects and spiders among dense undergrowth and dead leaves in deciduous forests. • The Worm-eating Warbler typically nests near water and on a slope, and is one of a small group of eastern warblers that nest on the ground. The female becomes completely still if she is approached while on the nest, relying on her striped crown for concealment. • The Worm-eating Warbler's song is a rapid trill that seems loudest in the middle and weaker at the beginning and end.

**ID:** buffy orange head and underparts; black stripes on crown and through eye; brownish olive upperparts; whitish undertail coverts.

**Size:** *L* 5 in; *W* 8½ in.

**Status:** locally common breeder in the Hudson Valley; migrants arrive in early May and depart by mid-September.

**Habitat:** steep, deciduous woodland slopes, ravines and swampy woodlands with shrubby understory cover.

**Nesting:** usually on a hillside or ravine bank, often near water; on the ground hidden under leaf litter; female builds a cup nest of decaying leaves and lines it with fine grass, moss stems and hair; female incubates 3–5 white eggs, speckled with reddish brown, for about 13 days.

**Feeding:** forages on the ground and in trees and shrubs; eats mostly small insects.

**Voice:** song is a rapid trill; call is a buzzy *zeep-zeep*.

**Similar Species:** *Red-eyed Vireo* (p. 233): gray crown; white "eyebrow"; red eyes; yellow undertail coverts. *Louisiana Waterthrush* (p. 302) and *Northern Waterthrush* (p. 301): darker upperparts; bold, white or yellowish "eyebrow"; dark streaking on white breast; lacks striped head.

**Best Sites:** John Boyd Thacher SP; Sterling Forest SP; Bear Mountain SP; Clarence Fahnestock SP; Ward Pound Ridge Reservation.

299

# OVENBIRD
*Seiurus aurocapilla*

The Ovenbird's loud and joyous "ode to teachers" is a common sound that echoes through deciduous and mixed forests in spring. Unfortunately, pinpointing the exact location of this resonating call is not always easy. An Ovenbird will rarely expose itself, and even when it does, active searching and patience is necessary to get a good look at it. What may sound like one long-winded Ovenbird may actually be two neighboring males singing and responding on the heels of each other's song. • The name "Ovenbird" refers to this bird's unusual, dome-shaped ground nest. An incubating female nestled within her woven dome usually feels so secure that she will choose to sit tight rather than flee when approached. Nests are so well camouflaged that few people ever find one, even though the nests are often located near hiking trails and bike paths. • Robert Frost was so moved by the Ovenbird's spring songs that he dedicated a poem to them entitled "Ovenbird." The genus and species names together translate as "golden-haired tail-waver."

**ID:** olive brown upperparts; white eye ring; heavy, dark streaking on white breast, sides and flanks; rufous crown bordered with black; pink legs; white undertail coverts; no wing bars.
**Size:** *L* 6 in; *W* 9½ in.
**Status:** common breeder from May to July; quite common migrant in early May and in September.
**Habitat:** *Breeding:* undisturbed, mature forests with a closed canopy and very little understory; often in ravines and riparian areas. *In migration:* dense riparian shrubbery and thickets; a variety of woodlands.

**Nesting:** on the ground; female builds an oven-shaped, domed nest of grass, bark, twigs and dead leaves and lines it with animal hair; female incubates 4–5 brown-spotted, white eggs for 11–13 days.
**Feeding:** gleans the ground for worms, snails, insects and occasionally seeds.
**Voice:** loud, distinctive *tea-cher tea-cher Tea-CHER Tea-CHER,* increasing in speed and volume; night song is an elaborate series of bubbly, warbled notes, often ending in *teacher-teacher;* call is a brisk *chip, cheep* or *chock.*
**Similar Species:** *Northern Waterthrush* (p. 301) and *Louisiana Waterthrush* (p. 302): bold yellowish or white "eyebrow"; darker upperparts; lacks rufous crown. *Thrushes* (pp. 260–67): all are larger and lack rufous crown outlined in black.
**Best Sites:** Allegany SP; Letchworth SP; John Boyd Thacher SP; Bear Mountain SP; Heckscher SP.

# NORTHERN WATERTHRUSH

*Seiurus noveboracensis*

Birders who are not satisfied with simply hearing a Northern Waterthrush in its nesting territory must literally get their feet wet if they hope to see one. This bird skulks along the shores of deciduous swamps or coniferous bogs, and the fallen logs, shrubby tangles and soggy ground may discourage human visitors. During the relatively bug-free months in spring and fall, birders can typically find migrating Northern Waterthrushes in drier, upland forests or along lofty park trails and boardwalks. Backyards featuring a small garden pond may also attract migrating waterthrushes. • Waterthrushes tip and teeter while walking, a habit that may be intended to disturb ground- and water-dwelling insects. • The voice of the Northern Waterthrush is loud and raucous for such a small bird, so it seems fitting that it was once known as the "New York Warbler," in reference to the city so well known for its decibels. The scientific name *noveboracensis* means "of New York."

**ID:** pale yellowish to buff "eyebrow"; dark streaking on pale yellowish to buff underparts; finely spotted throat; olive brown upperparts; pinkish legs; frequently bobs its tail.

**Size:** *L* 5–6 in; *W* 9½ in.

**Status:** fairly common breeder from May to July; widespread migrant, arriving in late April and departing in September.

**Habitat:** wooded edges of swamps, lakes, beaver ponds, bogs and rivers; also in moist, wooded ravines and riparian thickets.

**Nesting:** on the ground, usually near water; female builds a cup nest made of moss, leaves, bark shreds, twigs and pine needles; female incubates 4–5 brown-speckled, whitish eggs for 12–13 days.

**Feeding:** gleans foliage and the ground for invertebrates, frequently tossing aside ground litter with its bill; may also take aquatic invertebrates and small fish from shallow water.

**Voice:** song is a loud, 3-part *sweet sweet sweet, swee wee wee, chew chew chew chew;* call is a brisk *chip* or *chuck.*

**Similar Species:** *Louisiana Waterthrush* (p. 302): broader, white "eyebrow"; unspotted, white throat; buff orange wash on flanks. *Ovenbird* (p. 300): rufous crown bordered by black stripes; white eye ring; unspotted throat; lacks pale "eyebrow."

**Best Sites:** Allegany SP; Michigan Hollow–Spencer Marsh; Black Creek Marsh WMA; Bashakill WMA; Jamaica Bay Wildlife Refuge.

# LOUISIANA WATERTHRUSH

*Seiurus motacilla*

The Louisiana Waterthrush is often seen sallying along the shorelines of babbling streams and gently swirling pools in search of its next meal. This bird inhabits swamps and sluggish streams throughout much of its North American range, but where its range overlaps with that of the Northern Waterthrush, it inhabits shorelines near fast-flowing water. • The Louisiana Waterthrush has a larger bill, pinker legs, whiter "eyebrows" and less streaking on its throat than the Northern Waterthrush. Both waterthrushes are easily identified by their habit of bobbing their heads and moving their tails up and down as they walk, but the Louisana Waterthrush bobs its tail more slowly and also tends to sway from side to side. This bird's scientific name *motacilla* is Latin for "wagtail."

**ID:** brownish upperparts; long bill; pink legs; white underparts with buff orange wash on flanks; long, dark streaks on breast and sides; bicolored, buffy white "eyebrow"; clean white throat.

**Size:** *L* 6 in; *W* 10 in.

**Status:** fairly common breeder from May to July along streams south of the Adirondacks; migrants arrive in mid-April and depart by August.

**Habitat:** moist, forested ravines alongside fast-flowing streams; rarely along wooded swamps.

**Nesting:** concealed within a rocky hollow or within a tangle of tree roots; both adults build a cup nest of leaves, bark strips, twigs and moss; female incubates 3–6 brown-speckled, creamy white eggs for 12–14 days.

**Feeding:** gleans terrestrial and aquatic insects and crustaceans from rocks and debris in or near shallow water; dead leaves and other debris may be flipped and probed for food; occasionally catches flying insects over water.

**Voice:** song begins with 3–4 distinctive, shrill, slurred notes followed by a warbling twitter; call is a brisk *chick* or *chink*.

**Similar Species:** *Northern Waterthrush* (p. 301): yellowish to buff "eyebrow" narrows behind eye; underparts usually all yellowish or buff (occasionally all white); finely spotted throat; lacks buff orange flanks. *Ovenbird* (p. 300) and *thrushes* (pp. 260–67): lack broad, white "eyebrow."

**Best Sites:** Allegany SP; Letchworth SP; John Boyd Thacher SP; Five Rivers Environmental Education Center; Bear Mountain SP.

# KENTUCKY WARBLER

*Oporornis formosus*

Typically found in moist, deciduous woodlands, Kentucky Warblers spend much of their time on the ground, overturning leaves and scurrying through dense thickets in search of insects. These warblers are shy and elusive as they sing their loud springtime songs from secluded perches. As a general rule, male warblers sing most actively in the morning, feeding only intermittently, but quiet down in the afternoon and feed more actively. Once the young hatch, singing becomes rare as both males and females spend much of their time feeding the young. Unmated males, however, may continue to sing throughout the summer. The Kentucky Warbler's song may be confused with that of the Carolina Wren, but the Kentucky Warbler will sing the same song pattern repeatedly, while the Carolina Wren varies its song constantly. • Like waterthrushes and Ovenbirds, Kentucky Warblers bob their tails up and down as they walk.

**ID:** bright yellow "spectacles" and underparts; black crown, "side-burns" and "half mask"; olive green upperparts; pale pinkish legs.
**Size:** *L* 5–5½ in; *W* 8½ in.
**Status:** uncommon and local breeder from May to July in southeastern NY; very rarely reported as a migrant owing to small numbers.
**Habitat:** moist deciduous and mixed woodlands with dense, shrubby cover and herbaceous plant growth, including wooded ravines, swamp edges and creek bottomlands.

**Nesting:** on or close to the ground; pair builds a cup nest of grass, plant stems and leaves; female incubates 4–5 brown-speckled, creamy white eggs for 12–13 days.
**Feeding:** gleans insects while walking along the ground, flipping over leaf litter or by snatching prey from the undersides of low foliage.
**Voice:** *Male:* musical song is a series of 2-syllable notes: *chur-ree chur-ree;* call is a sharp *chick, chuck* or *chip.*
**Similar Species:** *Canada Warbler* (p. 308): dark, streaky "necklace"; bluish gray upperparts. *Hooded Warbler* (p. 306): black crown and throat. *Common Yellowthroat* (p. 305): black "mask."
**Best Sites:** Bashakill WMA; Bear Mountain SP.

# MOURNING WARBLER

*Oporornis philadelphia*

Although Mourning Warblers can be quite common in some locations, they are seen far less frequently than one might expect. These birds seldom leave the protection of their dense, shrubby, often impenetrable habitat, and they tend to sing only on their breeding territories. Riparian areas, regenerating clear-cuts and patches of forest that have been recently cleared by fire provide the low shrubs and sapling trees that these warblers rely on for nesting and foraging. Mourning Warblers are best seen during migration, when backyard shrubs and raspberry thickets may attract small, silent flocks. • The Mourning Warbler is the only member of the hooded *Oporornis* genus—which includes the Kentucky, Connecticut and MacGillivray's (*O. tolmiei*) warblers—whose breeding area overlaps that of all the others. • This bird's dark "hood" and black breast patch reminded pioneering ornithologist Alexander Wilson of someone dressed in mourning.

breeding

**ID:** yellow underparts; olive green upperparts; short tail; pinkish legs. *Breeding male:* blue gray "hood"; black upper breast patch; usually no eye ring, but may show broken eye ring. *Female:* gray "hood"; whitish "chin" and throat; may show thin eye ring.

**Size:** L 5–5½ in; W 7½ in.

**Status:** locally common breeder from May to July; absent south and east of the Catskills; uncommon migrant in May and September.

**Habitat:** dense, shrubby thickets, tangles and brambles, often in moist areas of forest clearings and along the edges of ponds, lakes and streams.

**Nesting:** on the ground at the base of a shrub or plant tussock or in a small shrub; bulky nest of leaves, weeds and grass is lined with fur and fine grass; female incubates 3–4 brown-blotched, creamy white eggs for about 12 days.

**Feeding:** forages in dense, low shrubs for caterpillars, beetles, spiders and other invertebrates.

**Voice:** husky, 2-part song is variable and lower-pitched at the end: *churry, churry, churry, churry, chorry, chorry;* call is a loud, low *check.*

**Similar Species:** *Connecticut Warbler* (p. 365): bold, complete eye ring; lacks black breast patch; long undertail coverts make tail look very short. *Nashville Warbler* (p. 279): bright yellow throat; dark legs.

**Best Sites:** Allegany SP; Letchworth SP; Ferd's Bog–Moose River Plains; Cherry Plain SP.

# COMMON YELLOWTHROAT

*Geothlypis trichas*

This energetic songster of our wetlands is a favorite among birders—its small size, bright plumage and spunky disposition quickly endear it to all who meet it. • The Common Yellowthroat favors shrubby marshes and wet, overgrown meadows, shunning the forest habitat preferred by most of its wood-warbler relatives. In May and June, the male Yellowthroat issues his distinctive song while perched atop a tall cattail or shrub. Observing a male in action will reveal the location of his favorite singing perches, which he visits in rotation. These strategic outposts mark the boundary of his territory, which is fiercely guarded from the intrusion of other males. • The Common Yellowthroat is one of New York's most common warblers.

**ID:** yellow throat, breast and undertail coverts; dingy white belly; olive green to olive brown upperparts; orangy legs. *Breeding male:* broad, black "mask" with white upper border. *Female:* no "mask"; may show faint, white eye ring.

**Size:** *L* 5 in; *W* 6½ in.

**Status:** common breeder from May to July, with some second broods into August; common migrant from late April through May and from September to October; rare in winter in small numbers on Long I.

**Habitat:** cattail marshes, riparian willow and alder clumps, sedge wetlands, beaver ponds and wet overgrown meadows; sometimes dry, abandoned fields.

**Nesting:** on or near the ground, often in a small shrub or among emergent aquatic vegetation; female builds a bulky, open cup nest of weeds, grass, bark strips, sedges and moss; female incubates 3–5 brown-blotched, creamy white eggs for 12 days.

**Feeding:** gleans vegetation and hovers for adult and larval insects, including dragonflies, spiders and beetles; occasionally eats seeds.

**Voice:** song is a clear, oscillating *witchety witchety witchety-witch;* call is a sharp *tcheck* or *tchet.*

**Similar Species:** male's black "mask" is distinctive. *Kentucky Warbler* (p. 303): yellow "spectacles"; all-yellow underparts; black "half mask." *Yellow Warbler* (p. 281): brighter yellow overall; yellow highlights on wings; all-yellow underparts. *Wilson's Warbler* (p. 307): bright yellow forehead, "eyebrow" and underparts; may show dark "cap." *Orange-crowned Warbler* (p. 278): dull, yellow olive overall; faint breast streaks. *Nashville Warbler* (p. 279): bold, complete eye ring; blue gray crown.

**Best Sites:** Allegany SP; Iroquois NWR–Tonawanda WMA–Oak Orchard WMA; Montezuma NWR; Jamaica Bay Wildlife Refuge; Jones Beach SP.

# HOODED WARBLER

*Wilsonia citrina*

Despite nesting low to the ground, Hooded Warblers require extensive mature forests, where fallen trees have opened gaps in the canopy, encouraging understory growth. • Different species of wood-warblers can coexist in a limited environment because they partition their food supplies, with each species foraging exclusively in certain areas. Hooded Warblers also partition between the sexes: males tend to forage in treetops, while females forage near the ground. • Unlike their female counterparts, male Hooded Warblers may return to the same nesting territory year after year. Once the young have left the nest, each parent takes on guardianship of half the fledged young. • When Hooded Warblers arrive on their wintering grounds, the males and females segregate—a practice unknown in any other warbler species—with males using mature forests, and females using shrubby and disturbed areas.

**ID:** bright yellow underparts; olive green upperparts; white undertail; pinkish legs. *Male:* black "hood"; bright yellow face. *Female:* yellow face; olive crown; may show faint traces of dark "hood."

**Size:** *L* 5½ in; *W* 7 in.

**Status:** fairly common breeder from May to July in western and southern NY; uncommon migrant in mid-May and in September.

**Habitat:** clearings with dense, low shrubs in mature upland deciduous and mixed forests; occasionally in moist ravines or mature white pine plantations with a dense understory of deciduous shrubs.

**Nesting:** low in a deciduous shrub; mostly the female builds an open cup nest of fine grass, bark strips, dead leaves, animal hair, spider webs and plant down; female incubates 4 brown-spotted, creamy white eggs for about 12 days.

**Feeding:** gleans insects and other forest invertebrates from the ground or shrub branches; may scramble up tree trunks or flycatch.

**Voice:** clear, whistling song is some variation of *whitta-witta-wit-tee-yo;* call note is a metallic *tink, chink* or *chip.*

**Similar Species:** *Wilson's Warbler* (p. 307), *Yellow Warbler* (p. 281) and *Common Yellowthroat* (p. 305): females lack white undertail feathers. *Kentucky Warbler* (p. 303): yellow "spectacles"; dark, triangular "half mask."

**Best Sites:** Allegany SP; Letchworth SP; Clarence Fahnestock SP; Bear Mountain SP; Bashakill WMA.

# WILSON'S WARBLER

*Wilsonia pusilla*

You are almost sure to catch sight of the energetic Wilson's Warbler at any migration hotspot. This lively bird flickers quickly through tangles of leaves and trees, darting frequently into the air to catch flying insects. Birders often become exhausted while pursuing a Wilson's Warbler, but the bird itself never seems to tire during its lightning-fast performances. • This bird may make brief stopovers in backyard shrubs during spring or fall migration. Though relatively common in migration, the Wilson's Warbler invariably moves farther north to nest, so it is rarely found as a breeder in New York. • The Wilson's Warbler is richly deserving of its name. Named after Alexander Wilson, this species epitomizes the energetic devotion that the pioneering ornithologist exhibited in the study of North American birds.

**ID:** bright yellow forehead, "eyebrow" and underparts; yellow green upperparts; small, dark bill; orange legs. *Male:* black "cap."
*Female:* "cap" is very faint or absent.
**Size:** *L* 4½–5 in; *W* 7 in.
**Status:** very rare breeder with only a handful of nestings reported; fairly common migrant in mid-May and in September.
**Habitat:** *Breeding:* riparian woodlands, willow and alder thickets, bogs and wet, shrubby meadows. *In migration:* woodlands or areas with tall shrubs.
**Nesting:** on the ground in moss or at the base of a shrub; female builds a nest of moss, grass and leaves; female incubates 4–6 brown-marked, creamy white eggs for 10–13 days.
**Feeding:** hovers, flycatches and gleans vegetation for insects.
**Voice:** song is a rapid chatter that drops in pitch at the end: *chi chi chi chi chet chet;* call is a flat, low *chet* or *chuck.*
**Similar Species:** male's black "cap" is distinctive. *Yellow Warbler* (p. 281): brighter yellow upperparts; male has reddish breast streaks. *Common Yellowthroat* (p. 305): female has darker face. *Kentucky Warbler* (p. 303): yellow "spectacles"; dark, angular "half mask." *Orange-crowned Warbler* (p. 278): dull yellow olive overall; faint breast streaks. *Nashville Warbler* (p. 279): bold, complete eye ring; blue gray crown.
**Best Sites:** Hamlin Beach SP; Letchworth SP; Black Creek Marsh WMA; Central Park (NYC); Prospect Park (NYC).

307

# CANADA WARBLER

*Wilsonia canadensis*

Male Canada Warblers, with their bold, white eye rings, have a wide-eyed, alert appearance. Both sexes are fairly inquisitive and will occasionally pop up from dense shrubs in response to passing hikers. These birds can be found in a wide variety of habitats, but you will almost always come across this "necklaced" warbler wherever there is a dense understory. • Canada Warblers live in open defiance of winter: they never stay in one place long enough to experience one! They are often the last of the warblers to arrive on their New York breeding grounds and the first to leave. As the summer nesting season in our region ends, these warblers migrate to South America. • Canada Warblers sing later than most warblers in the breeding season, and can even be heard singing while on migration.

**ID:** yellow stripe and white eye-rings form "spectacles"; yellow underparts (except white undertail coverts); blue gray upperparts; pale legs. *Male:* streaky black "necklace"; dark, angular "half mask." *Female:* blue green back; faint "necklace."
**Size:** *L* 5–6 in; *W* 8 in.
**Status:** common breeder from May to July upstate at higher elevations; common migrant in late May and August.
**Habitat:** *Breeding:* wet, low-lying areas of mixed forests with a dense understory, especially riparian willow-alder thickets; also cedar woodlands and swamps. *In migration:* woodlands or areas with tall shrubs.

**Nesting:** on a mossy hummock, upturned root or stump; female builds a loose, bulky cup nest of leaves, grass, ferns, weeds and bark; female incubates 4 brown-spotted, creamy white eggs for 10–14 days.
**Feeding:** gleans the ground and vegetation for beetles, flies, hairless caterpillars, mosquitoes and other insects; occasionally hovers.
**Voice:** song begins with 1 sharp *chip* note and continues with a rich, variable warble; call is a loud, quick *chick* or *chip*.
**Similar Species:** *Kentucky Warbler* (p. 303): yellow "spectacles" and undertail coverts; greenish upperparts; lacks black "necklace." *Northern Parula* (p. 280): white wing bars; broken, white eye ring; white belly.
**Best Sites:** Allegany SP; Letchworth SP; Ferd's Bog–Moose River Plains: John Boyd Thacher SP; Bear Mountain SP.

# YELLOW-BREASTED CHAT
*Icteria virens*

The unique Yellow-breasted Chat, measuring over 7 inches in length, is almost a warbler-and-a-half. Its bright yellow coloration and intense curiosity are typical warbler traits. Despite DNA evidence connecting this bird with the wood-warbler family, its odd vocalizations and noisy thrashing behavior suggest a closer relationship to the mimic thrushes such as the Gray Catbird and the Northern Mockingbird. Yellow-breasted Chats typically thrash about in dense undergrowth, and they rarely hold back their strange vocalizations, often drawing attention to themselves. • During courtship, the male advertises for a mate by launching off his perch to hover in the air with head held high and legs dangling, chirping incessantly until he drops back down.

**ID:** white "spectacles"; white jaw line; heavy, black bill; yellow throat and breast; olive green upperparts; white undertail coverts; long tail; gray black legs. *Male:* black lores. *Female:* gray lores.

**Size:** *L* 7½ in; *W* 9½ in.

**Status:** special concern; local breeder from May to July in southeastern NY; uncommon migrant in May and September; very rarely reported in winter on Long I.; unpredictable, as colonies appear and disappear.

**Habitat:** riparian thickets, brambles and shrubby tangles.

**Nesting:** low in a shrub or deciduous sapling; female builds a well-concealed cup nest of leaves, weeds, grasses and bark; female incubates 3–4 spotted, creamy white eggs for about 11 days.

**Feeding:** gleans insects from low vegetation; eats berries in fall.

**Voice:** song is an assorted series of whistles, "laughs," squeaks, grunts, rattles and mews; calls include a *whoit, chack* and *kook.*

**Similar Species:** none.

**Best Sites:** Bashakill WMA; Bear Mountain SP; Caumsett SP; Montauk Point SP; Central Park (NYC).

# SUMMER TANAGER

*Piranga rubra*

The northern limit of the Summer Tanager's breeding range lies south of our state, but each year small numbers of these dazzling birds make their way here. Most sightings are in spring and are the result of Summer Tanagers mistakenly traveling north past their nesting grounds. Summer and fall encounters are extremely rare, and though there are several nesting attempts on record, only one has ever been confirmed. • Summer Tanagers thrive on a wide variety of insects, but they are best known for their courageous attacks on wasps. These birds snatch flying bees and wasps from menacing swarms, and may even harass the occupants of a wasp nest to the point that the nest is abandoned, leaving the larvae inside free for the picking. • As is the case with other red tanager species, the males and females differ so much in appearance that they can be mistaken for different species altogether.

**ID:** *Male:* rose red overall; pale bill; immature male has patchy, red-and-greenish plumage. *Female:* grayish yellow to greenish yellow upperparts; dusky yellow underparts; may have orange or reddish wash overall.
**Size:** *L* 7–8 in; *W* 12 in.
**Status:** 1 confirmed nesting on Long I.; suspected breeding because of June and July sightings; uncommon migrant, most often seen in May and June on Long I.
**Habitat:** mixed woodlands, especially those with oak or hickory; riparian woodlands with cottonwoods.
**Nesting:** usually in a deciduous tree; female builds a shallow cup of grasses, leaves and bark; female incubates 3–5 brown-spotted, blue green eggs for 11–12 days; both adults feed the young.
**Feeding:** gleans insects from the tree canopy; may hover-glean or hawk insects in midair; also eats berries and small fruits; known to raid wasp nests.
**Voice:** song is a series of 3–5 sweet, clear, whistled phrases, like a faster version of the American Robin's song; call is *pit* or *pit-a-tuck.*
**Similar Species:** *Scarlet Tanager* (p. 311): smaller bill; male has black tail and wings; female has darker wings, brighter underparts and uniformly olive upperparts. *Northern Cardinal* (p. 332): red bill; prominent head crest; male has black "mask" and "bib." *Orchard Oriole* (p. 344) and *Baltimore Oriole* (p. 345): females have wing bars and sharper bills.
**Best Sites:** Central Park (NYC); Prospect Park (NYC); Jamaica Bay Wildlife Refuge; Jones Beach SP.

# SCARLET TANAGER

*Piranga olivacea*

Each spring, birders eagerly await the sweet, rough-edged song of the lovely Scarlet Tanager, which is often the only thing that gives away this unobtrusive forest denizen. The return of the brilliant red male to wooded ravines and traditional migrant stopover sites is always a much-anticipated event. • During the cold and rainy weather that often dampens spring migration, you may find yourself in the envious position of observing a Scarlet Tanager at eye level as it forages in the forest understory. At other times, however, this bird can be surprisingly difficult to spot as it darts through the forest canopy in pursuit of insect prey. • In Central and South America there are over 200 tanager species representing every color of the rainbow. The Scarlet Tanager migrates farther than any other tanager, most of which are sedentary birds in Central and South American forests.

♀

*breeding*

♂

**ID:** *Breeding male:* bright red overall with pure black wings and tail. *Nonbreeding male:* bright yellow underparts; olive upperparts; black wings and tail. *Female:* uniformly olive upperparts; yellow underparts; grayish brown wings.

**Size:** *L* 7 in; *W* 11½ in.

**Status:** common breeder from May to July; common and widespread migrant from April to May and from September to October.

**Habitat:** fairly mature, upland deciduous and mixed forests and large woodlands.

**Nesting:** on a high branch, usually in a deciduous tree; female builds a flimsy, shallow cup of grass, weeds and twigs; female incubates 2–5 brown-speckled, pale blue green eggs for 12–14 days.

**Feeding:** gleans insects from the tree canopy; may hover-glean or hawk insects in midair; may forage at lower levels during cold weather; also takes some seasonally available berries.

**Voice:** song is a series of 4–5 sweet, clear, whistled phrases like a slurred version of the American Robin's song; call is a *chip-burrr* or *chip-churrr*.

**Similar Species:** *Summer Tanager* (p. 310): larger bill; male has red tail and red wings; female has paler wings and is duskier overall, often with orange or reddish tinge. *Northern Cardinal* (p. 332): red bill, wings and tail; prominent head crest; male has black "mask" and "bib." *Orchard Oriole* (p. 344) and *Baltimore Oriole* (p. 345): females have wing bars and sharper bills.

**Best Sites:** Allegany SP; Letchworth SP; John Boyd Thacher SP; Bear Mountain SP; Connetquot River SP.

# EASTERN TOWHEE

*Pipilo erythrophthalmus*

Eastern Towhees are often heard before they are seen. These noisy foragers rustle about in dense undergrowth, craftily scraping back layers of dry leaves to expose the seeds, berries or insects hidden beneath, though they also take insects and fruit from vegetation above ground. They employ an unusual two-footed technique to uncover food items—a strategy that is especially important in winter when virtually all their food is taken from the ground. • Although you wouldn't guess it, this colorful bird is a member of the American Sparrow family—a group that is usually drab in color. • The Eastern Towhee and its similar-looking western relative, the Spotted Towhee, were once grouped together as a single species called the "Rufous-sided Towhee." • Eastern Towhees have red eyes, but white-eyed Eastern Towhees are more common in the southeastern states.

**ID:** rufous sides and flanks; white outer tail corners; white lower breast and belly; buff undertail coverts; red eyes; dark bill. *Male:* black "hood" and upperparts. *Female:* brown "hood" and upperparts.
**Size:** *L* 7–8½ in; *W* 10½ in.
**Status:** common breeder from May to July in all but high-elevation areas; common migrant in mid-April and in late October; small numbers overwinter on Long I.
**Habitat:** along woodland edges and in shrubby, abandoned fields.

**Nesting:** on the ground or low in a dense shrub; female builds a camouflaged cup nest of twigs, bark strips, grass, weeds, rootlets and animal hair; mostly the female incubates 3–4 brown-speckled, creamy white to pale gray eggs for 12–13 days.
**Feeding:** scratches at leaf litter for insects, seeds and berries; sometimes forages in low shrubs and saplings.
**Voice:** song is 2 high, whistled notes followed by a trill: *drink your teeeee;* call is a scratchy, slurred *cheweee!* or *chewink!*
**Similar Species:** *Dark-eyed Junco* (p. 329): much smaller; pale bill; black eyes; white outer tail feathers.
**Best Sites:** Allegany SP; Connecticut Hill WMA; John Boyd Thacher SP; Jones Beach SP; Connetquot River SP.

# AMERICAN TREE SPARROW

*Spizella arborea*

Most of us know these rufous-capped, spot-breasted sparrows as winter visitors to backyard feeders. The best time to see American Tree Sparrows, however, is in late March and April when they are in migration. As the small flocks migrate north, they offer bubbly, bright songs between bouts of foraging along the ground or in low, budding shrubs. • Although its name suggests a close relationship with trees or forests, the American Tree Sparrow actually prefers treeless fields and semi-open, shrubby habitats. This bird got its name because of a superficial resemblance to the Eurasian Tree Sparrow *(Passer montanus)* familiar to early settlers. Perhaps a more appropriate name for this bird would be "Subarctic Shrub Sparrow." With adequate food supplies, the American Tree Sparrow can survive temperatures as cold as −28° F.

**ID:** unstreaked, gray underparts; dark, central breast spot; pale rufous "cap"; rufous stripe behind eye; gray face; mottled brown upperparts; notched tail; 2 white wing bars; dark legs; dark upper mandible; yellow lower mandible. *Nonbreeding:* gray central crown stripe.

**Size:** *L* 6–6½ in; *W* 9½ in.

**Status:** very common winter resident; migrants arrive in late October and leave by late April.

**Habitat:** brushy thickets, roadside shrubs, semi-open fields and croplands.

**Nesting:** does not nest in NY.

**Feeding:** scratches exposed soil or snow for seeds in winter; eats mostly insects in summer; takes some berries and occasionally visits bird feeders.

**Voice:** song is a high, whistled *tseet-tseet* followed by a short, sweet, musical series of slurred whistles; song may be given in late winter and during spring migration; call is a 3-note *tsee-dle-eat.*

**Similar Species:** *Chipping Sparrow* (p. 314): clear, black eye line; white "eyebrow"; lacks dark breast spot. *Swamp Sparrow* (p. 326): white throat; lacks dark breast spot and white wing bars. *Field Sparrow* (p. 316): white eye ring; orange pink bill; lacks dark breast spot.

**Best Sites:** Hamlin Beach SP; Montezuma NWR; Cape Vincent–Pt. Peninsula; Five Rivers Environmental Education Center; Jones Beach SP.

# CHIPPING SPARROW

*Spizella passerina*

The Chipping Sparrow and the Dark-eyed Junco do not share the same tailor, but they must have attended the same voice lessons, because their songs are very similar. Though the rapid trill of the Chipping Sparrow is slightly faster, drier and less musical than the junco's, even experienced birders can have difficulty identifying this singer. • Chipping Sparrows commonly nest at eye level, so you can easily watch their breeding and nest-building rituals. They are well known for their preference for conifers as a nesting site and for hair as a lining material for the nest. By planting conifers in your backyard and offering samples of your pet's hair—or even your own—in backyard baskets in spring, you could attract nesting Chipping Sparrows to your area and contribute to their nesting success. • The Chipping Sparrow is the smallest and tamest of the sparrows. "Chipping" refers to this bird's call.

*breeding*

**ID:** *Breeding:* prominent rufous "cap"; white "eyebrow"; black eye line; light gray, unstreaked underparts; mottled brown upperparts; all-dark bill; 2 faint wing bars; pale legs. *Nonbreeding:* paler crown with dark streaks; brown "eyebrow" and "cheek"; pale lower mandible.
**Size:** *L* 5–6 in; *W* 8½ in.
**Status:** very common breeder from May to July; common migrant in April and from September to October; very rare in winter.
**Habitat:** open conifers or mixed woodland edges; often in yards and gardens with tree and shrub borders.
**Nesting:** usually at midlevel in a conifer; female builds a compact cup nest of woven grass and rootlets, often lined with hair; female incubates 4 darkly speckled, pale blue eggs for 11–12 days.

**Feeding:** gleans seeds from the ground and from the outer branches of trees or shrubs; prefers grass, dandelion and clover seeds; also eats adult and larval invertebrates; occasionally visits feeders.
**Voice:** song is a rapid, dry trill of *chip* notes; call is a high-pitched *chip.*
**Similar Species:** *American Tree Sparrow* (p. 313): dark central breast spot; rufous stripe extends behind eye; lacks white "eyebrow." *Swamp Sparrow* (p. 326): lacks white "eyebrow," wing bars and dark line behind eye. *Field Sparrow* (p. 316): rufous stripe extends behind eye; white eye ring; gray throat; orange pink bill; lacks white "eyebrow."
**Best Sites:** Allegany SP; Hamlin Beach SP; Durand-Eastman Park (Rochester); Central Park (NYC); Prospect Park (NYC).

# CLAY-COLORED SPARROW

*Spizella pallida*

For the most part, Clay-colored Sparrows go completely unnoticed because their plumage, habit and voice all contribute to a cryptic lifestyle. Even when males are singing at the top of their "air sacs," they are usually mistaken for buzzing insects. • Although it is subtle in plumage, the Clay-colored Sparrow still possesses an unassuming beauty. Birders looking closely at this sparrow to confirm its identity can easily appreciate its delicate shading, texture and form—features so often overlooked in birds with more colorful plumage. • The Clay-colored Sparrow is one of the few birds that will continue to sing into the heat of July. • A denizen of brushy, shrubby habitats, this species' range expanded in the early 20th century as land was cleared by logging and for agricultural purposes. In the last 30 years, however, there have been small but consistent declines in this bird's numbers because of modern agricultural practices and urbanization.

*breeding*

**ID:** unstreaked, white underparts; buff breast wash; gray nape; light brown "cheek" edged with darker brown; dark crown with pale central stripe; pale "eyebrow"; white "mustache" stripe bordered with brown; white throat; mostly pale bill.
**Size:** *L* 5–6 in; *W* 7½ in.
**Status:** uncommon breeder from May to July in northern and western NY; rare migrant on the coast from September to October.

**Habitat:** brushy open areas along forest and woodland edges; in forest openings, regenerating burn sites, abandoned fields and riparian thickets.
**Nesting:** in a grassy tuft or small shrub; female builds an open cup nest of twigs, grass, weeds and rootlets; mostly the female incubates 4 brown-speckled, bluish green eggs, for 10–12 days.
**Feeding:** forages for seeds and insects on the ground and in low vegetation.
**Voice:** song is a series of 2–5 slow, low-pitched, insectlike buzzes; call is a soft *chip.*
**Similar Species:** *Chipping Sparrow* (p. 314): breeding adult has prominent rufous "cap," gray "cheek" and underparts, 2 faint, white wing bars and all-dark bill.
**Best Sites:** Jones Beach SP; Fire Island National Seashore; Smith Point CP.

315

# FIELD SPARROW

*Spizella pusilla*

Deserted farmland may seem unproductive to some people, but to the Field Sparrow it is heaven. This pink-billed sparrow frequents overgrown fields, pastures and forest clearings. For nesting purposes it usually chooses pastures that are scattered with shrubs, herbaceous plants and plenty of tall grass. • The Field Sparrow has learned to recognize when its nest has been parasitized by the Brown-headed Cowbird. Because the unwelcome eggs are usually too large for this small sparrow to eject, the nest is simply abandoned. This sparrow may be so stubborn in refusing to raise young cowbirds that affected pairs of Field Sparrows may make numerous nesting attempts in a single season. • Unlike most songbirds, a nestling Field Sparrow will leave its nest prematurely if disturbed. • This sparrow is well known for its song—a pleasant combination of two or more languid whistles followed by a rapid trill.

**ID:** orange pink bill; gray face and throat; rusty crown with gray central stripe; rusty streak behind eye; white eye ring; 2 white wing bars; unstreaked, gray underparts with buffy red wash on breast, sides and flanks; pinkish legs.

**Size:** *L* 5–6 in; *W* 8 in.

**Status:** common breeder from May to July; common migrant from mid-March through April and from September to October; rare in winter.

**Habitat:** abandoned or weedy, overgrown fields and pastures; also woodland edges and clearings, extensive shrubby riparian areas and young conifer plantations.

**Nesting:** on or near the ground, often sheltered by a grass clump, shrub or sapling; female weaves an open cup nest of grass; female incubates 3–5 brown-spotted, whitish to pale bluish white eggs for 10–12 days.

**Feeding:** forages on the ground; takes mostly insects in summer and seeds in spring and fall.

**Voice:** song is a series of woeful, musical, downslurred whistles accelerating into a trill; call is a *chip* or *tsee*.

**Similar Species:** *American Tree Sparrow* (p. 313): dark central breast spot; dark upper mandible; lacks white eye ring. *Swamp Sparrow* (p. 326): white throat; dark upper mandible; lacks 2 white wing bars and white eye ring. *Chipping Sparrow* (p. 314): all-dark bill; white "eyebrow"; black eye line; lacks buffy red wash on underparts.

**Best Sites:** Nation's Road Grassland; Montezuma NWR; Ft. Edward Grassland; Five Rivers Environmental Education Center; Jones Beach SP.

# VESPER SPARROW

*Pooecetes gramineus*

For birders who live near grassy fields and agricultural lands with multitudes of confusing little brown sparrows, the Vesper Sparrow offers welcome relief— white outer tail feathers and a chestnut shoulder patch announce its identity whether the bird is perched or in flight. The Vesper Sparrow is also known for its bold and easily distinguished song, which begins with two sets of unforgettable, double notes: *here-here! there-there!* • When the business of nesting begins, the Vesper Sparrow scours the neighborhood for a potential nesting site. More often than not, this bird builds its nest in a grassy hollow at the base of a clump of weeds or small shrub. This setup provides camouflage and functions as a windbreak and an umbrella to protect the young. • "Vesper" is Latin for "evening," a time when this bird often sings.

**ID:** chestnut shoulder patch; white outer tail feathers; dark brown streaking on gray brown upperparts and creamy white underparts; pale yellow lores; white eye ring; pale legs.

**Size:** *L* 6 in; *W* 10 in.

**Status:** special concern; fairly common breeder from May to July at lower elevations; common migrant from late March through April and from October to November.

**Habitat:** open fields with shrubs, semi-open shrublands and grasslands; also in agricultural areas, particularly cornfields, open, dry conifer plantations and scrubby gravel pits.

**Nesting:** in a scrape on the ground, often under a canopy of grass or at the base of a shrub; loosely woven cup nest of grass is lined with rootlets, fine grass and hair; mostly the female incubates 3–5 brown-blotched, whitish to greenish white eggs for 11–13 days.

**Feeding:** walks and runs along the ground, picking up grasshoppers, beetles, cutworms, other invertebrates and seeds.

**Voice:** song is 4 characteristic, preliminary notes, with the second higher in pitch, followed by a bubbly trill: *here-here there-there, everybody-down-the-hill.*

**Similar Species:** *Other sparrows* (pp. 312–31): lack white outer tail feathers and chestnut shoulder patch. *American Pipit* (p. 272): thinner bill; grayer upperparts lack brown streaking; lacks chestnut shoulder patch. *Lapland Longspur* (p. 330): blackish or buff wash on upper breast; nonbreeding has broad, pale "eyebrow" and reddish edges on wing feathers.

**Best Sites:** Iroquois NWR–Tonawanda WMA–Oak Orchard WMA; Montezuma NWR; Ft. Edward Grassland; Nation's Road Grassland.

# SAVANNAH SPARROW

*Passerculus sandwichensis*

The Savannah Sparrow is one of the most common open-country birds in our region. At one time or another, most people have probably seen or heard one, although they may not have been aware of it—this bird's streaky, dull, brown-and-white plumage resembles so many of the other grassland sparrows that it is easily overlooked. • From early spring to early summer, male Savannah Sparrows belt out their distinctive, buzzy tunes while perched atop prominent shrubs, tall weeds or strategic fence posts. • Like most sparrows, Savannahs generally stay out of sight. When danger appears, they take flight only as a last resort, preferring to run swiftly and inconspicuously through the grass, almost like feathered voles. • The common and scientific names of this bird reflect its broad North American distribution: "Savannah" refers to the city in Georgia, while *sandwichensis* is derived from Sandwich Bay in the Aleutian Islands off Alaska.

**ID:** streaked, brown to gray brown upperparts; whitish to buff underparts; fine streaking on breast, sides and flanks; yellow lores; light jaw line; pinkish legs and bill; may show dark breast spot.

**Size:** *L* 5–6 in; *W* 6½ in.

**Status:** very common breeder from May to July; common migrant in March and April and in October; uncommon in winter; pale subspecies, "Ipswich Sparrow," is regular in small numbers in winter on Long I. barrier beaches.

**Habitat:** agricultural fields, especially hay and alfalfa, moist sedge and grass meadows, pastures, beaches, bogs and fens.

**Nesting:** on the ground in a shallow scrape well concealed by grass or a shrub; female builds an open cup nest woven from and lined with grass; female incubates 3–6 brown-marked, whitish to greenish or pale tan eggs for 10–13 days.

**Feeding:** gleans insects and seeds while walking or running along the ground; occasionally scratches.

**Voice:** song is a high-pitched, clear, buzzy *tea tea teeeeea today;* call is a high, thin *tsit.*

**Similar Species:** *Vesper Sparrow* (p. 317): white outer tail feathers; chestnut shoulder patch. *Lincoln's Sparrow* (p. 325): buff jaw line; buff wash across breast; broad, gray "eyebrow." *Grasshopper Sparrow* (p. 319): unstreaked breast. *Song Sparrow* (p. 324): dark "mustache" stripes; pale central crown stripe; rounded tail; lacks yellow lores.

**Best Sites:** Nation's Road Grassland; Montezuma NWR; Saratoga National Historical Park; Shawangunk Grasslands NWR; Jones Beach SP.

# GRASSHOPPER SPARROW

*Ammodramus savannarum*

The Grasshopper Sparrow is named not for its diet, but rather for its buzzy, insectlike song. During courtship flights, males chase females through the air, buzzing at a frequency that is usually inaudible to human ears. The males sing two completely different courtship songs: one ends in a short trill and the other is a prolonged series of high trills that vary in pitch and speed. • The Grasshopper Sparrow is an open-country bird that prefers grassy expanses free of trees and shrubs. Wide, well-drained, grassy ditches occasionally attract nesting Grasshopper Sparrows, so mowing or harvesting these grassy margins early in the nesting season may be detrimental to these birds. Convincing local landowners and state governments to delay cutting until mid-August or September would benefit the Grasshopper Sparrow. • The scientific name *Ammodramus* is Greek for "sand runner," while *savannarum* is Latin for "of the savanna," after this bird's grassy, open habitat.

**ID:** unstreaked, white underparts with buff wash on breast, sides and flanks; flattened head profile; dark crown with pale central stripe; buff "cheek"; mottled brown upperparts; sharp tail; pale legs; may show small yellow patch on edge of forewing.

**Size:** *L* 5–5½ in; *W* 7½ in.

**Status:** special concern; locally common breeder from May to July on Long I., Great Lakes Plain and lowlands across south-central NY; migrants arrive in May and are gone by September.

**Habitat:** grasslands and grassy fields with little or no shrub or tree cover.

**Nesting:** on the ground in a shallow depression, usually concealed by grass; female builds a small cup nest of grass; female incubates 4–5 creamy white eggs, blotched with gray and reddish brown, for 11–13 days.

**Feeding:** gleans insects and seeds from the ground and grass; eats a variety of insects, including grasshoppers.

**Voice:** song is a high, faint, buzzy trill preceded by 1–3 high, thin whistled notes: *tea-tea-tea zeeeeeeeeee*.

**Similar Species:** *Nelson's Sharp-tailed Sparrow* (p. 366): buff orange face and breast; gray central crown stripe; gray "cheek" and shoulders.

**Best Sites:** Nation's Road Grassland; Cape Vincent–Pt. Peninsula; Perch River WMA; Ft. Edward Grassland; Riverhead Sod Farms.

# HENSLOW'S SPARROW

*Ammodramus henslowii*

It is difficult to predict when you'll see the next Henslow's Sparrow in our region—this bird makes irregular visits here, often appearing one year but not the next. Some males have been known to occupy a field for a few weeks before suddenly disappearing, probably owing to the lack of a potential mate. The Henslow's unpredictability has made it a difficult species to study, and modern farming practices and loss of grassland habitat have led to a decline in Henslow's Sparrow populations to the point that it has become a priority for conservation in many parts of its range. • Henslow's Sparrows are known for their unusual habit of singing at night. In the daytime, the male Henslow's Sparrow throws back his streaky, greenish head as he hurls his distinctive song from atop a tall blade of grass or low shrub. Without the male's lyrical advertisements, the inconspicuous Henslow's Sparrow would be almost impossible to observe, as this bird spends most of its time foraging alone along the ground.

**Habitat:** large, fallow or wild, grassy fields and meadows with a matted ground layer of dead vegetation and scattered shrub or herb perches; often in moist, grassy areas.
**Nesting:** on the ground at the base of a grass clump or herbaceous plant; mostly the female builds an open cup nest of grass and weeds; female incubates 3–5 brown-marked, whitish to pale greenish white eggs for about 11 days.
**Feeding:** gleans insects and seeds from the ground.
**Voice:** weak, liquidy, cricketlike *tse-lick* song is distinctive, often given during periods of rain or at night.
**Similar Species:** *Other sparrows* (pp. 312–31): lack greenish face, central crown stripe and nape. *Grasshopper Sparrow* (p. 319): lacks dark "whisker" stripe and prominent streaking on breast and sides. *Savannah Sparrow* (p. 318): lacks buff breast.
**Best Sites:** unpredictable; Nation's Road Grassland; Ft. Edward Grassland; Shawangunk Grasslands NWR.

**ID:** flattened head profile; olive green face, central crown stripe and nape; dark crown and "whisker" stripes; rusty tinge on back, wings and tail; white underparts with dark streaking on buff breast, sides and flanks; thick bill; deeply notched, sharp-edged tail.
**Size:** *L* 5–5½ in; *W* 6½ in.
**Status:** threatened; uncommon and local breeder from May to July; rarely reported as a migrant, but arrives in May and departs in August.

# SALTMARSH SHARP-TAILED SPARROW

*Ammodramus caudacutus*

Confirming the specific identity of those little brown birds known as sparrows can be a challenge. Fortunately, all you have to do to identify the Saltmarsh Sharp-tailed Sparrow is look for the unique orange facial triangle that encompasses its gray ear patch and adjacent eye. Its streaky, buff-colored breast and sides also separate it from many of the sparrows that sport a clear, unstreaked breast. Another clue to its identity is its choice of habitat: the tidal salt marshes of the Atlantic Coast. • Unlike other sparrow species, breeding Saltmarsh Sharp-tails do not enter into a pair bond. The male does not defend a breeding territory or help females to raise young. Instead, the male flies through a marsh, occasionally stopping to attract a mate through song. After mating, the male moves on to search for other potentially interested mates while the female begins the business of raising young or in turn looks for another mate of her own. • Until 1995, this bird was classified with the Nelson's Sharp-tailed Sparrow as a single species called the "Sharp-tailed Sparrow."

**ID:** dark brown streaking on buffy breast and flanks; gray ear patch surrounded by orange facial triangle; gray central crown stripe; unstreaked, gray nape.

**Size:** *L* 5 in; *W* 7 in.

**Status:** locally common breeder from May to July in Long I. salt marshes; common migrant from April to May and from September to October; rare in winter.

**Habitat:** confined to freshwater and saltwater marshes along or adjacent to coast.

**Nesting:** in marsh vegetation just above the high-tide mark; female builds a bulky cup nest of grasses and seaweed; nest may be partially domed; female incubates 3–5 heavily brown-marked, pale greenish white eggs for 11–13 days and feeds the young alone.

**Feeding:** insects, other invertebrates and seeds are obtained by gleaning from the ground and marsh vegetation; occasionally probes for food in mud.

**Voice:** soft variety of trills, buzzes and other notes.

**Similar Species:** *Henslow's Sparrow* (p. 320): lacks gray nape and ear patch. *Other sparrows* (pp. 312–31): all lack orange facial triangle.

**Best Sites:** Jamaica Bay Wildlife Refuge; Marshlands Conservancy–Playland CP; Jones Beach SP; Shinnecock Inlet–Dune Rd.; Napeague Bay–Hither Hills SP.

# SEASIDE SPARROW
*Ammodramus maritimus*

Fortunate birders may delight in the view of a courting male Seaside Sparrow projecting his cheery, buzzing song from atop a nearby shrub or during a courtship flight. But for most observers, encounters with this bird may be brief and seemingly unrewarding, as most flushed birds flutter only a short distance before disappearing into the thick vegetation of their marshy home. Your best chance of meeting this secretive sparrow is to visit the tidal salt marshes of the Atlantic Coast and eastern Gulf Coast where tall stands of marsh grasses, rushes and shrubs provide ideal habitat. Foraging primarily on the ground, the Seaside Sparrow enjoys a diverse diet of insects, spiders, small aquatic invertebrates and seeds. • Small, widely separated populations of Seaside Sparrows living in slightly different salt marshes along the species' coastal range have produced a number of distinct subspecies or "races" that, given time, may develop into fully separate and unique species.

**ID:** long bill; yellow lores; white "chin"; gray "whisker" stripes; olive gray upperparts; streaked, pale gray underparts.

**Size:** *L* 6 in; *W* 7½ in.

**Status:** special concern; common but declining breeder from May to July; common migrant in April and from August to October; uncommon in winter.

**Habitat:** restricted to tidal salt marshes along the coast.

**Nesting:** in low marsh vegetation just above the high-tide mark; female builds cup-shaped nest of grasses and rushes with a sheltering canopy; female incubates 4–5 brown-speckled, pale greenish white eggs for 11–12 days; both adults feed the young.

**Feeding:** forages on the ground among marsh vegetation or at the water's edge for insects, invertebrates and seeds; occasionally probes in mud.

**Voice:** a series of soft notes followed by buzzes: *tup-tup zee-reeee.*

**Similar Species:** *Savannah Sparrow* (p. 318): lighter undersides; streaked head and back. *Song Sparrow* (p. 324): darker streaking; dark breast spot; lacks yellow lores. *Saltmarsh Sharp-tailed Sparrow* (p. 321): orange facial triangle.

**Best Sites:** Marshlands Conservancy–Playland CP; Jamaica Bay Wildlife Refuge; Jones Beach SP; Fire Island National Seashore; Shinnecock Inlet–Dune Rd.

# FOX SPARROW

*Passerella iliaca*

Like the Eastern Towhee, the Fox Sparrow eagerly scratches out a living, using both feet to stir up leaves and scrape organic matter along the forest floor. This large sparrow's preference for impenetrable, brushy habitat makes it a difficult species to observe, even though its noisy foraging habits often reveal its whereabouts. • The Fox Sparrow is generally agreed to be the best singer among the sparrows, and though its loud, whistled courtship songs are easily recognized, it doesn't sing while on migration. • Unlike other songbirds, which may filter through the region in a series of lingering waves, Fox Sparrows generally appear in our state for only a few short weeks before moving on to their nesting grounds farther north. • The overall reddish brown appearance of this bird inspired taxonomists to name it after the red fox. Fox Sparrows in other parts of North America look and sound somewhat different, causing experts to feel that they are different species.

**ID:** whitish underparts with heavy, reddish brown spotting and streaking that often converges into central breast spot; reddish brown wings, rump and tail; gray crown; brown-streaked back; gray "eyebrow" and nape; stubby, conical bill.
**Size:** *L* 6½–7 in; *W* 10½ in.
**Status:** common migrant in early April and from late October through November; uncommon in winter on the coast.
**Habitat:** riparian thickets and brushy woodland clearings, edges and parklands.

**Nesting:** does not nest in NY.
**Feeding:** scratches the ground to uncover seeds, berries and invertebrates; visits backyard feeders in migration and winter.
**Voice:** does not sing in migration; calls include *chip* and *click* notes.
**Similar Species:** *Song Sparrow* (p. 324): pale central crown stripe; dark "mustache"; dark brownish rather than reddish streaking and upperparts. *Hermit Thrush* (p. 265): longer, thinner bill; pale eye ring; dark breast spotting; unstreaked, olive brown and reddish brown upperparts; lacks heavy streaking on underparts.
**Best Sites:** Hamlin Beach SP; Montezuma NWR; Five Rivers Environmental Education Center; Jones Beach SP; Central Park (NYC).

# SONG SPARROW

*Melospiza melodia*

The Song Sparrow's heavily streaked, low-key plumage doesn't prepare you for its symphonic song. This well-named sparrow is known for the complexity, rhythm and emotion of its springtime rhapsodies, although some people will insist that the Fox Sparrow and the Lincoln's Sparrow carry the best tunes. • Young Song Sparrows, as well as many other songbirds, learn to sing by eavesdropping on their fathers or on rival males. By the time a young male is a few months old, he will have formed the basis for his own courtship tune. • In recent decades, mild winters and an abundance of backyard bird feeders have enticed an increasing number of Song Sparrows to overwinter here. • Most songbirds are lucky if they are able to produce one brood per year. In some years, Song Sparrows in our region will successfully raise three broods. • There are about 31 different subspecies of the Song Sparrow, from pale desert birds to larger and darker Alaskan forms.

**ID:** whitish underparts with heavy brown streaking that converges into central breast spot; grayish face; dark line behind eye; white jawline bordered by dark "mustache" stripes; dark crown with pale central stripe; mottled brown upperparts; rounded tail tip.

**Size:** *L* 5½–7 in; *W* 8½ in.

**Status:** very common breeder from April to July; common migrant from late March through April and in October; common in winter.

**Habitat:** shrubby areas, often near water, including willow shrublands, riparian thickets, forest openings and pastures.

**Nesting:** usually on the ground or low in a shrub or small tree; female builds an open cup nest of grass, weeds, leaves and bark shreds; female incubates 3–5 brown-blotched, greenish white eggs for 12–14 days; may raise 2–3 broods each summer.

**Feeding:** gleans the ground, shrubs and trees for cutworms, beetles, grasshoppers, ants, other invertebrates and seeds; also eats wild fruit and visits feeders.

**Voice:** song is 1–4 bright, distinctive introductory notes, such as *sweet, sweet, sweet,* followed by a buzzy *towee,* then a short, descending trill; calls include a short *tsip* and a nasal *tchep.*

**Similar Species:** *Fox Sparrow* (p. 323): heavier breast spotting and streaking; reddish rather than dark brownish streaking and upperparts; lacks pale central crown stripe and dark "mustache." *Lincoln's Sparrow* (p. 325): lightly streaked breast with buff wash; buff jaw line. *Savannah Sparrow* (p. 318): lightly streaked breast; yellow lores; notched tail; lacks grayish face and dark "mustache."

**Best Sites:** Beaver Meadow Nature Center; Beaver Lake CP; Five Rivers Environmental Education Center; Jamaica Bay Wildlife Refuge; Heckscher SP.

# LINCOLN'S SPARROW

*Merospiza lincolnii*

Though the Lincoln's Sparrow seems to be more timid than other sparrows, there is a certain beauty in its plumage that is greater than the sum of its feathers. Males will sit openly on exposed perches and sing their bubbly, wrenlike songs, but as soon as they are approached, they slip under the cover of nearby shrubs. When they are not singing their courtship songs, Lincoln's Sparrows remain well hidden in tall grass and dense, bushy growth. Their remote breeding grounds and secretive behavior conspire to keep this species one of the least-known sparrows. • If a female Lincoln's Sparrow is disturbed while sitting on her eggs, she will run quietly through the grass like a mouse, hoping both she and the nest will be passed over. If the young have hatched, the "broken-wing" method will be employed to draw the predator away. • This sparrow bears the name of Thomas Lincoln, a young companion of John J. Audubon on his voyage to Labrador.

**ID:** buff breast band, sides and flanks with fine, dark streaking; buff jaw stripe; gray "eyebrow," face and "collar"; dark line behind eye; dark, reddish "cap" with gray central stripe; white throat and belly; mottled, gray brown to reddish brown upperparts; very faint, white eye ring.
**Size:** *L* 5½ in; *W* 7½ in.
**Status:** fairly common breeder from May to July in Adirondack wetlands; uncommon migrant in May and from September to October.
**Habitat:** *Breeding:* shrubby edges of bogs, swamps, beaver ponds and meadows; also jack pine plains. *In migration:* brushy woodlands; shrubby fencerows.
**Nesting:** on the ground, often on soft moss or concealed beneath a shrub; female builds a well-hidden cup nest of grasses and sedges; female incubates 4–5 heavily speckled, greenish white to pale green eggs for 12–14 days.
**Feeding:** scratches at the ground to expose invertebrates and seeds; occasionally visits feeders.
**Voice:** song is a wrenlike musical mixture of buzzes, trills and warbled notes; calls include a buzzy *zeee* and a *tsup*.
**Similar Species:** *Song Sparrow* (p. 324): heavier breast streaking; dark "mustache"; lacks buff wash on breast, sides and flanks. *Savannah Sparrow* (p. 318): yellow lores; white "eyebrow" and jaw line. *Swamp Sparrow* (p. 326): generally lacks streaking on breast; more contrast between red and gray crown stripes.
**Best Sites:** Ferd's Bog–Moose River Plains; Bloomingdale Bog; Vischer Ferry Nature and Historic Preserve.

# SWAMP SPARROW

*Melospiza georgiana*

Swamp Sparrows are well adapted to life near water. These wetland inhabitants skulk among the emergent vegetation of cattail marshes, foraging for a variety of invertebrates, including beetles, caterpillars, spiders, leafhoppers and flies. Like other sparrows, they are unable to swim, but that is no deterrent—many of their meals are snatched directly from the water's surface as they wade through the shallows. • The Swamp Sparrow must keep a lookout for daytime predators such as Northern Harriers, Great Blue Herons and large snakes. At night, the key to survival is finding a secluded, concealing perch that will keep it safe from raccoons, skunks and weasels. • Male Swamp Sparrows are most easily seen in spring when they sing their familiar trills from atop cattails or shoreline shrubs, and both sexes can be seen in fall, often in the company of other sparrows.

*breeding*

**ID:** gray face and breast; reddish brown wings; brownish upperparts; dark streaking on back; white throat and jaw outlined by black stripes; dark line behind eye. *Breeding:* rusty "cap"; streaked, buff sides and flanks. *Nonbreeding:* streaked, brown crown with gray central stripe; more brownish sides.
**Size:** *L* 5–6 in; *W* 7½ in.
**Status:** common breeder from April to June; common migrant from March to April and from September to October; small numbers overwinter.
**Habitat:** cattail marshes, open wetlands, wet meadows and open deciduous riparian thickets.
**Nesting:** in emergent aquatic vegetation or shoreline bushes; female builds a cup nest of coarse grass and marsh vegetation, usually with a partial canopy and side entrance; female incubates 4–5 brown-marked, greenish white to pale green eggs for 12–15 days.
**Feeding:** gleans insects from the ground, vegetation and the water's surface; takes seeds in late summer and fall.
**Voice:** song is a slow, sharp, metallic trill: *weet-weet-weet-weet;* call is a harsh *chink.*
**Similar Species:** *Chipping Sparrow* (p. 314): clean white "eyebrow"; full, black eye line; uniformly gray underparts; white wing bars. *American Tree Sparrow* (p. 313): dark central breast spot; white wing bars; 2-tone bill. *Song Sparrow* (p. 324): heavily streaked underparts. *Lincoln's Sparrow* (p. 325): fine breast streaking; less contrast between brown and gray crown stripes.
**Best Sites:** Iroquois NWR–Tonawanda WMA–Oak Orchard WMA; Montezuma NWR; Bloomingdale Bog; Black Creek Marsh WMA; Bashakill WMA.

# WHITE-THROATED SPARROW

*Zonotrichia albicollis*

The handsome White-throated Sparrow is easily identified by its bold, white throat and striped crown. Two color morphs are common throughout our region: one has black and white stripes on the head; the other has brown and tan stripes. White-striped males are more aggressive than tan-striped males, and tan-striped females are more nurturing than white-striped females. These two color morphs are perpetuated because each morph almost always breeds with the opposite color morph. • In spring and fall, White-throated Sparrows can appear anywhere in our region in great abundance. Urban backyards dressed with brushy fenceline tangles and a bird feeder brimming with seeds can attract good numbers of these delightful sparrows. • *Zonotrichia* means "hairlike," a reference to the striped heads of birds in this genus; *albicollis* is Latin for "white neck"—not quite accurate, as it is the bird's throat and not its neck that is white.

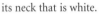

*white-striped morph*

**ID:** black and white (or brown and tan) head stripes; white throat; gray "cheek"; yellow lores; black eye line; unstreaked, gray underparts; mottled brown upperparts; grayish bill.

**Size:** *L* 6½–7½ in; *W* 9 in.

**Status:** common breeder at higher elevations from May to July; abundant migrant from April through May and in October; fairly common in winter.

**Habitat:** *Breeding:* semi-open coniferous and mixed forests, especially in regenerating clearings and along shrubby forest edges. *In migration:* woodlots, wooded parks and riparian brush.

**Nesting:** on or near the ground, often concealed by a low shrub or fallen log; female builds an open cup nest of grass, weeds, twigs and conifer needles; female incubates 4–5 brown-marked, greenish blue to pale blue eggs for 11–14 days.

**Feeding:** scratches the ground to expose invertebrates, seeds and berries; also gleans insects from vegetation and while in flight; eats seeds from bird feeders in winter.

**Voice:** variable song is a clear, distinct, whistled: *Old Sam Peabody, Peabody, Peabody;* call is a sharp *chink.*

**Similar Species:** *White-crowned Sparrow* (p. 328): pinkish bill; gray "collar"; lacks bold, white throat and yellow lores. *Swamp Sparrow* (p. 326): smaller; gray and chestnut on crown; streaked underparts; lacks head pattern.

**Best Sites:** Allegany SP; Braddock Bay; Bloomingdale Bog; Five Rivers Environmental Education Center; Jones Beach SP.

# WHITE-CROWNED SPARROW

*Zonotrichia leucophrys*

The large, bold, strongly patterned White-crowned Sparrow brightens brushy expanses and suburban parks and gardens with its cheeky song for a few short weeks in spring and fall. Most birders with well-stocked bird feeders should be especially familiar with this bird—besides being conspicuous in appearance, White-crowned Sparrows are tireless singers, even bursting into song under the light of the moon. • Many birders confuse this bird with the White-throated Sparrow, but the larger size and more erect stance of the White-crowned Sparrow helps to distinguish it. • White-crowns breed in the Far North, in alpine environments or along the California coast. This bird has a widespread distribution in North America, and populations in different parts of its range vary significantly in behavior and in migratory and nesting habits. • The White-crowned Sparrow is North America's most studied sparrow. Research on this bird has given science tremendous insight into bird physiology, homing behavior and the geographic variability of song dialects.

**ID:** black and white head stripes; black eye line; pink orange bill; gray face; unstreaked, gray underparts; pale gray throat; mottled, gray brown upperparts; 2 faint, white wing bars.
**Size:** *L* 7 in; *W* 9½ in.
**Status:** common migrant from mid-April through May and from September to October; rare but regular in winter.
**Habitat:** woodlots, brushy tangles and riparian thickets.

**Nesting:** does not nest in NY.
**Feeding:** scratches the ground to expose insects and seeds; also eats berries, buds and moss spore capsules; may take seeds from bird feeders.
**Voice:** song is a frequently repeated variation of *I gotta go wee-wee now*, often heard in spring migration; call is a high, thin *seet* or sharp *pink*.
**Similar Species:** *White-throated Sparrow* (p. 327): bold, white throat; grayish bill; yellow lores; browner overall.
**Best Sites:** Beaver Meadow Nature Center; Hamlin Beach SP; Stewart Park–Cayuga L.; Five Rivers Environmental Education Center; Jones Beach SP.

# DARK-EYED JUNCO

*Junco hyemalis*

Most Dark-eyed Juncos migrate south for the winter, but many remain even during the coldest years. Juncos usually congregate in backyards with bird feeders and sheltering conifers—with such amenities at their disposal, more and more juncos overwinter here. • Juncos spend most of their time on the ground, and they are readily flushed from wooded trails and backyard feeders. They rarely perch at feeders, preferring to snatch up seeds that are knocked to the ground by other visitors such as chickadees, sparrows, nuthatches and jays. • In 1973, the American Ornithologists' Union grouped five junco species into a single species called the Dark-eyed Junco. The five subspecies are closely related and have similar habits, but differ in coloration and range, though they interbreed where their ranges meet. New York is typically home to the "Slate-colored" complex of three subspecies. Birds found in the Adirondacks are clearly *hyemalis*, while Appalachian breeders include the *carolinensis* subspecies, and the western *cismontanus* winters here.

*"Slate-colored Junco"*

**ID:** white outer tail feathers; pale bill. *Male:* dark slate gray overall, except for white lower breast, belly and undertail coverts. *Female:* brown rather than gray.
**Size:** *L* 5½–7 in; *W* 9½ in.
**Status:** common breeder from May to July in high-elevation forests of the Catskills, Adirondacks and Appalachian Plateau; common migrant and winter visitor; peak numbers occur in April and October.
**Habitat:** *Breeding:* coniferous and mixed forests, especially in young jack pine stands, burned-over areas and shrubby regenerating clearings. *In migration and winter:* shrubby woodland borders; also backyard feeders.
**Nesting:** on the ground, usually concealed by a shrub, tree, root, log or rock; female builds a cup nest of twigs, bark shreds, grass and moss; female incubates 3–5 speckled, whitish to bluish white eggs for 12–13 days.
**Feeding:** scratches the ground for invertebrates; also eats berries and seeds.
**Voice:** song is a long, dry trill; call is a smacking *chip* note, often given in series.
**Similar Species:** *Eastern Towhee* (p. 312): larger; female has rufous sides, red eyes and grayish bill.
**Best Sites:** Allegany SP; Braddock Bay; Ferd's Bog–Moose River Plains; Cherry Plain SP; Jones Beach SP.

# LAPLAND LONGSPUR

*Calcarius lapponicus*

In winter, Lapland Longspurs wheel about in large numbers over our fields. From day to day, their movements are largely unpredictable, but they typically appear wherever open fields offer an abundance of seeds or waste grain. Flocks of longspurs can be surprisingly inconspicuous until approached—anyone attempting a closer look at the flock will be awed by the sight of the birds suddenly erupting into the sky, flashing their white outer tail feathers. • In fall, these birds arrive from their breeding grounds looking like mottled, brownish sparrows, and they retain their drab plumage throughout the winter months. When farmers work their fields in spring, lingering Lapland Longspurs have already molted into their bold breeding plumage, which they will wear through the summer. • Lapland Longspurs breed in northern polar regions, including the area of northern Scandinavia known as Lapland.

*nonbreeding*

**ID:** white outer tail feathers; pale yellowish bill. *Breeding male:* black crown, face and "bib"; chestnut nape; broad, white stripe curves down to shoulder from eye (may be tinged with buff behind eye). *Breeding female:* mottled brown-and-black upperparts; lightly streaked flanks; narrow, lightly streaked, buff breast band. *Nonbreeding male:* similar to female, but with faint chestnut on nape and diffuse black breast.
**Size:** *L* 6½ in; *W* 11½ in.

**Status:** fairly common winter visitor from October to April around the Great Lakes; rare winter visitor elsewhere.
**Habitat:** pastures, meadows and croplands.
**Nesting:** does not nest in NY.
**Feeding:** gleans the ground and snow for seeds and waste grain.
**Voice:** flight song is a rapid, slurred warble; musical calls; flight calls include a rattled *tri-di-dit* and a descending *teew*.
**Similar Species:** *Snow Bunting* (p. 331): black-and-white wing pattern. *Sparrows* (pp. 312–30): most have pale legs and lack distinctive head pattern.
**Best Sites:** Nation's Road Grassland; Cape Vincent–Pt. Peninsula; Essex-Westport; Ft. Edward Grassland; Smith Point CP.

# SNOW BUNTING
*Plectrophenax nivalis*

In early winter, when flocks of Snow Buntings descend on rural fields, their startling black-and-white plumage flashes in contrast to the snow-covered backdrop. It may seem strange that Snow Buntings are whiter in summer than in winter, but the darker winter plumage may help these birds absorb heat on clear, cold winter days. • Snow Buntings venture farther north than any other songbird in the world. A single individual, likely misguided and lost, was recorded not far from the North Pole in May 1987. • In winter, Snow Buntings prefer expansive areas, including grain croplands, fields and pastures, where they scratch and peck at exposed seeds and grains. They will also ingest small grains of sand or gravel from roadsides as a source of minerals and to help digestion. • Snow Buntings are definitely cold-weather songbirds, often bathing in snow in early spring and burrowing into it during bitter cold snaps to stay warm.

♂

♀

*nonbreeding*

**ID:** black-and-white wings and tail; white underparts. *Breeding male:* black back; all-white head and rump; black bill. *Breeding female:* streaky, brown-and-whitish crown and back; dark bill. *Nonbreeding male:* yellowish bill; golden brown crown and rump. *Nonbreeding female:* similar to male, but with blackish forecrown and darkly streaked, golden back.
**Size:** L 6–7½ in; W 14 in.

**Status:** common winter visitor from October to March.
**Habitat:** manured fields, feedlots, pastures, grassy meadows, lakeshores, roadsides and railroads.
**Nesting:** does not nest in NY.
**Feeding:** gleans the ground and snow for seeds and waste grain; also takes insects when available.
**Voice:** call is a whistled *tew*.
**Similar Species:** *Lapland Longspur* (p. 330) overall brownish upperparts; lacks black-and-white wing pattern. *Sparrows* (pp. 312–29): lack white wing and tail patches.
**Best Sites:** Hamlin Beach SP; Nation's Road Grassland; Cape Vincent–Pt. Peninsula; Essex-Westport; Ft. Edward Grassland.

331

# NORTHERN CARDINAL
*Cardinalis cardinalis*

A bird as beautiful as the Northern Cardinal rarely fails to capture our attention and admiration: it is often the first choice for calendars and Christmas cards. Most people can easily recognize this delightful year-round neighbor without the help of a bird field guide. • These birds prefer the tangled, shrubby edges of woodlands and are easily attracted to backyards with feeders and sheltering trees and shrubs. • Northern Cardinals form one of the bird world's most faithful pair bonds. The male and female remain in close contact year-round, singing to one another through the seasons with soft, bubbly whistles. The female is known to sing while on the nest, and it is believed that she is informing her partner whether or not she and the young need food. The male is highly territorial, and will even challenge his own reflection in a window or shiny hubcap! • The Northern Cardinal owes its name to the vivid red plumage of the male, which resembles the red robes of Roman Catholic cardinals.

**ID:** *Male:* red overall; pointed crest; black "mask" and throat; red, conical bill. *Female:* shaped like male; brown buff to buff olive overall; gray black "mask"; red bill, crest, wings and tail.
**Size:** *L* 7½–9 in; *W* 12 in.
**Status:** common year-round resident.
**Habitat:** brushy thickets and shrubby tangles along forest and woodland edges; also in backyards and suburban and urban parks.
**Nesting:** in a dense shrub, thicket or low in a coniferous tree; female builds an open cup nest of twigs, bark shreds, weeds, grass, leaves and rootlets; female incubates 3–4 brown-marked, whitish to greenish white eggs for 12–13 days.
**Feeding:** gleans seeds, insects and berries from low shrubs or while hopping along the ground.
**Voice:** song is a variable series of clear, bubbly whistled notes: *what cheer! what cheer! birdie-birdie-birdie what cheer!;* call is a metallic *chip*.
**Similar Species:** *Summer Tanager* (p. 310) and *Scarlet Tanager* (p. 311): lack head crest, black "mask" and throat and red, conical bill; Scarlet Tanager has black wings and tail.
**Best Sites:** Beaver Meadow Nature Center; Stewart Park–Cayuga L.; Five Rivers Environmental Education Center; Central Park (NYC); Heckscher SP.

# ROSE-BREASTED GROSBEAK

*Pheucticus ludovicianus*

It is difficult to miss the boisterous, whistled tune of the Rose-breasted Grosbeak. This bird's hurried, robinlike song is easily recognized, and is one of the more common songs heard in our deciduous forests through spring and summer. Although the female lacks the magnificent colors of the male, she shares his talent for beautiful song. Mating grosbeaks appear pleasantly affectionate toward each other, often touching bills during courtship and after absences. • Rose-breasted Grosbeaks usually build their nests low in a tree or tall shrub, but they typically forage high in the canopy where they can be difficult to spot. Luckily for birders, the abundance of berries in fall often draws these birds to ground level. • The species name *ludovicianus*, Latin for "of Louisiana," is misleading because this bird is only a migrant through Louisiana and other southern states.

*breeding*

♂

♀

**ID:** large, pale, conical bill; dark wings with small white patches; dark tail. *Male:* black "hood" and back; red breast and inner underwings; white underparts and rump. *Female:* bold, whitish "eyebrow"; thin crown stripe; brown upperparts; buff underparts with dark brown streaking.
**Size:** *L* 7–8½ in; *W* 12½ in.
**Status:** fairly common and widespread breeder from May to July; common migrant from late April through May and from September to October.
**Habitat:** deciduous and mixed forests.
**Nesting:** fairly low in a tree or tall shrub, often near water; mostly the female builds a flimsy cup nest of twigs, bark strips, weeds, grass and leaves; pair incubates 3–5 brown-speckled, pale greenish blue eggs for 13–14 days.
**Feeding:** gleans vegetation for insects, seeds, buds, berries and some fruit; occasionally hover-gleans or catches flying insects on the wing; may also visit feeders.
**Voice:** song is a long, melodious series of whistled notes, much like a fast version of a robin's song; call is a distinctive squeak.
**Similar Species:** male is distinctive. *Purple Finch* (p. 347): female is much smaller and has heavier streaking on underparts. *Sparrows* (pp. 312–31): smaller; all lack large, conical bill.
**Best Sites:** Allegany SP; Letchworth SP; John Boyd Thacher SP; Bear Mountain SP; Heckscher SP.

# BLUE GROSBEAK

*Guiraca caerulea*

Male Blue Grosbeaks owe their spectacular spring plumage not to a fresh molt but, oddly enough, to feather wear. While Blue Grosbeaks are wintering in Mexico and Central America, their brown feather tips slowly wear away, leaving the crystal blue plumage that is seen as they arrive on their breeding grounds. • Birders are advised to look carefully for the rusty wing bars that distinguish this bird from the similar-looking, and much more common, Indigo Bunting. Blue Grosbeaks are easy to overlook during country drives—at a distance their striking blue plumage seems black, and many people mistake them for cowbirds. • *Caerulea* is from the Latin for "blue," a description that does not do justice to this bird's true beauty.

**ID:** large, pale grayish, conical bill. *Male:* blue overall; 2 rusty wing bars; black around base of bill. *Female:* soft brown plumage overall; whitish throat; rusty wing bars; rump and shoulders faintly washed with blue.
**Size:** *L* 6–7½ in; *W* 11 in.
**Status:** uncommon spring and fall migrant to Long I.; rare migrant elsewhere in the state; most sightings occur in May; a couple of recent breeding records on Long I. may be the beginning of a northward expansion.
**Habitat:** thick brush, riparian thickets, shrubby areas and dense, weedy fields near water.

**Nesting:** on the ground or in a low bush; female builds a cup of grass, leaves, twigs and bark strips; female incubates 3–4 pale blue eggs for 11–13 days.
**Feeding:** gleans insects while hopping along the ground; occasionally takes seeds; may visit feeders.
**Voice:** sweet, melodious, warbling song with phrases that rise and fall; call is a loud *chink.*
**Similar Species:** *Indigo Bunting* (p. 335): smaller body and bill; male lacks wing bars; female has dark brown breast streaks. *Eastern Bluebird* (p. 260): slim bill; red-and-white underparts.
**Best Sites:** Jones Beach SP; Fire Island National Seashore.

# INDIGO BUNTING

*Passerina cyanea*

In the shadow of a towering tree, a male Indigo Bunting can look almost black. If possible, reposition yourself quickly to a place from which you can see the sun strike and enliven this bunting's incomparable indigo plumage—the rich shade of blue is rivaled only by the sky. • Raspberry thickets are a favored nesting location for many of our Indigo Buntings. The dense, thorny stems provide the nestlings with protection from many predators, and the berries are a convenient source of food. • The Indigo Bunting employs a clever and comical foraging strategy to reach the grass and weed seeds upon which it feeds. The bird lands midway on a stem and then shuffles slowly toward the seed head, which eventually bends under the bird's weight, giving the bunting easier access to the seeds. • Only male Indigo Buntings sing and they do not learn their musical warble from their fathers, but from neighboring males during their first spring.

*breeding*

**ID:** stout, gray, conical bill; black legs; no wing bars. *Breeding male:* blue overall; black lores; wings and tail may show some black. *Nonbreeding male:* similar to female, but usually with some blue in wings and tail. *Female:* soft brown overall; brown streaks on breast; whitish throat.
**Size:** L 5½ in; W 8 in.
**Status:** common, widespread breeder from May to July; fairly common migrant in May and September.
**Habitat:** deciduous forest and woodland edges, regenerating forest clearings, shrubby fields, orchards, abandoned pastures and hedgerows; occasionally along edges of mixed woodlands.

**Nesting:** in a small tree or shrub; female builds a cup nest of grass, leaves and bark strips; female incubates 3–4 white to bluish white eggs for 12–13 days.
**Feeding:** gleans low vegetation and the ground for insects, especially grasshoppers, beetles, weevils, flies and larvae; also eats the seeds of thistles, dandelions, goldenrods and other native plants.
**Voice:** song consists of paired, warbled whistles: *fire-fire, where-where, here-here, see-it see-it;* call is a quick *spit.*
**Similar Species:** *Blue Grosbeak* (p. 334): larger overall; larger, more robust bill; 2 rusty wing bars; male has black around base of bill; female lacks streaking on breast. *Eastern Bluebird* (p. 260): slim bill; red-and-white underparts.
**Best Sites:** Allegany SP; Montezuma NWR; Saratoga National Historical Park; Bear Mountain SP; Heckscher SP.

# DICKCISSEL

*Spiza americana*

Dickcissels are an irruptive species and may be common one year and absent the next. Arriving in suitable nesting habitat before the smaller females, breeding males bravely announce their presence with stuttering, trilled renditions of their own name. The territorial males perch atop tall blades of grass, fence posts or rocks to scour their turf for signs of potential mates or unwelcome males. Dickcissels are polygynous, and males may mate with up to eight females in a single breeding season. This breeding strategy means that the male gives no assistance to the females in nesting or brooding. • This "miniature meadowlark" has a special fondness for fields of alfalfa. Though Dickcissels eat mostly insects on their breeding grounds, seeds and grain form the main part of their diet on their South American wintering grounds, making them unpopular with local farmers. Each year large numbers of these birds are killed by pesticides in efforts to reduce crop losses, which may partially explain the Dickcissel's pattern of absence and abundance.

*breeding*

**Habitat:** abandoned fields, weedy meadows, croplands, grasslands and grassy roadsides.
**Nesting:** on or near the ground; well concealed among tall, dense vegetation; female builds a bulky, open cup nest of grass, weed stems and leaves; female incubates 4 pale blue eggs for 11–13 days.
**Feeding:** gleans insects and seeds from the ground and low vegetation.
**Voice:** song consists of 2–3 single notes followed by a trill, often paraphrased as *dick dick dick-cissel*; flight call is a buzzer-like *bzrrrrt*.
**Similar Species:** *Eastern Meadowlark* (p. 339): much larger; long, pointed bill; yellow "chin" and throat; black "necklace." *American Goldfinch* (p. 354): white or buff yellow bars on dark wings; may show black forecrown; lacks black "bib." *House Sparrow* (p. 356): female is smaller and lacks yellow on breast.
**Best Sites:** Jones Beach SP; Fire Island National Seashore.

**ID:** yellow "eye-brow"; gray head, nape and sides of yellow breast; brown upperparts; pale, grayish underparts; rufous shoulder patch; dark, conical bill. *Male:* white "chin"; triangular black "bib"; duller colors in non-breeding plumage. *Female:* duller version of male; white throat.
**Size:** *L* 6–7 in; *W* 9½ in.
**Status:** a few scattered breeding records; rare migrant in October, especially on coastal barrier islands; very rare in winter at feeders with House Sparrows.

# BOBOLINK

*Dolichonyx oryzivorus*

During the nesting season, male and female Bobolinks rarely interact with one another. For the most part, males perform aerial displays and sing their bubbly, tinkling songs from exposed grassy perches while the females carry out the nesting duties. Once the young have hatched, males become scarce, spending much of their time on the ground hunting for insects. Bobolinks once benefited from increased agriculture here, but modern practices, such as harvesting hay early in the season, continue to thwart the reproductive efforts of these birds. • At first glimpse, the female Bobolink resembles a sparrow, but the male, with his dark belly and his buff-and-black upperparts, is colored like no other bird in New York. • Some people think that the name of this bird is an abbreviation of "Robert of Lincoln," the title of a poem by American poet William Cullen Bryant, though others think it is a reference to the bird's song.

*breeding*

**ID:** *Breeding male:* black bill, head, wings, tail and underparts; buff nape; white rump and wing patch. *Breeding female:* buff brown overall; yellowish bill; streaked back, sides, flanks and rump; pale lores; dark eye line; pale central crown stripe bordered by dark stripes; whitish throat. *Nonbreeding male:* similar to breeding female, but darker above and rich golden buff below.
**Size:** *L* 6–8 in; *W* 11½ in.
**Status:** widespread, common breeder from May to July; very common migrant in May and from August to September.
**Habitat:** meadows and ditches with tall grass, hayfields and some croplands.
**Nesting:** on the ground, usually in a hayfield; well concealed in a shallow depression; female builds a cup nest of grass and weed stems; female incubates 5–6 darkly marked, grayish to light reddish brown eggs for 11–13 days.

**Feeding:** gleans the ground and low vegetation for adult and larval invertebrates; also eats many seeds.
**Voice:** song is a series of banjolike twangs: *bobolink bobolink spink spank spink,* often given in flight; also issues a *pink* call in flight.
**Similar Species:** male is distinctive. *Savannah Sparrow* (p. 318): dark breast streaking; yellow lores. *Vesper Sparrow* (p. 317): streaked breast; white outer tail feathers. *Grasshopper Sparrow* (p. 319): white belly; unstreaked sides and flanks.
**Best Sites:** Nation's Road Grassland; Montezuma NWR; Saratoga National Historical Park; Shawangunk Grasslands NWR; Jones Beach SP.

# RED-WINGED BLACKBIRD
*Agelaius phoeniceus*

Male Red-winged Blackbirds get an early start on the breeding season, often arriving in our marshes and wetlands in mid-March, a week or so before the females. In the females' absence, the males stake out territories through song and visual displays. The male's bright red shoulders and short, raspy song are his most important tools in the often intricate strategy he employs to defend his territory from rivals. A flashy and richly voiced male who has managed to establish a large and productive territory can attract several mates to his cattail kingdom. In field experiments, males whose red shoulders were painted black soon lost their territories to rivals that they had previously defeated. • After the male has wooed her, the female starts the busy work of weaving a nest amid the cattails. Cryptic coloration allows the female to sit inconspicuously upon her nest, blending in perfectly with the surroundings.

common in winter in western and southeastern NY.

**Habitat:** cattail marshes, wet meadows and ditches, croplands and shoreline shrubs.

**Nesting:** colonial; in cattails or shoreline bushes; female weaves an open cup nest of dried cattail leaves and grass; female incubates 3–4 darkly marked, pale blue green eggs for 10–12 days.

**Feeding:** gleans the ground for seeds, waste grain and invertebrates; also gleans vegetation for seeds, insects and berries; occasionally catches insects in flight; may visit feeders.

**Voice:** song is a loud, raspy *konk-a-ree* or *ogle-reeeee*; calls include a harsh *check* and a high *tseert*; female may give a loud *che-che-che chee chee chee*.

**ID:** *Male:* all black, except for large, red shoulder patch edged in yellow (occasionally concealed). *Female:* heavily streaked underparts; mottled brown upperparts; faint, red shoulder patch; pale "eyebrow."

**Size:** *L* 7–9½ in; *W* 13 in.

**Status:** common breeder from April to July; very common migrant from March to May and from August to October; fairly

**Similar Species:** male is distinctive when shoulder patch shows. *Rusty Blackbird* (p. 340): female lacks streaked underparts.

**Best Sites:** Iroquois NWR–Tonawanda WMA–Oak Orchard WMA; Montezuma NWR; Five Rivers Environmental Education Center; Jamaica Bay Wildlife Refuge; Jones Beach SP.

# EASTERN MEADOWLARK

*Sturnella magna*

The Eastern Meadowlark's trademark tune is the voice of rural areas, and it rings throughout spring from fence posts and powerlines, wherever grassy meadows and pastures are found. • The male's bright yellow underparts, black, V-shaped "necklace" and white outer tail feathers help attract mates. Females share these colorful attributes for a slightly different purpose: when a predator approaches too close to a nest, the incubating female explodes from the grass in a burst of flashing color. Most predators cannot resist chasing the moving target, and once the female has led the predator away from the nest, she simply folds away her white tail flags, exposes her camouflaged back and disappears into the grass without a trace. • The Eastern Meadowlark is not actually a lark, but a member of the blackbird family.

*breeding*

**ID:** yellow underparts; broad, black breast band; mottled brown upperparts; short, wide tail with white outer tail feathers; long, pinkish legs; yellow lores; long, sharp bill; blackish eye line and crown stripes border pale "eyebrow" and median crown stripe; dark streaking on white sides and flanks.
**Size:** *L* 9–9½ in; *W* 14 in.
**Status:** common, widespread breeder from April to July, except in mountains; common migrant from March to April and from September to October; fairly common in winter in southern NY.
**Habitat:** grassy meadows and pastures; also in some croplands, weedy fields, grassy roadsides and old orchards.
**Nesting:** in a depression on the ground, concealed by dense grass; female builds a domed grass nest with a side entrance, woven into surrounding vegetation; female incubates 3–7 brown-speckled, white eggs for 13–15 days.
**Feeding:** gleans grasshoppers, crickets, beetles and spiders from the ground and vegetation; extracts grubs and worms by probing its bill into the soil; also eats seeds.
**Voice:** song is a rich series of 2–8 clear, slurred, melodic whistles: *see-you at school-today* or *this is the year;* also gives a rattling flight call and a high, buzzy *dzeart.*
**Similar Species:** *Western Meadowlark* (p. 366): paler upperparts, especially crown stripes and eye line; yellow on throat extends onto lower "cheek"; different song and call. *Dickcissel* (p. 336): much smaller; solid dark crown; conical bill; white throat; lacks brown streaking on sides and flanks.
**Best Sites:** Nation's Road Grassland; Cape Vincent–Pt. Peninsula; Saratoga National Historical Park; Shawangunk Grasslands NWR; Jones Beach SP.

# RUSTY BLACKBIRD

*Euphagus carolinus*

The Rusty Blackbird owes its name to the rusty color of its fall plumage, but its name could just as well reflect this bird's grating, squeaky song, which sounds very much like a rusty hinge. • Unlike many blackbirds, Rusty Blackbirds nest in isolated pairs or very small, loose colonies in flooded woodlands and treed, boreal bogs, not in wetlands. • Rusty Blackbirds spend their days foraging along the wooded edges of fields and wetlands, occasionally picking through the manure-laden ground of cattle feedlots. At day's end, when feeding is curtailed, most birds seek the shelter of trees and shrubs and the stalks of emergent marshland vegetation. • Rusty Blackbirds are generally less abundant and less aggressive than their relatives, and they generally avoid human-altered environments.

*breeding*

**ID:** yellow eyes; dark legs; long, sharp bill. *Breeding male:* dark plumage; subtle green gloss on body; subtle bluish or greenish gloss on head. *Breeding female:* paler than male; plumage is without gloss. *Nonbreeding male:* rusty wings, back and crown. *Nonbreeding female:* paler than male; buffy underparts; rusty "cheek."
**Size:** *L* 9 in; *W* 14 in.
**Status:** uncommon breeder from May to July in the Adirondacks; fairly common migrant from March to April and from September to October in western NY, less common eastward; occurs rarely and in small numbers along the coast in winter.

**Habitat:** *Breeding:* treed bogs, fens, beaver ponds, wet meadows and the shrubby shorelines of lakes, rivers and swamps. *In migration:* marshes, open fields, feedlots and woodland edges near water.
**Nesting:** low in a shrub or small conifer; often above or very near water; female builds a bulky nest of twigs, grass and lichens with an inner cup of mud and decaying vegetation; female incubates 4–5 brown-blotched, pale blue green eggs for about 14 days.
**Feeding:** walks along shorelines gleaning waterbugs, beetles, dragonflies, snails, grasshoppers and occasionally small fish; also eats waste grain and seeds.
**Voice:** song is a squeaky, creaking *kush-leeeh ksh-lay;* call is a harsh *chack.*
**Similar Species:** *Common Grackle* (p. 341): longer, keeled tail; larger body and bill; more iridescent plumage. *European Starling* (p. 271): speckled appearance; dark eyes; yellow bill in summer.
**Best Sites:** Iroquois NWR–Tonawanda WMA–Oak Orchard WMA; Montezuma NWR; Chubb River Swamp; Black Creek Marsh WMA; Bashakill WMA.

# COMMON GRACKLE

*Quiscalus quiscula*

The Common Grackle is a poor but spirited singer. Usually while perched in a shrub, a male grackle will slowly take a deep breath to inflate his breast, causing his feathers to spike outward, then close his eyes and give out a loud, strained *tssh-schleek*. Despite his lack of musical talent, the male remains smug and proud, posing with his bill held high. • In fall, large flocks of Common Grackles are common in rural areas where they forage for waste grain in open fields. Smaller bands occasionally venture into urban neighborhoods where they assert their dominance at backyard bird feeders—even bullying Blue Jays will yield feeding rights to these cocky, aggressive birds. • The Common Grackle is easily distinguished from other blackbirds by its long, heavy bill and lengthy, wedge-shaped tail. • At night, grackles commonly roost with groups of European Starlings, Red-winged Blackbirds and even Brown-headed Cowbirds.

**ID:** iridescent plumage (bluish purple head and breast, bronze back and sides, purple wings and tail) often appears blackish; long, keeled tail; yellow eyes; long, heavy bill; female is smaller, duller and browner than male.

**Size:** *L* 11–13½ in; *W* 17 in.

**Status:** very common breeder and migrant from March to September; overwinters in southeastern NY and on Long I.

**Habitat:** wetlands, hedgerows, fields, wet meadows, riparian woodlands and along the edges of coniferous forests and woodlands; also shrubby urban and suburban parks and gardens.

**Nesting:** singly or in a small colony; in dense tree or shrub branches or emergent vegetation; often near water; female builds a bulky, open cup nest of twigs, grass, plant fibers and mud; female incubates 4–5 brown-blotched, pale blue eggs for 12–14 days.

**Feeding:** slowly struts along the ground, gleaning, snatching and probing for insects, earthworms, seeds, waste grain and fruit; also catches insects in flight and eats small vertebrates; may take some bird eggs.

**Voice:** song is a series of harsh, strained notes ending with a metallic squeak: *tssh-schleek* or *gri-de-leeek;* call is a quick, loud *swaaaack* or *chaack.*

**Similar Species:** *Rusty Blackbird* (p. 340): smaller overall; lacks heavy bill and keeled tail. *Red-winged Blackbird* (p. 338): shorter tail; male has red shoulder patch and dark eyes. *European Starling* (p. 271): very short tail; long, thin bill (yellow in summer); speckled appearance; dark eyes.

**Best Sites:** Braddock Bay; Montezuma NWR; Saratoga National Historical Park; Central Park (NYC); Prospect Park (NYC).

# BOAT-TAILED GRACKLE
*Quiscalus major*

Feathers fluffed, tail spread and wings fluttering above its back, the Boat-tailed Grackle issues its harsh, grating calls across the marsh landscape. A bill pointed skyward is a threatening posture that warns of impending attack if intruders dare enter the male's aggressively guarded territory. Sharing overlapping portions of their ranges and having remarkable similarities in appearance and habit, this bird and the Great-tailed Grackle of the southwest were considered to be the same species until the 1970s. One of the key pieces of evidence revealing their distinct identities was their failure to interbreed. The Boat-tailed Grackle is closely tied to the tidal waters of the Atlantic and Gulf coasts, where it finds everything it needs to thrive. This bold bird has been known to eat eggs from the unguarded nests of other birds, including the nests of birds much larger than itself, such as herons and rails.

**ID:** long, keeled tail; long bill; yellow eyes. *Male:* iridescent, blue green plumage (appears black). *Female:* brown upperparts; paler, orangy brown underparts; darker "mask," wings and tail.

**Size:** *Male: L* 17 in; *W* 23 in. *Female: L* 14 in; *W* 18 in.

**Status:** uncommon year-round resident in coastal marshes of Long I.; increasing and expanding eastward on Long I.

**Habitat:** usually near water, including salt marshes, beaches, flooded fields, mudflats and other oceanside habitats.

**Nesting:** colonial; in vegetation at the edge of a marsh or other water body; female builds bulky cup nest of rushes, grasses, plant stalks and mud; female incubates 3–4 pale blue eggs, scribbled with black, for 13–14 days and raises the young alone.

**Feeding:** forages by walking on land or in shallow water, thrusting its bill forward to snatch prey; omnivorous diet includes aquatic and terrestrial insects, crustaceans and other invertebrates; may also eat amphibians, fish, seeds, grain and the eggs and young of other birds.

**Voice:** varied calls include rattles, chatters, squeaks and a soft *chuck;* song consists of harsh *jeeb* notes repeated in series.

**Similar Species:** *Common Grackle* (p. 341): much smaller; yellow eyes; iridescent, purplish plumage.

**Best Sites:** Great Kills Park–Mt. Loretto (NYC); Jamaica Bay Wildlife Refuge; Shinnecock Inlet–Dune Rd.

# BROWN-HEADED COWBIRD

*Molothrus ater*

Historically, Brown-headed Cowbirds followed bison herds across the Great Plains—they now follow cattle—and the birds' nomadic lifestyle made it impossible for them to construct and tend a nest. Instead, cowbirds engage in "nest parasitism," laying their eggs in the nests of other songbirds. Many of the parasitized songbirds do not recognize that the eggs are not theirs, so they incubate them and raise the cowbird young as their own. Cowbird chicks typically hatch first and develop much more quickly than their nestmates, which are pushed out of the nest or outcompeted for food. • The expansion of livestock farming, the fragmentation of forests and the development of an extensive network of transportation corridors throughout North America have significantly increased the cowbird's range. It now parasitizes more than 140 species of birds, including species that probably had no contact with it before widespread human settlement.

**ID:** thick, conical bill; short, squared tail; dark eyes. *Male:* iridescent, green blue body plumage (appears glossy black); dark brown head.
*Female:* brown plumage overall; faint streaking on light brown underparts; pale throat.
**Size:** *L* 6–8 in; *W* 12 in.
**Status:** common breeder from April to July; common migrant from March to April and from September to October; fairly common in winter.
**Habitat:** open agricultural and residential areas including fields, woodland edges, utility cutlines, roadsides, fencelines, landfills, campgrounds, picnic areas and areas near cattle.

**Nesting:** does not build a nest; each female may lay up to 40 eggs per year in the nests of other birds, usually laying 1 egg per nest (larger numbers, up to 8 eggs in a single nest, are probably from several different cowbirds); brown-speckled, whitish eggs hatch after 10–13 days.
**Feeding:** gleans the ground for seeds, waste grain and invertebrates, especially grasshoppers, beetles and true bugs.
**Voice:** song is a high, liquidy gurgle: *glug-ahl-whee* or *bubbloozeee;* call is a squeaky, high-pitched *seep, psee* or *wee-tse-tse*, often given in flight; also a fast, chipping *ch-ch-ch-ch-ch-ch.*
**Similar Species:** *Rusty Blackbird* (p. 340): longer, slimmer bill; yellow eyes; longer tail; lacks contrasting brown head and darker body. *Common Grackle* (p. 341): much larger overall; longer, heavier bill; longer, keeled tail.
**Best Sites:** Beaver Meadow Nature Center; Braddock Bay; Ft. Edward Grassland; Jamaica Bay Wildlife Refuge; Heckscher SP.

# ORCHARD ORIOLE

*Icterus spurius*

Orchards may once have been favored haunts of this oriole, but since orchards are now heavily sprayed and manicured, it is unlikely that you will ever see this bird in such a locale. Instead, the Orchard Oriole is most commonly found in large shade trees that line roads, paths and streams. Smaller than all other North American orioles, the Orchard Oriole is one of only two oriole species commonly found in the eastern U.S. • These orioles are frequent victims of nest parasitism by Brown-headed Cowbirds. In some parts of its breeding range, over half of Orchard Oriole nests are parasitized by cowbirds. • Orchard Orioles are best seen in spring when eager males hop from branch to branch, singing their quick, musical courtship songs. • Male Orchard Orioles do not get their adult plumage until their second year; females and immature males look very similar except that the yearling males have a black "bib."

**ID:** *Male:* black "hood" and tail; chestnut underparts, shoulder and rump; dark wings with white wing bar and feather edgings. *Female* and *immature:* olive upperparts; yellow to olive yellow underparts; faint, white wing bars on dusky gray wings.
**Size:** *L* 6–7 in; *W* 9½ in.
**Status:** uncommon and local breeder in May and June; uncommon migrant from April to May and from July to September.
**Habitat:** open woodlands, suburban parklands, forest edges, hedgerows and groves of shade trees.
**Nesting:** in a deciduous tree or shrub; female builds a hanging pouch nest woven from grass and other fine plant fibers; female incubates 4–5 pale bluish white eggs, spotted with gray and brown, for 12–15 days.
**Feeding:** gleans insects and berries from trees and shrubs; probes flowers for nectar; may visit hummingbird feeders and feeding stations that offer orange halves.
**Voice:** song is a loud, rapid, varied series of whistled notes; call is a quick *chuck*.
**Similar Species:** *Baltimore Oriole* (p. 345): male has brighter orange plumage with orange in tail; female has orange overtones. *Scarlet Tanager* (p. 311): females have thicker, pale bills and lack wing bars.
**Best Sites:** unpredictable; Vischer Ferry Nature and Historic Preserve; Central Park (NYC); Prospect Park (NYC); Jones Beach SP.

# BALTIMORE ORIOLE

*Icterus galbula*

The male Baltimore Oriole has striking, Halloween-style, black-and-orange plumage that flickers like smoldering embers among our neighborhood tree-tops. As if his brilliant plumage was not enough to secure our admiration, he also sings a rich, flutelike courtship song and will vocalize almost continuously until he finds a mate. • This oriole doesn't suffer as much as the Orchard Oriole from nest parasitism by Brown-headed Cowbirds. Female Baltimore Orioles will eject cowbird eggs from the nest and both male and female orioles will react aggressively toward any adult cowbird that approaches their nest. • The city of Baltimore was first established as a colony by Irishman George Calvert, the Baron of Baltimore. This bird's name was chosen because the male's plumage mirrored the colors of the baron's coat of arms.

**ID:** *Male:* black "hood," back, wings and central tail feathers; bright orange underparts, shoulder, rump and outer tail feathers; white wing patch and feather edgings. *Female:* olive brown upperparts (darkest on head); dull yellow orange underparts and rump; white wing bar.
**Size:** *L* 7–8 in; *W* 11½ in.
**Status:** widespread, common breeder in May and June; common migrant from late April through May and in September; occasionally overwinters at feeders.
**Habitat:** deciduous and mixed forests, particularly riparian woodlands, natural openings, roadsides, orchards, gardens and parklands.

**Nesting:** high in a deciduous tree; female builds a hanging pouch nest of grass, bark shreds, rootlets and plant stems; female incubates 4–5 darkly marked, pale gray to bluish white eggs for 12–14 days.
**Feeding:** gleans canopy vegetation and shrubs for caterpillars, beetles, wasps and other invertebrates; also eats some fruit and nectar; may visit hummingbird feeders and feeding stations that offer orange halves.
**Voice:** song consists of slow, loud, clear whistles: *peter peter peter here peter;* calls include a 2-note *tea-too* and a rapid chatter: *ch-ch-ch-ch-ch.*
**Similar Species:** *Orchard Oriole* (p. 344): male has darker chestnut plumage; female is olive yellow and lacks orange overtones. *Scarlet Tanager* (p. 311): female has thicker, pale bill and lacks wing bars.
**Best Sites:** Beaver Meadow Nature Center; Stewart Park–Cayuga L.; Five Rivers Environmental Education Center; Central Park (NYC); Jones Beach SP.

# PINE GROSBEAK

*Pinicola enucleator*

The Pine Grosbeak is a large finch that inhabits subarctic and boreal forests across North America. Every so often flocks of these birds find their way south to our region in winter and may show up in your backyard if you have fruit-bearing trees or offer sunflower seeds. These erratic winter invasions thrill local naturalists—the Pine Grosbeak's bright colors and exciting flock behavior are always a welcome sight. These invasions are not completely understood, but it is thought that cone crop failures or changes to forest ecology caused by logging, forest fires or climatic factors may force these hungry finches southward in search of food. Much of their survival depends on the availability of conifer seeds, so Pine Grosbeaks are always in search of a good crop. • During nesting, adult Pine Grosbeaks develop "gular pouches," throat pouches that allow them to carry food to nestlings. • *Pinicola* is Latin for "pine dweller," and *enucleator* is Latin for "one who takes off shells."

**ID:** stout, dark, conical bill; 2 white wing bars; black wings and tail. *Male:* rosy red head, upperparts and breast; gray sides, flanks, belly and undertail coverts. *Female* and *immature:* gray overall; yellow or russet wash on head and rump.
**Size:** *L* 8–10 in; *W* 14½ in.
**Status:** rare to common winter visitor; absent some years; occurs most often from November to March.
**Habitat:** conifer plantations and deciduous woodlands with fruiting mountain-ash and crabapple; also backyard feeders.
**Nesting:** does not nest in NY.

**Feeding:** gleans buds, berries and seeds from trees; also forages on the ground; visits feeders in winter.
**Voice:** song is a short, sweet, musical warble; call is a 3-note whistle with a higher middle note; short, muffled trill is often given in flight; chatters when feeding in flocks.
**Similar Species:** *White-winged Crossbill* (p. 350): much smaller; lacks stubby bill and prominent gray coloration. *Red Crossbill* (p. 349): lacks stubby bill and white wing bars. *Evening Grosbeak* (p. 355): female has pale bill, dark "whisker" stripe, tan underparts and broad, white wing patches. *House Finch* (p. 348) and *Purple Finch* (p. 347): smaller; lack white wing bars.
**Best Sites:** Durand-Eastman Park (Rochester); Cape Vincent–Pt. Peninsula; Essex-Westport; Crown Point SP.

# PURPLE FINCH

*Carpodacus purpureus*

The Purple Finch's gentle nature and simple but stunning plumage endears it to many birders. Fortunately, bird admirers in our region have many opportunities to meet this charming finch. • The courtship of the Purple Finch is a gentle and appealing ritual. The liquid, warbling song of the male bubbles through conifer boughs, announcing his presence to potential mates. Upon the arrival of an interested female, the colorful male dances lightly around her, beating his wings until he softly lifts into the air. • Flat, table-style feeding stations with nearby tree cover are sure to attract Purple Finches, and erecting one may keep a small flock in your area over winter. • "Purple" *(purpureus)* is simply an inaccurate description of this bird's reddish coloration. Roger Tory Peterson said it best when he described the Purple Finch as a "sparrow dipped in raspberry juice." Only the male is brightly colored, however, and the female is a rather drab, unassuming bird by comparison.

**ID:** *Male:* pale bill; raspberry red (occasionally yellow to salmon pink) head, throat, breast and nape; back and flanks are streaked with brown and red; reddish brown "cheek"; red rump; notched tail; pale, unstreaked belly and undertail coverts. *Female:* dark brown "cheek" and jaw line; white "eyebrow" and lower "cheek" stripe; heavily streaked underparts; unstreaked undertail coverts.
**Size:** *L* 5–6 in; *W* 10 in.
**Status:** common breeder from May to July upstate, especially at higher elevations; common migrant from March to April and from September to October; scarce winter visitor, except common in irruption years.
**Habitat:** *Breeding:* open coniferous and mixed forests. *In migration* and *winter:* coniferous, mixed and deciduous forests, shrubby open areas and feeders with nearby tree cover.
**Nesting:** in a conifer; female builds a cup nest of twigs, grass and rootlets; female incubates 4–5 darkly marked, pale greenish blue eggs for about 13 days.
**Feeding:** gleans the ground and vegetation for seeds, buds, berries and insects; readily visits table-style feeding stations.
**Voice:** song is a bubbly, continuous warble; call is a single metallic *cheep* or *weet*.
**Similar Species:** *House Finch* (p. 348): squared tail; male has brown flanks and lacks reddish "cap"; female lacks distinct "cheek" patch. *Red Crossbill* (p. 349): larger bill with crossed mandibles; male has more red overall and whitish undertail coverts.
**Best Sites:** Letchworth SP; Whetstone Gulf SP; Ferd's Bog–Moore River Plains; Bloomingdale Bog; Essex-Westport.

# HOUSE FINCH
*Carpodacus mexicanus*

A native of western North America, the House Finch was brought to eastern parts of the continent as an illegally captured cage bird known as the "Hollywood Finch." In the early 1940s, New York pet shop owners released their birds to avoid prosecution and fines, and it is the descendants of those birds that have colonized New York. In fact, the House Finch is now commonly found throughout the continental U.S. and southern Canada and has been introduced to Hawaii. • The resourceful House Finch is the only bird that has been aggressive and stubborn enough to successfully outcompete the House Sparrow, which also prospers in urban environments. In the West, the House Finch is often found in natural settings as well as urban centers, while in the East it is seldom found outside urban and suburban settings. • The male House Finch's plumage can vary in color from light yellow to bright red, but females will choose the reddest males with which to breed.

**ID:** streaked undertail coverts; streaked, gray brown back; square tail. *Male:* brown "cap"; bright red "eyebrow," forecrown, throat and breast; heavily streaked flanks and belly. *Female:* indistinct facial patterning; heavily streaked underparts.
**Size:** *L* 5–6 in; *W* 9½ in.
**Status:** very common year-round resident; breeds from April to July.
**Habitat:** cities, towns and agricultural areas.
**Nesting:** in a cavity, building, dense foliage or abandoned bird nest; especially in evergreens and ornamental shrubs near buildings; mostly the female builds an open cup nest of grass, twigs, leaves and feathers, often adding string and other debris; female incubates 4–5 sparsely marked, pale blue eggs for 12–14 days.

**Feeding:** gleans vegetation and the ground for seeds; also takes berries, buds and some flower parts; often visits feeders.
**Voice:** song is a bright, disjointed warble lasting about 3 seconds, often ending with a harsh *jeeer* or *wheer;* flight call is a sweet *cheer,* given singly or in series.
**Similar Species:** *Purple Finch* (p. 347): notched tail; male has more burgundy red "cap," upper back and flanks; female has distinct "cheek" patch. *Red Crossbill* (p. 349): bill has crossed mandibles; male is more red overall and has darker wings.
**Best Sites:** Tifft Nature Preserve; Durand-Eastman Park (Rochester); Five Rivers Environmental Education Center; Central Park (NYC); Jones Beach SP.

# RED CROSSBILL

*Loxia curvirostra*

Red Crossbills are the great gypsies of our bird community, wandering through forests in search of pine cones. They may breed at any time of year if they discover a bumper crop—it's not unusual to hear them singing and see them nest-building in midwinter. Their nomadic ways make them difficult birds to find, and even during years of plenty there is no guarantee that these birds will put in an appearance. Winter is typically the time to see crossbills in our region, and in some years, large flocks suddenly appear. • The crossbill's oddly shaped bill is an adaptation for prying open conifer cones. While holding the cone with one foot, the crossbill inserts its closed bill between the cone and scales and pries them apart by opening its bill. Once a cone is cracked, a crossbill uses its nimble tongue to extract the soft, energy-rich seeds hidden within.

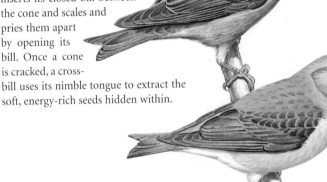

**ID:** bill has crossed tips. *Male:* dull orange red to brick red plumage; dark wings and tail; always has color on throat. *Female:* olive gray to dusky yellow plumage; plain, dark wings.

**Size:** *L* 5–6½ in; *W* 11 in.

**Status:** irruptive; uncommon breeder from March to June in the Adirondacks, though breeding may be as early as February or as late as November; occasionally breeds in other parts of the state after winter irruptions.

**Habitat:** coniferous forests and plantations; favors red and white pine, but also found in other pine and spruce-fir forests.

**Nesting:** high in a conifer; female builds an open cup nest of twigs, grass, bark shreds and rootlets; female incubates 3–4 sparsely marked, pale bluish white eggs for 12–18 days.

**Feeding:** eats primarily conifer seeds (especially pine); also eats buds, deciduous tree seeds and occasionally insects; often licks road salt or minerals in soil and along roadsides; rarely visits feeders.

**Voice:** distinctive *jip-jip* call note, often given in flight; song is a varied series of warbles, trills and *chip* notes.

**Similar Species:** *White-winged Crossbill* (p. 350): 2 broad, white wing bars. *House Finch* (p. 348) and *Purple Finch* (p. 347): conical bills; lighter brownish wings; less red overall; lack red on lower belly.

**Best Sites:** Ferd's Bog–Moose River Plains; Paul Smiths Visitor Interpretive Center (Adirondack Park); Bloomingdale Bog; Chubb River Swamp; Whiteface Mt.

# WHITE-WINGED CROSSBILL

*Loxia leucoptera*

People are often amazed by the variety of color and the many different shapes of bird bills. Although this bird's bill lacks the colorful flair of the tropical toucan or the massive proportions of the hornbill, the White-winged Crossbill's well-designed mandibles combine function with artistry. This bill arrangement is shared by only one other bird species in North America, the Red Crossbill. The White-winged Crossbill eats primarily spruce and tamarack seeds, and its unique bill is adapted for prying open conifer cones. • The presence of a foraging group of White-winged Crossbills high in a spruce tree creates an unforgettable shower of conifer cones and crackling chatter. Like many finches, White-winged Crossbills can be abundant one year, then absent the next.

**ID:** bill has crossed tips; 2 bold, white wing bars. *Male:* pinkish red overall; black wings and tail. *Female:* streaked, brown upperparts; dusky yellow underparts slightly streaked with brown; dark wings and tail.

**Size:** *L* 6–7 in; *W* 10½ in.

**Status:** uncommon, irruptive, nomadic breeder; breeds from January to August in the Adirondacks, but may breed in other parts of the state after irruptions.

**Habitat:** coniferous forests, primarily spruce, fir, tamarack and eastern hemlock; occasionally townsites and deciduous forests.

**Nesting:** in a conifer; female builds an open cup nest of twigs, grass, bark shreds, leaves and moss; female incubates 2–4 brown-flecked, whitish to pale blue green eggs for 12–14 days.

**Feeding:** prefers conifer seeds (mostly spruce and tamarack); also eats deciduous tree seeds and occasionally insects; often licks salt and minerals from roads when available.

**Voice:** song is a high-pitched series of warbles, trills and *chip* notes; call is a series of harsh, questioning *cheat* notes, often given in flight.

**Similar Species:** *Red Crossbill* (p. 349): lacks white wing bars; male is deeper red (less pinkish). *Pine Siskin* (p. 353): smaller; yellow highlights on wing; lacks crossed bill. *Pine Grosbeak* (p. 346): stubby, conical bill; thinner wing bars; male has gray sides; female is very gray. *House Finch* (p. 348) and *Purple Finch* (p. 347): conical bills; lighter brownish wings; less red overall.

**Best Sites:** Ferd's Bog–Moose River Plains; Bloomingdale Bog; Chubb River Swamp; Whiteface Mt.

# COMMON REDPOLL

*Carduelis flammea*

A predictably unpredictable winter visitor, the Common Redpoll is seen in varying numbers—it might appear in flocks of hundreds or thousands, or in groups of a dozen or fewer, depending on the year. • Renowned for their effective winter adaptations, redpolls can endure colder temperatures than any other songbird. Because they do not have much body fat, they maintain a high metabolic rate and eat almost constantly to avoid dying from hypothermia—redpolls continually glean waste grain from bare fields or stock up on seeds at winter feeders. Their focus on food helps make wintering redpolls remarkably fearless of humans. Highly insulative feathers also help these birds to withstand bitter cold, especially when the feathers are fluffed out to trap layers of warm, insulating air.

*nonbreeding*

**ID:** red forecrown; black "chin"; yellowish bill; streaked upperparts, including rump; lightly streaked sides, flanks and undertail coverts; notched tail. *Male:* pinkish red breast. *Female:* whitish to pale gray breast.
**Size:** *L* 5 in; *W* 9 in.
**Status:** irregular, sometimes common, winter visitor from November to April.
**Habitat:** open fields, meadows, roadsides, utility cutlines, railroads, forest edges and backyards with feeders.
**Nesting:** does not nest in NY.

**Feeding:** gleans the ground, snow and vegetation in large flocks for seeds in winter; often visits feeders.
**Voice:** song is a twittering series of trills; calls are a soft *chit-chit-chit-chit* and a faint *swe-eet;* indistinguishable from the Hoary Redpoll's songs and calls.
**Similar Species:** *Hoary Redpoll* (p. 352): generally paler and plumper overall; unstreaked or partly streaked rump; usually has faint or no streaking on sides and flanks; bill may look stubbier; lacks streaking on undertail coverts. *Pine Siskin* (p. 353): heavily streaked overall; yellow highlights on wings and tail.
**Best Sites:** Cape Vincent–Pt. Peninsula; Robert Moses SP; Essex-Westport.

# HOARY REDPOLL

*Carduelis hornemanni*

Interspersed within a group of Common Redpolls, you might see a bird that has noticeably less streaking and is lighter in color. As you compare the ambiguous field marks used to distinguish Hoary Redpolls from Common Redpolls, you may be drawn into the "Great Redpoll Debate" with fellow birders. Some say the only way to differentiate the two species is to look at the amount of streaking on the rump: Hoary Redpolls have very little and Common Redpolls are heavily streaked. • Hoary Redpolls are well adapted to life in cold northern climates. They possess a special pouch in the esophagus, the esophageal diverticulum, which allows them to store greater quantities of energy-rich seeds than they are able to digest at one time. Even so, when seed crops fail or icy winds become intolerably cold, Hoary Redpolls will move south, where they occasionally "irrupt" every few years. • This bird's scientific name honors Jens Wilken Hornemann, one of Denmark's leading botanists, who helped organize an expedition to Greenland, where the first scientific specimen of this bird was collected.

*nonbreeding*

**Status:** very rare winter visitor from November to April; invariably occurs with Common Redpolls.
**Habitat:** open fields, meadows, roadsides, utility power lines, railroads, forest edges; backyards with feeders.
**Nesting:** does not nest in NY.
**Feeding:** gleans the ground, snow and vegetation for seeds and buds; occasionally visits feeders in winter.
**Voice:** song is a twittering series of trills; calls are a soft *chit-chit-chit-chit* and a faint *swe-eet;* indistinguishable from the Common Redpoll's songs and calls.
**Similar Species:** *Common Redpoll* (p. 351): streaked rump, sides, flanks and undertail coverts; generally darker and slimmer overall. *Pine Siskin* (p. 353): heavily streaked overall; yellow highlights on wings and tail.
**Best Sites:** Cape Vincent–Pt. Peninsula; Robert Moses SP; Essex-Westport.

**ID:** red forecrown; black "chin"; yellowish bill; frosty white plumage overall; lightly streaked upperparts, except for unstreaked rump; unstreaked underparts (flanks may have faint streaking); notched tail. *Male:* pinkish-tinged breast. *Female:* white to light gray breast.
**Size:** *L* 5–5½; *W* 9 in.

# PINE SISKIN
*Carduelis pinus*

Y<sup></sup>ou can spend days, weeks or even months in pursuit of Pine Siskins, only to meet with frustration, aching feet and a sore, crimped neck. The best way to meet these birds is to set up a finch feeder filled with black niger seed in your backyard and wait for them to appear. If the feeder is in the right location, you can expect your backyard to be visited by Pine Siskins much of the year, but particularly in winter. • Tight flocks of these gregarious birds are frequently heard before they are seen. Once you recognize their characteristic rising *zzzreeeee* calls and boisterous chatter, you can confirm the presence of these finches simply by listening. • Aside from the Pine Siskin's occasional flashes of yellow, its wardrobe is drab and sparrowlike. For those who get to know it, this bird's behavior reveals a gentle nature that radiates the playfulness and enthusiasm of a goldfinch.

**ID:** heavily streaked under-parts; yellow high-lights at base of tail feathers and on wings (easily seen in flight); dull wing bars; darker, heavily streaked upperparts; slightly forked tail; indistinct facial pattern.
**Size:** *L* 4½–5½ in; *W* 9 in.
**Status:** uncommon breeder; unpredictable, but occurs most often in the Adirondacks from April to June; irruptive visitor from September to May anywhere in the state.
**Habitat:** *Breeding:* coniferous and mixed forests; urban and rural ornamental and shade trees. *Winter:* coniferous and mixed forests, forest edges, meadows, roadsides, agricultural fields and backyards with feeders.

**Nesting:** usually loosely colonial; in a conifer; female builds a loose cup nest of twigs, grass and rootlets; female incubates 3–5 darkly dotted, pale blue eggs for about 13 days.
**Feeding:** gleans the ground and vegetation for seeds (especially thistle seeds), buds and some insects; attracted to road salts, mineral licks and ashes; regularly visits feeders.
**Voice:** song is a variable, bubbly mix of squeaky, raspy, metallic notes, sometimes resembling a jerky laugh; call is a buzzy, rising *zzzreeeee*.
**Similar Species:** *Common Redpoll* (p. 351) and *Hoary Redpoll* (p. 352): red forecrowns; lack yellow on wings and tail. *Purple Finch* (p. 347) and *House Finch* (p. 348): females have thicker bills and no yellow on wings or tail. *Sparrows* (pp. 312–31): all lack yellow on wings and tail.
**Best Sites:** Hamlin Beach SP; Cape Vincent–Pt. Peninsula; Paul Smiths Visitor Interpretive Center (Adirondack Park); Essex-Westport; Jones Beach SP.

# AMERICAN GOLDFINCH

*Carduelis tristis*

American Goldfinches are bright, cheery songbirds that are commonly seen in weedy fields, along roadsides and among backyard shrubs throughout summer and fall. Goldfinches seem to delight in perching upon late-summer thistle heads as they search for seeds to feed their offspring. It's hard to miss their familiar, jubilant *po-ta-to-chip* calls as they flutter over parks and gardens with their distinctive, undulating flight style. • The American Goldfinch is one of the latest songbird breeders, nesting in late summer and early fall. • It is enjoyable to observe a flock of goldfinches raining down to ground level to poke and prod the heads of dandelions. These birds can look quite comical as they attempt to step down on the flower stems to reach the crowning seeds.

*breeding*

**Habitat:** weedy fields, woodland edges, meadows, riparian areas, parks and gardens.

**Nesting:** in a deciduous shrub or tree, often in a hawthorn, serviceberry or sapling maple; female builds a compact cup nest of plant fibers, grass and spider silk; female incubates 4–6 pale bluish white eggs for 12–14 days.

**Feeding:** gleans vegetation for seeds, primarily thistle, birch and alder, as well as for insects and berries; commonly visits feeders.

**Voice:** song is a long, varied series of trills, twitters, warbles and hissing notes; calls include *po-ta-to-chip* or *per-chic-or-ee*, often delivered in flight, and a whistled *dear-me, see-me.*

**Similar Species:** *Evening Grosbeak* (p. 355): much larger; massive bill; lacks black forehead. *Yellow Warbler* (p. 281): thin bill; lacks black forehead and wings.

**Best Sites:** Beaver Meadow Nature Center; Braddock Bay; Five Rivers Environmental Education Center; Bear Mountain SP; Jones Beach SP.

**ID:** *Breeding male:* black "cap" (extends onto forehead), wings and tail; bright yellow body; white wing bars, undertail coverts and tail base; orange bill and legs. *Nonbreeding male:* olive brown back; yellow-tinged head; gray underparts. *Female:* yellow green upperparts and belly; yellow throat and breast.

**Size:** *L* 4½–5½ in; *W* 9 in.

**Status:** occurs year-round; common breeder from June to September; very common migrant from March to April and from October to November; common to abundant in winter.

# EVENING GROSBEAK

*Coccothraustes vespertinus*

One chilly winter day, a flock of Evening Grosbeaks descends unannounced upon your backyard bird feeder filled with sunflower seeds. You watch the stunning gold-and-black grosbeaks with delight, but soon come to realize that these birds are both an aesthetic blessing and a financial curse. Evening Grosbeaks will eat great quantities of expensive birdseed, then suddenly disappear in late winter. These birds are generally encountered every two to three years in large, wintering flocks. • The massive bill of this seed eater is difficult to ignore. In French, *gros bec* means "large beak," and any seasoned bird bander will tell you that the Evening Grosbeak's bill can exert an incredible force per unit area—it may be the most powerful bill of any North American bird. • It was once thought that the Evening Grosbeak sang only in the evening, a fact that is reflected in both its common and scientific names (*vespertinus* is Latin for "of the evening").

**ID:** massive, pale, conical bill; black wings and tail; broad, white wing patches. *Male:* black crown; bright yellow "eyebrow" and forehead band; dark brown head gradually fades into golden yellow belly and lower back. *Female:* gray head and upper back; yellow-tinged underparts; white undertail coverts.

**Size:** *L* 7–8½ in; *W* 14 in.

**Status:** locally common breeder from May to July in the Adirondacks; irregular in winter with large flocks moving from place to place.

**Habitat:** *Breeding:* coniferous and mixed forests and woodlands; occasionally deciduous woodlands, suburban parks and orchards. *Winter:* coniferous, mixed and deciduous forests and woodlands; parks and gardens with feeders.

**Nesting:** in a conifer; female builds a flimsy cup nest of twigs and lines it with rootlets, fine grass, plant fibers, moss and pine needles; female incubates 3–4 darkly blotched and scrawled, pale blue to blue green eggs for 11–14 days.

**Feeding:** gleans the ground and vegetation for seeds, buds and berries; also eats insects and licks mineral-rich soil; often visits feeders for sunflower seeds.

**Voice:** song is a wandering, halting warble; call is a loud, sharp *clee-ip* or a ringing *peeer*.

**Similar Species:** *American Goldfinch* (p. 354): much smaller; small bill; smaller wing bars; male has black "cap." *Pine Grosbeak* (p. 346): female is gray overall with black bill and smaller wing bars.

**Best Sites:** Paul Smiths Visitor Interpretive Center (Adirondack Park); Chubb River Swamp; Essex-Westport.

355

# HOUSE SPARROW

*Passer domesticus*

For most of us, the House Sparrow is the first bird we meet and recognize in our youth. Although it is one of our most abundant and conspicuous birds, many generations of House Sparrows live out their lives within our backyards with few of us ever knowing much about this omnipresent neighbor. • House Sparrows were introduced to North America in the 1850s around Brooklyn, as part of a plan to control the numbers of insects that were damaging grain and cereal crops. Contrary to popular opinion at the time, this sparrow's diet is largely vegetarian, so its impact on crop pests proved to be minimal. Since then, this Eurasian sparrow has managed to colonize most populated areas on the continent, and has benefited greatly from close association with humans. Unfortunately, its aggressive behavior has helped it to usurp territory from many native bird species, especially in rural habitats. • House Sparrows are not closely related to the other North American sparrows, but belong to the family of Old World Sparrows or "Weaver Finches."

**ID:** *Breeding male:* gray crown; black "bib" and bill; chestnut nape; light gray "cheek"; white wing bar; dark, mottled upperparts; gray underparts. *Nonbreeding male:* smaller black "bib"; pale bill. *Female:* plain gray brown overall; buffy "eyebrow"; streaked upperparts; indistinct facial pattern; grayish, unstreaked underparts.
**Size:** *L* 6–6½ in; *W* 9½ in.
**Status:** very common year-round resident, mostly associated with human-altered environments, such as cities, suburbs and farms.
**Habitat:** townsites, urban and suburban areas, farmyards and agricultural areas, railroad yards and other developed areas; absent from undeveloped and heavily wooded areas.
**Nesting:** often communal; in a human-made structure, ornamental shrub or natural cavity; pair builds a large, dome-shaped nest of grass, twigs, plant fibers and litter; pair incubates 4–6 gray-speckled, whitish to greenish white eggs for 10–13 days.
**Feeding:** gleans the ground and vegetation for seeds, insects and fruit; frequently visits feeders for seeds.
**Voice:** song is a plain, familiar *cheep-cheep-cheep-cheep;* call is a short *chill-up.*
**Similar Species:** female is distinctively drab with light stripe over eye; most native sparrows have streaked breasts or streaked or reddish "caps."
**Best Sites:** widespread in cities, suburbs, parks and farms.

# OCCASIONAL BIRD SPECIES

The following is a selection of 40 accidental and casual species that occur in New York State. For a full listing of these species, please refer to the checklist (pp. 370–74).

## ROSS'S GOOSE
*Chen rossii*

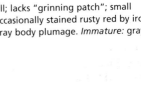

This diminutive "Snow Goose look-alike" first occurred in New York 20 years ago. Birders have since become more vigilant and are seeing these small geese with more regularity, usually in spring and almost always with Snow Geese.

**ID:** white overall; black wing tips; dark pink feet and bill; lacks "grinning patch"; small bluish or greenish "warts" on base of bill; plumage is occasionally stained rusty red by iron in the water. *Blue morph:* very rare; white head; blue gray body plumage. *Immature:* gray plumage; dark bill and feet.
**Size:** *L* 21–26 in; *W* 3¾ ft.

## EARED GREBE
*Podiceps nigricollis*

*nonbreeding*

A rare but regular winter visitor, this western diver is seen annually on the Great Lakes or the Atlantic Coast from November to April. Winter-plumaged Horned Grebes look very similar, and the Eared Grebe can be easily overlooked.

**ID:** thin, all-dark bill with slightly uptilted lower mandible. *Breeding:* thin, black neck, "cheek," forehead and back; reddish flanks; gold "ear" tufts; slightly raised black crown; red eyes. *Nonbreeding:* dark back, head and neck with some white on foreneck, "chin" and behind ear; fluffy white hind end.
**Size:** *L* 12–14 in; *W* 16 in.

## MANX SHEARWATER
*Puffinus puffinus*

There are records for this offshore "tubenose" in every month, though it is observed mostly from May to October. It has been seen on occasion from Long Island's south shore beaches.

**ID:** dark upperparts; white underparts; white wing linings; white on throat extends to white crescent behind eye; long, slender bill with hooked tip. *In flight:* white underparts; dark wing border; white undertail coverts; stiff-winged, flap-and-glide flight.
**Size:** *L* 12–15 in; *W* 30–35 in.

## LEACH'S STORM-PETREL
*Oceanodroma leucorhoa*

Breeding as close as Massachusetts, this small oceanic wanderer is seen only rarely offshore from May to November, usually after storms. The few inland records are of hurricane-driven birds.

**ID:** white rump patch often partially divided in half by dark, narrow band; long, forked tail. *In flight:* narrow, pointed wings with sharp bend at "wrist"; distinctive, erratic, zigzagging flight with alternating flaps and glides.
**Size:** *L* 7½–9 in; *W* 19 in.

# BROWN PELICAN
*Pelecanus occidentalis*

*breeding*

Northward expansion of this large, unmistakable bird has made this species an almost annual visitor along Long Island's south shore in summer. This bird is usually seen singly, but may appear in small groups of a dozen or more birds. Numbers in the Great Lakes region can be astonishing.

**ID:** grayish brown body; very large bill. *Breeding:* yellow head; white foreneck; dark brown nape. *Nonbreeding:* white neck; yellow wash on head; pale gray brown pouch. *1st-year:* uniformly dusky; buff-tipped head and neck contrast with pale underparts; lacks upperwing contrast of adult; requires several years to reach maturity.
**Size:** *L* 4 ft; *W* 7 ft.

# SWAINSON'S HAWK
*Buteo swainsoni*

Perhaps as a result of the increasing popularity of hawk watching, this rare vagrant from the West is being seen more often in our state. Most sightings are of light-morph birds, and this buteo occurs most often in April and May. Half of the spring records are from Braddock Bay.

**ID:** *Light morph:* dark "bib"; white belly; white wing linings contrast with dark flight feathers. *Dark morph:* dark overall; brown wing linings blend with flight feathers. *In flight:* long, pointed wings; narrowly banded tail; dark flight feathers; holds wings in a shallow "V."
**Size:** *L* 19–22 in; *W* 4½ ft.

*light morph*

# GYRFALCON
*Falco rusticolus*

*gray morph*

This species is a rare winter visitor, and most records are from the Great Lakes and Lake Champlain regions. All three color morphs, gray, brown and white, have been seen, with white being the rarest. When a Gyrfalcon shows up in December, it often stays into March. Take care when identifying this bird because of possible confusion with the Peregrine Falcon. Escaped falconers' birds are also a possibility.

**ID:** long tail extends beyond wing tips when perched; tail may be barred or unbarred. *Gray morph:* dark gray upperparts; streaking on white underparts. *Brown morph:* dark brown upperparts; streaking on white underparts. *White morph:* pure white head, breast and rump; white back and wings have dark flecking and barring. *Immature:* darker and more heavily streaked than adult; gray (rather than yellow) feet and cere.
**Size:** *Male: L* 20–22 in; *W* 4 ft. *Female: L* 22–25 in; *W* 4½ ft.

# BLACK RAIL
*Laterallus jamaicensis*

This secretive, sparrow-sized rail bred sparingly in Long Island salt marshes in the 1930s. Rediscovered in one of these marshes in the 1960s, the species is believed to be breeding again in small numbers in New York. This bird is more likely to be heard than seen, and because it is nocturnal and its habitat is full of ticks and mosquitoes, few birders will pursue it.

**ID:** short, black bill; small, stocky body; large feet; blackish upperparts with white flecking; chestnut nape; dark grayish black underparts with white barring on flanks; red eyes.
**Size:** *L* 6 in; *W* 9 in.

# KING RAIL
*Rallus elegans*

This large rail favors freshwater marshes and its population has declined greatly in its northern range. It may still breed in our state, as evidenced by the two or three reports each year from western New York, most often from Iroquois NWR. It is occasionally found on Christmas bird counts in southeastern New York.

**ID:** long, slightly downcurved bill; buff or tawny edges on black back feathers; rufous shoulders and underparts; strongly barred, black-and-white flanks; grayish brown "cheek." *Immature:* similar plumage patterning with lighter, washed-out colors.
**Size:** *L* 15 in; *W* 20 in.

# BLACK-NECKED STILT
*Himantopus mexicanus*

This unmistakable black-and-white wader with long, bubblegum-colored legs is a rare vagrant that turns up nearly every year, most often from April to July. Most sighting are on Long Island, not surprising since this species has recently begun breeding in New Jersey.

**ID:** very long, pinkish red legs; dark upperparts; clean white underparts; long, straight, needlelike bill; small, white "eyebrow"; male is blacker above than female.
**Size:** *L* 14–15 in; *W* 30 in.

# CURLEW SANDPIPER
*Calidris ferruginea*

One of the rare but regular vagrants from Europe, this sandpiper is most often observed from July to September on the mudflats of Long Island's coastal marshes. The Jamaica Bay Wildlife Refuge accounts for more than half of the state's records.

**ID:** long, black, downcurved bill; black legs; clean white undertail coverts; white rump; bold, white upperwing stripe. *Breeding:* rich chestnut overall; dark mottling on crown and back; female is paler. *Nonbreeding:* pale gray upperparts; darker gray wings; whitish underparts; white "eyebrow"; brownish wash on head.
**Size:** *L* 8–9 in; *W* 18 in.

# RUFF
*Philomachus pugnax*

From May to September, this midsized sandpiper from Eurasia can show up almost anywhere, though Long Island is the most likely locale. Males in breeding plumage are easy to identify, but the much drabber females, called Reeves, take some skill to find in a multispecies flock of shorebirds.

**ID:** plump body; small head; yellow green to orange legs; yellow or black bill; gray brown upperparts. *Breeding male:* black, white or orangy neck ruff, usually flattened, but erected during courtship; dark underparts. *Breeding female:* dark blotches on underparts. *In flight:* thin, white wing stripe; oval, white rump is divided by dark central stripe.

*nonbreeding*

**Size:** *Male: L* 10–12 in; *W* 21 in. *Female: L* 8–10 in; *W* 21 in.

# GREAT SKUA
*Stercorarius skua*

A 1977 taxonomy change confused all previous records that were considered to be of this species. Skuas are far-offshore Atlantic gull relatives, and those seen from fishing boats in late fall and winter are generally assumed to be Great Skuas, a Northern Hemisphere breeder. This bird is not likely to be seen from shore, and few birders venture out to sea in winter.

**ID:** pale streaking on dark brown upperparts; pale brown underparts; dark, hooked bill. *In flight:* white patch on upperwing.
**Size:** *L* 22 in; *W* 4½ ft.

# SOUTH POLAR SKUA
*Stercorarius maccormicki*

Since the 1977 taxonomic split, which separated the South Polar Skua from the Great Skua, birders have been much more careful to look for subtle distinguishing characteristics and have documented this Southern Hemisphere breeder in offshore waters in summer. How many sightings there were of this species before its taxonomy was understood is anyone's guess.

**ID:** white wing patch; dark, hooked bill. *Dark morph:* dark gray brown overall; yellowish nape. *Light morph:* pale body; pale streaking on dark wings.
**Size:** *L* 21 in; *W* 4¼ ft.

*dark morph*

# LONG-TAILED JAEGER
*Stercorarius longicaudus*

This High Arctic skua, as Europeans call jaegers, is a rare migrant in offshore waters in fall and spring, with most records in May, June and September. It is occasionally seen from Great Lakes vantage points during fall migration.

**ID:** long central tail feathers; dark "cap"; clean white throat and belly; yellow "collar"; gray upperparts; dark flight feathers. *Juvenile:* dark "chin" and throat; dark barring on sides, flanks and rump; mottled underwing linings; brown upperparts; short, rounded tail streamers.
**Size:** *L* 20–23 in; *W* 3¼ ft.

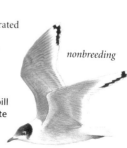

*light morph breeding*

# FRANKLIN'S GULL
*Larus pipixcan*

The one or two reports each year of this species are concentrated in the Great Lakes region in fall, most often in October and November. Known as "Prairie Dove" in our continent's mid-section, this gull is most apt to be seen in our region in the Niagara Gorge.

*nonbreeding*

**ID:** gray mantle; white underparts; full or partial "hood"; broken, white eye ring. *Breeding:* black head; orange red bill and legs; breast may have pinkish tinge. *Nonbreeding:* white on face and throat; black "hood." *In flight:* black crescent through white wing tips.
**Size:** *L* 13–15 in; *W* 3 ft.

# CALIFORNIA GULL
*Larus californicus*

A very rare vagrant from the West, this species was first recorded in our state 25 years ago in southwestern New York. As many as three individuals show up each winter in the Niagara region. It is a careful observer that can pick one out of a large flock of very similar Herring Gulls.

**ID:** dark eyes. *Breeding:* clean white head; narrow, red eye ring. *Nonbreeding:* dark gray mantle; white spots on black wing tips; greenish gray legs and feet; 1 red and 1 black spot on lower mandible. *1st-winter:* dark brown, becoming paler on underparts; black-tipped, pink bill; dull pink legs; long wing tips.
**Size:** *L* 18–20 in; *W* 4–4½ ft in.

*nonbreeding*

# THAYER'S GULL
*Larus thayeri*

Currently considered a valid species, this gull is sometimes considered a subspecies of either the Herring Gull or the Iceland Gull. Usually reported from December through February, it takes a great deal of skill (or a good imagination) to separate this visitor from the High Arctic from the thousands of other gulls at a landfill or at the most reliable site, the Niagara River.

*nonbreeding*

**ID:** *Nonbreeding:* pink feet; pale gray mantle; dark eyes; red spot near tip of lower mandible; variably heavy "winter streaking" on head, neck and upper breast; black upperwing tips with a few white spots; underwing tip is entirely pale except for dark tips to most outer primaries. *1st-winter:* pale gray brown; slim, all-dark or nearly all-dark bill; primaries slightly darker than upperparts; pale base to outer tail feathers.
**Size:** *L* 22–25 in; *W* 4½ ft.

# IVORY GULL
*Pagophila eburnea*

This species is an extremely rare vagrant from December to January, and reports of immatures outnumber those of adults three to one. Except for the confirmation of several expert birders, the record of an Ivory Gull visiting an inland, suburban birdfeeder and staying for a day eating quickly proffered canned sardines would not have been believed.

**ID:** pure white plumage; black legs; orange-tipped, gray bill. *Immature:* dark face; dark spots on flight feathers.
**Size:** *L* 17 in; *W* 3 ft.

*nonbreeding*

# SANDWICH TERN
*Sterna sandvicensis*

This southern species used to be a rare and irregular visitor to Long Island, almost invariably in summer after tropical storms. Every year through the 1990s, though, this tern was observed from Long Island beaches in summer independent of storms.

**ID:** yellow-tipped, black bill; black legs; deeply forked tail; dark wedge on upperwing primaries; dark border on underwing primaries. *Breeding:* black "cap" with shaggy crest. *Nonbreeding:* white forehead. *Juvenile:* shorter crest; less deeply forked tail; mottled upperparts.
**Size:** *L* 14–16 in; *W* 34 in.

*breeding*

# SOOTY TERN
*Sterna fuscata*

Any time a hurricane travels as far north as New York, birders watch for this oceanic wanderer off Long Island beaches. A rare vagrant that may travel in the eye of a hurricane for long distances, this dark tern has appeared on upstate lakes, reservoirs and rivers.

*breeding*

**ID:** sooty black crown and back; white underparts and throat; black eye line; thin bill; deeply forked black tail with narrow white outer edges. *Immature:* dark brown; white blotches on back and wings; dark sooty brown head, throat and breast.
**Size:** *L* 16 in; *W* 30 in.

# DOVEKIE
*Alle alle*

The "Little Auk" of Europe is a rare winter visitor to far offshore waters from November to March. Most of the onshore and the couple of dozen inland reports were all of birds blown in by very strong nor'easters, mostly in November and December. Long Islanders have found these small alcids in their yards after the strongest of these storms.

*nonbreeding*

**ID:** stocky body; stubby bill; black upperparts with some white on back and trailing edge of wings; white underparts. *Breeding:* black neck and breast. *Nonbreeding:* white throat and breast; black "collar"; black rump.
**Size:** *L* 8 in; *W* 15 in.

# THICK-BILLED MURRE
*Uria lomvia*

This species is a very rare and irregular winter visitor, and most records are from Montauk Point. Take great care in identifying this bird because it is easily confused with the rare Common Murre and the often-seen Razorbill. Individuals that have been sickened by spilled oil at sea are sometimes picked up on beaches in the winter.

*nonbreeding*

**ID:** *Breeding:* black upperparts; white underparts; short, thick, black bill. *Nonbreeding:* white "chin" and throat.
**Size:** *L* 18 in; *W* 28 in.

# NORTHERN HAWK OWL
*Surnia ulula*

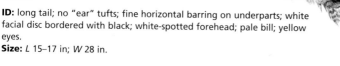

This very rare winter visitor is easily seen because it tends to sit upright on the top of a tree in the middle of open country. Sometimes irruptive and found in a number of places in New York, these owls are most often seen from December through March.

**ID:** long tail; no "ear" tufts; fine horizontal barring on underparts; white facial disc bordered with black; white-spotted forehead; pale bill; yellow eyes.
**Size:** *L* 15–17 in; *W* 28 in.

# GREAT GRAY OWL
*Strix nebulosa*

Sometimes irruptive and totally unpredictable, this large owl is a very rare winter visitor to northern parts of the state. Though sometimes seen only on one day, some individuals have stayed in one locality for weeks.

**ID:** gray plumage; large, rounded head; no "ear" tufts; small yellow eyes; well-defined concentric rings in facial disc; black "chin" bordered by white; long tail.
**Size:** *L* 24–33 in; *W* 4½–5 ft.

# RUFOUS HUMMINGBIRD
*Selasphorus rufus*

Any hummingbird that is seen after the departure of the Ruby-throats in September should be carefully scrutinized. With more feeders being stocked into the fall, some of the western hummingbird species are being observed in the East. There have been several reliable records of this species in the past few years, most from the Metropolitan New York area.

**ID:** long, thin, black bill; mostly rufous tail. *Male:* orange brown back, tail and flanks; iridescent, orange red throat; green crown; white breast and belly; some adult males have green backs. *Female:* green back; red-spotted throat; rufous sides and flanks contrast with white underparts.
**Size:** *L* 3¼–3½ in; *W* 4½ in.

# SAY'S PHOEBE
*Sayornis saya*

One of the mysteries of migration is why some western birds stray eastward in the fall. The Say's Phoebe is one of these. Most observations of this very rare vagrant occur in September and October, though at least one bird has been seen as late as January.

**ID:** apricot buff belly and undertail coverts; dark tail; gray brown breast and upperparts; dark head; no eye ring; very faint wing bars; constantly bobs its tail.
**Size:** *L* 7½ in; *W* 13 in.

# ASH-THROATED FLYCATCHER
*Myiarchus cinerascens*

A very rare vagrant from September to November, this species is apparently being seen with increasing frequency in the eastern U.S. This bird can be easily confused with several related species, so perhaps the increase in Ash-throated Flycatcher sightings is attributable to the array of good field guides available to the modern birder.

**ID:** gray brown upperparts; gray throat and breast; yellow belly and undertail coverts; stout, dark bill; fluffy crown; 2 whitish wing bars; no eye ring; ample, dark brown tail shows some rufous in the webbing.
**Size:** *L* 7–8 in; *W* 12 in.

# WESTERN KINGBIRD
*Tyrannus verticalis*

The Western Kingbird is a rare but regular fall visitor to coastal beaches, with some staying into January. This species is seen almost every year, and sometimes as many as three birds at a time have been observed. There are only a handful of spring records and it is much rarer at upstate locations.

**ID:** gray head and breast; white "chin"; black bill; ashy gray upperparts; dark gray "mask"; concealed, orange red crown; yellow belly and undertail coverts; white outer feathers on square-ended, black tail.
**Size:** *L* 8–9 in; *W* 15–16 in.

# SCISSOR-TAILED FLYCATCHER
*Tyrannus forficatus*

Three-quarters of the 40 or so records of this species are from Long Island, mostly from May to July and from September to November. These rare vagrants are most likely on the move because most sightings are of one-day duration.

**ID:** whitish to grayish head, back and breast; salmon pink underwing linings, flanks and lower underparts; bright pink "wing pits"; dark wings and extremely long outer tail feathers give forked appearance in flight. *Immature:* duller, shorter-tailed version of adult; brownish back.
**Size:** *L* 13 in (male's tail is up to 9 in long); *W* 15 in.

# LOGGERHEAD SHRIKE
*Lanius ludovicianus*

This species is drastically reduced in numbers and now endangered in our state, and the last breeding record in New York was in the late 1980s from the St. Lawrence Plain area. It is still seen very occasionally on Long Island during fall migration and in the Great Lakes Plain region in spring.

**ID:** black tail and wings; gray crown and back; extensive black "mask" extends above bill; dark, hooked bill; white underparts; barred flanks. *In flight:* white wing patches; white-edged tail.
**Size:** *L* 9 in; *W* 12 in.

# CAVE SWALLOW
*Petrochelidon fulva*

Southwestern race

A "be on the watch for" accidental wanderer, this swallow has staged incursions into several northern states in the past couple of years, typically in November. It has recently shown up on the Great Lakes shore and on Long Island. There are two subspecies, a Caribbean and a Southwestern, and careful observation is needed to determine this swallow's origin.

**ID:** stubbier than other swallows; cinnamon forehead, throat, nape, and rump; dark blue crown and back; dark wings; buffy flanks; whitish underparts; squared-off tail; Caribbean subspecies is darker than Southwestern.
**Size:** *L* 5½ in; *W* 13 in.

# NORTHERN WHEATEAR
*Oenanthe oenanthe*

A rare vagrant and apparently increasing, this tundra nester may show up anywhere in the state, most likely in the fall. September accounts for nearly two-thirds of all our records. This is an open-country bird and appears at home on beaches and open fields.

**ID:** white rump and tail base; pale cream belly. *Breeding male:* gray "cap," nape and back; thick, black eye line; cinnamon breast; black wings and tail tip. *Female* and *nonbreeding male:* gray brown "cap," nape and back; dark brown wings and tail tip.
**Size:** *L* 6 in; *W* 12 in.

*breeding*

# VARIED THRUSH
*Ixoreus naevius*

The popularity of bird feeding may account for most of our records of this species—almost all of the 70 or so records are from backyard feeders in December and January. This rare vagrant is a relative of the American Robin and is found primarily in the Pacific Northwest. Listening to the birding hotlines is the best way to find out where this bird can be seen.

**ID:** dark upperparts; orange "eyebrow"; orange throat and belly; 2 orange wing bars. *Male:* black breast band; deep blue black upperparts. *Female:* similar to male but with muted colors; brown upperparts; fainter breast band.
**Size:** *L* 9½ in; *W* 16 in.

# CONNECTICUT WARBLER
*Oporornis agilis*

A notorious skulker, this rare migrant may be more common than our recorded sightings indicate. The several reports each August and September are from western New York and Long Island, while most of the few reported spring migrants are seen west of Syracuse. More people see these birds caught in banding nets than see them in their dense, brushy habitat.

*breeding*

**ID:** yellow underparts; olive green upperparts; long undertail coverts make tail look short; bold, white eye ring; pink legs; longish bill. *Breeding male:* blue gray "hood." *Female:* gray brown "hood"; light gray throat.
**Size:** *L* 5–6 in; *W* 9 in.

# LARK SPARROW
*Chondestes grammacus*

Long Island's barrier beaches mirror this open-country sparrow's home, and better than 90 percent of this rare fall visitor's appearances have been made from August to October on Long Island. A few birds have also overwintered in this relatively mild marine climate.

**ID:** distinctive "helmet," white throat, "eyebrow" and crown stripe with a few black lines on chestnut red head; unstreaked, pale breast with dark central spot; rounded tail with white corners; soft brown, mottled back and wings.
**Size:** *L* 6 in; *W* 11 in.

# NELSON'S SHARP-TAILED SPARROW
*Ammodramus nelsoni*

Sharp-tailed Sparrow taxonomy has been confused for a long time, with at least five named subspecies now classified into two species. The Nelson's Sharp-tailed Sparrow is an uncommon fall migrant to both inland freshwater marshes and coastal salt marshes. From August to October, the inland races are seen along the Great Lakes Plain, while the maritime race moves along the coast. A few of these sparrows winter on Long Island alongside the Saltmarsh Sharp-tailed Sparrow.

**ID:** buff orange face, breast, sides and flanks; gray "cheek," central crown stripe and nape; dark line behind eye; light streaking on sides and flanks; white stripes on dark back; white to light buff throat; white belly.
**Size:** *L* 5–6 in; *W* 7 in.

# HARRIS'S SPARROW
*Zonotrichia querula*

Nesting in north-central Canada and wintering on the southern Great Plains, this rare vagrant is truly lost in New York. This species is most often seen at backyard feeders from October to May, and about one-third of these handsome sparrows stay the winter.

**ID:** *Breeding:* black crown, throat and "bib"; gray face; white under-parts; pink orange bill; black streaks on flanks; mottled upperparts. *Nonbreeding:* brown face; buff flanks.
**Size:** *L* 7–8 in; *W* 10–11 in.

*nonbreeding*

# WESTERN MEADOWLARK
*Sturnella neglecta*

*breeding*

A very rare spring and summer visitor to western New York, this species can only be distinguished from the Eastern Meadowlark by its voice. It's no surprise, then, that most reliable reports are from April to July, when the birds are singing. Most of the almost annual occurrences are from the Great Lakes Plain area east to Oswego and Onondaga Counties.

**ID:** yellow underparts; broad, black "necklace"; mottled brown upperparts; short, wide tail with white outer tail feathers; long, pinkish legs; yellow lores; brown crown stripes and eye line border pale "eyebrow"; black streaking on white flanks; long, sharp bill.
**Size:** *L* 8–10 in; *W* 14–15 in.

# YELLOW-HEADED BLACKBIRD
*Xanthocephalus xanthocephalus*

This beautiful, lemon-fronted blackbird is a rare vagrant that can show up anywhere and anytime. The hundred or so docu-mented occurrences are evenly divided between downstate and upstate areas, and this bird has been seen in all seasons, with fewer sightings in summer than the rest of the year. A marsh bird in its usual range, it shows up in suburban backyards with amazing regularity.

**ID:** *Male:* yellow head and breast; all-blackish body; white wing patches; black lores; stout, sharply pointed, black bill; long tail. *Female:* dusky brown overall; dingy yellow breast, throat and "eyebrow"; hints of yellow in face.
**Size:** *L* 8–11 in; *W* 15 in.

# SELECT REFERENCES

American Ornithologists' Union. 1998. *Check-list of North American Birds.* 7th ed. (and its supplements). American Ornithologists' Union, Washington, D.C.

Andrle, Robert F., and Janet R. Carroll. 1988. *The Atlas of Breeding Birds in New York State.* Cornell University Press, Ithaca, NY.

Choate, E.A. 1985. *The Dictionary of American Bird Names.* Rev. ed. Harvard Common Press, Cambridge, MA.

Cox, Randall T. 1996. *Birder's Dictionary.* Falcon Publishing, Inc., Helena, MT.

Drennan, Susan Roney. 1981. *Where to Find Birds in New York State.* Syracuse University Press, Syracuse, NY.

Kaufman, K. 1996. *Lives of North American Birds.* Houghton Mifflin Co., Boston.

Kaufman, K. 2000. *Birds of North America.* Houghton Mifflin Co., New York.

Levine, Emanuel. 1998. *Bull's Birds of New York.* Cornell University Press, Ithaca, NY.

National Geographic Society. 1999. *Field Guide to the Birds of North America.* 3rd ed. National Geographic Society, Washington, D.C.

Sibley, D.A. 2000. *National Audubon Society: The Sibley Guide to Bird Life and Behavior.* Alfred A. Knopf, New York.

Sibley, D.A. 2000. *National Audubon Society: The Sibley Guide to Birds.* Alfred A. Knopf, New York.

Sibley, D.A. 2002. *Sibley's Birding Basics.* Alfred A. Knopf, New York.

*Brown Pelican*

# GLOSSARY

**accipiter:** a forest hawk (genus *Accipiter*), characterized by a long tail and short, rounded wings; feeds mostly on birds.

**brood:** *n.* a family of young from one hatching; *v.* to incubate eggs.

**brood parasite:** a bird that lays its eggs in other birds' nests.

**buteo:** a high-soaring hawk (genus *Buteo*), characterized by broad wings and a short, wide tail; feeds mostly on small mammals and other land animals.

**cere:** a fleshy area at the base of the bill that contains the nostrils.

**clutch:** the number of eggs laid by the female at one time.

**dabbling:** a foraging technique used by some ducks, in which the head and neck are submerged but the body and tail remain on the water's surface; dabbling ducks can usually walk easily on land, can take off without running and have brightly colored speculums.

**diurnal:** most active during the day.

**"eclipse" plumage:** a cryptic plumage, similar to that of females, worn by some male ducks in fall when they molt their flight feathers and consequently are unable to fly.

**endangered:** a species that is facing extirpation or extinction in all or part of its range.

**extinct:** a species that no longer exists.

**extirpated:** a species that no longer exists in the wild in a particular region but occurs elsewhere.

**flushing:** when frightened birds explode into flight in response to a disturbance.

**flycatching:** a feeding behavior in which the bird leaves a perch, snatches an insect in midair and returns to the same perch; also known as "hawking" or "sallying."

**hawking:** attempting to capture insects through aerial pursuit.

**irruption:** a sporadic mass migration of birds into an unusual range.

**kettle:** a large concentration of hawks, usually seen during migration.

**lek:** a place where males gather to display for females in the spring.

**mantle:** the area of the body that includes the back and upper sides of the wings.

**molt:** the periodic shedding and regrowth of worn feathers (often twice a year).

**nocturnal:** most active at night.

**peep:** a sandpiper of the *Calidris* genus.

**pelagic:** inhabiting or occurring on the open ocean.

**polyandry:** a mating strategy in which one female breeds with many males.

**polygyny:** a mating strategy in which one male breeds with many females.

**precocial:** a bird that is relatively well developed at hatching; precocial birds usually have open eyes, extensive down and are fairly mobile.

**primaries:** the outermost flight feathers of a bird's wing.

**raft:** a gathering of birds resting on the water.

**raptor:** a carnivorous (meat-eating) bird; includes eagles, hawks, falcons and owls.

**riparian:** habitat along rivers or streams.

**sexual dimorphism:** a difference in plumage, size or other characteristics between males and females of the same species.

**special concern:** a species that has characteristics that make it particularly sensitive to human activities or disturbance, requires a very specific or unique habitat or whose status is such that it requires careful monitoring.

**speculum:** a brightly colored patch on the wings of many dabbling ducks.

**stage:** to gather in one place during migration, usually when birds are flightless or partly flightless during molting.

**stoop:** a steep dive through the air, usually performed by birds of prey while foraging or during courtship displays.

**syrinx:** a bird's voice organ.

**taxonomy:** the system of classification of animals and plants.

**thistle feeder:** a feeder that dispenses thistle (niger) seed; especially attractive to finches.

**threatened:** a species likely to become endangered in the near future in all or part of its range.

**understory:** the shrub or thicket layer beneath a canopy of trees.

**vagrant:** a bird that has wandered outside its normal migration range.

**vent:** the single opening for excretion of uric acid and other wastes and for sexual reproduction; also known as the "cloaca."

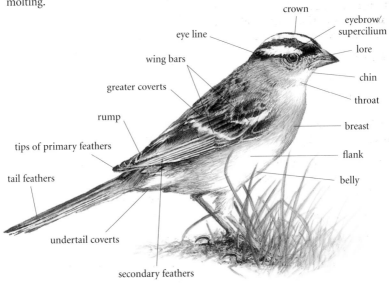

crown
eyebrow/supercilium
eye line
lore
wing bars
chin
greater coverts
throat
rump
breast
tips of primary feathers
flank
tail feathers
belly
undertail coverts
secondary feathers

# CHECKLIST

The following checklist contains 460 species of birds that have been officially recorded in New York State. Species are grouped by family and listed in taxonomic order in accordance with the A.O.U. *Check-list of North American Birds* (7th ed.) and its supplements.

Accidental and casual species (those that are not seen on a yearly basis) are listed in *italics*. In addition, the following risk categories are also noted: extinct or extirpated (ex), endangered (en), threatened (th) and special concern (sc). We wish to thank the New York State Ornithological Association for their kind assistance in providing the information for this checklist.

## Waterfowl (Anatidae)
- ❏ *Fulvous Whistling-Duck*
- ❏ Greater White-fronted Goose
- ❏ Snow Goose
- ❏ *Ross's Goose*
- ☑ Canada Goose
- ❏ Brant
- ❏ *Barnacle Goose*
- ❏ Mute Swan
- ❏ Tundra Swan
- ❏ Wood Duck
- ❏ Gadwall
- ❏ Eurasian Wigeon
- ❏ American Wigeon
- ❏ American Black Duck
- ☑ Mallard
- ❏ Blue-winged Teal
- ❏ *Cinnamon Teal*
- ❏ Northern Shoveler
- ❏ Northern Pintail
- ❏ Green-winged Teal
- ❏ Canvasback
- ❏ Redhead
- ❏ Ring-necked Duck
- ❏ Tufted Duck
- ❏ Greater Scaup
- ❏ Lesser Scaup
- ❏ King Eider
- ❏ Common Eider
- ❏ Harlequin Duck
- ❏ *Labrador Duck (ex)*
- ❏ Surf Scoter
- ❏ White-winged Scoter
- ❏ Black Scoter
- ❏ Long-tailed Duck
- ❏ Bufflehead
- ❏ Common Goldeneye
- ❏ Barrow's Goldeneye
- ❏ *Smew*
- ❏ Hooded Merganser
- ❏ Common Merganser
- ❏ Red-breasted Merganser
- ❏ Ruddy Duck

## Grouse & Allies (Phasianidae)
- ❏ Gray Partridge
- ❏ Ring-necked Pheasant
- ❏ Ruffed Grouse
- ❏ Spruce Grouse (en)
- ❏ *Greater Prairie-Chicken (ex)*
- ☑ Wild Turkey

## New World Quail (Odontophoridae)
- ❏ Northern Bobwhite

## Loons (Gaviidae)
- ❏ Red-throated Loon
- ❏ *Pacific Loon*
- ❏ Common Loon (sc)
- ❏ *Yellow-billed Loon*

## Grebes (Podicipedidae)
- ❏ Pied-billed Grebe (th)
- ❏ Horned Grebe
- ❏ Red-necked Grebe
- ❏ *Eared Grebe*
- ❏ *Western Grebe*

## Albatrosses (Diomedeidae)
- ❏ *Yellow-nosed Albatross*

## Petrels & Shearwaters (Procellariidae)
- ❏ Northern Fulmar
- ❏ *Herald Petrel*
- ❏ *Mottled Petrel*
- ❏ *Black-capped Petrel*
- ❏ Cory's Shearwater
- ❏ Greater Shearwater
- ❏ Sooty Shearwater
- ❏ *Manx Shearwater*
- ❏ *Audubon's Shearwater*

## Storm-Petrels (Hydrobatidae)
- ❏ Wilson's Storm-Petrel
- ❏ *White-faced Storm-Petrel*
- ❏ *Leach's Storm-Petrel*

## Tropicbirds (Phaethontidae)
- ❏ *White-tailed Tropicbird*
- ❏ *Red-billed Tropicbird*

## Gannets & Boobies (Sulidae)
- ❏ *Brown Booby*
- ❏ Northern Gannet

## Pelicans (Pelecanidae)
- ❏ American White Pelican
- ❏ *Brown Pelican*

## Cormorants (Phalacrocoracidae)
- ❏ Double-crested Cormorant

❏ Great Cormorant

## Darters (Anhingidae)
❏ *Anhinga*

## Frigatebirds (Fregatidae)
❏ *Magnificent Frigatebird*

## Herons (Ardeidae)
❏ American Bittern (sc)
☑ Least Bittern (th)
☑ Great Blue Heron
❏ Great Egret
❏ Snowy Egret
❏ Little Blue Heron
❏ Tricolored Heron
❏ *Reddish Egret*
❏ Cattle Egret
❏ Green Heron
❏ Black-crowned Night-Heron
❏ Yellow-crowned Night-Heron

## Ibises (Threskiornithidae)
❏ *White Ibis*
❏ Glossy Ibis
❏ *White-face Ibis*
❏ *Roseate Spoonbill*

## Storks (Ciconiidae)
❏ *Wood Stork*

## Vultures (Cathartidae)
☑ Black Vulture
☑ Turkey Vulture

## Kites, Hawks & Eagles (Accipetridae)
❏ Osprey (sc)
❏ *Swallow-tailed Kite*
❏ *White-tailed Kite*
❏ *Mississippi Kite*
❏ Bald Eagle (th)
❏ Northern Harrier (th)
☑ Sharp-shinned Hawk (sc)
❏ Cooper's Hawk (sc)

❏ Northern Goshawk (sc)
❏ Red-shouldered Hawk (sc)
❏ Broad-winged Hawk
❏ *Swainson's Hawk*
❏ Red-tailed Hawk
❏ Rough-legged Hawk
❏ Golden Eagle (en)

## Falcons (Falconidae)
❏ American Kestrel
❏ Merlin
❏ *Gyrfalcon*
❏ Peregrine Falcon (en)

## Rails, Gallinules & Coots (Rallidae)
❏ *Yellow Rail*
❏ *Black Rail (en)*
❏ *Corn Crake*
❏ Clapper Rail
❏ *King Rail (th)*
❏ Virginia Rail
❏ Sora
❏ *Purple Gallinule*
❏ *Azure Gallinule*
❏ Common Moorhen
❏ American Coot

## Cranes (Gruidae)
❏ Sandhill Crane

## Plovers (Charadriidae)
❏ *Northern Lapwing*
❏ Black-bellied Plover
❏ American Golden-Plover
❏ *Wilson's Plover*
❏ Semipalmated Plover
❏ Piping Plover (en)
❏ Killdeer

## Oystercatchers (Haematopodidae)
❏ American Oystercatcher

## Stilts & Avocets (Recurvirostridae)
❏ *Black-necked Stilt*

❏ American Avocet

## Sandpipers & Allies (Scolopacidae)
❏ Greater Yellowlegs
❏ Lesser Yellowlegs
❏ *Spotted Redshank*
❏ *Wood Sandpiper*
❏ Solitary Sandpiper
❏ Willet
❏ Spotted Sandpiper
❏ Upland Sandpiper (th)
❏ *Eskimo Curlew (ex)*
❏ Whimbrel
❏ *Eurasian Curlew*
❏ *Long-billed Curlew*
❏ *Black-tailed Godwit*
❏ Hudsonian Godwit
❏ *Bar-tailed Godwit*
❏ Marbled Godwit
❏ Ruddy Turnstone
❏ Red Knot
❏ Sanderling
❏ Semipalmated Sandpiper
❏ Western Sandpiper
❏ *Red-necked Stint*
❏ *Little Stint*
❏ Least Sandpiper
❏ White-rumped Sandpiper
❏ Baird's Sandpiper
❏ Pectoral Sandpiper
❏ *Sharp-tailed Sandpiper*
❏ Purple Sandpiper
❏ Dunlin
❏ *Curlew Sandpiper*
❏ Stilt Sandpiper
❏ *Broad-billed Sandpiper*
❏ Buff-breasted Sandpiper
❏ *Ruff*
❏ Short-billed Dowitcher
❏ Long-billed Dowitcher
❏ Wilson's Snipe
❏ American Woodcock
❏ Wilson's Phalarope

# CHECKLIST

❏ Red-necked Phalarope
❏ Red Phalarope

**Gulls & Allies (Laridae)**
❏ *Great Skua*
❏ *South Polar Skua*
❏ Pomarine Jaeger
❏ Parasitic Jaeger
❏ *Long-tailed Jaeger*
☑ Laughing Gull
❏ *Franklin's Gull*
❏ Little Gull
❏ Black-headed Gull
❏ Bonaparte's Gull
❏ *Black-tailed Gull*
❏ *Mew Gull*
❏ Ring-billed Gull
❏ *California Gull*
❏ Herring Gull
❏ *Thayer's Gull*
❏ Iceland Gull
❏ Lesser Black-backed Gull
❏ *Slaty-backed Gull*
❏ Glaucous Gull
❏ Great Black-backed Gull
❏ Sabine's Gull
❏ Black-legged Kittiwake
❏ *Ross's Gull*
❏ *Ivory Gull*
❏ Gull-billed Tern
❏ Caspian Tern
❏ Royal Tern
❏ *Sandwich Tern*
❏ Roseate Tern (en)
❏ Common Tern (th)
❏ Arctic Tern
❏ Forster's Tern
❏ Least Tern (th)
❏ *Bridled Tern*
❏ *Sooty Tern*
❏ *White-winged Tern*
❏ Black Tern (en)
❏ Black Skimmer (sc)

**Alcids (Alcidae)**
❏ *Dovekie*
❏ *Common Murre*
❏ *Thick-billed Murre*
❏ Razorbill

❏ Black Guillemot
❏ *Long-billed Murrelet*
❏ *Ancient Murrelet*
❏ *Atlantic Puffin*

**Pigeons & Doves (Columbidae)**
☑ Rock Pigeon
❏ *White-winged Dove*
☑ Mourning Dove
❏ *Passenger Pigeon (ex)*

**Parrots (Psittacidae)**
❏ Monk Parakeet

**Cuckoos (Cuculidae)**
❏ Black-billed Cuckoo
❏ Yellow-billed Cuckoo

**Barn Owls (Tytonidae)**
❏ Barn Owl

**Owls (Strigidae)**
❏ Eastern Screech-Owl
❏ Great Horned Owl
❏ Snowy Owl
❏ *Northern Hawk Owl*
❏ *Burrowing Owl*
❏ Barred Owl
❏ *Great Gray Owl*
❏ Long-eared Owl
❏ Short-eared Owl (en)
❏ *Boreal Owl*
❏ Northern Saw-Whet Owl

**Nightjars (Caprimulgidae)**
❏ Common Nighthawk (sc)
❏ Chuck-will's-widow
❏ Whip-poor-will (sc)

**Swifts (Apodidae)**
❏ Chimney Swift

**Hummingbirds (Trochilidae)**
☑ Ruby-throated Hummingbird

❏ *Anna's Hummingbird*
❏ *Calliope Hummingbird*
❏ *Rufous Hummingbird*

**Kingfishers (Alcedinidae)**
☑ Belted Kingfisher (Hudson River)

**Woodpeckers (Picidae)**
❏ *Lewis's Woodpecker*
☑ Red-headed Woodpecker (sc)
☑ Red-bellied Woodpecker
❏ Yellow-bellied Sapsucker
☑ Downy Woodpecker
☑ Hairy Woodpecker
❏ American Three-toed Woodpecker
❏ Black-backed Woodpecker
☑ Northern Flicker
☑ Pileated Woodpecker

**Flycatchers (Tyrannidae)**
❏ Olive-sided Flycatcher
❏ Eastern Wood-Pewee
❏ Yellow-bellied Flycatcher
❏ Acadian Flycatcher
❏ Alder Flycatcher
❏ Willow Flycatcher
❏ Least Flycatcher
❏ *Hammond's Flycatcher*
❏ Eastern Phoebe
❏ *Say's Phoebe*
❏ *Vermilion Flycatcher*
❏ *Ash-throated Flycatcher*
❏ Great Crested Flycatcher
❏ *Western Kingbird*
☑ Eastern Kingbird
❏ *Gray Kingbird*
❏ *Scissor-tailed Flycatcher*
❏ *Fork-tailed Flycatcher*

**Shrikes (Laniidae)**
- ❏ *Loggerhead Shrike (en)*
- ❏ Northern Shrike

**Vireos (Vireonidae)**
- ❏ White-eyed Vireo
- ❏ *Bell's Vireo*
- ❏ Yellow-throated Vireo
- ❏ Blue-headed Vireo
- ❏ Warbling Vireo
- ❏ Philadelphia Vireo
- ❏ Red-eyed Vireo

**Jays & Crows (Corvidae)**
- ❏ Gray Jay
- ☑ Blue Jay
- ❏ *Black-billed Magpie*
- ❏ American Crow
- ❏ Fish Crow
- ❏ Common Raven

**Larks (Alaudidae)**
- ❏ *Sky Lark (ex)*
- ❏ Horned Lark (sc)

**Swallows (Hirundinidae)**
- ❏ Purple Martin
- ☑ Tree Swallow
- ❏ Northern Rough-winged Swallow
- ❏ Bank Swallow
- ❏ Cliff Swallow
- ❏ *Cave Swallow*
- ❏ Barn Swallow

**Chickadees and Titmice (Paridae)**
- ☑ Black-capped Chickadee
- ❏ Boreal Chickadee
- ☑ Tufted Titmouse

**Nuthatches (Sittidae)**
- ❏ Red-breasted Nuthatch
- ☑ White-breasted Nuthatch
- ❏ *Brown-headed Nuthatch*

**Creepers (Certhiidae)**
- ❏ Brown Creeper

**Wrens (Troglodytidae)**
- ❏ *Rock Wren*
- ❏ Carolina Wren
- ❏ *Bewick's Wren*
- ❏ House Wren
- ☑ Winter Wren
- ❏ Sedge Wren (th)
- ❏ Marsh Wren

**Kinglets (Regulidae)**
- ❏ Golden-crowned Kinglet
- ❏ Ruby-crowned Kinglet

**Gnatcatchers (Sylviidae)**
- ❏ Blue-gray Gnatcatcher

**Thrushes (Turdidae)**
- ❏ *Northern Wheatear*
- ☑ *Eastern Bluebird*
- ❏ *Mountain Bluebird*
- ❏ *Townsend's Solitaire*
- ❏ Veery
- ❏ Gray-cheeked Thrush
- ❏ Bicknell's Thrush (sc)
- ❏ Swainson's Thrush
- ❏ Hermit Thrush
- ❏ Wood Thrush
- ❏ *Fieldfare*
- ❏ *Redwing*
- ☑ *American Robin*
- ❏ *Varied Thrush*

**Mockingbirds & Thrashers (Mimidae)**
- ☑ Gray Catbird
- ☑ Northern Mockingbird
- ❏ *Sage Thrasher*
- ❏ Brown Thrasher

**Starlings (Sturnidae)**
- ☑ European Starling

**Wagtails & Pipits (Motacillidae)**
- ❏ American Pipit

**Waxwings (Bombycillidae)**
- ❏ Bohemian Waxwing
- ❏ Cedar Waxwing

**Wood-Warblers (Parulidae)**
- ❏ Blue-winged Warbler
- ❏ Golden-winged Warbler (sc)
- ❏ Tennessee Warbler
- ❏ Orange-crowned Warbler
- ❏ Nashville Warbler
- ❏ Northern Parula
- ❏ Yellow Warbler
- ❏ Chestnut-sided Warbler
- ❏ Magnolia Warbler
- ❏ Cape May Warbler
- ❏ Black-throated Blue Warbler
- ❏ Yellow-rumped Warbler
- ❏ *Black-throated Gray Warbler*
- ❏ Black-throated Green Warbler
- ❏ *Townsend's Warbler*
- ❏ Blackburnian Warbler
- ❏ Yellow-throated Warbler
- ❏ Pine Warbler
- ❏ Prairie Warbler
- ❏ Palm Warbler
- ❏ Bay-breasted Warbler
- ❏ Blackpoll Warbler
- ❏ Cerulean Warbler (sc)
- ❏ Black-and-white Warbler
- ❏ American Redstart
- ❏ Prothonotary Warbler
- ❏ Worm-eating Warbler
- ❏ *Swainson's Warbler*
- ❏ Ovenbird
- ❏ Northern Waterthrush
- ❏ Louisiana Waterthrush
- ❏ Kentucky Warbler
- ❏ *Connecticut Warbler*
- ❏ Mourning Warbler
- ❏ *MacGillivray's Warbler*
- ❏ Common Yellowthroat

- ❏ Hooded Warbler
- ❏ Wilson's Warbler
- ❏ Canada Warbler
- ❏ *Painted Redstart*
- ❏ Yellow-breasted Chat (sc)

## Tanagers (Thraupidae)
- ❏ Summer Tanager
- ❏ Scarlet Tanager
- ❏ *Western Tanager*

## Sparrows & Allies (Emberizidae)
- ❏ *Green-tailed Towhee*
- ❏ *Spotted Towhee*
- ❏ Eastern Towhee
- ❏ *Cassin's Sparrow*
- ❏ *Bachman's Sparrow*
- ❏ American Tree Sparrow
- ❏ Chipping Sparrow
- ❏ Clay-colored Sparrow
- ☑ Field Sparrow
- ❏ Vesper Sparrow (sc)
- ❏ *Lark Sparrow*
- ❏ *Lark Bunting*
- ❏ Savannah Sparrow
- ❏ Grasshopper Sparrow (sc)
- ❏ *Baird's Sparrow*
- ❏ Henslow's Sparrow (th)
- ❏ *Le Conte's Sparrow*
- ❏ *Nelson's Sharp-tailed Sparrow*

- ❏ Saltmarsh Sharp-tailed Sparrow
- ❏ Seaside Sparrow (sc)
- ❏ Fox Sparrow
- ☑ Song Sparrow
- ❏ Lincoln's Sparrow
- ❏ Swamp Sparrow
- ❏ White-throated Sparrow
- ❏ *Harris's Sparrow*
- ❏ White-crowned Sparrow
- ❏ *Golden-crowned Sparrow*
- ☑ Dark-eyed Junco
- ❏ Lapland Longspur
- ❏ *Smith's Longspur*
- ❏ *Chestnut-collared Longspur*
- ❏ Snow Bunting

## Grosbeaks & Buntings (Cardinalidae)
- ☑ Northern Cardinal
- ☑ Rose-breasted Grosbeak
- ❏ *Black-headed Grosbeak*
- ❏ Blue Grosbeak
- ❏ *Lazuli Bunting*
- ❏ Indigo Bunting
- ❏ *Painted Bunting*
- ❏ Dickcissel

## Blackbirds & Allies (Icteridae)
- ☑ Bobolink
- ☑ Red-winged Blackbird

- ❏ Eastern Meadowlark
- ❏ *Western Meadowlark*
- ❏ *Yellow-headed Blackbird*
- ❏ Rusty Blackbird
- ❏ *Brewer's Blackbird*
- ☑ Common Grackle
- ❏ Boat-tailed Grackle
- ☑ Brown-headed Cowbird
- ❏ Orchard Oriole
- ❏ *Bullock's Oriole*
- ❏ Baltimore Oriole

## Finches (Fringillidae)
- ❏ *Brambling*
- ❏ Pine Grosbeak
- ☑ Purple Finch
- ☑ House Finch
- ❏ Red Crossbill
- ❏ White-winged Crossbill
- ❏ Common Redpoll
- ❏ Hoary Redpoll
- ❏ Pine Siskin
- ☑ American Goldfinch
- ❏ *European Goldfinch (ex)*
- ❏ Evening Grosbeak

## Old World Sparrows (Passeridae)
- ☑ House Sparrow

*Common Grackle*

# INDEX OF SCIENTIFIC NAMES

This index references only the primary species accounts.

# INDEX

# INDEX OF COMMON NAMES

Page numbers in boldface type refer to the primary, illustrated species accounts.